PORTRAITS OF LITERACY ACROSS FAMILIES, COMMUNITIES, AND SCHOOLS

Intersections and Tensions

PORTRAITS OF LITERACY ACROSS FAMILIES, COMMUNITIES, AND SCHOOLS

Intersections and Tensions

Edited by

Jim Anderson
Maureen Kendrick
Theresa Rogers
Suzanne Smythe
University of British Columbia

 LAWRENCE ERLBAUM ASSOCIATES, PUBLISHERS
2005   Mahwah, New Jersey   London

Lawrence Erlbaum Associates, Inc., Publishers
10 Industrial Avenue
Mahwah, New Jersey 07430
www.erlbaum.com

Cover design by Kathryn Houghtaling Lacey

Library of Congress Cataloging-in-Publication Data

Portraits of literacy across families, communities, and schools : intersections and tensions /
edited by Jim Anderson . . . [et al.].
    p.   cm.
Includes bibliographical references and index.
ISBN 0-8058-4859-2 (cloth)
ISBN 0-8058-4860-6 (paper)
1. Literacy—Social aspects—Cross-cultural studies—Congresses.   2. Education,
Bilingual—Social aspects—Cross-cultural studies—Congresses.   3. Critical pedagogy—
Cross-cultural studies—Congresses.   I. Anderson, Jim, 1950–

LC149.P65   2005
302.2′244—dc22   2004056424
                                                                                          CIP

Books published by Lawrence Erlbaum Associates are printed on acid-free paper,
and their bindings are chosen for strength and durability.

Printed in the United States of America
10 9 8 7 6 5 4 3 2 1

Contents

Foreword

Victoria Purcell-Gates
University of British Columbia

Finally, we are beginning to map the terrain of literacy development and literacy practice! We researchers are slowly filling in the picture of what literacy *is*, *how* development occurs, *what* the relationships are among different instructional systems dedicated to teaching literacy skills, and the myriad ways in which these skills are put into practice. This edited volume provides multiple portraits of this complex picture and thus contributes significantly to the scientific and analytic understanding of literacy—a process and product so crucial to lives, economies, governments, and well-being of people the world over.

Perhaps to some of us, it seems a simplistic truism that to understand literacy development, you must understand literacy itself. And to understand literacy, it seems (again, simplistically obvious) you need to understand how, where, and why it is practiced. However, until recently, literacy research, policy, and funding focused myopically on literacy instruction alone. This resulted in a system of thought and a system of instructional policy that is closed, with no feedback beyond itself. Why this has remained the scenario is truly a mystery. Looking at any other practice and instruction in that practice, one can readily see the folly of designing instruction without knowing how that instruction is paying off in practice or, even more insidious, the very nature of the practice itself. Can you imagine the instructional staff of a football team, for example, teaching the rudiments of football and never really knowing what an actual game looks like? Never watching films of different games? What about automobile driving instructions? With little knowledge or interest in actual driving behaviors, conditions, or purposes, how effective would these lessons be?

If nothing else, the work in the past 20 years by sociologists, anthropologists, and literacy studies scholars has demonstrated that literacy is conceived of and practiced in different ways by different peoples and that these practices are shaped and patterned by social and cultural factors and contexts such as social domains (religion, work, home, and so on), cultural values and beliefs, historical patterns, and power relations. The seminal work of Brian Street, David Barton and Mary Hamilton, Denny Taylor, and others has opened up an entire area of knowledge and insight for literacy scholars. Despite instruction in the skills of reading and writing that is essentially the same in educational institutions around the world, the actualization of those school-acquired skills looks remarkably different, and those different literacy practices are patterned in ways that are predicted not by schooling so much as by social factors.

Unfortunately, the blinders that have restricted the vision of those in charge of instructional issues, as well as a good number of literacy researchers focused only on schools, remain firmly in place, despite this opening up of the picture and construct of literacy. Even more unfortunately, the fundamental role of power has become more visible in dominant governments during the last few years, and the solipsistic cycle of literacy instruction was closed completely, with literacy itself now defined as measured by instruction in literacy.

Saying something is so, though, does not make it so! The authors and editors of this volume, taking a lead from the little boy who pointed out that the king was wearing no clothes, have built on Street's, Barton and Hamilton's, and Taylor's early work and have begun to document what literacy actually looks like in action and in different contexts with different players. This collection of work adds to a few other such efforts. This work is not done. But it is continuing, and we need many more studies and volumes such as this one to build our knowledge base—a full picture of literacy as a process and as a product.

One of the aspects of this work that particularly interests me, and one that I hope will interest others, is that of better understanding the relationships among instructional schemes in the skills of reading and writing and the ways that those skills are taken up and transformed by students in their lived-in cultures outside of the culture of school. Although we have a beginning body of work that documents impressive mismatches between textual practices in and out of school, we have very little research and analytic insight into how students who get even rudimentary instruction in reading and writing become readers and writers in their own lives, meeting their own social and cultural demands for literacy, and living their lives with the mediation of print. Furthermore, how do students who receive virtually no instruction in literacies other than print (e.g., visual, graphic, sound) become creators and users of multisemiotic systems in their lives? Again, we, as scholars of literacy, must persevere in seeking a fuller picture of literacy development and literacy practice. To do anything less, I believe, is scientifically unethical and socially irresponsible.

Enjoy the work contained in this volume. It is important and desperately needed. Consider it as part of the slowly emerging picture and join us in working on its completion.

Preface

Our intention is for this book to stimulate debate and critical thought, and draw readers' attention to the ideological nature of literacy education across a broad range of literacy contexts. The book represents a departure from conventional wisdom in that it crosses traditional boundaries between the studies of family, community, and school literacies. It offers a unique global perspective on multiple literacies, from theory to case studies of various settings. These examples suggest ways we all mould literacy practices by simultaneously shaping relationships and identity, and by privileging particular literacy practices in particular situations. The implicit dialogue within the book among the chapter authors, writing across the traditionally distinct fields of family, community, adult, and school literacies, highlights the interconnections between these literacy sites and stimulates the pursuit of a more integrated and interdisciplinary approach to literacy education. Moreover, this critical and dialogic orientation serves to challenge and extend many conventional notions surrounding literacy education in communities, schools, and families.

Out of respect for the literacy practices of the different countries of origin of the authors, and in keeping with the international character and multiple/situated literacies orientation of the book, we have retained the original spellings used in the different chapters. Thus the reader might notice what appear to be inconsistencies in spelling.

Acknowledgments

This volume had its genesis in the *Portraits of Literacy: Critical Issues in Family/Community/School Literacies* conference held at the University of British Columbia. Sincere appreciation is extended to the following for their support of that conference: Fatima Pirbhai-Illich, the conference coordinator, the Social Sciences and Humanities Research Council of Canada, Literacy B.C., The British Columbia Ministry of Advanced Education (C2T2), The National Literacy Secretariat, Human Resources Development Canada, The President's Office at the University of British Columbia, The Faculty of Education, The Department of Language and Literacy Education, The Department of Educational Studies, the Public Knowledge Project, and graduate students from various departments who were instrumental in ensuring the success and the daily organization of this event. We also thank Naomi Hamer for her assistance in preparing this manuscript, and the three reviewers for their feedback and suggestions. Special thanks also to Naomi Silverman, our editor at Lawrence Erlbaum Associates, for her support, encouragement, guidance, and patience. Finally, we thank our families for their support and encouragement throughout this process.

Chapter 1

Portraits of Literacy Across Families, Communities, and Schools: An Introduction

Maureen Kendrick
Theresa Rogers
Suzanne Smythe
Jim Anderson
University of British Columbia

Over the past few decades, there has been a dramatic shift in thinking about literacy and the relationship of literacy practices across home, community, and school contexts. Until recently, research in literacy has been largely the domain of linguistics and psychology. Street (1984) posited that this research contributed to the autonomous model of literacy that has dominated our conceptions of, and discourse about, literacy for most of the last century. According to Street, the autonomous model regards literacy as an individualized skill that can be measured and calibrated to adapt to social structures, including the school, the workplace, and the economic imperatives of the day. However, more recent ethnographic, sociolinguistic, and critical sociological work has prompted a shift among many educators and researchers toward the view that reading and writing are not just a set of cognitive/linguistic skills, but complex social practices (e.g., Baker & Luke, 1991; Barton, Hamilton, & Ivanic, 2000; Bloome & Green, 1984; Dyson, 1997, 2001; Purcell-Gates, 1997). That is, there is considerable variation in literacy practices, in the meanings ascribed to literacy, and in the ways in which literacy practices are carried out in different contexts. Thus, literacy cannot be measured in terms of "high" or "low" but rather according to the institutional contexts and power relationships that shape literacy uses.

In light of this new interdisciplinary focus on what constitutes literacy practices across diverse contexts, the editors of this volume sponsored an international conference in July 2002 at the University of British Columbia in Vancouver, Canada (for online proceedings see http://www.pkp.ubc.ca/literacyconference/). Our goal was to encourage dialogue among practitioners, researchers, graduate students, and members of the larger community and to stimulate public engagement in literacy issues that cross the traditional borders of family, community, and school contexts. This volume represents some of the key papers from that conference, as well as contributions from additional scholars whose work illustrates the rich variation of language and literacy practices evident in global contexts.

In this collection, portraits of literacy from Bangladeshi homes in London, England to primary schools in Johannesburg, South Africa and from a middle school in Karachi, Pakistan to a First Nations community in Northern Ontario, Canada illustrate diverse, situated, and contested literacy beliefs and practices across homes, communities, and schools. Three overarching and interrelated perspectives on literacy inform or, in some cases, are challenged by the scholars who contributed to this volume: critical literacy, social or situated literacy, and multiple literacies. The roots of critical literacy can be traced to the works of Freire (1970) and Freire and Macedo (1987). Central to this perspective is the notion that literacy can, and should be, emancipatory and transformational, enabling those who live on the economic, political, and social margins of society to participate fully and meaningfully. Another tenet of a critical literacy perspective is that learning how to interpret and act on the world in socially just ways is equally important to learning how to read and write words. Historically, critical literacy has taken varying local forms based on distinctive cultural standpoints and political interests at both national and transnational levels (Luke, 2002). For example, in Australia, South Africa, Canada, the United Kingdom, and the United States, critical literacy projects have typically focussed on key dialectical tensions between societal demands for students to engage with dominant discourses, genres, and practices and the need for them to engage critically with such texts and practices.

Advocates of a situated social literacy perspective argue that literacy is a complex set of social practices and thus the uses to which it is put, how it is acquired or learned, and indeed, what it means to be literate are determined by the sociocultural context in which literacy occurs (Barton, Hamilton, & Ivanic, 2000; Heath, 1983; Street, 1995). From this perspective, literacy is examined within the complex networks of social practices (Heath, 1983; Scollon & Scollon, 1981; Scribner & Cole, 1981; Solsken, 1993) and defined within the context of communities (Ferdman, 1990; Heath, 1983; Scribner, 1988), classrooms (Bloome, 1989), and families (Taylor, 1983; Taylor & Dorsey-Gaines, 1988). Emanating from cultural anthropology and sociolinguistic research traditions, this perspective challenges the assumption that literacy skills and knowledge are generic and easily transferable from one context to another.

Although the term *multiliteracies* has recently come to the forefront in the literacy field (e.g., Cope, Kalantzis, & New London Group, 2000), we propose that the perspective that there are multiple ways of representing meaning, in addition to print, has been acknowledged for some time. For example, theorists such as Dyson (1997), Harste, Woodward, and Burke (1984), Hodge and Kress (1988), and Kress (1993, 1997) adopt a semiotic framework to interpret the multiple and integrated ways—including print—that young children use to represent and construct meaning. These multiple forms of literacy include visual arts, play, and drama, as well as various digital multimedia literacies. Likewise, the importance of the meaning carrying and meaning making functions of graphs, charts, diagrams, and other modes of representation in various disciplinary texts has been recognized for some time (e.g., Early & Tang, 1991; Herber, 1970; Lemke, 1990). Moreover, systemic functional linguists have shown how different genres necessitate different reading stances as well as specialized knowledge of composing within them (Halliday, 1969, 1975a, 1975b; Martin & Halliday, 1981). However, even with this rich set of theory and research supporting the notion that literacy consists of social, cultural, political, and multimodal practices, we believe that the perception of literacy as generic or as a universal set of psycholinguistic skills and abilities, transferable from one context to another, is still pervasive both in literacy learning and teaching in school and other institutions, and among the general populace.

Although each of the authors in this collection uses and challenges the frameworks of critical literacy, situated social literacy, and multiple literacies, they do so from unique contexts and perspectives. We have organized the volume into four parts that reflect their distinctive contexts: Part I focuses on family literacy contexts; Part II presents early and youth literacy contexts; Part III showcases work in adult and community literacy; and Part IV highlights current literacy policy issues. Within and across these sections, we highlight the salient themes as well as intersections and tensions evident in the careful examination of literacy practices in these diverse contexts. Four themes in particular are taken up across these chapters. The first theme focuses on the location and politics of social contexts and how these shape the meanings of literacy and related practices taken up by participants. Integral to this theme are the ways in which various groups in society legitimize the meanings of literacy, thereby creating a struggle for power in relation to who defines literacy, who does literacy education, and whose literacy research counts. The second theme highlights the need for researchers and educators to interrogate the relative salience of literacy in relation to social, cultural, and political practices in promoting social change and social justice. A third theme concentrates on identity positions connected with ethnicity, class, gender, language, and culture, and the key ways in which individuals position themselves in relation to literacy, and the ways in which they are positioned by literacy. The final theme highlights tensions across the continuum of social institutional and more locally situated literacy practices that illustrate the hegemonic and less permeable nature of institutional literacies and discourses. We revisit these themes at the end of this chapter.

FAMILY LITERACIES

In Part I, the intersections and tensions at the forefront of family literacy are illuminated across three global contexts: Britain, Australia, and Canada. Evident in most of the chapters in this section is the tension between "school literacy" and literacy as practiced in families and communities. Although the concept that the family is a site for literacy learning and engagement seems a given in each of the chapters, it is also apparent that the term *family* connotes widely different meanings to these participants, practitioners, and researchers, as does the term *literacy* itself. Finally, the issue of whose voices count in family literacy research and practice is raised in several of the chapters in this section.

For example, in chapter 2, Gregory borrows Padmore's (1994) term *guiding light* to refer to individuals who play a very important role in children's literacy development. She offers portraits of young Bangladeshi-origin siblings, showing ways in which they fulfil this role of guiding light as they read together in London's East End. When parents are unfamiliar with the language and culture of the school, siblings may become very special guiding lights in their siblings' and parents' literacy lives, as they help them to negotiate this system. Gregory's study joins a growing body of scholarship that problematizes the notion that parents will be the exclusive "teachers" in families, particularly those who move to live in a new country. Some of these studies show how siblings assist each other by sharing a common language and cultural knowledge; others demonstrate the contribution of siblings to each other's social, cognitive, and emotional development. However, the role of siblings as unique teachers of *school literacy practices* has hitherto not been a focus of attention. Gregory shows how older siblings take ownership of school learning and present it in an understandable form to their younger siblings during play at home, and investigates what transformations occur during this teaching and what can be learned about collaboration and cognition.

Whereas Gregory focuses on the role of siblings in Bangladeshi family literacy contexts in East London, Cairney (chapter 3) shifts attention to the mismatch between the discursive and literacy practices of the home and the school in Australia. As he points out, schools privilege a limited set of texts, particular interactional patterns, and restricted definitions of, and expectations for, literacy. Furthermore, he shows how literacy practices are not neutral, but rather characterized by complex power relationships. Employing qualitative research data gathering methods in one secondary school and three elementary schools, he documents the literacy practices of 35 students across family and school contexts. He found that there was considerable variability in the visibility of literacy across families but less variability in terms of literacy practices within or across schools. Furthermore, children had more choice and greater control over literacy at home than at school. Cairney argues that in order to meet the diverse literacy needs of children, educators must pay attention to their discursive, instructional, and textual practices. He concludes by arguing that making changes in the ways that we "do" literacy in schools is a process of negotiating and sharing power with the communities and families with whom we should be working.

Anderson, Smythe, and Shapiro (chapter 4) report on a case study in British Columbia, Canada based on the Parents As Literacy Supporters (PALS) family literacy program. Similar to Cairney, their chapter is framed within a sociocultural perspective. The authors raise questions about the generalizability and applicability of family literacy research conducted in the 1970s and 1980s in culturally diverse, multilingual communities. A major aim of the PALS developers was to have the program reflect a social contextual orientation, while at the same time recognizing and facilitating parents' desires to support their children's early literacy development in school. In reflecting on her role as a PALS facilitator in two inner city schools, Smythe documents the challenges inherent in transposing a family literacy program from one context to another. She demonstrates that each site requires ongoing negotiation and accommodation. This case study also documents that PALS was effective in helping teachers come to know and understand the parents and communities with whom they work. Indeed, the relationships that developed were synergistic in that while the families learned from the teachers and the school, the teachers and the school benefited from working intensively with the families.

In relation to the PALS pilot program, Stacey Cody (Snapshot 1) reflects on her experiences as a parent participant. Her case speaks to the importance of family literacy programs honouring the strengths that participants bring. Although we need to be cautious about taking on fervour about programs such as PALS, it is evident from Stacey that this program also helped her develop personally. Proponents of social contextual approaches to family literacy programs, such as Auerbach, envision encouraging participants to engage in transformational and political work. In her unassuming and somewhat understated way, Stacey Cody embodies this potential. Interestingly, this chapter affirms the importance of print literacy as argued by Phillips and Sample in their chapter but also points to the ways in which literacy, in a Freirian sense, can be personally liberating and transformational.

Arguing that children are socialized into literacy and that the family is a key site for this socialization, Phillips and Sample (chapter 5) draw from a longitudinal study of a family literacy program in Edmonton, Alberta meant to enhance children's and parents' literacy development, as well as parents' ability to assist their children's literacy development. Drawing on the concept of intergenerational literacy and data from the study, they argue that family literacy programs must provide parents with the knowledge, skills, and strategies they need to support children's early language and literacy development to ensure success in school. Phillips and Sample share five case studies to illustrate their struggle to learn from the parents how they think about their past experiences, perceived vulnerabilities, contingencies for poverty, loneliness, and what it means to do without in their current lives, yet to have very clear hopes for their children to do better. An overarching assumption of the authors (and indeed of many family literacy educators) is that literacy is a means to financial, political, and social self-improvement, which challenges the perspective advocated by Auerbach (chapter 18, this volume) and others who argue that literacy in and of itself cannot address many of the social and economic factors that people who are marginalized and dispossessed face in our society.

Shifting attention to family literacy practitioners, Ruth Hayden and Maureen Sanders (Snapshot 2) present an insider's view on the difficulties in sustaining family literacy programs. These authors maintain that the voices of program providers have scarcely been evident. In this snapshot, they capture a number of issues that confront the family literacy field including chronic underfunding, unrealistic expectations in terms of outcomes and program evaluation, and problems with dissemination of research and evaluation in family literacy. The authors argue that the feminization of the family literacy field (which we see as very much related to some of the other issues they raise) is being largely ignored. They call for greater collaboration among family literacy practitioners and researchers, and the critical need to listen to the voices of those who work "in the trenches," so to speak.

EARLY AND YOUTH LITERACIES

In Part II, issues relating to early and youth literacies across the diverse contexts of South Africa, Pakistan, and Canada become the focal point. The six chapters in this section raise important questions about pedagogical practices, definitions of literacy across formal and informal learning contexts, and the privileging of school literacies and language-based modes of representation. Each of the chapters provides unique examples of how children and adolescents move beyond school-defined modes of expression by fusing multiple signs systems and multiple literacies as a means of expressing and exploring complex understandings of themselves, literature, and the world. The question of which reader and writer identities are available to children in school contexts echoes throughout each of the chapters and raises the important question of how institutions position learners in relation to literacy. The chapters also bring under scrutiny the privileging of language-based modes of communication and institutionalised literacies.

In the first chapter in this section, Prinsloo and Stein (chapter 6) highlight some of the tensions between home and school literacies in their chapter focussing on literacy learning in three preschools and a primary school in South Africa. Through case study discussions of four early literacy learning sites, they explore questions such as: What are the limits and uses of reading and writing? How do small children learn about these limits in the early years? What kinds of readers and writers are they set up to become and what are the consequences for their later learning? The three preschools are in urban townships around Cape Town, serving children from working class or unemployed parents, and the primary school is on the borders of Johannesburg and serves children from informal settlements. The remarkable variations found across these different sites were not, they argue, a function of the differences children brought to these institutions. Rather, the differences resulted from the distinct ways in which the teacher in each site invented the notion of literacy and the consequences of this invention for the children's engagement with literacy pedagogy.

In keeping with this focus on children's identities and literacy learning, Maguire and her colleagues (chapter 7) invite us into the lives of young multilingual children in Montreal, Canada. They explore the children's multiple school experiences, with a focus on how they negotiate multiple literacies in heritage language contexts and how this impacts their identity constructions and representations of self. Through an embedded case design, involving comparisons within and across classroom and family settings, the authors delineate the perspectives and changing circumstances of multilingual learners themselves, their interpretations of these circumstances, and the chameleon-like character of such literacy portraits. They argue that when different languages and cultures intersect in classrooms and playground spaces, and when these differences go unrecognized, it is critical for children to be able to define their identities on their own terms. Maguire and her colleagues also discuss the implications for the teaching and learning of immigrant children in heritage language contexts, and for policymakers and community leaders interested in multilingual children's lived experiences and sociocultural contexts.

Whereas Maguire et al. focus on heritage language contexts, Masny (chapter 8) presents a comprehensive conceptualization of literacies, in-

cluding multiple literacies, global education, and additive bilingualism in
Canadian Francophone and minority language contexts. Her framework
opens up possibilities for literacy as a process of becoming—of "reading
the world, the word, and oneself in a postmodern world." Her chapter
also illuminates the tensions concerning minority communities in an era
of globalization. The intention is to provoke debate about the ways learners conceptualize and are conceptualized by multiple literacies. She argues that while difference and plurality in a minority language community "trouble the boundaries" of both community and self, learning to
read critically the world, the word, and self presents new possibilities for
"becoming" in the world.

Kendrick, McKay, and Moffatt (chapter 9) examine the portrayal of literacy identities in young Western Canadian children's drawings about reading and writing. The drawings are viewed as moments in the children's literacy histories that reveal individual identities and literacy learning
experiences across the broad and unique contexts of children's lives. Recent research on social identity and literacy suggests students' ideas of how
reading and writing relate to various social identities may be a significant
factor in their decisions to engage in particular literacy practices, particularly school-based literacy practices. Given that early experiences with literacy often lead students to form specific learner identities, understanding
young children's constructions of self in relation to literacy is of particular
concern. The authors highlight the difficulty of eliciting young children's
ideas and conceptualizations using traditional modes of inquiry such as talk
or writing. Their use of drawings as a research method demonstrates how
children use modes other than language to represent their conceptualizations of the literacies in their lives.

Building on these concepts of identity, context, and pedagogy, Rogers
and Schofield (chapter 10) contribute needed perspectives on multiple
literacies pedagogy as it relates to youth. The authors argue that as the parameters and expectations for youth literacies expand, we need increasingly sophisticated theoretical and practical approaches to designing curricula for students who do not succeed or have been marginalized in
traditional secondary schools. Based on a review of current theory and practices in youth literacy programming in and out of school, they make a
strong case for arts-based and multimedia approaches that accommodate
the particular language and literacy histories, identities, and resistances of
students, and are sensitive to their social lives. Their collaborative work in
an alternative youth literacy program in the Lower Mainland of British Columbia (see also Schofield & Rogers, 2004) illustrates this approach with examples of student digital video projects. Drawing on the work of social, multiple, and critical literacy theorists, as well as work in the areas of biography,
imagination, and critical geography, they reconceptualize these youth liter-

acy practices as including the imaginative and fluid visual and spatial practices that cross students' lives inside and outside school.

As a student in the alternative program described by Rogers and Schofield, Scott Moloney (Snapshot 3) provides a unique perspective on youth literacies. He describes his decision to continue his education after a brief time on the streets, and his discovery that there can be "more to school than the building." Through exploring music and video as additional means for expression (he was already a poet), Moloney tries to capture and share "a small piece of the truth" with the hope that people will "maybe do something" to make the world a better place, and to learn to succeed.

Norton (chapter 11) focuses on the Youth Millennium Project in Karachi, Pakistan. She adopts a critical literacy perspective, which assumes that students use texts to make sense of the world, that the meanings of texts are not fixed, and that the notion of "text" is not confined to the written word, but includes oral, visual, and graphic representations of meaning. The Youth Millennium Project, which encourages students to address global issues by examining social issues at the local level, is a contemporary example of critical literacy in action. The project involves over 10,000 school-aged children in 80 countries. In documenting Pakistani middle school students' implementation of the project, Norton sought to determine what vision of social change informed the students' choice to work with Afghan refugee children. Her chapter addresses two particularly interesting findings: the students' conceptions of literacy, which included a sophisticated understanding of the role of literacy for the progress of a democratic nation, and their understanding of English as an international language that could potentially connect Pakistan to the world. She concludes with a rich discussion of the practical and theoretical implications of her research, including the "politics of location" as a way of explaining the meaning of language and literacy in the lives of these students.

COMMUNITY AND ADULT LITERACIES

Part III focuses on diverse community and adult literacy learning contexts in Canada, the United States, and Britain. These five chapters all illustrate the ways in which dominant discourses about literacy—which include an emphasis on individual cognitive skills, print literacies, and academic, institutional or "schooled" literacy practices—marginalize children, adolescents, and adults. For instance, in these dominant discourses, rich Aboriginal literacy practices and beliefs (e.g., reading the landscape and the importance of educating a person's whole being) continue to be unrecognized and unsupported. In a similar way, the needs of women in and outside of institutions remain underarticulated and undervalued, as do pedagogies that recognize trauma and provide avenues for asserting positionality and power. This section closes with a call to recognize the many subfields that constitute what we call literacy and take up questions that cut across and recognize the rich contexts and populations served in order to integrate our research and practice.

To begin, Hare (chapter 12) draws on the narratives of the elders in a First Nations (Anishinaabe) community in Northern Ontario to illustrate how they have constructed multiple meanings for literacy. As Western notions of literacy (or "knowing papers") and various forms of assimilation came to be more highly valued in their residential and day school experiences, they experienced a consequent loss of their own language, identity, and ways of knowing. However, Hare also notes examples of the appropriation of Western literacy to assert their own positions or subvert the system. She uses a historical framework to explain the social and political forces that led to these changes and suggests directions for both policy and practice that would promote Aboriginal language and literacy while ensuring that First Nations peoples have access and opportunity in school literacy. Such policies and practices, she argues, would include a "far more inclusive understanding of literacy [that honors] the languages, narrative traditions, and rich symbolic and meaning making systems of Aboriginal culture."

In chapter 13, Ningwakwe/Rainbow Woman, executive director of the National Indigenous Literacy Association, complements Hare's chapter by pointing out the limits of a Western view of literacy and proposes a "Medicine Wheel" model of Canadian Aboriginal literacy that takes into account the Spirit, Heart, Mind, and Body to counteract the more reductionist views of literacy that focus solely on the mind or on cognitive outcomes. She further elaborates on this model with a rainbow motif in which each color stands for a type of literacy, such as the language of origin of First Nations peoples, the balance of emotions, creativity across sign systems, and the skills of technology, offering a unique and culturally relevant model of literacy.

Echoing the work of Hare and Ningwakwe, but in a very different North American context, Horsman (chapter 14) reports on a collaborative, action research project that explores the impact of violence on literacy learning. This work is carried out with literacy workers in Canada and the United States who are attempting to enact changes to their programs based on her earlier research findings. These findings show that for literacy programs to design successful learning situations for the many women who have experienced trauma in their lives, they need to take into account more fully the impact of trauma on learning. In the study described here, Horsman focuses on the discourses that shape understandings and forms of organization within literacy programs to explore how these discourses enable or constrain the ability to address the impact of violence in the women's lives. World Education, one of the key collaborators in this research, is supporting the work of six literacy organizations in New England as they engage in extensive interventions to strengthen the possibility for successful learning for survivors of violence in the face of traditional discourses of violence and schooling.

Further supporting the notion that dominant institutional discourses and practices shape literacy practices, Bloome (chapter 15) draws on his work in the Mass Observation Project in England to develop his thesis that writing is a socially structured, hierarchical process. The Mass Observation Project, which began in 1937, was designed to encourage members of the public to write about their lives; the writing data were supplemented by interviews, observations, and surveys. Bloome focuses on Mrs. Wright, a middle-aged woman from a working-class community employed in a midmanagement position in a public service company. Although she enjoyed writing in school, as a student, Mrs. Wright was not seen as a competent writer because of difficulties with grammar and spelling. In her workplace, where her job entailed writing complex texts in a variety of genres, she was not seen as occupying the position of writer and indeed did not see herself as a writer because of her position in the hierarchy of the company. Bloome notes that much writing is invisible, unvalued, and in most cases, unrecognized within institutions. He argues that the ways in which writing is hierarchically structured within these institutions need to be challenged and changed to eliminate the bottlenecks of access that prevent so many people from positioning themselves as writers or being seen as legitimate writers within their workplaces.

In the last chapter of this section, Quigley (chapter 16) describes the world of literacy education as comprised of a multiplicity of subdisciplines, professional terms and language(s), goals, purposes, and approaches (e.g., literacy as reading, vocational literacy, critical literacy) and as concerned with a range of learner populations (e.g., family literacy, adolescent literacy, workplace literacy, early literacy, etc.). He argues that there is a need for research that addresses common problems such as: How, when, and where do youth and adults learn on their own locally and informally? What are the participation patterns across populations in terms of gender, ethnicity, and cognitive development? and What approaches lead to learner progress? His chapter explores the terrain of the field of literacy and makes the case for more practitioner research as one way to build a better informed and more integrated field.

LITERACY POLICY ISSUES

The two chapters that comprise the final section suggest important implications for literacy policy research and development. Both chapters report on ethnographic studies: Duff on the uses of literacy in workplace and school settings (broadly defined) and Auerbach on the subordination of literacy within the broader learning aims in social movements and community settings. In drawing attention to the interplay among context, identity, and power, they each question the primary role attributed to literacy within economic, educational, and social reform initiatives. Indeed, both studies decentre literacy as a focus of intervention and foreground the political and social aspects of learning in a global world, thus pointing to potentially new ways to conceptualize family, school, and community literacies in the 21st century.

Duff (chapter 17) provides an overview of trends in the use of English as it proliferates as a global language, producing, as she observes, an unprecedented scale of English language learning internationally. Drawing on a range of studies in domains such as globalization and employment, secondary and postsecondary instruction, workplace and community settings, Duff argues that while English is taking its place as "the global official language" of business and commerce, education, and popular culture, this position is far from uncontested, and indeed as English dominates, movements to assert local and national languages, such as that of French in Quebec, grow alongside it, stimulating multilingualism and multiple literacies. Moreover, the uses of English in specific contexts, such as workplaces, are complex and challenge educators and policymakers to closely link instruction and policies to local dynamics rather than broad and generalized English instruction. In calling attention to these complexities, Duff reminds us of the multilingual and multicultural realities of a globalized world and the need for language educators, researchers, and policymakers to recognize the complexities these produce in our framing of education strategies.

Auerbach (chapter 18) concludes the volume with a provocative call to reexamine the central positioning of literacy as a force for social change, which she argues underpins the work of proponents of multiple literacies as well as critical educators such as herself. She argues that both these stances require a reexamination because they contribute to a new form of the "literacy myth" whereby literacy is seen as a motor force for social change, rather than as the actual struggles for social change that take place in social movements and community settings. Auerbach draws on a range of examples of these to suggest that in successful initiatives, literacy plays a subordinate role to the issues and activities identified by participants. She thus articulates a vision of a "pedagogy of not-literacy" that asks literacy educators, researchers, and activists to recognize the limitations of literacy education, but at the same time become more engaged in learning with and in movements for social change.

INTERSECTIONS AND THEMES

Evident within and across these multiple and varied portraits of literacy, which represent the voices of practitioners, researchers, graduate students, and members of the larger community, are several overlapping themes.

The authors in this volume elucidate the intersections and tensions across family, community, and school literacies. They challenge taken-for-granted meanings of literacy and relationships of power in literacy theory, practice, and research and problematize how individuals position themselves and are positioned by multiple literacies and languages. The implication of this work is a renewed attention to the hegemony of institutionalized literacies and language-based modes of representation that call on researchers and educators to carefully examine how literacy practices are framed socio-culturally and sociopolitically. In this final section, we discuss the ways in which these themes are addressed across the chapters.

The Meanings of Literacy and the Struggle for Power

The first theme that runs across several of the chapters in this volume re-lates to the meanings of literacy and the struggle for power. We note that many of the authors illustrate the ways the location and the social and polit-ical relationships of particular contexts shape the definitions and broader meanings of literacy, as well as the literacy practices taken up by partici-pants. For instance, in elaborating Aboriginal definitions of literacies, in their expansiveness and emphasis on reading the land as well as elements of body, spirit, and mind, Hare and Ningwakwe remind us that many literacy scholars and educators, even when articulating a multiple literacies per-spective, take for granted Western definitions of literacy. Chapters such as Kendrick et al.'s and Rogers and Schofield's remind us that children and youth may define and enact literacy practices in ways different from adults and more in relation to their own developing identities.

Related to how literacy gets defined are a set of questions about who has power in various literacy education contexts: who "does" literacy edu-cation, whose voices and perspectives are taken into account, and whose literacy research counts. The snapshots included in this volume begin to speak to these questions: Hayden and Sanders, for example, raise ques-tions about funding for literacy practitioners, issues of training and pro-fessional development, and accountability, arguing that those who do family literacy work are often women who are beset by many demands but who receive little financial or research support. Horsman also argues that in order to include and meet the needs of women literacy learners, society needs to do the work of recognizing violence and trauma and its effects on learning, by taking into account the stories and lives of women as lived in the discourses of literacy. Transforming literacy work is thus also a project of transforming society. Quigley suggests that valuing practitioner re-search has the potential to integrate and better inform this and many other areas of literacy work.

Positioning and Being Positioned by Literacy

The question of how individuals position themselves and are positioned by literacy, as these are made available through specific discourses and contexts, is taken up by a number of authors. Both Maguire and Masny, in their chapters on heritage language and learning and minority language communities, draw attention to the identity struggles inherent in learning and speaking languages other than English in a globalized world. Bloome discusses how one learner positions herself in relation to writing, and in turn, how she becomes positioned by writing considered to be "invisible" within the institutional walls of her workplace. Phillips and Sample also focus on issues of identity in their discussion of how parents' perceptions of themselves shift and change as a result of their participation in a family literacy program. In two of the snapshots included in this volume, both Cody and Moloney provide very personal accounts of identity that illustrate the learners' perceptions of their own literacy learning. Finally, Kendrick et al.'s and Rogers and Schofield's studies of the various ways in which students interact through symbolic and linguistic forms carry strong messages about how children and youth see themselves and others as members of particular discourse communities.

The Hegemony of Institutionalised Literacies and Language-Based Modes of Representation

The tensions across the continuum of social, institutional, and more locally situated literacy practices that illustrate the hegemonic and less permeable nature of institutional literacies and discourses is a third theme addressed across a number of chapters. Authors such as Gregory, Maguire, and Kendrick et al. call for a more "textured" notion of literacies as neither vernacular nor dominant but sometimes one or the other or both. The broad tendency in Western society to privilege school-based literacies over other less formal literacies is challenged by authors such as Anderson et al., Cairney, Gregory, Prinsloo and Stein, and Rogers and Schofield. Dichotomies between inside school/outside school literacies and the tensions associated with transplanting literacy and language practices and values from one context to another are confronted by Norton in her examination of Pakistani schoolchildren's perceptions of English as the cure-all for social problems. Bloome grapples with institutional practices that constrain (or expand) reader–writer positions according to class and gender across institutions of family and workplace.

An issue related to the hegemony of institutionalized literacies is that at the core of current literacy development paradigms are the literate behaviors traditionally associated with learning to decode and encode print. Hare and Kendrick et al. draw attention to the institutionalized privileging of linguistic modes of representation over other ways of knowing, such as reading the landscape, drawing, and image production. Despite recent rhetoric about the importance of sociocultural context and semiotics in language and literacy policy debates, policy continues to focus almost exclusively on oral and written language with little or no reference to other modes of representation. Moreover, although a growing number of language and literacy educators and theorists are calling for a multiple literacies perspective, much of the current literacy research itself continues to be grounded in a verbocentric approach.

Sociocultural and Sociopolitical Framing of Language and Literacy Practices

The fourth theme brings us full circle to the first. The sociocultural and sociopolitical framing of language literacy practices is integrally related to the projects of social change and social justice. The purpose of the majority of academic books with literacy as the subject is to make claims about the vital and ever increasing importance of literacy to the economic, political, social, and cultural well-being of a society. But how important is literacy really in terms of making a difference? Duff argues that in the context of globalization, educators and policymakers need to connect language and literacy instruction to local social and political needs and issues. Auerbach asks to what extent we can claim that literacy is central to "everything" without restating the literacy myth. She suggests that forces of globalization that argue for the need for more, and more complex, literacy skills are far from benign; indeed, multinational corporations often invoke the discourses of "flexibility" and "adaptability" in ways that mirror desired multimodal literacies, but in ways that can exploit and marginalize certain groups. Norton points out that people recognize that literacy is important, but that conceptions of literacy are located within geopolitical and historical perspectives, as well as the "imagined worlds" of individuals and groups. A key question these chapters raise is how literacy researchers and educators can recognize and engage with political and economic agendas that impact as much on a multiple literacies model as they do on the autonomous literacy model.

CONCLUSION

We want this book to stimulate debate and critical thought, and draw readers' attention to the ideological nature of literacy education across a broad range of literacy contexts. The book represents a departure from conventional wisdom in that it crosses traditional boundaries among the study of family, community, and school literacies. It offers a unique global perspective on multiple literacies, from theory to case studies of various settings. These examples suggest ways we all mould literacy practices by simultaneously shaping relationships and identity, and by privileging particular literacy practices in particular situations. The implicit dialogue within the book among the chapter authors writing across the traditionally distinct fields of family, community, adult, and school literacies highlights the interconnections between these literacy sites and stimulates the pursuit of a more integrated and interdisciplinary approach to literacy education. Moreover, this critical and dialogic orientation serves to challenge and extends many conventional notions surrounding literacy education in communities, schools, and families.

REFERENCES

Baker, C., & Luke, A. (Eds.). (1991). *Towards a critical sociology of reading pedagogy.* Amsterdam: John Benjamins.

Barton, D., Hamilton, M., & Ivanic, R. (2000). *Situated literacies: Reading and writing in context.* London: Routledge.

Bloome, D. (1989). Locating the learning of reading and writing in classrooms: Beyond deficit, differences and effectiveness models. In C. Emilhovich (Ed.), *Locating learning: Ethnographic perspective on classroom research* (pp. 87–114). Norwood, NJ: Ablex.

Bloome, D., & Green, J. (1984). Directions in the sociolinguistic study of reading. In P. D. Pearson, R. Barr, M. Kamil, & P. Mosenthal (Eds.), *Handbook of reading research* (pp. 395–422). New York: Longman.

Cope, B., Kalantzis, M., & New London Group. (2000). *Multiliteracies: Literacy learning and the design of social futures.* London: Routledge.

Dyson, A. H. (1997). *Writing superheroes: Contemporary childhood, popular culture, and classroom literacy.* New York: Teachers College Press.

Dyson, A. H. (2001). Where are the childhoods in childhood literacy: An exploration in outer (school) space. *Journal of Early Childhood Literacy, 1*(1), 9–39.

Early, M., & Tang, G. (1991). Helping ESL students cope with content-based tasks. *TESL Canada Journal, 8,* 34–44.

Ferdman, B. M. (1990). Literacy and cultural identity. *Harvard Educational Review, 60,* 181–204.

Freire, P. (1970). *Pedagogy of the oppressed.* New York: Continuum.

Freire, P., & Macedo, D. (1987). *Literacy: Reading the word and the world.* South Hadley, MA: Bergin & Garvey.

Halliday, M. A. K. (1969). Relevant models of language. *Educational Review, 22*(1), 26–37.

Halliday, M. A. K. (1975a). *Explorations in the functions of language.* London: Edward Arnold.

Halliday, M. A. K. (1975b). *Learning how to mean.* New York: Elsevier North-Holland.

Harste, J., Woodward, V., & Burke, C. (1984). *Language stories and literacy learning.* Portsmouth, NH: Heinemann Educational Books.

Heath, S. B. (1983). *Ways with words: Language, life, and work in communities and classroom.* Cambridge: Cambridge University Press.

Herber, H. (1970). *Teaching reading in content areas.* Englewood Cliffs, NJ: Prentice Hall.

Hodge, R., & Kress, G. (1988). *Social semiotics.* Cambridge, England: Polity Press.

Kress, G. (1993). Against arbitrariness: The social production of the sign as a foundational issue in critical discourse analysis. *Discourse and Society, 4*(2), 169–193.

Kress, G. (1997). *Before writing: Rethinking the paths into literacy.* London: Routledge.

Lemke, J. (1990). *Talking science: Language, learning and values.* Norwood, NJ: Ablex.

Luke, A. (2002). *Critical literacy and globalization: Between the diasporic and cosmopolitan.* Keynote address, NCTE Assembly for Research 2002 Midwinter Conference, New York City.

Martin, J., & Halliday, M. A. K. (1981). *Readings in systemic linguistics.* London: Batsford Academic and Educational.

Padmore, S. (1994). Guiding lights. In M. Hamilton, D. Barton, & R. Ivanic (Eds.), *Worlds of literacy* (pp. 143–157). Clevedon: Multilingual Matters.

Purcell-Gates, V. (1997). *Other people's words: The cycle of low literacy.* Cambridge, MA: Harvard University Press.

Schofield, A., & Rogers, T. (2004). At play in the fields of ideas: The lives and multiple literacies of youth in an alternative school. *Journal of Adolescent and Adult Literacy, 48*(3), 238–248.

Scollon, R., & Scollon, S. (1981). *Narrative, literacy and face in interethnic communication.* Norwood, NJ: Ablex.

Scribner, S. (1988). Literacy in three metaphors. In E. Kingsten, B. Knoll, & M. Rose (Eds.), *Perspectives on literacy* (pp. 71–81). Carbondale, IL: Southern Illinois University Press.

Scribner, S., & Cole, M. (1981). *The psychology of literacy.* Cambridge, MA: Harvard University Press.

Solsken, J. W. (1993). *Literacy, gender, and work in families and in schools.* Norwood, NJ: Ablex.

Street, B. (1984). *Literacy in theory and practice.* Cambridge: Cambridge University Press.

Street, B. (1995). *Social literacies: Critical approaches to literacy development, ethnography and education.* London: Longman.

Taylor, D. (1983). *Family literacy: Young children learning to read and write.* Exeter, NH: Heinemann.

Taylor, D., & Dorsey-Gaines, C. (1988). *Growing up literate: Learning from inner-city families.* Portsmouth, NH: Heinemann.

FAMILY LITERACIES

Chapter *2*

Guiding Lights: Siblings as Literacy Teachers in a Multilingual Community

Eve Gregory
Goldsmiths College, University of London

Jahanara, aged 11, and her younger sister Shahana, 8, live in Spitalfields, in the East End of London. They are both bilingual in Sylheti,[1] which they speak to their parents and grandparents, and English, which they speak in school, to friends, and to each other. On this occasion, Jahanara is reading a story in English to Shahana at home:

> *Jahanara: Kora's new pet. Kora lived in a small house beside the lake. At the back of the house there was a big hill. Lots of blackberry grew there. One fine day, she sneaked out to pick the berries. . . . Soon her bucket was half-full. As Kora was about to get up again, she heard a noise, a bark or a cry. Looking around, she saw something moving in the grass. "What could it be?" she screamed. She walked slowly, very slowly, over to the spot when she saw that it was a small fox cub. It looked up at her but did not move . . . She bent down and saw it was caught in a trap . . . Leaving her blackberries behind, Kora picked up the cub and made for home. "What have you got there?" asked her mother. . . . Her mother was a nurse . . . She washed the fox's leg with hot water and put a bandage on it . . . The happy girl lifted the fox up in her arms. She looked up and saw the mist on the hill . . . "I'll call it Misty" she said.*
>
> *Jahanara: Now on to the questions. What was at the back of Kora's house? Tell me.*
>
> *Shahana: A hill with blackberries*
>
> *Jahanara: OK, I'll accept that . . . Write that in a full sentence after I've gone through with you.*

---

[1]Sylheti is generally regarded to be a dialect of Bengali, spoken by the people of Sylhet in the northeastern corner of Bangladesh. Literacy is learned by these children in standard Bengali, which the children understand but do not speak.

Jahanara: How did her mother help the fox?

Shahana: . . . (inaudible)

Jahanara: Say it again.

Shahana: She banded the fox neck leg.

Jahanara: Banded?

Shahana: The fox leg.

Jahanara: How can she banned the fox leg?

Shahana: Because she was a nurse.

Jahanara: There is no such thing as banned as such. If I was the king, I would have banned the cigarette. You mean bandage or plaster?

Shahana: Bandage. (Gregory, 2001, pp. 312–313)

The term *guiding light* has been used to refer to individuals who play a very important role in our literacy development (Padmore, 1994). When parents are unfamiliar with the language and culture of the school, siblings may become very special guiding lights in younger children's literacy lives. Recent studies are beginning to highlight the special role that may be played by older siblings in linguistic minority families where parents do not speak the new language (Azmitia & Hesser, 1993; Gregory, 1998; Perez et al., 1994; Volk, 2001; Zukow, 1989). These studies all call into question the notion that parents will be the exclusive "teachers" in families who move to live in a new country. Some show how siblings assist each other by sharing a common "language" and "cultural recipes" (Azmitia & Hesser, 1993); others demonstrate the contribution of siblings to each other's social, cognitive, and emotional development (Dunn, 1989; Ervin-Tripp, 1989). However, the role of siblings as unique teachers of *school literacy practices* has hitherto not been a focus of attention. In this chapter, I offer portraits of young Bangladeshi-origin siblings, showing ways in which they fulfil this role as they read together in London's East End. I show how older siblings take hold of school learning and present it in an understandable form to their younger siblings during play at home. I investigate what transformations might occur during this "teaching" and what we might learn from these about collaboration and cognition.

THEORETICAL PERSPECTIVES

The work presented here draws on perspectives that originate in different disciplines and research traditions. The first perspective comes from what is now known as the New Literacy Studies. These studies cut across linguistics, anthropology, sociology, and psychology to unite researchers challenging the notion of a "great divide" between literacy and orality. Researchers in

New Literacy Studies argue that there is no single, monolithic, autonomous literacy: Rather, there are "literacies" or "literacy practices" whose character and consequences are different in each context. Literacy practices are, then, aspects not just of culture but also of power structures (Barton & Hamilton, 1998; Baynham, 1995; Street, 1984). Viewed in this way, school-sanctioned literacy, or "**Literacy**" to which Street (1995, p. 14) refers, is just one of a multiplicity of literacies (or literacy practices) that take place in people's lives, in different domains, and for a variety of purposes and in different languages.

From the New Literacy Studies, I borrow and extend Baynham's (1995) term *mediator of literacy* to refer particularly to siblings close in age. Baynham defines a mediator as "a person who makes his or her skill available to others, on a formal or informal basis, for them to accomplish specific literacy purposes" (p. 39). Siblings, however, play a more important role than simply offering literacy skills. They initiate younger members of the family into whole new discourses (Gee, 1996) comprising ways of behaving, valuing, and expressing new opinions, beliefs, and views. Through their caregiving, they open up new cultural worlds, worlds entered by their siblings who "apprentice" themselves to the older role model. Thus childhood initiation into literacy is viewed as a collaborative group activity rather than a dyadic activity between parent and child. I have used Padmore's (1994) term *guiding lights* to refer to those special mediators who are siblings close in age (p. 143). The guiding lights in Padmore's study generally tended to be grandparents, aunts, or friends, but her starting point was adults with reading difficulties reflecting on their childhood experiences.

A second perspective draws on and extends the powerful metaphor of *scaffolding* (Bruner, 1986) from early childhood studies. This metaphor describes how adults or older experts provide a scaffold to assist the young child; the scaffold is slowly dismantled as the child becomes competent in a task. This interpretation of the learning process complements that promoted earlier by Vygotsky (1978), who sees the adult as assisting the child across the zone of proximal development (ZPD), which is the space between what the child is capable of alone or with adult assistance (in other words, what she or he will be capable of alone tomorrow). Rogoff (1990) and her colleagues (Rogoff, Mistry, Goncu, & Mosier, 1993) develop the scaffolding concept by referring to *guided participation* between infants and adults. Their interpretation stresses the *active* role played by the child, as well as the different nature of adult assistance according to the cultural background of the family. Siblings will, of course, interact differently from adults. Although older sisters and brothers are conceptually and linguistically more advanced than their younger siblings, I refer in this research to a *synergy* taking place (Gregory, 2001), whereby the younger child *questions* and the older *practises*, but both teach and learn equally from each other. This distinguishes their relationship from the traditional scaffolding role.

A third and important perspective informing this study is that of syncretism as used by cultural anthropologists (Cole, 1996; Gregory, Long, & Volk, 2004). This view stresses that young children are not entrapped within practices they may be familiar with from home, but actively transform different activities and practices to create new forms. The siblings introduced in this chapter reveal a complex heterogeneity of traditions, whereby reading practices from school, Qur'anic, and Bengali language, and literacy classes are blended, resulting in a form that is both new and dynamic. I refer to this type of blending as *syncretic literacy*, which merges not simply linguistic codes or texts but different activities. In this chapter, we see a complex interplay between the methods, materials, and role relationships of school and community language and literacy lessons through games and "play school" sessions conducted by siblings at home. The conclusion to this chapter illustrates further the specific features of work belonging to "syncretic literacy studies" (Gregory, Long, & Volk, 2004).

Thus the theoretical framework within which this chapter is situated encompasses work from linguistics and adult literacy (Barton & Hamilton, 1998; Gee, 1996), psychology and cultural psychology (Cole, 1996; Rogoff, 1990; Vygotsky, 1978) and cultural anthropology (Duranti, Ochs, & Ta'ase, 2004; Gregory, 2001). Each contributes a different but complementary understanding of children learning literacy within a social and cultural context.

THE CONTEXT: CHILDREN OF BANGLADESHI
BRITISH ORIGIN IN EAST LONDON

This chapter introduces findings from research conducted in a primary school with 99% Bangladeshi British intake in Spitalfields, East London.[2] The district of Spitalfields has a long tradition of receiving immigrants: the Huguenots during the 18th century, followed by Jews from Eastern Europe during the later half of the 19th and early 20th centuries. Today, their place has been taken by families from Bangladesh, and the streets in the area reflect their Muslim religion and culture. The families come almost uniquely from the Sylhet area of Bangladesh. They speak Sylheti, a dialect of Bengali in which they learn the written form. Many families came to live in the

[2]Data used in this chapter are drawn from a much larger bank of data collected in an ESRC-funded research project *Siblings as Mediators of Literacy in Two East London Communities* (R 000 222487) (1998–1999) whereby the home and school literacy practices of 10 pairs of Bangladeshi London and the same number of Anglo siblings were studied. Fuller accounts of this work can be found in Gregory (2001), Williams (2004), and Williams and Gregory (2001).

United Kingdom during the 1970s and 1980s. At the turn of the 21st century, therefore, children in primary schools were mostly born in London;
youngsters grow up speaking Sylheti to their grandparents and possibly
their parents and English to their siblings and Anglo friends. In terms of
health, housing, and income, the district is one of the poorest in the country. Unemployment is high among the older generation, whose English often is not fluent, and those who manage to find employment mostly remain
together working as tailors or in restaurants in the immediate vicinity. However, families place great importance on the language and culture of their
origin, and children regularly attend both Qur'anic and Bengali language
and literacy classes after school.

In the Spitalfields school, eight families, each with an older child in Years
5 or 6 (i.e., aged 10–11) and a younger child in school (i.e., aged 4–8), took
part in the research. The families, whose sizes ranged from eleven children
to three, lived in rented accommodation in blocks of flats. We[3] collected a
wide range of data types over one year, including interviews with children,
parents, teachers, and head teachers, regular recordings of class literacy
hour sessions, group discussions, and children's literacy diaries.

Of particular interest were the home recordings. Each family was provided with a tape recorder, and the children were asked to record themselves at home, taking part in a play activity that involved reading or writing.
They chose a range of activities: singing songs, reciting rhymes, reading to
younger siblings and crucially, playing school. In this chapter, I present
data from these recordings (especially playing school) and audiotaped
classroom literacy lessons to analyse particularly the importance of both the
school "reading culture" and individual classroom "lessons" in children's
home literacy lives. In so doing, I show how siblings play a unique role as
guiding lights in teaching younger children what counts as literacy in
school. Interactions presented reveal the skill of the older siblings in transforming classroom discourse into play, thus rendering school learning into
an enjoyable and easily understandable task.

The skills shown by siblings are unpacked and analysed in terms of *procedural, academic,* and *cultural* knowledge. Procedural knowledge refers to the
routines and rituals, whether linguistic or behavioural, that children need
to know for successful classroom interaction to take place. Street and Street
(1995, p. 121) highlight these in the words of one teacher who says to her
class, "Now you are in school, use your school voice." Academic knowledge
relates to the skills or teacher-led learning that might be grammar, spelling,
mathematics, or any other subject of the curriculum. Cultural knowledge

---

[3]Ann Williams and Ali Asghar worked as researchers on this project, which was directed by
Eve Gregory.

refers to either knowledge about traditional literature, poetry, or stories from the host country or the way of interacting with the teacher in the classroom (teacher might be "madam," etc.; Gregory, 1993). On each occasion, I present children's "play school" as well as the actual classroom sessions in which the older child participated, highlighting how "work" is transformed at home for the younger child.

PROCEDURAL KNOWLEDGE

> Listen, before we start, cross your legs. Before we start, let's get the rules sorted out. Wait till I ask you a question. Sometimes I'll say you can all answer or read or sometimes put your hand up. Don't just call out when I'm trying to get another child looking for words. So . . . it's a lovely book. The title. You can all call out the title. (Gregory & Williams, 2000, p. 182)

In this excerpt, Mrs. Kelly is carefully initiating her class into literacy in her multilingual classroom in London. The procedural knowledge here indicates "what counts as literacy" in the classroom as far as the organisation of time, space, and work practices are concerned. In other words, procedures ". . . set the boundaries of literacy itself and assert its place within a culturally defined authority structure" (Street, 1995, p. 122). Formulae for successful participation in the reading session form an important part of this, as shown in the opening formulae in both home and classroom sessions.

Farjana Teaching Her Younger Sister

In this excerpt, we see ways in which Farjana structures the learning context through her opening moves as she engages in Playing School. Farjana is age 10 and her sister Farhana is age 8.

1. Farjana: Hello, my name is Farjana. Today a bit of English, then a story and last of all a spelling test. OK, for English we're working on signs and notices. The title is: Where would you see these notices. This is what you have to do. I have put signs and some answers. All you have to do is to choose a sign and then put a circle around what you think is the right answer. OK, here's your sheet, Farhana. You understand what to do?	
	2. Farhana: Yes.

3. Farjana: Here, off you go.
   OK, let's see how you've done it. Danger
   Stay Out—you put it in a mine field.
   Correct, 1 point. Please do not touch—
   toy shop. No, I thought it'll be going to
   a shop with expensive things. Now, Look
   before you cross—a busy road. Correct,
   2 points. This way to the dolphins—in
   a zoo, correct, OK. Now it's time for a
   story, your favourite story, Monty the
   Monster Mouse.

Farjana clearly signals the organisation of the lesson and begins working through her plan. She identifies the topic, draws attention to the elements of the task, and checks whether her instructions have been understood. She then goes through the task in detail. She emphasises that the "class" is engaged in an ongoing sequence of learning activities and is approaching learning as a joint enterprise: "For English we're working on signs and notices" . . . "Let's see how you've done it." Finally, she allocates rewards (points) for answering correctly before she moves smoothly to the next lesson: "OK. Now it's time for a story, your favourite story, Monty the Monster Mouse."

Farjana's Teacher

Farjana's teacher begins a literacy lesson in a similar way by focusing on learning and academic purpose:

1. Teacher: OK. Who's ready? I must say
   I'm really pleased to see some of you
   testing each other on your spellings
   whilst you're waiting . . . (attendance
   register taken)
   "Good morning, Miss . . ."
   Put your hands up please if you have
   not done your science homework . . .
   (repeated) You haven't . . . Why not?
   Did you forget we were doing science last
   week? (child replies) Maybe you should
   start it a bit earlier . . . Well, it's science
   again tomorrow, Thursday. You'd better
   have it finished by then.

Right, we're going to look at a different poem again this morning. What sort of poem have we been looking at over the past 2 weeks? What sort of poetry? Can you remember the name?	
	2. Child: Narrative.
3. Teacher: <u>Narrative</u> poetry. But what does 'narrative' actually mean? It's another of those long words. What does it actually mean, Farjana?	
	4. Farjana: Story.
5. Teacher: It's a <u>story</u> poem.	

Like Farjana, the teacher reinforces the child's engagement in directed learning activities (spelling tests) and emphasises the status of such activities in the classroom, checks the organisation of children's homework, and refers to previous learning activities jointly undertaken by the class: "What sort of poem have we been looking at . . . ?" Although consciously building a classroom culture based on explicit explanations and questioning, she is aware that her children are familiar with her style from both their Bengali and Qur'anic lessons (Gregory, 1996). Crucially, procedural knowledge is not the focus of attention but is constantly intertwined with academic and cultural knowledge.

LEARNING AS ACADEMIC KNOWLEDGE

Since the introduction in Britain of the National Curriculum in 1989 and the National Literacy Strategy in 1998,[4] the transmission of particular kinds of academic knowledge has been paramount during literacy lessons in the primary school. Teaching has become considerably more focused on the gathering of factual knowledge that can be tested regularly rather than personal knowledge gained through experimentation and finding things out for oneself. Literacy lessons have adopted a precise structure. For 1 hour per day, children engage in activities that are largely teacher-led, where word, sentence, and phonic skills are often drilled repeatedly, to be tested in national exams at ages 7, 11, and 14. Next, we see how Wahida takes this factual knowledge on board in two different contexts.

---

[4]The National Literacy Strategy was introduced into all schools in England by David Blunkett of the Labour Government in 1998. One hour of directed structured literacy activities per day are obligatory from Year 1 (age 5). These are tested at age 7 and later at 11 in the primary school.

The Excitement of Academic Knowledge:
Wahida and Her Sister Sayeeda

Wahida is also 11 and her sister Sayeeda 8. This episode forms a small part of a "lesson" lasting almost an hour that covers maths, science, and the animal world, as well as various types of reading, comprehension, and spelling. First, we eavesdrop on her science "lesson":

Wahida: Welcome back, children. Now we're going to do science. We're going to do electricity—about circuits because tomorrow or the next day we're going to make circuits of our own. So I'm going to show you how to make a circuit and then you're going to do it by yourselves. You always need wires, battery, bulb, switch—you can always make a switch by yourselves so it doesn't matter . . . and if so you need a crocodile clip. When you make a circuit, you always need a good battery to light, obviously. You need the two wires to touch the two sides of the battery. And the bulb needs a bulb holder to sit up . . . the wire has a . . . a metal stuff so it can touch the bulb's screw for it to light . . . the metal. So that's when it lights up. Then you can make your own switch whenever you want. If you want to make one switch you can do . . . That's how I know how to make a switch. You need a card with two pins and you wrap . . . and you wrap the paper clip around the one pin and then when you want the bulb to light up easily you need the wire's, erm, er silver bits to touch the pins so it . . . for the paper clip to go with the wire and then you wrap it . . . when you touch the paper clip to the other pin it lights up. So you're going to make your own circuit today. So you can start now. OK? (Gregory & Williams, 2000, pp. 201–202)

Wahida's linguistic and academic knowledge and skills are striking, especially when we consider that she entered school 5 years earlier speaking and understanding very little English. It is clear that she uses her "lesson" to practise; she weaves procedural information—"So I'm going to show you how to make a circuit and then you're going to do it by yourselves"—with academic knowledge—"You need a card with two pins and you wrap . . . and you wrap the paper clip around the one pin. . . ." Yet her practice also serves another purpose: Sayeeda, her younger sister, is extremely impressed by her older sister's skills. She listens and responds modestly. In time, she, too, will "teach" her younger sister in a similar way.

The second excerpt could come straight from a school literacy lesson where grammar now has pride of place. The learning of homophones has taken on a surprising importance in the literacy curriculum, and it is possible to go from one school to the next and observe almost identical lessons at the same time of the day.

42. Now we're going to do homophones. Who knows what's a homophone is? No one? OK. I'll tell you one and then you're going to do some by yourselves.
Like watch—one watch is your time watch, like what's the time, watch. And another watch is I'm watching you, I can see you. OK? So Sayeeda, you wrote some in your book, haven't you? Can you tell me some please. Sayeeda, can you only give me three please.

43. Oh I have to give five.

44. No, Sayeeda, we haven't got enough time. We've only another five minutes to assembly. And guess who's going to do assembly—Miss Kudija.

44. OK.

45. OK? So tell me one.

46. Son is the opposite of daughter

47. Yeah

48. and sun is . . . um . . . its shines on the sky so bright.

49. Well done! That's one correct one. The next one?

50. The cell means you go . . . to jail . . . in prison . . . you're going to prison and another sell means the selling money . . . they are giving money.

51. The last one is ?

52. Hear. Hear is you're hearing something . . . people are telling you something and here is come here, come.

53. Well done! Now you can go to assembly. Sayeeda line up in order. Otherwise you'll come back and do lines. So remember your order. OK? Well done, Sayeeda, you're in your correct order and Miss Kudija is going to take you down because I have to do some more things.

It is clear from these excerpts that Wahida's knowledge and skills in this specialist area of language and literacy come directly from the teacher's classroom practice. However, Wahida adjusts her demands to a child of Sayeeda's age, realising that the work on homophones in her own classroom is too complex for an 8-year-old. Words such as "shipwright" to rhyme with "right" and "write" (see the next example) are not attempted, and the homophones practised are indeed those used by teachers of Sayeeda's age group. She thus provides an excellent illustration of Vygotsky's (1978) argument that the best teaching leads children across the zone of proximal development (the space between what is possible alone and what can be achieved with the help of another, more experienced person). One of Wahida's skills here is her ability to pitch the level of difficulty just at the right point, to stretch her sister's knowledge. Like Farjana and her younger sister, we see how Wahida could almost be her sister's real teacher. The curriculum is clearly focused, the discourse shows respect from both teacher and learner, and praise is given where deserved.

The Excitement of Academic Knowledge: Wahida's Teacher

81. Teacher: 'Right'. Can you tell me why that's a homophone, Sultana? What's the other word that sounds like it? How would you spell that? Sorry, can't hear you. A. can you spell it for me?	
	82. A: 'w-r-i-g-h-t'
83. Teacher: 'w-r-i-g-h-t'. Do you agree with him, M?	
	84. Chorus: Yes.
85. Teacher: What do you think, Hasira?	
	86. H: 'w-r-i-t-e'
87. Teacher: Excellent, Hasira. Although, M. is right, aren't you M? Because what's that word? (inaudible) <u>No</u>. This is the 'write' that you write in your book (pointing)	
	88. Chorus: Or the left and right side.
89. Teacher: No. This is the left and right side. But where did we come across this 'wright'. Let's go back to Noah's Ark.	
	90. Children (excitedly): Shipwright.

91. Teacher: Yes, and a shipwright named 'Arkwright' wasn't it? I was just wondering, 'Where have they got '<u>wright</u>' from' and I remembered it was from the other poem that we read. Excellent!	
	92. Children: Three.
93. Teacher: We've got <u>three</u> different ways of making that sound. 'Right, write, wright'. Three homophones.	

Wahida's teacher displays all the attention to detail that makes her such an excellent role model for her pupil to follow. She is flexible in her approach, realising her own errors and learning from the children themselves. This is most clear as she suddenly realises that the children have remembered "shipwright" and "Arkwright" from a previous lesson; she had initially forgotten it herself (87), but takes their choral "Yes" (84) very seriously and re-thinks. This type of negotiation is part of the classroom culture.

LITERACY AS PART OF THE WIDER CULTURE

The National Literacy Strategy in Britain also places great store by the teaching and learning of Western literature and poetry. However, Wahida and Farjana's teacher also introduces her class to poetry from across the world. She realises that European poetry and literature are extremely difficult for her 100% Bangladeshi British class, owing not only to the complexity of language structures, but also the inaccessibility of the cultural and historical knowledge required. Consequently, she aims to give her pupils "ownership" of poetry by encouraging listening carefully and reciting by heart before going on to write their own piece.

Learning a Culture Through Poetry:
Farjana's Teacher in School

On this occasion, Farjana's class has been discussing "rap" as a poetic form and are now learning and practising a rap poem together:

55. Teacher: What was it that anyone found difficult at our first reading?	
	56. Child: The reading.

57. Teacher: You just found the reading a bit hard. What made it hard?

58. Child: Making it fast.

59. Teacher: Yes. When you couldn't get it faster. That's a good point. How do you think W? could improve that? What could she do?

60. Child: Read it slower.

61. Teacher: We could read it slower to help her. What else? Maybe we could do a copy. Maybe you might like to take a copy home to practise. You could read it to your mum, couldn't you? OK. I'm pointing to it, just to help you keep up with me. (in chorus, whole poem started with 'If you're old enough to go to school' but halted after a couple of lines. The teacher hesitates when the children cannot read the poem fast enough and with the correct rhythm). There's a very fine line, isn't there, between keeping the pace up for the rhythm and it not sounding very nice. Let me just have a go on my own. 'So if by chance . . .' (reads to end) What did my voice lack? What did my voice not have very much of? Yes, ??

62. Child: Expression.

63. Teacher: Expression. It didn't sound like I was very interested in that poem, did it? I think I need to try again, to get some expression into it. 'So if by chance, while in the playground or the park . . .' (read again with more emphasis and expression)

Farjana's teacher takes a very formal approach and has very high expectations of the children's ear for rhythm and rhyme in a language that is not their mother tongue. However, she knows that they are accustomed to reciting and practising prayers and other important texts in both their Qur'anic and Bengali classes and calls on their excellent memory skills for this task. She acknowledges the potential difficulty of the task, and explores ways of dealing with this. She also makes herself a participant in finding a solution: "I think I need to try again. . . ." We might say that both the children and their teacher syncretise the literacy practices from their English, Bengali, and Qur'anic classes. The poem itself and the rap form that are the starting point of the lesson are part of Black Anglo–American culture, yet the rhythm and repetition could place it within Bengali or Qur'anic traditions. It is, indeed, the rhythm and sounds of the poem that may appeal most to the children, as the activities mentioned are very different from those within the children's experience.

Poetry at Home: Farjana as Initiator of a New Culture

As part of her English "lesson," Farjana also turns to poetry. This is a regular part of her "lesson" and usually involves the younger child in listening, reciting, and then writing her own piece.

31. Farjana: OK very nice. Now I'm going to have to do a poem and memorize it. You looked at it. Now we're going to do a short poem and memorize it. So it's not too hard. Unless you want it to be difficult for you, you do the longest poem on earth. All right. OK. We'll have a short one, like we had in the poetry book. They had really the short one, didn't they? Some were complicated, some weren't. But I did read the easy ones. And there were some with <?> number. So you could do a numbered one as long as it . . . it doesn't have to be short, if you do numbered one I know it's going to be long. Isn't it? OK. Off you go . . . OK. Everybody should finish by now. Are you finished, Farhana?

32. Farhana: Yes.

33. Farjana: Let's see. It doesn't look finished. While you're doing yours, I'll read my poem, I done <?> OK. My poem.
I don't like working but I do like playing
Everytime I think of anything bad I start praying
I don't like working, but of course I like to <?> praying.

Now OK. I forgot to say something before all of you wrote your poems.
If <?> every poem does not have to
rhyme. It could be about anything, like
I did about praying, playing and working. That's it. OK. I'll read my poem
once again so we'll have an idea. But
mine's do rhyme actually
because I couldn't think of any other
words. OK—my poem.
I don't like working but I do like
playing
Every time I think of anything bad I
start praying
I don't like worry <?> (or 'working'?)
But of course I like praying.
OK. Some of the words did rhyme, but
in the real poems you don't quite . . .
some poetry have it and some don't.
So because when I didn't know all poems don't have to rhyme, I get the
niggling thought ain't it strange why
would it be called a poem if it does
not rhyme. But I did find out all
poems don't have to rhyme. OK
Farhana have you finished yours?

34. Farhana: Yes.

35. Farjana: Would you like to read it
anybody.

36. Farhana: Traffic lights
The red light at the top says
you have to stop
Red light and amber be-
tween say get ready for free
Green below says you can go.

37. Farjana: OK. Very good. But I'm sorry
I didn't say that it doesn't have to
rhyme and you had to think twice as
much. Still it's very nice. OK.

Just like her teacher (and her teacher of Bengali, where children are also
learning poems from their Bengali primer), Farjana reassures her "pupil"
that writing a poem and memorising it will be difficult but manageable. She
also gives the opportunity for her "pupil" to choose the level of difficulty: "it
doesn't have to be short. . . ." She makes herself a participant in learning

about whether poems are required to rhyme. A focus on rhyming and memorisation is also part of Farjana's community class experience, and here she integrates the negotiation around learning that characterises classroom discourse in her primary classroom.

CONCLUSION

In this chapter, I examined some of the home and school literacy and learning practices in the lives of young second-generation Bangladeshi British girls whose home is in East London. The chapter shows ways in which the powerful literacy practices of the school extend into the homes of children who are also participating in very different literacies in different languages in their community classes (Bengali and Qur'anic). It thus illustrates the argument made by others working within the New Literacy Studies that literacy practices are a reflection not just of culture but of the power structures in our society. Despite regular attendance at both Bengali and Qur'anic classes,[5] the children all chose to act out and practise only their English lessons. The chapter also shows the very special role played by siblings close in age as literacy mediators in initiating their younger siblings into the wider school discourses (Gee, 1996) or ways of behaving, valuing, and expressing new opinions, beliefs, and views. Farjana and Wahida mediate the procedural, academic, and cultural knowledge needed for success in school. When Farjana demarcates different sections of her "lesson," allocates points for getting something correct, praises, and reminds, she directs the younger child to crucial procedures to which she must pay attention. Likewise, Wahida enables Sayeeda to "practise what they [she] already know[s]" (Cole, 1985, p. 157) by rehearsing the academic language of science and homophones at home before needing it in school. Finally, by listening to her older sister's poems and making up her own simple poems at home, Farjana will begin to recognise what counts as poetry in her English classroom.

These examples are but a few from numerous others taking place in the homes of the Bangladeshi London children.[6] We could say that the older siblings are simply expert imitators of the language and pedagogic style of their teachers and are, therefore, able to "play" school literacy practices as well as the role of teacher in their interaction with younger children. Play is,

---

[5]Although it would be inappropriate to act out practices taking place at the mosque, there is no reason why the children should not have chosen to act out Bengali classes. When questioned about this, they responded that they never did so.

[6]A similar argument can also be made for the Anglo London children in the study whose home literacy practices also reflect the aims of the head teacher of the school. In their case, however, a number of different activities were taped revealing the broad variety of informal literacies taking place in their out-of-school lives.

of course, of crucial importance in their learning (Williams, 2004), as the children not only imitate but transform school practices, extending and exaggerating them (for example, through giving "lines" for bad behaviour) as well as syncretising them with styles used in Qur'anic and Bengali classes.

The chapter thus provides an example of what is now referred to as "Syncretic Literacy Studies" in early childhood (Gregory, Long, & Volk, 2004). These studies share the following beliefs:

1. Young children are active members of different cultural and linguistic groups and appropriating membership to a group is not a static or a linear process.

2. Children do not remain in separate worlds but acquire membership of different groups *simultaneously*, that is, they live in "simultaneous worlds" (Kenner, 2003).

3. Simultaneous membership means that children syncretise the languages, literacies, narrative styles, and role relationships appropriate to each group and then go on to transform the languages and cultures they use to create new forms relevant to the purpose needed.

4. Young children who participate in cross-linguistic and cross-cultural practices call on a greater wealth of metacognitive and metalinguistic strategies. These strategies are further enhanced when they are able to *play out different roles and events*.

5. Play is a crucial feature of children's language and literacy practice with siblings, grandparents, and peers.

6. The mediators, often bicultural and/or bilingual, play an essential role in early language and literacy learning. Studies investigate different forms of scaffolding, guided participation, or synergy as young and older children or adults work and play together.

Syncretic Literacy Studies, therefore, go beyond issues of method, materials, and parental involvement toward a wider interpretation of literacy, including what children take culturally and linguistically from their families and communities (*prolepsis*), how they gain access to the existing *funds of knowledge* in their communities through *finely tuned scaffolding* by mediators, and how they transform existing languages, literacies, and practices to create new forms (*syncretism*). This whole process takes place within the wider sociocultural framework.

In this chapter, both the older siblings and their teacher's lessons reveal a syncretism of each other's practices. Both draw on recitation, repetition, and strict role relationships between teacher and learner, yet both retain the concern for the individual linked with child-centred learning. The teacher's use of whole class teaching might well reflect a focus on *the family as a group entity* rather than *family members as individuals.* (See also work on Central Mexican families by Zukow, 1989; families from Senegal by Whittemore & Beverly, 1989; and the Solomon Isles by Watson-Gegeo & Gegeo, 1989.) It is almost as if the teacher and older sibling are colluding together in initiating family learning. If, indeed, collusion were taking place, it is clear that teachers have found the perfect partners, for, far more than parents, siblings are able to pitch their lessons at exactly the right level, showing how "culture and cognition create each other" (Cole, 1985, in Rogoff, 1990, p. 14) as they rehearse the cultural world of the school.

ACKNOWLEDGMENTS

This research was funded by the ESRC (Siblings as mediators of literacy in two East London communities: R000222487, 1998–2000). I thank Ann Williams and Ali Asghar for their work on this project and Charmian Kenner for her assistance in analysing data collected. I am also grateful to all the families and teachers participating in the project.

REFERENCES

Azmitia, M., & Hesser, J. (1993). Why siblings are important agents of cognitive development: A comparison of siblings and peers. *Child Development, 64,* 430–444.

Baynham, M. (1995). *Literacy practices: Investigating literacy in social contexts.* London: Longman.

Barton, D., & Hamilton, S. (1998). *Local literacies: Reading and writing in one community.* London: Routledge.

Bruner, J. (1986). *Actual minds, possible worlds.* Cambridge, MA: Harvard University Press.

Cole, M. (1985). The zone of proximal development: Where culture and cognition create each other. In J. V. Wertsch (Ed.), *Culture, communication and cognition: Vygotskian perspectives* (pp. 146–162). Cambridge: Cambridge University Press.

Cole, M. (1996). *Cultural psychology: A once and future discipline.* Cambridge, MA: Harvard University Press.

Dunn, J. (1989). Siblings and the development of social understanding in early childhood. In P. G. Zukow (Ed.), *Sibling interaction across cultures: Theoretical and methodological issues* (pp. 106–116). New York: Springer Verlag.

Duranti, A., Ochs, E., & Ta'ase, E. (2004). Change and tradition in literacy instruction in a Samoan American community. In E. Gregory, S. Long, & D. Volk (Eds.), *Many pathways to literacy: Young children learning with siblings, grandparents, peers and communities* (pp. 159–170). London: Routledge.

Ervin-Tripp, S. (1989). Sisters and brothers. In P. G. Zukow (Ed.), *Sibling interaction across cultures: Theoretical and methodological issues.* New York: Springer Verlag.

Gee, J. P. (1996). *Social linguistics and literacies.* London: Routledge.

Gregory, E. (1993). What counts as literacy in the early years' classroom? *British Journal of Educational Psychology, 63,* 213–229.

Gregory, E. (1996). *Making sense of a new word: Learning to read in a second language.* London: Sage.

Gregory, E. (1998). Siblings as mediators of literacy in linguistic minority communities. *Language and Education, 1*(12), 33–55.

Gregory, E. (2001). Sisters and brothers as language and literacy teachers: Synergy between siblings playing and working together. *Journal of Early Childhood Literacy, 1*(3), 301–322.

Gregory, E., & Williams, A. (2000). *City literacies: Learning to read across generations and cultures.* London: Routledge.

Gregory, E., Long, S., & Volk, D. (2004). *Many pathways to literacy: Early learning with siblings, grandparents peers and communities.* London: Routledge.

Kenner, C. (2004). Living in simultaneous worlds: Difference and integration in bilingual script learning. *International Journal of Bilingual Education and Bilingualism, 7*(1), 43–61.

Padmore, S. (1994). Guiding lights. In S. Hamilton, D. Barton, & R. Ivanic (Eds.), *Worlds of literacy* (pp. 143–156). Clevedon, Avon: Multilingual Matters.

Perez, D., Barajas, N., Dominiguez, M., Juarez, R., Saab, M., Vergara, F., & Callanan, M. (1994). Siblings providing one another with opportunities to learn. *Focus on Diversity, 5*(1), 1–5.

Rogoff, B. (1990). *Apprenticeship in thinking: Cognitive development in social context.* New York: Oxford University Press.

Rogoff, B., Mistry, J., Goncu, A., & Mosier, C. (1993). Guided participation in cultural activity by toddlers and caregivers. *Monographs of the Society for Research in Child Development, 58*(8), Serial No. 236.

Street, B. V. (1984). *Literacy in theory and practice.* Cambridge: Cambridge University Press.

Street, B. V. (1995). *Social literacies.* London: Longman.

Street, B. V., & Street, J. (1995). The schooling of literacy. In B. V. Street (Ed.), *Social literacies* (pp. 106–131). London: Longman.

Volk, D. (2001). Many differing ladders, many ways to climb . . . Literacy events in the bilingual classroom, homes, and community of three Puerto Rican kindergartners. *Journal of Early Childhood Literacy, 1*(2), 193–224.

Vygotsky, L. (1978). *Mind in society. The development of higher psychological processes.* Cambridge, MA: Harvard University Press.

Watson-Gegeo, K. A., & Gegeo, D. W. (1989). The role of sibling interaction in child socialisation. In P. G. Zukow (Ed.), *Sibling interaction across cultures: Theoretical and methodological issues.* New York: Springer Verlag.

Whittemore, R. D., & Beverly, E. (1989). Trust in the Mandinka way: The cultural context of sibling care. In P. G. Zukow (Ed.), *Sibling interaction across cultures. Theoretical and methodological issues.* New York: Springer Verlag.

Williams, A. (2004). "Right, get your book bags!" Siblings playing school in multi-ethnic London. In E. Gregory, S. Long, & D. Volk (Eds.), *Many pathways to literacy: Early learning with siblings, grandparents, peers and communities.* London: Routledge.

Williams, A., & Gregory, E. (2001). Siblings bridging literacies in multilingual contexts. *Journal of Research in Reading, 23*(3), 248–265.

Zukow, P. G. (1989). *Sibling interaction across cultures.* New York: Springer Verlag.

Chapter 3

Literacy Diversity: Understanding and Responding to the Textual Tapestries of Home, School, and Community

Trevor H. Cairney
University of New South Wales

As part of a national research project concerned with the relationship between the literacy of home and school (Cairney & Ruge, 1998), case studies were conducted of four schools and selected families. The purpose was to try to understand incongruities between discourse experiences in the varied contexts that make up children's lives and the impact this has on school learning. In one of the schools, Woodgate Elementary,[1] an Indigenous Australian teacher provided a valuable metaphor to help understand how some students struggle with the instructional discourses of schooling. As I sat talking on one of our regular visits about our desire to understand why so many of his indigenous students struggled at school, he exclaimed, "You know, I just think that often these kids don't get it." When asked to elaborate, he replied that students often had trouble understanding ("getting") what the intentions of the curriculum activities were each day. He continued:

> Just last week I was trying to teach the Koori[2] kids some maths and I thought I'd try to use a concrete example. And some of the kids just didn't get it. I was trying to explain some basic subtraction using the example of eating oranges—to make it real. The conversation went something like this. I said to them, "Now I want you to tell me what would happen if I had 5 oranges and

---

[1]The place and personal names have been changed to preserve anonymity.

[2]"Koori" is an Aboriginal word that is used by some indigenous Australians who live along the east coast.

41

then gave 3 of them away?" Out of the blue, Sharon pipes up next to me and says: "Where are the oranges?" I ignored her. I asked again, "How many would I have left?" She piped up again, "What'd you do with them oranges?" I said to her (quietly, and as an aside), "There aren't any oranges really." She came back at me, "What'd you do with them?" I said to her (a bit frustrated by now), "There aren't any oranges!" She comes back again, "Why'd you give 'em away, we could've eaten them oranges."

Ralph was experiencing something that teachers experience daily, a mismatch between the curriculum purpose, the discourse practices required by the task, and the discourse experiences of the student. Sharon was struggling to enter into the discourse required as part of this lesson. The purpose for which literacy was being used and the expected learning outcome were not evident to her. As well, she was being required to engage in dialogue about a real-life experience purely to illustrate a mathematical concept, and this was unknown territory for her. When this type of mismatch occurs, a lack of student responsiveness can be interpreted in many ways. For example, some teachers see it as inadequacy on the part of the student or perhaps even inattentiveness and disobedience.

In our work at multiple sites over the last 13 years, we found that some students struggle to understand and use appropriate discourse practices. This, in part, reflects the increasing diversity of linguistic experiences that students bring with them from equally diverse cultural backgrounds. In the face of increased diversity, teachers find it difficult to know how to acknowledge and build on this linguistic and cultural diversity. Our work has shown us that the way in which literacy is supported and valued in the multiple contexts that children experience daily is critical to developing more responsive and effective curricula. There is great tension here, for after all, schools were created so that children living in poverty might gain skills for life. As well, for some children, school is still a refuge and an important way for them to overcome injustices in their lives. School isn't home, nor should it be, but we must understand how the differences between these two key sites affect children's educational chances.

ACKNOWLEDGING AND RESPONDING TO CULTURAL DIVERSITY IN THE CLASSROOM

In countries like Australia, Canada, and the United States, most urban classrooms have increasing cultural diversity. For some teachers, the majority of children in their class are from non-English-speaking backgrounds. Hence, classrooms are active sites for encountering and negotiating culture. Modern classrooms are places where students and their teachers construct and take for granted multiple definitions of teacher, student, knowledge, values, and so on (Cairney, 1991; Fernie, Kantor, & Klein, 1988; Green, Kantor, & Rogers, 1991).

They are also places where the classroom practices can be dominated by a limited range of literacy practices. This can be experienced as a limited range of texts to be read and written, set scripts that frame interaction between the teacher and students, and limited definitions of what it means to be literate (Cairney & Ashton, 2002). Ralph's insight about students "not getting it" was related to Sharon and other students not responding appropriately to an instructional approach embedded in specific discourse practices that he was privileging.

Au (1993) suggested that each classroom is characterised by its own culture, that is, "a dynamic system of values, beliefs, and standards, developed through understandings which the teacher and the students have come to share" (p. 9). Literacy in classrooms is not just a set of culturally neutral literacy activities. To view literacy as a series of isolated tasks that can moved from one classroom to another without modification is to miss the point that literacy is more than just a limited range of reading and writing events that can be reproduced for any class in any context.

Early work by Heath (1983) helped us to understand the variations that occur in literacy across specific groups. She was able to show us that talk associated with literacy within the home is related to differences in culture and language. In the last decade we have also learned that the way teachers shape classroom discourse can at times be limited in scope and not reflective of the diversity of student language and culture (Cairney, Lowe, & Sproats, 1995; Cairney & Ruge, 1998; Freebody, Ludwig, & Gunn, 1995; Gutierrez, 1993).

Literacy practices[3] vary considerably from family to family (Cairney & Ruge, 1998), as well as within families. Such variations have a relationship to factors as diverse as age, gender, social class, ethnicity, and so on (Cairney, Ruge, Buchanan, Lowe, & Munsie, 1995). Although there are similarities in the literacy practices of differing families in relation to the artefacts of literacy (e.g., specific texts, forms of writing), and the literacy events experienced (e.g., school homework is common), there is also great variation in the purposes for which literacy is used, the way children's liter-

[3]Literacy *practices* are the general cultural ways of utilizing literacy that people draw on in a literacy event. According to Barton (1991), "Literacy *events* are the particular activities in which literacy has a role: They may be regular repeated activities." Street (1995) explored the distinction between literacy practices and literacy events by arguing that whenever people engage in a literacy event they have "culturally constructed models of the literacy event in [their] minds" (p. 133). He used the term *literacy practices* "to indicate this level of the cultural uses and meanings of reading and writing. Literacy practices [refer] not only to the event itself but the conceptions of the reading and writing process that people hold when they are engaged in the event" (p. 133).

acy is supported, the demonstrations of literacy observed, attitudes toward literacy, the role that family members play in children's literacy learning, and the value placed on literacy learning (Cairney, 1994, 2000, 2003).

In contrast to these findings are those from other projects that have shown that there is far less diversity in the literacy of schooling (Cairney, Lowe, & Sproats, 1995; Freebody, Ludwig, & Gunn, 1995) than in communities. It seems that to be a teacher in any school demands specific ways of using language, behaving, and interacting, and adherence to sets of values and attitudes (Gee, 1990). It would also seem that often curriculum is not well matched to student needs.

Coe (1995) argues that schools fail to recognise that literacy is situated, that it varies according to the context and purposes for which it is used, and that a person may be highly literate within one situation and not in another. Bourdieu (1977) goes much further, suggesting that schools actually inconsistently tap the social and cultural resources of society, privileging specific groups by emphasising particular linguistic styles, curricula, and authority patterns.

Such perspectives draw heavily on the work of critical theorists, sociolinguistics, and cultural studies, and recognise that power relationships are also part of literacy practices. These researchers suggest that some families and individuals are disadvantaged (and others advantaged) by power relationships that fail to value the funds of knowledge that they bring to school (see Moll, 1992; Moll, Amanti, Neff, & Gonzalez, 1992). This collective work has helped us to identify "the social practices by which schools, families and individuals reproduce, resist and transform hierarchies of social relations and their positions within them" (Solsken, 1993, p. 7). Furthermore, it has enabled research and educational initiatives concerned with family literacy to be critiqued in new ways.

Willis (1995) argued that children from cultural and linguistic minority groups continue to have difficulty in achieving school success because the dominant pedagogical approaches are based on "a narrow understanding of school knowledge and literacy, which are defined and defended as what one needs to know and how one needs to know it in order to be successful in school and society" (p. 34). The Indigenous teacher described in the introduction to this chapter might well have been observing students who were being disadvantaged due to the limited way in which literacy was being defined and experienced and the power relationships within which they were embedded. This possibility is given some support by the observations made by several researchers interested in Native Americans and their experience of schooling.

For example, several researchers have investigated the impact of differences between the cultural beliefs and expectations of Native Americans and those of mainstream cultural groups (Deyhle & LeCompte, 1994; Locust, 1988; McCarty, 1987). Locust (1988) and Deyhle and LeCompte (1994) found that cultural differences in expectations and approaches, such as conflict of beliefs with the education system, result in the low school achievement of Native American children in middle schools. The latter found, through case study work in a middle school, that some features of the educational structure and pedagogy were actually congruent with Navajo culture, but others were not. They concluded that "Navajo children face conflict not only because their parents' conceptions of proper ways to raise children are different from those of Anglo Saxon parents, but also because of a related set of differences in attitudes and beliefs about stages in child development" (p. 157). In essence, although teachers at their school were committed to their students, cultural differences other than language were often ignored, not noticed, or seen as irrelevant. Hence there were few variations to teaching approaches to accommodate the Navajo children, and parental involvement was mainly a vehicle for the school to transmit its views on schooling and parental roles.

In conclusion, what this research shows is that the match and mismatch in language and literacy between home/community and school is of vital importance in addressing the specific needs of all students, but in particular, those who experience difficulties with literacy and schooling.

SOME INSIGHTS FROM OUR WORK

Before summarising the key insights from our work over the last 13 years, I need to explain the path that we traversed in our research. The work that I have conducted with research staff and postgraduate students has been in three broad phases (see Table 3.1). The first phase was concerned with developing parent education programs, before implementing and evaluating them. This work was in response to the perceived needs of specific schools and their communities. It was well intentioned, provided good results, and was well received by schools and communities, but it failed to sufficiently acknowledge home and community literacy. The second phase was concerned with exploring how schools build more effective partnerships with their communities. This work helped us to understand the richness of family literacy and the limitations and tokenism of many home/school initiatives. The third phase involved an exploration of the differences between the literacy practices of home and school and the implications that such differences have for the school's success.

In the rest of this chapter I concentrate on the third phase of our work and describe the findings of one key study that has shaped much of our re-

TABLE 3.1
Summary of Major Phases of Our Research 1990–2003

Phase	Focus	Selected Key Publications
1	Development of parent education programs	Cairney & Munsie, 1991 Cairney, 1994 Cairney & Munsie, 1995b Cairney, 1995b
2	Building partnerships between home & school	Cairney & Munsie, 1995a Cairney, Ruge, Buchanan, Lowe, & Munsie, 1995 Cairney, 1996 Cairney & Ruge, 1996
3	Exploring the match and mismatch between home & school literacy	Cairney, 1997 Cairney & Ruge, 1998 Cairney, 2000 Cairney & Ashton, 2002

cent work (Cairney & Ruge, 1998). This project involved two major phases. In the first, case studies were conducted of four schools (one secondary and three elementary) that had been identified as adopting innovative strategies to acknowledge and respond to differences in the language and literacy practices of the communities they serve.

The second phase involved detailed observation and discourse analysis of the literacy practices of 35 case study children as they moved in and out of home, school, and community contexts. These students were chosen to reflect diversity in culture, age, gender, ability, and social class.

The method of tracking individual students through their real-world literacy contexts involved the collection of the following forms of data:

- Interview data from students, parents, teachers, and other community support workers.
- Student, parent, and teacher self-reporting of their own literacy practices utilising time sampling techniques.
- Observation of literacy practices at school, home, and in the community utilising participant observation, self-audiotaping of interactions and videotaping (e.g., homework, story reading, playing literacy-related games, discussion of school activities).
- Audio recording of specific literacy events (e.g., story reading at home and school; homework discussion at home and school; research/project work discussion and completion at home and school).
- Data on student achievement to enable comparisons to be made between high- and low-achieving students.

The project also involved the recruitment of child and family members as coresearchers to collect data and meet regularly with the researchers to help to interpret it. This involved the coresearchers in the recording of a range of home literacy events and the collection of artifacts. The interactions discussed in this chapter were drawn from a total of 130 recorded home literacy events (Cairney & Ruge, 1998).

Observations were conducted in a total of eight classrooms across the three participating primary schools. In addition, classroom observations were conducted across seven subject areas in Years 7 and 9 in the participating secondary school.

A total of 82 days of classroom observation were conducted across the four schools and led to a number of insights concerning the literacy of home and school. We have reported in great detail in other publications the precise nature of our observations of literacy. These include the types of practices observed at school and home as well as the identification of specific forms of literacy[4] and constructions of literacy[5] in both contexts. In this chapter I report the general findings for this 2-year project.

OUR GENERAL FINDINGS ON THE NATURE OF LITERACY

Our interest in this project was not simply to describe the literacy practices that we saw; however, a brief description of what we observed is of relevance to what I say later in the chapter about differences across contexts and how schools should respond to diversity.

Literacy at Home

A total of 35 students in 27 families were involved in this phase of the project; they represented a diverse range of cultural and linguistic backgrounds, as well as socioeconomic circumstances. Not surprisingly, our observations in their homes indicated a diverse range of literacy practices. In all homes, there was evidence of rich literacy. Family members read and wrote a variety of texts for a vast range of purposes. We reached the following conclusions:

---

[4]Cairney and Ruge (1998) identified four purposes for, or forms of, literacy: literacy for establishing and maintaining relationships, literacy for accessing or displaying information, literacy for pleasure and/or self-expression, and literacy for skills development.

[5]Cairney and Ruge (1998) identified four different constructions of literacy at home and at school, each with its own patterns of interaction, roles, and relationships: literacy as knowledge, literacy as performance, literacy as negotiated construction of meaning, and literacy as "doing school."

- There was considerable literacy variation and diversity across and within families.
- Literacy interactions between siblings and other family members were frequent.
- There was variation in literacy "visibility" across homes, that is, it was more evident in some homes than others.
- Home literacy practices and values were influenced by parents' past experiences.
- There was considerable variation across families in the types of literacy resources.
- There was a high level of access to IT and multimedia at home.
- Specific literacy practices could form part of significantly different literacy events across different families.
- School literacy practices were dominant in homes, accounting for a great deal of the literacy we observed.
- Writing at home was more strongly influenced by school practices than reading.

One important finding from this study was that specific literacy practices may contribute to, and constitute part of, different literacy events in different contexts depending on the understandings and purposes of the participants. For example, the intended purpose of a newsletter from school may be to give parents access to information about school policies or activities. Alternatively, the intended purpose may be to maintain communication between home and school and thereby develop the relationship between families and the school. However, in reading the newsletter at home, families may have very different purposes and "use" the newsletter in different ways (e.g., one family used it for oral reading practice).

Cairney and Ruge (1998) also found that the families in their study differed greatly in the extent to which literacy was *visible* in everyday life, ranging from the ever pervasive nature of literacy in one family home, to the seemingly rare occurrence of literacy events in another household. There was considerable variation in the amount and types of literacy resources available in each home. One home had literally thousands of books, whereas another had a collection of less than 10 battered books in a cupboard that couldn't be easily accessed. Some homes displayed the drawings and written texts of their children everywhere, whereas in others it was difficult to find such texts. In some homes, parents were regularly reading and writing texts for multiple purposes, whereas in others, we observed little use of literacy by adults.

One of the striking features of literacy practices in the homes of many of the families in this study was the extent to which "school literacy" dominated home contexts. That is, the particular types and uses of literacy usually associated with schooling were prominent in many families. This prominence was manifested primarily in the amount of time spent on homework activities and, to a lesser extent, siblings "playing school" (see Cairney, 2003; Cairney & Ruge, 1998; and Freebody, Ludwig, & Gunn, 1995). We also found from our observations and interviews with parents that the literacy practices promoted for children were strongly shaped by the parents' experience of school literacy as well as the desire to equip children for school success (Cairney & Ruge, 1998).

Literacy at School

Our observations of eight classrooms in three primary schools, and seven subject areas in Years 7 and 9 of a secondary school, also provided evidence of varied literacy practices. However, although there was considerable variation between the literacy practices in the primary classrooms and the way literacy was used in the varied discipline-based secondary classrooms, we found less variation than expected across the primary classrooms and even from one subject to another in the secondary school. Our general findings were as follows:

- There was less diversity and variation in literacy within and across schools than in families.
- There was an emphasis on learning how to do literacy as opposed to using literacy for learning as part of authentic tasks, particularly in primary schools.
- There was less access to IT and multimedia in schools than homes.
- Literacy interactions between students and between students and the teacher were rare.
- Literacy practices were predominantly directed toward learning how to successfully engage in school tasks.

It was clear from our investigations that, apart from homework activities that were similar across home and school contexts, there were significant differences between literacy practices and events at home and at school. These differences were: the major purposes for literacy use in different contexts, the extent to which literacy activities remained within the child's control, the relevance and difficulty of literacy activities, and the dominant "view of text" at home and at school.

In home and community contexts, literacy events and practices (other than "school literacy" practices) were almost always embedded in everyday activities. The major purposes for literacy use in these contexts were to es-

tablish and maintain relationships and to meet practical needs in organising everyday life. There was little emphasis specifically on the development
of literacy skills outside homework. In contrast, and perhaps not surprisingly, the major emphasis in school contexts (especially primary classrooms) was on the use of literacy for the purpose of developing literacy
skills. That is, the development of literacy was an end in itself, and classroom events and activities were structured to achieve that end. Although
there was some evidence of literacy being used for establishing or maintaining relationships, and for organisational purposes, these were peripheral to
the main events and activities in all of the classrooms observed in this study.

In contrast, children's literacy practices at home tended to remain much
more within the child's control. Even when parents gave considerable help
with homework, they were more likely (than teachers) to allow the child to
maintain a significant measure of control over what would be done, as well
as when and how it would be done. In the classroom observations in this
study, teachers were far more prescriptive and children were given little
choice and control over activities. This is consistent with other studies. For
example, Freebody et al. (1995) also found that parents permitted greater
participation rights in literacy interactions than teachers did at school.

Literacy practices at home were also often more suited to their interests,
and more challenging, than literacy practices at school. This finding is related to the issue of teachers maintaining almost sole control over children's activities at school. Children were given little opportunity at school
to select activities or topics that interested them, and the dominance of
whole-class activities meant that some children were rarely challenged by
more difficult or complex tasks. Stuart (Year 1) showed his frustration in
the following interview comment:

Stuart:	If I was Prime Minister of Australia, it'd be quite hard to decide what to do for the kids, because I don't want them to be locked up in school. Probably, maybe, yeah, if I was . . . Education Minister I'd try and make it that the teachers have to give the kids interesting activities, but it takes a fair while to do that.
Interviewer:	Do you mean it takes the teachers a long while to prepare them?
Stuart:	No, it takes the kids a fair while to do and it's a fun activity, so they'll like doing it for a long time.

Finally, the predominant "view of text" seemed to be different in home
and school contexts. In home contexts, texts were viewed mainly as resources, secondary to the accomplishment of a particular purpose. In classrooms, however, texts were seen as primary objects, as "sources of knowledge or bases for inference" (Baker & Luke, 1991, p. 169) or as bases for
the display of literacy knowledge.

UNDERSTANDING AND RESPONDING
TO DIFFERENCE

The experiences of Sharon and other participants involved in our various studies demonstrate that successfully negotiating "school literacy" involves learning the norms and expectations and ways of participating that are valued and reproduced in school contexts.

In our sample of families, the students who were most academically successful were generally those whose family literacy practices reproduced school literacy practices. Those who were less academically successful did not share the home dominance of school literacy.

The work that we have been conducting over the past 13 years in Australia has had an overriding metaquestion driving it: Why does school literacy empower some and disempower others? Whether school literacy empowers children or not is a question that requires us to understand the relationship between the school literacy practices that particular children encounter, and the home literacy practices of those same children.

The research discussed in this chapter demonstrates that there are differences between home and school literacy practices in the way literacy is defined and supported. However, it also demonstrates that these differences vary greatly across home and school contexts.

One important finding of this study is that children from minority language and cultural backgrounds are not the only ones who may find school literacy disempowering. Knowing that a student is a member of a particular subgroup (e.g., a member of a socioeconomically disadvantaged family; a recent Vietnamese immigrant; a third-generation Australian-born "native" Arabic speaker; etc.) does not necessarily entitle us to assume anything about that student's literacy practices or ways of participating in the cultural practices of the group.

This research has shown other forms of unexpected diversity. For example, some children like Stuart, from more dominant and mainstream cultures, encounter a more restricted range of literacy practices at school than the literacy practices in which they engage at home.

As Clegg (cited in Gilbert & Low, 1994) argued, "empowering" students through school literacy is not simply a matter of improving students' skills in reading and writing, it is about changing the relational structures so that the whole basis of institutional power is transformed. I add that these changes are multidimensional and far from unidirectional. It isn't simply about changing home or school, but rather the relational structures and discourse practices that are privileged. This largely requires teachers to diversify classroom practices and increasingly acknowledge and build on the diversity of discourse practices of home and community, rather than simply replacing one set of literacy practices with another.

In concrete terms, this means that empowering children like Sharon does not mean teaching them how to interact "appropriately" so that their knowledge will be accepted and privileged. Rather, it means accepting their knowledge regardless of how they interact, and in so doing, changing the relational structures in which the power is based.

Sharon's teacher, Ralph, was provided with a critical decision to make when she responded "inappropriately" to his question. At first he rejected her response, but eventually he allowed her to share her knowledge with the class. Such critical incidents are defining moments in classroom inter-action. Although Sharon had missed the purpose of the interaction framed by the teacher, Ralph needed to include her in the interaction without sim-ply dismissing her knowledge as irrelevant.

A teacher's handling of such discourse moments is critical for learners struggling to make sense of curriculum. As Corson (1991) pointed out, ed-ucation can routinely repress, dominate, and disempower language users whose practices differ from the norms that it establishes. Ralph was able to respond in such a way that Sharon was included, rather than repressed and excluded from the learning process.

Matches between home and school literacy events and practices allow children to develop situated expertise that can enhance and support the development of "school literacy." However, mismatches in home and school literacy practices (particularly in terms of authority structures and concepts of knowledge) constrain children's development of nonschool literacies. School achievement may be ensured, but empowerment is not.

It is clear from the evidence provided in our research that families and schools differ markedly in their literacy practices and values. What is also clear is that there are significant differences among families in the way they define and use literacy. Just as Ralph needed to understand Sharon's needs and background, schools generally need to understand families and the communities within which they are situated. There is a need for genuine di-alogue between schools and their communities. This involves more than simply giving information and advice to families about how they can con-form to school curricula.

Given all that has been reported in this chapter, there is one logical next question to ask: What implications does this work have for schools and teachers? More specifically, how might schools and teachers respond?

Responding as Teachers

Individual teachers need to observe and understand literacy discourse prac-tices within their classrooms and to appreciate the differences that may ex-ist between these and home literacy practices. In many ways, the actual liter-acy events that are planned are secondary to the nature of the interaction that takes place, the definitions of literacy privileged or marginalised, the way we choose texts and set topics, and so on. The following are just some of things that teachers need to consider in light of our findings. In essence, teachers need to be less concerned about the actual events planned and more concerned with factors such as the following.

The Way We Question Students. What types of questions do we ask? How do we direct such questions? Do we direct our questions more to some students than others? Are there differences in the type of questions that we use for children with different backgrounds, abilities, gender, and so forth?

The Way We Permit Interaction. How do we structure our classrooms for interaction? Do the spatial arrangements limit interaction or open up new possibilities? Do our practices lead to some children receiving and responding to more questions? Do some find specific forms of interaction (e.g., class-based lessons, group work, teacher interviews, formal class presentations) more difficult than others? Does there appear to be any relationship between level of interaction and factors such as gender, ethnicity, physical location in classroom space, and so on?

The Forms of Cooperation Permitted or Not Permitted. How frequently do we vary the way students work together? Do we privilege individual learning, small group work, whole class lessons? Do we actively create opportunities for students to work with students of different ability levels, life experiences, interests, genders, and so forth? How do we limit or enhance forms of cooperation and collaboration?

The Language of Instruction We Use. How frequently do teachers vary the language of instruction? Do we privilege specific discourse forms (e.g., exposition, anecdote, narrative, question and answer)? Do we modify the language we use for specific individuals, groups, instructional contexts? What impact do some of these variations have for specific students?

The Knowledge We Privilege in Classrooms. How do we make decisions about the knowledge we share, or that we encourage students to seek? How does our interpretation of curriculum guidelines limit or expand possibilities? How do we attempt to draw on the rich knowledge resources of home and community?

The Text Types We Use. How do we make decisions about the texts we use? How do the texts we use and the text forms that we request as written tasks reflect a diversity of genres and cultural traditions? Do the topics or themes of the texts privileged match the interests and needs of all students? How do we actively seek a balance?

The Very Instructional Approaches We Use. Are there specific instructional practices used more frequently than others? If so, is this justified? Do some practices privilege specific students because of their learning styles, gender, cultural backgrounds, and so forth?

The preceding questions are meant to challenge teachers to reflect on and evaluate the discourse practices that are evident in the classroom. They also signal my belief that teachers, students, and parents need to understand the way each defines, values, and uses literacy as part of cultural practices. Such mutual understanding offers the potential for schooling to be adjusted to meet the diverse needs of learners.

Responding as Schools

Just as individual teachers have a responsibility to understand and respond to the diversity of the families they teach, schools also need to respond to community diversity. What the project that has been the focus of this chapter demonstrates is that schools that effectively respond to cultural diversity share some important characteristics. To make these key characteristics clear, I contrast two different school responses to observations of student difference, the first based on our observations of what happened at one primary school in our sample, St. Joseph's, and the second based on observations at a second primary school from another study. In doing so, I provide a pointer to the different ways in which teachers and schools can respond to the social and cultural complexity of their students and communities. I am aware of the difficulties such dichotomous comparisons can have, and that they can oversimplify what one observes. In spite of this, I believe that the comparison (see Table 3.2) is helpful.

Notwithstanding the dangers of such categorical comparisons, the contrast between these two schools and their response to diversity is instructive. We need to look at such responses, reflect on them, and interrogate the differences between each and the impact that this has on the lives of individual children and families.

Over the 6 years prior to our study, St. Joseph's School had implemented major structural as well as pedagogical changes. The introduction of a bilingual program and the use of across-the-grade language groups, the development of explicit teaching strategies, and the emphasis on different learning styles, resulted in substantial changes to the entire teaching/learning program at the school.

TABLE 3.2

Comparison of Responses to Key Factors Relating to School
Effectiveness in Social and Culturally Diverse Communities

Factors	School 1 Response	School 2 Response
Key staff	• Recent higher education experience	• Few with recent higher education experience
	• Key agents for change	• Key agents for maintenance
	• Facilitators	• Experts
Process of change	• Engaged staff in dialogue about issues	• Assessed the need for resources
	• Joint staff curriculum planning	• Provided new resources to staff members
	• Team-based strategies utilised	• Communicated ideas and information
	• Collaboration valued	• Individual development sought
Observation of difference	• Difference seen as a source of richness to build on	• Difference seen as a resource to use
	• "Funds of knowledge" as a platform	• Difference seen as a hurdle to overcome
Students' first language	• Encouraged	• Ignored
	• Valued as important to English literacy	• Seen as an impediment to English literacy
Definition of literacy	• Multiple literacies	• Unitary literacy
	• Reading & writing integrated with other sign systems	• Reading and writing seen as separate language skills
	• A focus on language and meaning	• A focus on skills
Expectations of students	• High	• Low
	• Capable of learning anything	• Impeded by difference
	• Difference as a rich resource	• Difference as deficit
Expectations of parents	• Important to children's learning	• Important to the school's agendas
	• To support their children	• To support the school
	• To use multiple languages	• To use English at home

At St. Joseph's School, staff were "contesting the traditional discourses" in the sense that they were developing new shared discourses to which everyone (students and teachers alike) had equal access. Through the teaching of text types, in particular, and the establishment of a common language across classrooms, they were explicitly teaching all children forms of discourse and shared thinking that were valued in this particular context.

The experiences of St. Joseph's School parallel the experiences of Richmond Road School, which has been described by Cazden (1989) and May (1995) as an effective multilingual, multicultural school in New Zealand. In recounting the development of innovative practices at Richmond Road, May reported:

> Those who were not willing to listen to other viewpoints soon became disillu-
> sioned. Those who were not willing to concede previously held positions of
> power met similar opposition. However, those who were able to make these
> accommodations have progressed towards establishing different discourses;
> discourses which are contesting the traditional hierarchies associated with
> school organization (and the power relations implicit in these) and ascribing,
> in the process, status to all participants. (p. 13)

Schooling in Australia, as in the United States, is "built upon a narrow understanding of school knowledge and literacy, which are defined and de-fended as what one needs to know and how one needs to know it in order to be successful in school and society" (Willis, 1995, p. 34).

In many schools, it would appear that the discourse strategies and peda-gogy that are familiar to the culture of teachers remain the preferred or dominant discourses because they are successful in promoting school achievement for the majority of students. That is, the legitimacy and per-petuation of such discourses is based on their success with students from the dominant culture.

Those children who do not succeed, then, are seen as failing (in part) because they are unable to access the dominant discourses (Au, 1993). Cul-tural differences other than language tend to be ignored, rendered invisi-ble, or considered to be irrelevant (Deyhle & LeCompte, 1994). In such schools, teachers are unlikely (and unwilling) to reject traditional dis-courses as they seem to serve the majority.

Reyes (1992) argues that teachers fail to cater to the needs of minority students because most teachers "are members of the dominant culture, im-plementing programs designed primarily for mainstream students" (p. 437). She suggests that many teachers treat culturally and linguistically di-verse students as "exceptions to the norm, as students who should be assimi-lated into the dominant group, rather than accommodated according to their own needs" (p. 437).

At St. Joseph's School, however, there was no "dominant culture" group to be served by the perpetuation of the traditional discourses of schooling. Even those few students in the school who were from English-speaking backgrounds were, almost without exception, socioeconomically disadvan-taged and at risk of educational failure. Thus, teachers at St. Joseph's School were able, to a large extent, to set aside their preferred discourses and to develop new shared discourses.

Erickson (1993) argues that, "Whatever the reasons for school failure may be in schools, it is necessary for educators to transform routine practice and symbol settings in their own school settings" (p. 28). Teachers at St. Joseph's School went some way toward redefining school literacy in their own context, and hence transformed routine practice in significant ways. Au (1993) suggests that redefining school literacy may be achieved through expanding the types of texts students read and write, as well as changing the nature of instructional activities and implementing culturally responsive instruction. This was part of what St. Joseph's did, but not all of it.

The key to the success of St. Joseph's School was not the strategies (pedagogical changes) or the language groups (structural changes), and not the specific discourses that had been constructed, but rather the process of negotiation, the willingness to set aside preferred or traditional discourses in order to negotiate new ones.

To take the discourses constructed at St. Joseph's School and impose these on other schools would simply reinforce the existing reproductive processes. However, as Erickson (1993) points out: "If schools . . . are active agents in the processes of reproduction and contestation of dominant social relations, then understanding what they do and acting upon them becomes of no small moment" (p. 44). In a sense each teacher, and indeed every school, must ask their own questions designed to evaluate what discourse practices they privilege, for whom, and why.

What can be learned from St. Joseph's School is how to challenge the existing reproductive processes so that they are not power-driven, nor success-based, but rather negotiated constructions that empower all.

> Clegg argue[d] that power is not a property held by persons, as some forms of episodic agency would have it, but that power is *relational*, and is the product of structured sets of relations among people, relations which are not attributable to or created by particular people, but are more historically, institutionally and discursively produced. (Gilbert & Low, 1994, p. 7)

Thus, "empowering" students through school literacy is not simply a matter of improving students' skills in reading and writing; it is about changing the relational structures so that the whole basis of institutional power is transformed.

In the second phase of our research, we found that mismatches identified between home and school literacies were not so much in terms of literacy practices, but in terms of authority and concepts of knowledge. Matches between home and school literacy events and practices allow children to develop situated expertise that enhances or supports the development of "school literacy."

However, mismatches in home and school literacy practices (particularly in terms of authority structures and concepts of knowledge) also constrain children's development of nonschool literacies. School achievement may be ensured, but empowerment is not.

The findings of this study strongly support Connell's (1994) argument
that it is misleading to assume that problems in school achievement concern only a disadvantaged minority of students. Educational change is not
something to be "done to" minority groups, and effective programs cannot
exist as add-ons to the "real" work of schools.

What is needed is fundamental change in student–teacher–parent relationships. The key to this is the development of more effective partnerships
between homes and schools that acknowledge the diverse needs of all students, recognise the way power and resources are unevenly distributed, and
in the process open up the discourses of schooling to critique and reconstruction. Such partnerships require five essential conditions to be met.
When entering into genuine partnerships, we need to:

KNOW our communities and their people, be in contact with them, and
be open and dialogic in our approach to them.

UNDERSTAND our communities—do more than maintain contact;
seek to understand their languages, cultures, and social fabric.

ACKNOWLEDGE the significant "funds of knowledge" they bring and
contribute.

VALUE our communities and what their people have to offer—not in to-
ken ways but by listening to parents and community members.

LEARN from our communities as well as providing opportunities for
them to learn about our goals and key strategies.

CONCLUSION

Our research over the last 13 years has enabled us to learn a great deal
about the importance of families and the home as sites for literacy development. We know that children experience multiliteracies at home, and that
literacy is defined, used, and supported in accordance with social and cultural differences. As well, we know that literacy in the home and community
is more diverse than we once thought. However, it is evident from our work
that much still needs to be done in understanding family literacy practices.
We still know little about the diversity of literacy experiences outside school.
We know even less about the way in which the multiliteracies of life interact
and shape each other and the people who use them (Cairney, 2003).

In a recent publication (Cairney, 2003), I suggest that there are three
main reasons for the gaps in our knowledge. First, much previous research
uses definitions of literacy that are limited and that restrict observations to a
more limited range of literacy practices than are identified from what we
know of school literacy practices. Second, our attempts to observe family lit-

eracy have typically been driven by a desire to know how the family supports literacy learning at school. Third, we have used limited methods to assess home literacy practices that fail to identify the depth and breadth of the authentic practices that take place. Except for a small number of significant ethnographies and case studies, few offer much depth, and most research has involved limited time with families. There is a great need for researchers to understand these limitations and embark on projects that seek to overcome them.

As well as these generic issues, there are many specific factors to consider. We need, for example, more studies that consider how gender, social class, and culture interact with issues of literacy practice. Are the experiences of some students at home and school influenced by secondary factors such as language background, gender, and so on? We also need to give considerable attention to the impact of school literacy on home literacy. Rather than simply examining family and community literacy to gain lessons for school literacy, we need to consider the synergistic relationship between the two contexts and the roles that students play as mediators between them.

Another critical need is to consider how multimedia and digital literacy demands are changing the literacy of home and community and what this means for traditional school literacy. Although literacy practices appear to be changing (see for example Cairney, 1995b; Cope & Kalantzis, 2000; Lankshear, 1997; Makin & Jones-Diaz, 2002), we know little of the impact this will have on the way schools teach literacy and the discourse practices that will be privileged.

Finally, much has been said in recent times about how literacy is implicated in power relationships, but little is known about how this operates in classrooms. Although we know that literacy is not culturally and ideologically neutral (Street, 1995), we know much less about the precise nature of its ideological impacts across home and school contexts. We need to know more about the relationship of family literacy to life and public institutions such as schools. What our work shows is that there are complex relationships between the literacies of home and school that have impacts for some students in some circumstances. Understanding these impacts and responding to them is the stuff of which good literacy teaching is made.

REFERENCES

Au, K. (1993). *Literacy instruction in multicultural settings.* Fort Worth: Harcourt Brace Jovanovich College Publishers.

Baker, C., & Luke, A. (1991). *Toward a critical sociology of reading pedagogy.* Philadelphia: John Benjamins.

Barton, D. (1991). *Literacy: An introduction to the ecology of written language.* Oxford: Blackwell.

Bourdieu, P. (1977). Cultural reproduction and social reproduction. In J. Karabel & A. H. Halsey (Eds.), *Power and ideology in education* (pp. 473–486). New York: Oxford University Press.

Cairney, T. H. (1991). *Text meets text, reader meets writer*. Bloomington, IN: ERIC Clearing House, ED 322 476, Jan.

Cairney, T. H. (1994). Family literacy: Moving towards new partnerships in education. *Australian Journal of Language and Literacy, 17*(4).

Cairney, T. H. (1995a). Developing parent partnerships in secondary literacy learning. *Journal of Adolescent and Adult Literacy, 38*(7), 520–526.

Cairney, T. H. (1995b). *Pathways to literacy*. London: Cassell.

Cairney, T. H. (1996). Developing partnerships with families in literacy learning. In S. Wolfendale & K. Topping (Eds.), *Family involvement in literacy: Effective partnerships in education* (pp. 131–146). London: Cassell.

Cairney, T. H. (1997). Acknowledging diversity in home literacy practices: Moving towards partnerships with parents. *Early Child Development and Care, 127–128*, 61–73.

Cairney, T. H. (2000). The construction of literacy and literacy learners. *Language Arts, 77*(6), 496–505.

Cairney, T. H. (2003). Literacy within family life. In N. Hall, J. Larson, & J. Marsh (Eds.), *Handbook of early childhood literacy* (pp. 85–98). London: Sage Publications.

Cairney, T. H., & Ashton, J. (2002). Three families, multiple discourses: Examining differences in the literacy practices of home and school. *Linguistics and Education, 38*(3), 303–345.

Cairney, T. H., Lowe, K., & Sproats, E. (1995). *Literacy in transition: An investigation of the literacy practices of upper primary and junior secondary schools* (Vols. 1–3). Canberra: Department of Employment, Education & Training.

Cairney, T. H., & Munsie, L. (1991, April). *Talking to literacy learners: A parent education project*. ERIC Clearinghouse, ED 332158.

Cairney, T. H., & Munsie, L. (1995a). *Beyond tokenism: Parents as partners in literacy*. Portsmouth, NH: Heinemann.

Cairney, T. H., & Munsie, L. (1995b). Parent participation in literacy learning. *The Reading Teacher, 48*(5), 392–403.

Cairney, T. H., & Ruge, J. (1996). Bridging home and school literacy: In search of more effective partnerships. *The Forum of Education, 51*(1), 103–115.

Cairney, T. H., & Ruge, J. (1998). *Community literacy practices and schooling: Towards effective support for students*. Canberra: Department of Employment, Education & Training.

Cairney, T. H., Ruge, J., Buchanan, J., Lowe, K., & Munsie, L. (1995). *Developing partnerships: The home, school and community interface* (Vols. 1–3). Canberra: Department of Employment, Education & Training.

Cazden, C. (1989). Richmond Road: A multilingual/multicultural primary school in Auckland, New Zealand. *Language and Education, 3*, 3.

Coe, R. M. (1995). *What students aren't learning at school: Assessing students' ability to situate their discourses*. Paper presented at the American Educational Research Association Annual Conference, San Francisco.

Connell, R. W. (1994). Poverty and education. *Harvard Educational Review, 64*(2), 125–149.

Cope, B., & Kalantzis, M. (2000). A pedagogy of multiliteracies: Designing social futures. In B. Cope & M. Kalantzis (Eds.), *Multiliteracies: Literacy learning and the designing of social futures* (pp. 9–38). Melbourne: Macmillan Publishers Australia Pty Ltd.

Corson, D. (1991). Language, power and minority schooling. *Language and Education, 5*(4), 231–253.

Deyhle, D., & LeCompte, M. (1994). Cultural differences in child development: Navajo adolescents in middle schools. *Theory Into Practice, 33*(3), 156–166.

Erickson, F. (1993). Transformation and school success: The politics and culture of educational achievement. In E. Jacob & C. Jordan (Eds.), *Minority education: Anthropological perspectives* (pp. 335–356). Norwood, NJ: Ablex.

Fernie, D., Kantor, R., & Klein, E. (1988). Becoming students and becoming ethnographers in a preschool. *Journal of Childhood Research in Education, 3*(2), 95–110.

Freebody, P., Ludwig, C., & Gunn, S. (1995). *Everyday literacy practices in and out of schools in low socio-economic status urban communities: A descriptive and interpretive research program.* Canberra: Department of Education, Employment and Youth Affairs.

Gee, J. (1990). *Social linguistics and literacies: Ideology in discourses.* London: The Falmer Press.

Gilbert, R., & Low, P. (1994). Discourse and power in education: Analysing institutional processes in schools. *Australian Educational Researcher, 21*(3), 1–23.

Green, J., Kantor, R., & Rogers, T. (1991). Exploring the complexity of language and learning in the classroom. In B. Jones & L. Idol (Eds.), *Educational values and cognitive instruction: Implications for reform* (Vol. 2, pp. 333–364). Hillsdale, NJ: Lawrence Erlbaum Associates.

Gutierrez, K. D. (1993). How talk, context, and script shape contexts for learning: A cross-case comparison of journal sharing. *Linguistics and Education, 5*(3, 4), 335–365.

Heath, S. B. (1983). *Ways with words: Language, life, and work in communities and classrooms.* New York: Cambridge University Press.

Lankshear, C. (1997). *Changing literacies.* Buckingham: Open University Press.

Locust, C. (1988). Wounding the spirit: Discrimination and traditional American belief systems. *Harvard Educational Review, 55*(3), 315–330.

Makin, L., & Jones-Diaz, C. (2002). *Literacies in early childhood: Challenging views, challenging practice.* Sydney: Maclennan & Petty.

May, S. (1995). Deconstructing traditional discourses of schooling: An example of school reform. *Language and Education, 9*(1), 1–29.

McCarty, T. L. (1987). School as community: The Rough Rock demonstration. *Harvard Educational Review, 59*(4), 484–503.

Moll, L. (1992). Literacy research in community and classrooms: A sociocultural approach. In R. Beach, J. Green, M. Kamil, & T. Shanahan (Eds.), *Multidisciplinary perspectives on literacy research* (pp. 211–244). Urbana, IL: National Council of Teachers of English.

Moll, L., Amanti, C., Neff, D., & Gonzalez, N. (1992). Funds of knowledge for teaching: Using a qualitative approach to connect homes and classrooms. *Theory Into Practice, 31*(2), 132–141.

Reyes, M. de la Luz. (1992). Challenging venerable assumptions: Literacy instruction for linguistically different students. *Harvard Educational Review, 62*, 427–446.

Solsken, J. W. (1993). *Literacy, gender and work: In families and in schools.* Norwood, NJ: Ablex.

Street, B. (1995). *Social literacies: Critical approaches to literacy development, ethnography and education.* London: Longman.

Willis, A. I. (1995). Reading the world of school literacy: Contextualising the experience of a young African American male. *Harvard Educational Review, 65*(1), 30–48.

Chapter 4

Working and Learning With Families, Communities, and Schools: A Critical Case Study

Jim Anderson
Suzanne Smythe
Jon Shapiro
The University of British Columbia

It's 1:00 on a pleasant March afternoon. We are in the staff room of Valley School in Vancouver, British Columbia, having just concluded another session in the family literacy program called PALS. The focus of today's session was on reading with children. The kindergarten teachers, Suzanne, the program facilitator, and I are discussing several of the issues that arose as we worked with a group of parents over the last several hours. One of the teachers comments that some of the parents seemed concerned with the selection of children's books that we incorporated into the classroom learning centres today. Indeed, during the debriefing and follow-up discussion, one of the parents commented that her son really enjoys an old "reader" that they had purchased at a yard sale; we noted the affirmative nods. Our talk then turns to the dearth of children's books available in languages other than English and the challenges of trying to rectify this situation in a school where more than a dozen language groups are represented. The school bell signals the beginning of the afternoon session and the teachers busily head off to their classrooms. I write a note to myself: "We must address the question from the parent about her daughter's fascination with making signs and notices and displays and her comment that her child is not interested in storybooks, at the next session."

In this chapter, we share some of the insights, dilemmas, questions, and critical reflections that emerged as we conceptualised, developed, and implemented a family literacy initiative called PALS, or Parents As Literacy Supporters (Anderson & Morrison, 2003).

FAMILY LITERACY: AN OVERVIEW

That the family can be an important context for young children's literacy learning is now considered axiomatic. Ethnographic research (e.g., Gregory, 2001; Taylor, 1983) reveals the ways children use print and other forms of representation for a variety of purposes and functions embedded in the daily lived experiences of family life. Ironically, at one time, educators advised families to leave the teaching of reading to the schools. However, in the 1970s and 1980s, a shift began to occur, due, we believe, to a flurry of research that clearly demonstrated that many young children had acquired considerable literacy knowledge prior to formal instruction at school. Suddenly, parents became children's first and most important teachers of literacy. During the 1980s and 1990s, family literacy programs proliferated. They were held up as a panacea to the growing concern about the "literacy deficit" in Western industrialized countries, brought to the fore in the 1980s with the Southam report in Canada (Southam Literacy Survey, 1987) and consolidated through the OECD (Organization for Economic Development)-sponsored International Adult Literacy Survey in 1994. This research allowed some proponents of family literacy intervention programs to argue that large percentages of the population could not function properly in a "knowledge-based" economy, and an intergenerational response (Sticht, 1983) was required to stop the transmission of illiteracy to further generations. Indeed, in the introduction to an edited volume on family literacy published by the International Reading Association, former First Lady Barbara Bush wrote that family literacy programs were potentially the solution to the "literacy problem" in the United States (Bush, 1995). Similar proclamations about "breaking the cycle of literacy" were strewn throughout a review of family literacy program in Canada (Thomas, 1998).

Despite this rhetoric and the proliferation of family literacy programs, such programs have come under considerable scrutiny and powerful critiques from a number of sources. Auerbach (1989, 1995), for example, contended that many family literacy programs are based on deficit notions of family aimed at working class and immigrant families and ignore the sociocontextual realities and literacy practices of the families and communities for whom they are designed. Many family literacy programs are seen as promoting a narrow range of school-like literacy practices (Whitehouse & Colvin, 2001). For example, as Pellegrini (1991) suggested, and as we have argued elsewhere (e.g., Anderson, Smythe, & Lynch, 2003), storybook reading is promoted as the literacy event "par excellence" both in school and in family literacy programs. However, the centrality of the role of storybook reading in literacy development has been questioned on empirical (Scarborough & Dobrich, 1994) and philosophical (e.g., Carrington & Luke, 2003) grounds. As well, concern has arisen that mothers are framed in family literacy research and programs as surrogate teachers, responsible for imparting to their children the literacy skills valued by the schools, while their own literacy needs and aspirations go unrecognised (Mace, 1998). Similarly, Smythe and Isserlis (2002) point out that the use of the neutral terms *family* or *parent* to describe family literacy participants are somewhat disingenuous inasmuch as most family literacy programs, by design or by default, place the onus on mothers to insure that their children are ready for, and are successful at, literacy in school.

Educators and researchers have also raised concerns that many of the studies in early literacy from the 1970s and 1980s (e.g., Baghban, 1984; Doake, 1988) that inform the family literacy field were "case studies, chronologies and descriptions" (Adams, 1990, p. 336) written by "parent academics" (Heath & Thomas, 1984, p. 51). These studies tended to portray children immersed in literate surroundings from birth and enculturated into the discursive practices privileged by schools (Blackledge, 1999). Furthermore, educators tend to generalize from research often without the benefit of replication in different contexts. A case in point is Sulzby's (1985) classic and often cited study on children's retelling of favorite storybooks. This work categorized the emergence of storybook reenactments from "oral language like" to "written language like"; it was conducted with kindergarten children from middle-class families in the midwestern United States. However, Anderson and Matthews (1999) found that the kindergarten children from working class homes in a rural area of British Columbia with whom they worked did not demonstrate the same developmental trajectory as the children in the Sulzby study. In fact, none of the children had progressed to the "written language like" category that nearly all of the children in the original study had by June of the kindergarten year. Viewed from a literacy-as-social-practices perspective, then, we believe family literacy programs tend to borrow heavily from, and to promote uncritically, the literacy practices of middle-class, Caucasian homes that are also valued and reinforced in school (Heath, 1983).

Conceptualizing and Developing PALS

It is against this backdrop that PALS was developed. PALS had its genesis when the mayor of a small city in British Columbia invited the developers to participate in a program that would assist parents in supporting their children's literacy development. We entered the partnership cognizant of the issues and perspectives just highlighted and committed to attempting to work with the community in a manner that met their needs but also, as far as possible, reflected the sociocultural approach that Auerbach (1989) envisioned. We were also influenced by ethnographic research (e.g., Barton, Hamilton, & Ivanic, 2000; Heath, 1983) that describes literacy as complex social practices embedded in particular sociocultural milieus and that vary considerably across contexts. Furthermore, we wanted PALS to reflect a multiliteracies perspective (New London Group, 1996). Thus, it was serendipitous that parents also wanted to include a session on technology and literacy, or "computers," as they put it.

We were also mindful and respectful of alternative perspectives, especially those of Delpit (1995) and Edwards (1995), who passionately call for educators to teach parents and children from outside the mainstream culture the "ways with words" (Heath, 1982) and the literacy practices of the school while also valuing and supporting the vernacular language and literacies (see also Phillips & Sample, chapter 5, this volume).

PALS was seen as part of a larger, interagency community development initiative in economically depressed, inner city areas. Parents, early childhood educators, and administrators have all been involved in the development and evolution of the program. PALS is designed for 3- to 5-year-olds and their parents and/or other caregivers. The program consists of 12 to 15 two-hour sessions held about every 2 weeks commencing in October and ending in May. Session topics typically include learning the alphabet, early mathematics or numeracy development, learning to write, environmental print, technology and literacy, and reading with children. Sessions begin with the families, facilitators, and teachers sharing food together. Then, the facilitator and the parents spend about half an hour discussing the topic (e.g., early numeracy) that is the focus of the session while the children go to their classroom(s). Parents, children, and teachers then spend an hour in the classroom(s) at a number of literacy and learning centers, each containing a different activity reflecting the topic of the day. Sessions conclude with a group discussion based on parents' observations of their children's learning in the classroom. A book or other materials and resources, such as mathematics activities and games, are handed out at the end of each session for parents to take home. About a third of the sessions are kept "open" to address topics and issues important to particular parent groups. For example, the parents in one school wanted an extra session to learn more about the role of computers in learning to read and write, whereas in another school parents wanted a session devoted to children and television. Books, materials such as crayons, glue, and scissors, and writing materials such as pencils, paper, and markers, as well as a set of dice and other materials that can promote numeracy are provided. Different possibilities for using these materials are discussed; however, great care is taken to honor and value that which parents already do with their children. For example, no effort is made to teach parents to read to their children in particular or prescribed ways.

We developed PALS in a manner that we hoped was responsive to some of the criticisms of family literacy programs, and that reflected current thinking that literacy is situated and social and that it has multiple forms.

We also wanted to insure that the program meets the needs of the parents with whom we worked. Having worked in program and curriculum development and implementation previously, however, we were also cognizant that when our intentions met with the everyday lives of families, schools, and teachers, we would learn much that would give us cause to reflect and re-evaluate our work. Next, Suzanne shares some of the insights she gained as she implemented the program in two inner city schools over the course of two school years.

INSIGHTS FROM THE INSIDE: CRITICAL
REFLECTIONS ON FACILITATING
A FAMILY LITERACY PROGRAM

I joined the PALS project in 2000 as a facilitator in two inner city schools, Valley School and Mountain School.[1] Both schools served large immigrant communities, and the kindergarten classes were designed to meet the language and literacy needs of children who spoke English as a Second or Additional Language. Mountain School also served a large aboriginal community, although at the time, the kindergarten curricula did not include any special provisions to meet the learning interests of these children.

Kindergarten curriculum and pedagogy in British Columbia are (ostensibly) guided by *The Primary Program* (2000). This document articulates a child-centered orientation to literacy learning and teaching. Children are portrayed as learning through approximation and risk taking, with the teacher's role as a facilitator. An integrated approach to curriculum is favoured, and teachers are encouraged to organize curriculum and instruction around themes.

My role required that I work closely with kindergarten teachers, resource teachers, and the school principal in each school to plan each of the 13 PALS sessions to meet the needs of culturally and linguistically diverse families living in two of Vancouver's poorest neighbourhoods. It also involved recruiting families, facilitating one session every 2 weeks or so in each school, and documenting the themes, ideas, and issues emerging from each of these sessions. The first stages of the planning took place with kindergarten teachers before we met the parents and were therefore guided by what the teachers thought parents knew (and didn't know) about supporting their children's literacy.

At the time I was hired as the PALS facilitator, I was a first-year doctoral student, designing a thesis on the topic of mothering and literacy from feminist and historical perspectives. I had worked for 10 years in Vancouver

---

[1] All names except those of the authors are pseudonyms.

and Johannesburg, South Africa as an adult educator and family literacy facilitator and so I brought to the role considerable experience in literacy work with adults and children in out-of-school settings. However, when I first began to meet with school board officials and teachers, I felt somewhat of an outsider. I had not interacted with the formal school system in Canada since I graduated from secondary school 20 years earlier. Among the many people associated with the PALS project, I was, along with many of the parents, the only one not trained as a teacher for the K–12 system. I therefore had to learn the particular ways in which early literacy and the goals of kindergarten were currently framed in the formal school system. I also had to work to maintain my own credibility among teachers and administrators as someone who was knowledgeable about literacy issues, but worked outside the school system.

In the second year as a PALS facilitator, my own daughter started kindergarten at a school close to the PALS pilot schools. I was thus able to bring my own experiences as a "new parent" in the system to the PALS sessions. It is against this backdrop of my own shifting identities as a literacy educator and mother, and the particular salience of the kindergarten year as one of transition and thus conflicting identities for many families, particularly socially and economically marginalized families, that I analysed and interpreted the data presented here.

The data I draw on for this section are based on over 40 three-hour PALS sessions with parents, teachers, and children, and 15 planning sessions with teachers that took place in two schools between September 2000 and June 2002. I documented the questions and discussions that surrounded PALS topics, observations of parents in classrooms, critical incidents, and events that marked significant shifts in my views as a facilitator, as well as those of the PALS researchers, parents, and teachers. The data are extensive and detailed and suggest a variety of themes worthy of elaboration. In keeping with the aims of this book, however, we focus on three ideas that researchers claim are either underdocumented in the literature on home–school relations, or that require further exploration from the lenses of power and identity.

The first theme explores the interplay of home and school literacies, specifically focusing on the ideas about literacy promoted in PALS and the possibilities and limitations of these for reflecting on literacy instruction in classrooms and home settings. The second theme highlights the paradox between the assumptions and expectations placed on parents as the "first and most important educators" and what we were able to learn from families about the role of literacy and "parental involvement" in the context of their everyday lives. The third theme questions the prescribed role of parents as "their child's first educators" in the context of the forms of power that shape their participation in their children's classrooms.

Interplay of Home and School Literacies

Each of the 13 PALS sessions was organized around a children's storybook. PALS had been piloted in two inner city schools in a neighbouring but much smaller city with a less diverse population. At the beginning of the first year, I chose to provide the same set of books that had been used in the pilot program. These books were selected because they were fairly well-known children's books such as *Rosie's Walk* (Hutchins, 1968) and, pragmatically, because they were inexpensive and within our limited budget. Parents in the PALS Vancouver group were less than enamoured with these books. In fact, most of them had much broader tastes in the books they chose for their children. A trip to the local library suggested that, contrary to our assumptions, many families used library services quite often. The community library provided essential Internet service for parents looking for work and wanting to communicate with family members who lived far away. Unlike the school libraries, the public libraries held collections in languages of neighbourhood families, such as Vietnamese, Spanish, Chinese, Hindi, and Punjabi. On one library visit with a group of parents, I documented the materials parents chose:

> Sami goes directly to books on drawing, intending to teach her child to draw. Khatija decides to come back with her daughter to choose, but takes out a number of books for herself. Anne takes out recipe books, books on First Nations, an "Arthur" video. Tran chooses bilingual Vietnamese–English storybooks for her children. For herself, she chooses a novel in Vietnamese by an author well known to herself and the other Vietnamese parents. She also takes out a book on craft projects and paper making to do with her children. (Field notes, Mountain School, January 15, 2002)

The visit to the library offered insight into the literate lives of parents. As mentioned previously, family literacy projects encourage parent literacy to the extent that they read stories to their children. However, Mountain School parents' book choices reflected parent interest in a broader genre of reading material than that of the storybooks we offered in PALS or that are offered in most classrooms. Almost all the books lent themselves to collaborative activities with their children and are either bilingual or in languages other than English. When I was able to find affordable copies of multilingual or home language books to distribute during PALS sessions, these were snapped up.

Parent and teacher discourses on the meanings and purposes of storybook reading also differed. During the topic dedicated to storybook reading in Valley School, we started off with a discussion about stories that parents knew as children and the elements that make a good story. Many parents said that storytelling, rather than storybook reading, had been a feature of their own childhoods. Of course, this phenomenon depended on where the parents were from and their ages, reflective of the shifting and changing nature of literacies over time and in the context of changing economies, family structures, and the organization of work. Whereas parents spoke of stories as ways to connect to their children, of educating children in "ways of living," teachers talked about ways to use stories to develop literacy skills, and to extend their potential with the use of puppets, storyboards, and questioning techniques. In the schooling context, storybooks were seen more as instructional tools to promote the development of specific literacy skills, although there is not a lot of evidence that such is the case, especially with nonmainstream families (Anderson, Anderson, Lynch, & Shapiro, 2003).

One teacher modelled to parents pedagogical strategies for reading stories at home. Using *Clifford, the Big Red Dog* (Bridwell, 1963), she showed parents how to prompt children for background experience, draw attention to the print and illustrations, and ask a number of comprehension and prediction questions. An excerpt from my facilitator's notes reflects on that pedagogical strategy:

> Should parents be encouraged to use pedagogical strategies for sharing stories at home? Is the role of stories and the ways of telling/sharing them in homes and community settings, quite different to those told or "used" in school settings? I am reminded of an observation by a multicultural worker for one of the school boards, who said that for many families a story is told and that's it: You listen to it, or read it, and then you take what you need from it. Modelling to parents how to deconstruct the narrative, what questions to ask the children to "get at" the meaning can really kill a story. It turns the parent–child relationship, and the story itself, into something else. (Field notes, Mountain School, November 15, 2000)

Sometimes I asked parents what they thought of the book that they had taken home the previous session. Some would say they "liked it," whereas others were silent. In an effort to probe this issue, I truthfully told them that I often found it hard to find time to read to my daughter. Consequently, some parents agreed that sometimes there just isn't time. There are also other learning activities to attend to, such as attending Saturday school instruction in families' first languages (known locally as Heritage Language Schools) and completing homework for these, or attending Sunday school, the mosque, or temple, or caring for other children, and working. Interestingly, some parents said their children prefer the graded readers sent home by the school as part of the school district's early literacy strategy. The children enjoyed showing their parents their knowledge of the text, and parents were assured that indeed their children were learning to read. For many of the parents, the controlled vocabulary and language structures of the graded readers supported their children's emerging English reading skills.

These insights into home literacy and learning raised important points for reflection and exploration in PALS. One of the main goals of the project, and an idea to which we returned repeatedly with parents, was that literacy is not just learned in school, but is integral to home and community life. However, much early literacy research and programming equate early literacy with storybook reading practices, and parental involvement in literacy as primarily reading books to their children. This raised the need to perhaps make more visible to parents and teachers the many ways parents support literacy at home beyond storybook reading.

Another PALS session focused on technology to provide an introduction to the use of computers in supporting early literacy, both at home and in the classroom. Whereas this session was highly valued in the schools in a neighbouring school district—one group asked for a second session devoted to technology, as was previously mentioned—it had mixed reception in the schools in which I worked. Mountain School did not have sufficient resources or support staff to use computers in classrooms, and Valley School did not want to encourage computer use among young children. As an alternative in the latter school, we discussed issues related to the computer such as criteria for good software, safety and security, and the uses of computers in education. We strived for a critical, balanced attitude toward computer use among children, and talked about places parents could learn computer skills and access computers in the community. Contrary to our assumption that most families did not have home computers, we found that most families did indeed have a home computer and were perhaps more knowledgeable about computer games and programmes than the teachers and myself. Moreover, the technology sector was a growing industry in Vancouver at the time and many of the parents were enrolled in courses to qualify as technicians, software designers, and so on. The Internet and e-mail were especially important to new immigrant families as an affordable means for communicating with family and friends, including those in their own countries. Thus, although the schools did not generally encourage computer use in the kindergarten classroom, it became clear that many children were engaged in a broad range of computer literacies at home. This paradox was expressed in an excerpt from my notes:

> The reluctance to introduce young children and parents to computers raises different things for me. On the one hand, I can appreciate the concern over too much computer play among young children. But on the other hand, Luke and Luke's (2001) image of teachers as being "techno-phobic" and harkening back to an image of childhood "before the fall" stays with me. Is it the computer use that is in itself "bad" for children or is it that what they may be learning is harder to assimilate into the school's early literacy curricula? (Field notes, Valley School, February 23, 2002)

The sessions on community print helped to broaden notions of literacy. On a walk around the neighbourhood with parents, teachers, and children, we paid closer attention than usual to the print around us. We discovered heritage markers, labelling historical sites that most of us who lived in the neighbourhood had not noticed before. Many children focused on street addresses, trying to predict what number would come next. On a busy business strip, children were able to read the many "open" and "closed" signs in storefronts by the end of the walk. When we returned to the classroom and asked the children to draw a sign they remembered, many chose "Beware of Dog" because, as one child explained, "Maybe a dog will bite us." The pattern was similar in each school: Children came back to the classroom happy and excited from fresh air, exercize, and a chance to show their knowledge of their community.

The book *Signs* (Goor & Goor, 1983) framed the community print session. This book features some of the more common traffic signs people are likely to encounter in large cities. However, many parents and teachers took their own pictures of signs during the walk and in Mountain School, the project teacher made a poster of these in an effort to better reflect the neighbourhood surrounding the school. Unlike the monolingual English signs published book, the signs in the community were in Korean, Vietnamese, Italian, and Chinese as well as English, and reflected great variety in genre and uses; the signs told their own story about the people who lived there. For example, we passed a vegetable stall filled with fruit and vegetables that the teachers and some children did not recognize. The names of the produce were in Vietnamese. One parent explained the health and medicinal properties of some of the fruit and how to cook it, thus sharing her cultural knowledge and identity in ways that are not always available to her in structured work or learning environments.

This opportunity to explore the literacies of a neighbourhood with families suggests that, more than just supporting "print awareness," these activities invite closer reflection with children and their families on the ways in which literacies intersect and are shaped by broader social and historical events, local patterns of immigration and settlement, and individual family histories. Thus, trips to the library, sessions on computer literacy, and the community walk each brought forth a paradox between advice for supporting children's learning and families' everyday lives.

Literacy and Everyday Lives

Sessions on literacy and play and on parenting that one of the groups requested led to discussions about the home context for learning and provided valuable lenses for reflecting on the standard advice offered to parents for supporting their children's learning. The sessions on the links between play and literacy were particularly salient in bringing out cultural, social, and pedagogical issues surrounding learning. The aim of the session was to encourage parents to value play as a form of learning and as a context for literacy development. The typical kindergarten curriculum is based on this interconnection, though many parents resist this, feeling that children "have plenty of time at home to play—school is a place to work" (Field notes, Mountain School, October 21, 2001). However, after visiting their children's classrooms, one parent remarked, "It is a good experience to see my son in class. Very interesting that they are playing but learning—like doing ABC puzzles." Parents also talked about the contrast in the play-based approaches they saw in the class and the ways they had been taught. One parent commented, "[I]n my country children are afraid to go to school, sitting in rows all the time, the teacher very angry. Here my child wants to go to school even when she is sick" (Field notes, Mountain School, October 21, 2001).

In Valley School, efforts on the part of teachers and the facilitator to encourage outdoor play and exercise led to a discussion of children's spaces. Parents pointed out that many parks in the neighbourhood were not safe, sometimes there were hypodermic needles on the ground, and there was always the fear of strangers approaching their children. For many families who had recently immigrated to Vancouver from Asia, Eastern Europe, and the Middle East, the need in North America to supervise one's children constantly and not to be able to share this task with other neighbours or extended family was a new and unwelcome reality. Parents also said that it was hard to find time to go to parks because of work responsibilities and the needs of other children. One of the take-home activities for the play topic was play dough. Feedback the following week led to more insights about children's spaces and families' lives. One parent complained that play dough got stuck in the carpet, suggesting that recommended "creative" messy play is impractical in a small, rental apartment. Anderson, Fagan, and Cronin (1998) reported a similar response from the parents with whom they worked. That group, when pressed, explained that the government agency responsible for overseeing the public housing projects where they lived regularly conducted inspections and families were admonished for the "untidiness" that children's play with materials like play dough generates. It emerged, too, that the parents in PALS expressed concerns over who their children play with in school, and the desire to know more about what was happening on the school playground at recess and lunchtime was one reason some parents attended PALS.

Thus, the topic of play brings out many of parents' anxieties and insights into the social organization of children's lives in North America. Access to, and time for, safe play is not equally distributed across all families or neighbourhoods in Vancouver, and thus saying "let your children play" is much easier said than done. Far more valuable was the discussion of strategies to support children's play on a community level. We talked about ways to make playgrounds safer and more accessible for children, shared information about family drop-in gym programs in the community, and ways that parents could connect with others to share child-raising tasks. This did not rectify the difficulties of providing children with spaces for play, but it did help to shift the issue from one of individual family choice to one of collective experiences and possible strategies.

Parents chose the topic of parenting skills as one of the "open" sessions in the PALS programme in one of the schools. The school nurse spoke to parents about the kinds of home routines that children need to learn well in school. The session was conducted in English, with translation taking place in small groups. Her recommendations included eating dinner early, making sure children get at least 12 hours of sleep per night, deciding with the child what the bedtime routine will be (e.g., teeth first or book first), and the need for children to go to sleep by themselves. Parents were advised not to allow TV in the morning, to eat breakfast early, and then enjoy quiet time together with their child, reading a story, taking a slow walk to school, and some play time on the playground as a reward. Above all, parents were reminded that they were the ones in charge; it was they who had the power to decide and enforce routines.

The nurse's ideas precipitated considerable discussion among the group as they considered her advice in light of daily life. One parent told the nurse that she works at McDonald's at night so her husband puts the children to sleep. But because there are several children with several bedtimes, he doesn't have lots of time to read stories. She phones during her shift to remind her children to get to bed. But when she comes in late, the children wake up because they want to see their mom. Another parent said that her child does not get 12 hours a night, but seems to be doing fine. Another pointed out that she has three children and they live in a one-bedroom apartment, so how could she put one child to bed before the others?

When the nurse left, the conversation about parenting continued. Some parents questioned whether they really were in charge of their children's routines, noting that they use bargains or threats, promises and punishments on a regular basis. Some parents wondered if being in charge was even desirable, saying that Chinese parents, for example, don't tend to think about their role in this way. The teachers and I made a point of deconstructing the image of "ideal" parenting that had been presented. One teacher said her child didn't need lots of sleep; her doctor said that it was very normal for some children to need only 7 or 8 hours a night. Also, finding time in the morning for a story and walk to school was not possible for the teachers and other parents who had to get to work and wouldn't be possible for all parents either.

The storybook for that session was *No, David!* (Shannon, 1998). We read and discussed the story in light of the nurse's presentation. One parent remarked that in the story, the mother was always saying no, but never said why she was saying no. She said that it was important that parents show the child that they do not like what the child is doing, not that they do not like the child. Other parents asked her to explain this, then agreed it was an important distinction. In this way, the conversation shifted from routines over which parents had little control to the complex emotional relationships we have with our children. An excerpt from field notes taken following this session suggests the value of drawing on stories and the collective experiences of the group, rather than on advice-driven approaches to discussing parenting and literacy:

> Sharing our parenting stories, the values we have, the circumstances each of us are in, helped to break down the notion that there is a right way and a wrong way to parent. We also talked about the fact that all families need support and that asking for help was fine. So we ended with a feeling that there are some good parenting ideas out there but families need to do what works for them, and trust themselves. (Field notes, Valley School, March 15, 2002)

Parents in the Classroom

The third theme relates to the experiences of parents in schools. This builds on the themes of home and school literacies and the paradoxes between advice for supporting literacy and everyday life discussed thus far, as it illustrates the quite different ways that teachers and parents relate to children as "children's educators."

As described in the introduction, a key component of the PALS programme is parent visits to the classroom. During this hour, parents are invited to help facilitate the learning centres and interact with their own children as well as children whose parents do not attend PALS. In both schools, this "hands-on" form of parental involvement in the classrooms was new to the teachers, the parents, and the children. In Mountain School, teachers at first felt uncomfortable with parents' presence and sometimes forgot to introduce visiting parents to the children. Perhaps as a result, parents tended to stay along the edges of the activities, watching rather than participating in the learning activities. In subsequent sessions, we made a point of offering parents more support in the classroom, by sharing more explicitly the goals of the activities and ways they could work with the children. Some parents found it easy to get involved; others were not sure how to start. Language was a barrier in this respect, as some centres required parents to read to children or to listen to them read in English, a difficult and confusing experience for parents who do not read English. Over time, however, parents seemed to

find a niche for themselves, as these field notes, written at the halfway point
of the programme in Mountain School, suggest:

> The centers went well today, parents seem to be getting more comfortable in
> the class, getting to know how their own child interacts in the classroom.
> Many are getting to know all the children and are calling them by name, feel-
> ing more comfortable leading activities. But the initial discomfort, and the
> need for me to be really proactive in involving and supporting parents, sug-
> gests that although parents are constructed as their "child's first educator,"
> the practices that surround this role are very different in a classroom than in
> the home or community. (Field notes, Mountain School, February 12, 2001)

In Valley School, however, teachers were more open to shifting and
adapting their classroom management methods and their attitudes toward
parents in the classroom to make the experience work for everyone. Thus,
when some parents said that they worried their presence was more of a dis-
traction to their children and to the teachers, they were assured that their
presence was valuable in itself, even if the children were, at first, more excited and distractible when their parents were present. Possibly because the
teachers in Valley School attended the discussion period with parents that
followed the classroom visits (the Mountain School teachers opted to return to their classrooms and not attend the debriefing session) and often
the recess breaks as well, they developed relationships with parents that
seemed to translate to more comfortable interactions in the classroom.

Quite unexpectedly for teachers in Valley School, the participation of
parents in the classroom led to the formation of alliances in support of
smaller class sizes and the need for special education assistance in the classrooms, both of which were under threat due to a wave of education funding
cutbacks. For example, following discussion on the difficulties children had
with estimation problems in mathematics, one parent observed, "You need
two teachers in the class, not one, because it is necessary to talk to each
child about what she is doing."

The ensuing discussion focused on issues of class size and why it is important to keep the ratio of children to teachers low, to 20, particularly in the
early grades. Many parents said they had heard the term *class size* before but
were never sure what it meant. They then offered to sign a petition being
circulated calling for smaller class sizes and to write a letter for a campaign
under way to protest cuts to education.

Often, literacy is presented to parents as a specific package of skills they
can support at home. However, parents who visit classrooms also get a sense
of the diverse approaches to literacy instruction in schools, and thus the diverse meanings and understandings of literacy even within one school. In
Mountain School, parents visited one of two kindergarten classes in which a
session on early writing was taking place. The teachers did not plan their

approach together, nor did they design centres in which parents could participate as is intended in the PALS program. Thus, parents observed "typical" but very different lessons. One teacher invited children to write a story in their journals, focusing on content and expression, and encouraging children to use invented spelling, models of writing found around the classroom, and the help of peers. The lesson in the other classroom was a structured, whole class activity in which children were asked to copy verbatim from a story that had been written on a large sheet of newsprint. Children were asked to read this text several times and then reproduce it in their writing books, paying particular attention to punctuation, spelling, and spacing. During the discussion that followed, parents shared what each had seen in their children's classrooms. They identified the differences in each approach and weighed the possible benefits and drawbacks of each. One parent summarized that "both ways had their place." It was first important for children to figure out how the language worked by "playing with it and then learn how to do it correctly." Others said that the success of the approach depends very much on each child's way of learning, so approaches need to vary: "If the same method is used all the time, some children will fall behind or become confused" (Parent comment, Field notes, Valley School, March 15, 2001).

Parents, as one teacher remarked, "don't miss much." Our observations concluded that parental involvement in the classroom can make the work of public schools more visible, and thus promote advocacy for the improvement of conditions for quality teaching/learning. It can also stimulate important discussions about the diversity of literacy practices and instruction in schools. However, if parental involvement in their children's classrooms is to be ethical and enjoyable, it must take into account the unequal power relations between teachers and parents. Regardless of the efforts to welcome and support parents' presence in the classroom, I found as a facilitator that when parents entered their children's classrooms, their knowledge of their children and their particular parenting styles were difficult to integrate and validate in the context of prevailing methods of classroom management and instruction. This is not necessarily a critique of classroom instruction, but rather the recognition that parents are not teachers in the sense of the professionalized role of a teacher working within a particular institutional culture. This distinction is not often made, or indeed recognized, in family literacy research or programmes.

We found that we could be more supportive of parents' involvement in the classroom if we provided and modelled a range of ways for parents to participate. Some parents may want to watch, others will dive in, some will not want to work with their own children, others will spend the whole time with their own child. In essence, parents need to be allowed to be parents (and not be expected to be teachers) in the classroom.

The kindergarten year is a time of transition for young children as well as for their families. It is a time when family cultures and histories, so important in shaping literacy practices and the meaning and expectations for children's education, meet with the institutionally driven practices and expectations of schooling. The extent to which schools acknowledge and embrace this conflict, and recognize the adjustments and demands that families are faced with, seems to determine the smoothness of this transition. Indeed, as the data suggests, PALS was effective in acknowledging and giving space for the negotiation of this transition, albeit among a small but significant number of parents. Teachers had the opportunity to move from stereotypical images of parents to engagement with real, complex people, much like themselves. In both schools, at the end of the year, the conversations between teachers and parents had shifted from more dydactic advice to parents to joint inquiry. Parents reflected on their own shifts in thinking. One parent said that at the beginning of the year, she was most concerned over how her child would fit in and learn English and succeed in the "new" system. Now, her concern was how she was going to maintain the family's language and values, as her child integrates more successfully than her parents into the new culture and language.

The programme also raises broader questions about the role of schools in the community. Some of the most successful sessions were built around discussions about families' lives outside of school. As the year went by, many parents asked the facilitator and teachers about ways they could access education programmes or update or "Canadianize" their qualifications. For many parents, PALS sessions provided the only adult time they got outside their family to talk about education, ideas, and events that are happening both in the school and in the community. Parents were very interested in information on child care, drop-in centres, and after-school programs. This kind of networking and information sharing falls outside the formal curricula for PALS and for most early literacy initiatives, but seemed important to parents.

LEARNING WITH AND FROM FAMILIES: TEACHERS' PERSPECTIVES

Given the context described earlier, and the fact that the formal involvement of the facilitator and the researchers in the 2-year PALS pilot was coming to an end, and teachers would be continuing with PALS in their own classrooms the following year, we thought it important to try to understand these teachers' perceptions of PALS. We conducted interviews with each of the teachers around questions such as: What did you learn about the parents and the community as a result of your participation in PALS? What did you learn about yourself as a teacher? Several themes emerged from these interviews.

Learning About Families' Lives

From the outset, it is important to point out that the teachers were dedicated and caring individuals, having chosen to dedicate significant planning and work time to the PALS project. Initially, some of the teachers expressed concerns about parents who were unable to attend all sessions or were late for sessions. However, this concern seemed to dissipate somewhat as it came to light that some parents were working night shifts, others had irregular part-time jobs, and some encountered difficulties with transportation, as they did not own automobiles. The latter problem was exacerbated for parents when a mass transit strike occurred in the middle of the program. Indeed, we sensed that as the program progressed and rapport with parents developed, the teachers became more aware of the daily lived realities of the parents and attendance became less of an issue. One teacher exemplified these developing understandings quite nicely when she commented, "I got more insight into the lives of the parents" [through her participation in PALS]. Nevertheless, one teacher in particular still voiced concerns about attendance after 2 years of working in PALS and after listening to parents talk about the challenges they encountered daily.

Each teacher expressed the view that participating in the PALS program helped her (all of the teachers were women) to know the children better. One reported, "I learned a lot about the children's expectations and personalities by watching them with their parents." Another teacher commented, "I learned how different they all are—how they come to school with such different knowledge, different experiences, and different language abilities." We believe that this focus on the children's interactions with other significant adults provided teachers with additional insights into working with the individual children in the kindergarten classrooms. The notion of individual differences has long been promoted in teacher training programs and in official curriculum documents. However, we speculate that the social and situated nature of literacy learning and teaching that underpins PALS, combined with the opportunity afforded the teachers to discuss cultural, social, and pedagogical issues in a safe environment over time, contributed to their deepening understandings of the children both as individuals and as part of a wider social and cultural network.

Developing Intercultural Understandings

Most of the teachers reported that they now felt more comfortable working with parents from different cultural and linguistic groups and that they had developed new insights, especially in terms of the parents' values, beliefs, and expectations of schooling and discourse practices. For example, one teacher cited the example of being called "teacher." Many new immigrants initially used the honorific "Teacher," instead of addressing the teacher as "Ms. Jones," for example. She found this frustrating until a discussion with parents about how different cultural groups use names allowed her and the other teachers to see that parents used the term as a sign of respect. During this discussion, parents also shared the importance of getting children's and parents' names correct on the class lists that appear early in the school year. Parents explained how to determine a first and second name of a child in their respective cultures, instead of assuming that the child's last name is that of the father, as is the usual practice in many Canadian schools. This discussion provided the teachers with a practical, culturally responsive action they could take the following school year to make the transition for children and parents easier. Indeed, this growing cultural sensitivity was affirmed by one of the teachers who commented, "I enjoyed hearing about the experiences parents bring with them [to the country and school]." She continued that through the program, she had developed "insights from different cultural groups."

From the teachers' perspectives, the parents had also developed new knowledge and insights about the curriculum and the learning potential of young children. One reported, ". . . they seemed to change their views about the educational significance of our play-based kindergarten curriculum. They learned it is different here, not deficient." This latter comment reflected the initial feeling among some parents that the play-based kindergarten curriculum did not constitute "real" learning. Teachers believed that as a result of the relationships that had evolved, parents indicated more willingness "to trust the teacher" and the process. We sensed that because of their deepening understanding of the lived experiences of the parents, the teachers also developed more trust in them. Parents also shared with the teachers some of the activities they did in the home with their children, and the teachers, as a group, thought that this two-way exchange of information "always helps the kids."

Family Literacy and School: Possibilities for Synergy

Teachers also noticed the relationship or lack of relationship that the PALS program had with other programs in the schools. For example, through discussion in PALS, teachers began to recognise a need for greater schoolwide articulation of beliefs, expectations, and visions regarding the primary literacy curriculum. According to one teacher, PALS highlighted the "difference between our approach and the approaches of the Grade 1 teachers," leading them to declare, "We have different philosophies. This has always been something we were aware of as individuals, but now we have a group awareness of it—something that identifies us." The kindergarten teachers began to plan for better communication between themselves and the Grade 1 teachers in order to ease the transition for parents and children.

Family Literacy and Reflective Practice

The teachers involved with PALS learned quite a lot about themselves, both as professionals and as people. They learned that they were "open to new ideas" and some saw their involvement as a wonderful professional development opportunity where they learned more about learning centres, about professional collaboration, and about working in culturally responsive ways with parents. For example, one teacher explained, "I got to know the concerns of the parents and realized the kinds of transitions they have gone through and the stresses they are experiencing [as new immigrants]. I became much more aware of differences in childrearing [practices]."

One teacher commented how much she enjoyed working with the parents because she learned how to open up and become more comfortable with a group of adults. For another, learning that she could effectively communicate with parents gave her confidence: "It allowed me to see my strengths and helped me see what I am trying to do and why I am doing it." Finally, one teacher reported, "PALS helps me in my journey to let go of control. Having parents in the room, knowing that people may not do what I would do or want them to do was a liberating experience."

LOOKING BACK, LOOKING AHEAD

We believe that this critical look back at the PALS program has provided insights that will guide our own work and that of others interested in the family as a site for literacy teaching and learning.

First, it is obvious that attempting to transpose a family literacy model from one context to another is very difficult. What is highly valued and appreciated in one context is not appropriate in another. For example, we wonder about the value and use of the books that we provided the families we worked with in Mountain and Valley Schools. Yet, in another community, these books were highly valued by parents and teachers. As noted, the sessions devoted to technology were also received quite differently in the two contexts. The difficulties inherent in implementing a program such as PALS, which aims to build on strengths, was brought home to us when we eventually had to withdraw from one school in the same geographic area as Mountain and Valley Schools because it was perceived that we were not being directive enough in teaching parents specific skills to teach their children. On the other hand, we are encouraged by the manner in which other communities have adapted PALS to fit their context.

As we reported elsewhere (Anderson, Shapiro, Smythe, & Morrison, 2003), it appears, based on comparisons of pre and post measures of early literacy development such as storybook reenactment (Sulzby, 1985), early writing, and *Concepts of Print* (Clay, 1992), that PALS contributed positively to children's early literacy development, though much more modestly than other studies (e.g., Jordan, Porche, & Snow, 2000). However, we believe that there were other very important outcomes that fall outside standard evaluation parameters, but that nevertheless contribute to home–school relationships and learning. For example, in the environmental print walk, it became obvious that parents, teachers, and children were learning a great deal about their community as they explored it together. Likewise, the parents also valued the sharing of information about community resources that permeated many of the sessions. And it was apparent that the parents had gained considerable insight into teaching and learning in the context of child-centered curriculum and pedagogy in kindergarten classrooms.

It is important to note that the teachers who were involved in implementing PALS also believed that they had benefited and learned from their participation in the program. This is an interesting finding, as family literacy is usually seen as a way of enhancing children's learning. In fact, the impact that family literacy programs can have on teachers, other child-care workers, schools, and preschools is an underresearched and undertheorized area worthy of further study. Our sense is that PALS helped the teachers begin to reflect on their own practices, especially in issues of cross-cultural understanding, communication with parents, and inclusiveness.

We saw little evidence, however, of the literacy practices of the families and communities being incorporated into the school curriculum. As was mentioned earlier, central to PALS was the notion that literacy learning occurs not just in school but in communities and families as well. However, if we want these vernacular literacies incorporated into school literacy curricula, it might be that we have to make very explicit specific strategies that teachers can employ to build on the "funds of [literacy and language] knowledge" (Moll, Amanti, Neff, & Gonzalez, 1992) of families and communities. We are currently working with a First Nations teacher in Langley, B.C. on such a project.

As we shared in this chapter, there are considerable tensions and many issues that arise when family literacy initiatives attempt to explore and build on the intersections between school and community literacy practices. It is humbling to confront just how much we still have to learn about working with communities. This is hard work. But we are encouraged by the way in which PALS has evolved and been adapted to fit the goals of different communities. For example, in Abbotsford B.C., PALS is being offered to a group of newly immigrated Indo-Canadians. Sessions are run in the evenings, according to the preference of the parents, and are conducted in

Punjabi, their first language. First Nations communities have also adapted the program to fit their context, as, for example, is the case of the Dene Community of Fort Providence in the North West Territories in Canada (see http://www.nwt.literacy.ca/resource/famnews/apr03/page7.htm). In other First Nations communities, emphasis is placed on the culture of the communities; for example, oral story telling is promoted.

Research with children demonstrates that they are particularly adroit at crossing boundaries and at importing literacy practices from one context into another. In her foundational work, Dyson (2003) has shown that when given the opportunity and encouragement, young children from marginalized communities are very adept at incorporating aspects of their social worlds into their classroom literacy learning. Likewise, in her ethnographic work in inner city London, Gregory (2001; Gregory, chapter 2, this volume) documents how children borrow the routines and practices from school and integrate it into their literacy play at home. Although the bifurcation between "school literacy" and "social" or "local" or "out of schools literacies" is of theoretical interest and importance, we speculate that children and their families engage in hybridised forms of literacy, borrowing and using aspects of school literacy and out of school literacy as they attempt to make sense of reading and writing and other forms of representation in their daily lives.

We believe that PALS has made at least a small difference in the lives of some of the children, parents, and teachers with whom we have worked. It is thus fitting that in Snapshot 1 (pp. 87–89, this volume), Stacey Cody, a parent with whom we worked in the initial pilot program of PALS, shares how the program affected her.

REFERENCES

Adams, M. (1990). *Beginning to read: Thinking and learning about print.* Cambridge, MA: Massachusetts Institute of Technology.

Anderson, J., Anderson, A., Lynch, J., & Shapiro, J. (2003). Storybook reading in a multicultural society: Critical perspectives. In A. van Kleeck, S. Stahl, & E. Bauer (Eds.), *On reading books to children: Parents and teachers* (pp. 203–230). Mahwah, NJ: Lawrence Erlbaum Associates.

Anderson, J., Fagan, W. T., & Cronin, M. (1998). Insights in implementing family literacy programs. In E. G. Sturtevant, J. Duggan, P. Linder, & W. Linek (Eds.), *Literacy and community* (pp. 269–277). Commerce, TX: College Reading Association.

Anderson, J., & Matthews, R. (1999). Emergent storybook reading revisited. *Journal of Research in Reading, 22,* 293–298.

Anderson, J., & Morrison, F. (2003). *Parents As Literacy Supporters (PALS): A culturally responsive family literacy program.* Langley, British Columbia: Langley School District.

Anderson, J., Shapiro, J., Smythe, S., & Morrison, F. (2003, May). *Assessment issues in family literacy programs.* Paper presented at the annual conference of the Canadian Society for the Study of Education, Halifax, Nova Scotia.

Anderson, J., Smythe, S., & Lynch, J. (2003). Family literacy. In J. Ponzetti (Ed.), *International encyclopedia of marriage and families* (2nd ed., pp. 601–605). New York: Macmillan Reference USA.

Auerbach, E. (1989). Toward a social-contextual approach to family literacy. *Harvard Educational Review, 59*, 165–181.

Auerbach, E. (1995). Deconstructing the discourse of strengths in family literacy. *Journal of Reading Behaviour, 27*, 643–661.

Baghban, M. (1984). *Our daughter learns to read and write.* Newark, DE: International Reading Association.

Barton, D., Hamilton, M., & Ivanic, R. (2000). *Situated literacies: Reading and writing in context.* London: Routledge.

Blackledge, A. (1999). Language, literacy and social justice: The experience of Bangladeshi women in Birmingham, UK. *Journal of Multilingual and Multicultural Development, 20*, 179–193.

Bridwell, N. (1963). *Clifford, the big red dog.* Toronto: Scholastic.

Bush, B. (1995). Foreword. In L. Morrow (Ed.), *Family literacy: Connections in schools and communities.* Newark, DE: International Reading Association.

Carrington, V., & Luke, A. (2003). Reading homes and families from postmodern to modern. In A. van Kleeck, S. Stahl, & E. Bauer (Eds.), *On reading books to children: Parents and teachers* (pp. 231–267). Mahwah, NJ: Lawrence Erlbaum Associates.

Clay, M. (1992). *The early detection of reading difficulties.* Auckland, New Zealand: Heinemann.

Delpit, L. (1995). *Other people's children: Cultural conflict in the classroom.* New York: New Press.

Doake, D. (1988). *Reading begins at birth.* Richmond Hill, Ontario: Scholastic.

Dyson, A. (2003). *The brothers and sisters learn to write: Popular literacies in childhood and school cultures.* New York: Teachers College Press.

Edwards, P. (1995). Empowering low-income mothers and fathers to share books with young children. *Reading Teacher, 48*, 558–564.

Goor, R., & Goor, N. (1983). *Signs.* New York: Crowell.

Gregory, E. (2001). Sisters and brothers as language and literacy teachers: Synergy between siblings playing and working together. *Journal of Early Childhood Literacy, 1*, 301–322.

Heath, S. B. (1982). What no bedtime story means: Narrative skills at home and school. *Language in Society, 11*, 49–76.

Heath, S. B. (1983). *Ways with words.* New York: Cambridge University Press.

Heath, S. B., & Thomas, C. (1984). The achievement of preschool literacy for mother and child. In H. Goelman, A. Oberg, & F. Smith (Eds.), *Awakening to literacy* (pp. 51–72). Portsmouth, NH: Heinemann Educational Books.

Hutchins, P. (1968). *Rosie's walk.* New York: Macmillan.

Jordan, G., Porche, M., & Snow, C. (2000). Project EASE: Easing children's transition to kindergarten literacy through planned parent involvement. *Reading Research Quarterly, 35*, 524–546.

Luke, A., & Luke, C. (2001). Adolescence lost, childhood regained: Early intervention and the emergence of the techno-subject. *Journal of Early Childhood Literacy, 1*, 92–103.

Mace, J. (1998). *Playing with time: Mothers and the meaning of literacy.* London: UCL Press.

Moll, L., Amanti, C., Neff, D., & Gonzalez, N. (1992). Funds of knowledge for teaching: Using a qualitative approach to connect homes and classrooms. *Theory Into Practice, 31*, 132–141.

New London Group. (1996). A pedagogy of multiliteracies: Developing social futures. *Harvard Education Review, 66*, 60–92.

Pellegrini, A. (1991). A critique of the concept of at risk as applied to emergent literacy. *Language Arts, 68*, 380–385.

The primary program: A framework for teaching. (2000). Victoria, British Columbia: The Queens Printers.

Scarborough, H., & Dobrich, W. (1994). On the efficacy of reading to pre-schoolers. *Developmental Review, 14,* 245–302.

Shannon, D. (1998). *No, David!* New York: Blue Sky Press.

Smythe, S., & Isserlis, J. (2002). Regulating women and families: Mothering discourses in family literacy texts. *English Quarterly, 34,* 28–36.

Southam Literacy Survey. (1987). *Literacy in Canada: A research report.* Ottawa: Southam Communications (prepared by The Creative Research Group, Toronto).

Sticht, T. (1983). *Literacy and human resources development at work: Investing in the education of adults to improve the educability of children* (HumRRO Professional Paper 2-83). Alexandria, VA: Human Resources Research Organization.

Sulzby, E. (1985). Children's emergent reading of favourite storybooks: A developmental study. *Reading Research Quarterly, 20,* 458–481.

Taylor, D. (1983). *Family literacy: Young children learning to read and write.* Portsmouth, NH: Heinemann.

Thomas, A. (1998). *Family literacy in Canada: Profiles of effective practice.* Welland, Ontario: Soleil Publishing.

Whitehouse, M., & Colvin, C. (2001). "Reading" families: Deficit discourse and family literacy. *Theory Into Practice, 40,* 212–219.

Snapshot 1

A SINGLE MOTHER'S JOURNEY OF REDISCOVERY

Stacey Cody
Langley, British Columbia

I was born in Halifax, Nova Scotia in 1971. I grew up in a very small community called Caribou Gold Mines. My earliest memories of literacy are with my mother. She read story books to me, wrote poetry, sang songs, played games, and we loved to make up stories together. I was very lucky to have such a positive literacy role model. I now reside in Langley City with my 8-year-old daughter, Mickenzie. She attends Grade 3 in an inner city school called Nicomekl Elementary. I work as a Data Entry Clerk for Sprott-Shaw Community College in Langley.

I came to PALS (Parents As Literacy Supporters) quite reluctantly in its first year running, January 2000. I say reluctantly because I had just pulled my daughter from preschool where she had a bad experience. My faith in education was absolutely gone. I was now prepared to keep her at home for good with me where I would teach her. One afternoon I ran into a parent from Mickenzie's old preschool, and she handed me a pamphlet for PALS. I took it home and threw it in the garbage; I was not about to take Mickenzie back into a school. Although I had always read with Mickenzie and was teaching her at home, I could see how much she was missing the interaction she had experienced at preschool. I went in search of another PALS pamphlet, and called Fiona Morrison to see about signing Mickenzie and myself up for the next session. Fiona was great on the phone, and I remember wondering to myself, could this be okay?

We had missed the first session but attended the second. I was so apprehensive; Mickenzie was so excited. The session began with a lunch; there were lots of people in the room, unfamiliar people. After lunch the kids went off with a teacher to the kindergarten classroom. I started wondering what I was doing there. I already knew how to read; I had read to Mickenzie from the day I found out I was pregnant with her. I recognized the importance of literacy. Both Jim Anderson and Fiona Morrison (the developers of the PALS program who were implementing it as a pilot project) were very friendly and extremely respectful of all those in the room. That spoke volumes to me. The last thing I needed after having had a bad experience with a teacher was to be talked down to.

Mickenzie could speak of nothing else, she was hooked. I knew that we would be going back and I was excited about what the next session may hold in store for us. Already I was letting my guard down and learning to trust the school again. The next sessions were even greater than the first.

I learned so many new things about supporting Mickenzie's literacy. In everything we do, literacy is there. I learned one of the most valuable lessons, not to critique everything she did while reading, writing, and playing. That was a very hard lesson for me to learn, as I have always supported, encouraged, and validated all that Mickenzie has done. We all want the best for our children, but they need to be able to make mistakes and learn from them. I just cannot thank Fiona and Jim enough for teaching me that lesson.

PALS helped me realize how much more of an impact I can have on my own daughter as well as others. The program restored my faith in teachers and school. I saw the importance of using my voice to advocate for Mickenzie and the other children of our community. There are some very important roles that you can play at your child's school. You can join your school's PAC (parents advisory council), become a Read-To-Me volunteer, and many others.

PALS gave me the confidence to run for School Board Trustee in the last local civic elections. Although I lost by five hundred votes, I still felt very proud that I had taken a chance on myself and given it a whirl. Mickenzie was so proud of me—what a feeling for a mom to experience. I will run again, and again Mickenzie will be by my side, cheering me on and lending a hand as before. I have had the privilege of speaking at the International Reading Association conference in San Francisco and in Vancouver. I presented at the CSSE (Canadian Society for the Study of Education) in Halifax and numerous workshops in many different communities. Today, I sit on the Board of Directors as Treasurer for the LLA (Langley Literacy Association) and am still locally involved in my community and my daughter's school. You see, PALS is truly a program where not only the children walk away with something new, but the parents walk away with the gift of knowing you have the power to enhance your child's learning.

Parents need to be aware that they have the opportunity to be their child's first teacher in their life and that does not need to end when they hit the school system. Continue to be that teacher, nurture and encourage their learning in all that they do. There will always be teachers that believe there is no room for parents in their classroom; I challenge you to push through that. I believe that parent involvement is an integral part of our children's education, as do many others, teachers included.

Some of the strengths that I see in a family literacy program such as PALS are food, child care, respect, and freebies. The reason I mention food is because food seems to bring people together, it relaxes people, and communities have been doing this for centuries. Child care is huge; how can one participate in a program with small children without adequate free care on site? Respect may be the biggest strength of all. Without it I believe there would not be eager participants wanting to learn. Everyone likes free stuff, adults and children alike. It makes for a fun and happy environment.

People need to keep in mind that illiteracy holds no dollar value. It is not only the poor or less fortunate that do not read. Everyone deserves to know the joy of reading a book. I believe that if we can eradicate the social stigma of illiteracy, that we will live in a literate world where all can enjoy the magic of reading.

One voice can make a difference; let that be your voice. If there is just one thing you take from what I've shared with you, I hope it is my love for literacy and children that encourages you to take an active role in your child's education and in their lives. There is nothing greater you can share with a child than reading.

Chapter 5

Family Literacy: Listen to What the Families Have to Say

Linda M. Phillips
Heather L. Sample
University of Alberta

It was a Wednesday morning, a cold big blue-sky day on the Prairies. It was a typical day at the office until the phone rang. I answered but there was no response, though I sensed a person on the line. Several seconds went by before Lori spoke; her breathing was quickened and she hesitatingly asked for help, "with her children's ABCs."

In 2003, Yaden and Paratore, in the *Handbook of Research on Teaching the English Language Arts*, referred to family literacy as a *research diaspora*. They went on to say that the defining feature is the lack of consensus on the most fundamental elements in the state of knowledge in family literacy (p. 533). Fundamental elements included definitions, participants, practices, measures, and research. Two other major reviews of family literacy (Purcell-Gates, 2000) and intergenerational literacy within families (Gadsden, 2000) laid out with exquisite precision the status quo. Both reviewers concluded that existing research on family literacy is inadequate but appeared to differ on fundamental presuppositions. Purcell-Gates, with qualification, acknowledges the benefits of family literacy programs, whereas Gadsden and others are concerned that family literacy interventions detrimentally change the ways families interact with their children.

It is not our purpose to canvass these major reviews nor to contest the positions of either side of the debate, but rather to rely on them as an evidentiary backdrop to provide evidence that we must build on the wishes of the families in order to achieve successful family literacy programs. We do not have to have agreement on, nor acceptance of, what constitutes family literacy in order to appreciate the importance of parents asking for help with their "children's ABCs." These parents hold beliefs about their own life circumstances and about the future life circumstances of their young children, about what affected them and what they think will affect their children, and about what they believe and think they can change for their children. These beliefs and understandings are at the heart of family literacy.

Cutting across these beliefs and understandings is the fundamental issue that breaks with everyday experiences are necessary to get beyond the here and now, to build on their local and social literacies (Barton & Hamilton, 1998; Street, 1995) in order to move more deeply and further into the world on paper, wherein written language is the representation of thought beyond the here and now (Olson, 1994). In this chapter, we propose that families' beliefs and understandings of why literacy is important to their children's development are critical to the success of family literacy programs. We approach this proposition by presenting a number of family cases from an ongoing national longitudinal study of family literacy, but first we begin with some background to put the substance of the debate into its scholarly context, and give a general account of it. This account is necessary in order to highlight the significance of the voices of families because they hold a key to moving forward with family literacy programs and development. Finally, we discuss some research implications of taking a familial perspective on issues surrounding family literacy programs.

FAMILY LITERACY

There is general consensus within the literature that literacy goes beyond the simple acquisition of reading and writing skills that are transferable to every literacy context or need (Phillips, 2002). Literacy includes many social and cultural dimensions that influence learners' (adults and children) adaptations to the literacy tasks demanded of them.

Family literacy, as an educational movement, has acknowledged the importance of the family as the core environment for the promotion of literacy learning. Born in 1857, Adelaide Sophia Hunter Hoodless, the first known Canadian Family Educator, made the prescient statement, "A nation cannot rise above the level of its homes" (British Columbia Women's Institute, 1892). Then, as now, the most pathetic victims of poverty and social ills were women and children. Hoodless is known for her directness: "Educate a boy and you educate a man, but educate a girl and you educate a family" (BCWI, 1892). She saw education as a means of implementing social reform and worked tirelessly to promote the education of families. After nearly 100 years, Hoodless was finally honored as a family educator with a stamp bearing her image released by Canada Post in 1993. Nearly the same length of time has passed for family literacy to become a topic worthy of discussion in educational settings.

From the outset, *family literacy* has been a term that means different things to different people (Durkin, 1966; Sticht & McDonald, 1989; Taylor & Dorsey-Gaines, 1988; Teale, 1986). The view presented by Tracey (1995) captures many of the concepts and includes (a) the ways literacy is used within and across families in both mainstream and other cultural settings; (b) the nature of the development, implementation, and evaluation of programs designed to facilitate the literacy growth of family members; and (c) the interconnectedness of literacy use in the home and community and children's future academic achievement in school. We use the term *family literacy* to refer to the second concept of literacy programs for family members.

BASIS FOR FAMILY LITERACY PROGRAMMING

The logic of family literacy programming is based on research suggesting a strong link between home experiences and later literacy achievement. Home environment has been demonstrated to be an important factor in early linguistic and cognitive development. It is also recognized that children are socialized into literacy and that this socialization begins with the family (Heath, 1983; Morrow, 1989; Nickse, 1989; Paratore, 2001, 2002; Purcell-Gates, 2000; Purcell-Gates & Dahl, 1991; Sénéchal, Thomas, & Monker, 1995; Sulzby & Teale, 1991; Taylor, 1982; Teale & Sulzby, 1986).

There is evidence to suggest that children's emergent literacy development is constrained by the ways in which their families use print (Scarborough, Dobrich, & Hager, 1991; Sénéchal & LeFevre, 2002). For example, Sénéchal, LeFevre, Thomas, and Daley (1998) have shown that children may be exposed to informal and/or formal literacy experiences at home. In the case of informal literacy experiences, "the goal is the message contained in the print," such as what the story is about, and not the formal literacy experiences where the goal is "to focus more on the print per se," such as the identification of particular letters (p. 102). The informal precedes the formal, but both are necessary if children are to acquire literacy. Otherwise, even if children's homes are rich in oral language, they may have difficulty acquiring literacy and may not develop knowledge of written registers. One way to develop such knowledge is through shared book reading. Particular strategies have been identified that can make shared book reading more effective in increasing children's vocabulary and language knowledge (Evans, Shaw, & Bell, 2000). Such strategies include the use of language that takes children beyond the here and now, promotes the development of language skills expected for use in school, and provides experiences that overflow into and make meaningful other areas of life (DeTemple, 2001). Variations in the level and nature of literacy activities in the home account for some of the differences in the ways children understand and produce decontextualized print (Snow, 1983).

Given the preceding points, we know that at least some of the difference in literacy achievement can be explained by variation with print experiences. It is at this point that ideological differences emerge. Questions have been raised about the appropriateness of intervening in the literacy practices of families. Family literacy programs that teach parents mainstream ways of relating to print have been criticized for transmitting the culture of school literacy through the vehicle of the family instead of enhancing the family's home literacy (Auerbach, 1989). Concerns have been raised that some family literacy programs are predicated on deficiencies in family literacy practices and attitudes (Auerbach, 1995). There are those who assert that family literacy interventions imply that families bear primary responsibility for any literacy, economic, and educational problems they may face. The fear is that this implication will divert attention away from social and political factors that may play a greater role (Auerbach, 1995; Taylor & Dorsey-Gaines, 1988).

Advocates of family literacy programs, however, endorse strongly the positive benefits of intervention, particularly for lower income families headed by parents with low levels of literacy. This endorsement is supported by research showing that it is difficult for these parents to support, as much as they might like, their children's literacy development and to pass on positive attitudes about schooling and the importance of learning to read and write (Newman & Beverstock, 1990). Family literacy advocates have noted also that many of these parents want to know how to help their children with literacy and resent not being taught specific strategies on how to read with their children (Edwards, 1991, 1995). Supporters of family literacy programs strive to demonstrate that interventions can meet a need that the families themselves recognize and can do so in ways that are respectful of their cultural and personal values.

FEATURES OF FAMILY LITERACY PROGRAMS

Family literacy programs share common features. According to Neuman (1998), family literacy programs offer literacy instruction to members of families, involve participants in curriculum planning and development, create supportive learning environments, provide opportunities for the formation of family and social networks, and actively collaborate with other social and educational services.

Family literacy programs that incorporate early-childhood programming and adult education along with an element of parents and children working together have been referred to as *comprehensive* programs (Wasik, Dobbins, & Herrmann, 2001). These programs presume that the skills learned and practiced by the adult and the child produce an intergenerational and/or reciprocal transfer of skills (Neuman, 1998) and vary in the relative emphasis on the child and adult components (Hendrix, 1999). Within the child-focused component, developmentally appropriate experiences are offered to promote language and literacy learning. The experiences are designed not only to impart skills but also to encourage a positive attitude toward learning. The adult literacy instruction is typically geared to the goals of the individuals, either relating to parent–child learning or to employment (Brizius & Foster, 1993). The joint parent–child activities are focused on families learning how to become a greater part of the world of print and are designed to promote interactions that lead to greater understanding, communication, and skill gains.

Facilitators promote parents' awareness of their own knowledge and capabilities for helping their children (Rodriguez-Brown & Meehan, 1998). They also provide opportunities for lower income parents and children to learn and practice strategies demonstrated to be successful for middle income parents and children. In these cases, family literacy facilitators serve as coaches for participating families as they acquire new skills, which may include techniques for book sharing, questioning, language facilitation, and providing positive feedback to children (Wasik et al., 2001). Many programs also specifically seek to provide opportunities for parents to support parents, provide time for sharing of experiences, and discuss ways to overcome obstacles to family learning.

Family literacy advocates have recognized the need to develop a range of models that respond to different family structures and build on the strengths and history of each cultural group. Where different program models are not feasible, programs are urged to be sensitive to cultural differences and to build on the diversity of the participants and the assets of each cultural group (Brizius & Foster, 1993). Programs have also been tailored to the needs of families through collaboration with education, social service, health, and employment programs. Family literacy programs also typically provide support services such as transportation, child care, and appropriate scheduling for participants.

EVIDENCE FOR THE SUCCESS OF FAMILY LITERACY PROGRAMS

Much of the information used to justify family literacy interventions initially came from research into individual program components and from positive anecdotal reports. For example, the children's component of family literacy programs was most often defended in terms of the success of other initiatives that promoted early childhood development. Adult programming was likewise connected to research into the benefits of adult education. Synergistic effects of parents and children learning together were often assumed or bolstered by anecdotal reports.

In 1991 the National Center for Family Literacy (NCFL) in the United States published a summary of the positive outcomes of family literacy programs. The Center concluded that the initiatives increased the developmental skills of preschool children and the parenting skills and educational levels of participating parents. Positive effects on the parent–child relationships were documented. Parents were described as becoming familiar with and comfortable in the school setting and as providing a role model for the child by showing interest in education. Although the NCFL study provided some indications of the success of family literacy programs, it was acknowledged that additional research was needed (Brizius & Foster, 1993).

Despite an ongoing call for additional investigations into the efficacy of family literacy, research has continued to lag behind practice. This lag is troubling because of the critical role the evaluation process should play in informing practice. Family literacy providers need to be able to identify what, if any, difference their programs make in the lives of participants and in their community. They also have a need to assess individual progress of the parent and child participants and factors affecting that progress. The effectiveness of each component of family literacy must be ascertained along with possible interactive and reciprocal effects of combinations of components. All of this information is useful in determining ways to improve family literacy programs so that they better serve participating families. Demonstrating the value of family literacy programs through research is also necessary to compete effectively for resources.

Several difficulties in conducting literacy research with very young children and with parents of low educational levels are acknowledged. One is that reliable and valid literacy measurement at ages 2 to 5 years is difficult to obtain because it is a time when children's understanding of literacy is still emerging, and their progress is uneven (Phillips, Norris, & Mason, 1996). A second difficulty is that many parents with low levels of education have less than positive attitudes about schooling and literacy activities and may choose not to participate in programs if required to participate in evaluations of their reading. These barriers are not insurmountable. Outcomes for participating children can be determined by using multiple measures of their vocabulary and early reading development. Parents may be less reluctant to participate in program evaluation if they are met on their own terms and care is taken to use nonthreatening methods of data collection.

There has been a dearth of studies on the efficacy of family literacy programs within high quality research parameters. An exception was the study conducted by the National Foundation for Educational Research (NFER) on the British Skills Agency (BSA) Family Literacy Demonstration Programmes in the United Kingdom (Brooks, Gorman, Harman, Hutchison, & Wilkin, 1996). We are currently engaged in a longitudinal, quasiexperimental, cross-sectional control group study extending across 6 years of the *Learning Together* program adapted from the British model. In addition to the standard measures used in quantitative research, we conducted extensive parent interviews on what parents say they want to learn in order to help their children.

The 13-week *Learning Together* program adapted for use in a Canadian context by our partners, the Centre for Family Literacy, includes eight units with sessions for adult, child, and joint adult and child components. The units build on what the parents want to learn and focus on creative play, developing language for literacy, and games used to give parents alternative ways to interact with children, beginning with books, early reading, writing and drawing, environmental print walks, question and answer for parents, and end-of-course celebration. A genuine effort is made to interweave culturally, linguistically, personally, and socially appropriate information for the different audiences within a common element. For example, in unit 5, "early reading," the parent program includes the stages of children's early reading, learning how reading and talking together helps children to learn to read and discussing the importance of "kid watching." Activities for the parents include highlighting environmental print, developing an alphabet scrapbook, writing about their shared reading experiences with their children, and a range of other activities. For the same unit, the children's program addresses the children becoming aware of the print around them and its purposes, recognizing letters and words, sequencing ideas, and making connections among letters/sounds and meaning. Activities include rhymes, songs, and finger plays with rebus or written versions of some of their favorites, reading pattern books, and finding first letters of their names in other words. The joint session for this unit provided for an environmental print walk and the recording of what was seen during the excursion (Hayden & Phillips, 2000). Concurrent with and essential to the ongoing longitudinal study is an exploration of what the families and children bring to the *Learning Together* program.

WHAT DO FAMILIES BRING TO FAMILY LITERACY PROGRAMS?

Gadsden (2000) says, ". . . there is no appropriate, prototypical model of family structure" (p. 874), and we agree. In our current study, we have a total of 183 urban and rural families of low income and low educational backgrounds with children aged 3–5+ years considered to be at risk for future school achievement. Ninety-eight percent of the families include mothers and the remaining 2% include child-care providers, grandmothers, and fathers and their children and stepchildren. The mothers range in age from 21 to 46 years with 50% being in their 20s, 36% in their 30s, and 10% in their 40s. The grandmothers are in their 60s, the fathers are in their 30s, and the child-care providers are in their early 20s.

Forty-seven percent of all family literacy participants are single, 44% are married, and the rest are either widows or living in common-law relationships. Sixty-nine percent are Caucasian, 13% are Aboriginal, and Chinese, Kurdish, Jamaican, Spanish, and South African families complete the picture. The number of children per family ranges from one to six and the average number is 2.5 children. A very high percentage (53%) of all the mothers reported pregnancy as either the cause of leaving school early or a consequence shortly thereafter. Some are from arranged marriages, some from war-torn countries where girls are not permitted an education, some are from families with alcohol and drug addiction problems, others are from poor and broken families, and some just quit school.

The many constellations of families and ethnic groups within our study add diversity and interest. Despite the diversity, we have found that most families are extraordinarily univocal in what they bring to family literacy programs. They bring a reflective, informed, and determined perspective that clusters around five points, and these include:

1. They acknowledge a complicated longing and disabling regret that they did not complete high school.
2. They see themselves as victims of unfortunate life circumstances but are ready to move on in the interest of their children.
3. They acknowledge a lack of capital in either money, land, or acquired knowledge but they are not deterred.
4. They declare that there is a "book world" beyond the one they see every day and they want it for their children.
5. They want the opportunity for their children and grandchildren "to be able to read and write" and to be "better than me."

These five points are not mutually exclusive. For brevity we have integrated the first three as remembering the past and acknowledging the present, and the last two as planning for the future beyond the here and now. We discuss each and appeal to five cases, selected at random from the 183 families who participated in our extensive interviews and visits with them, in order to emphasize what they bring to family literacy programs.

Remembering the Past and Acknowledging the Present

Among the families in the *Learning Together* program, there is a straightforward and matter-of-fact acknowledgment of lack of capital in money, land, or acquired knowledge and an unmistakable regret for not completing high school. But these families, without exception, are not deterred and they want to provide for and create opportunities for their children that they themselves did not have. These families do not lack initiative when it comes to their children, and their educational goals are unequivocal, as evidenced by the stories that follow.

Meet Lori, a Cree, who called to join our program. She is 29 and grew up in several foster homes in a large prairie city. She left school after she had spent 6 or 7 years there, became involved in drugs and was pregnant at an early age. She is a single mom with three children, and her oldest son, at the age of 12, is addicted to drugs and has been taken into foster care. Referring to her oldest son, Lori says, "He wanted to learn his ABCs. He wanted to learn them really bad. Well, I tried. I would say them with him and sing the song but he never could tell which one from which one. Like, how do you teach that, that's what I want to know so my littlest boy learns his ABCs." Despite very difficult life circumstances, Lori says, "I don't want my kids to be like me, I want them to have options." There is literacy in Lori's home: She takes her children to the library for books and they read together each night, she uses recipes to cook, and enjoys doing quite complex beadwork. Lori wants her children to learn their ABCs so that they can be successful in school and have "at least a chance to break out of drugs and poverty." Lori is shy and it was a difficult step for her to call our program. She attends the program, enjoys meeting other moms, is delighted to see what her children are learning, and is now talking excitedly about learning to use the computer.

Marie, a Caucasian, is 26 and grew up in a small eastern Canadian town. Her mom's mental health was not good, there was no mention of a dad, and the next sibling was 20 years older. She left high school before completion: "I was always alone at home, so I cut out of there." Marie is a single mom with two little girls ages 3 and 5 years. The girls' dad committed suicide and Marie is currently battling cancer. She has kept a journal daily since she was 20. Marie is a very determined, open, direct, and wise woman. She is single-minded about the importance of her daughters' education: "I want my daughters to get the best, I want them to be able to enjoy the world beyond here. They can do that only if they become a part of the world of books. I want them to know they can do anything they set their minds to." Marie says, "I never talk down to my children. I don't want them to suffer the stigma attached to children who come from battered, welfare homes so

I take my oldest girl by bus to a school in a neighbourhood where we are going to live someday. 'Cause, I know they won't stand a chance in the school here. Kids here don't matter, they're welfare kids."

Marie does not have any family in the city. She is lonely but determined to learn as much as she can to help her girls. Marie met Tina in the *Learning Together* program, they became good friends, and now they are both going to upgrading classes. Marie is effusive about how much the program helped her and her children: "My youngest girl talks so proudly and confidently now, she knows all her ABCs and finds them everywhere we go, she's reading words now, she can count and add, and she reads to her doll. The girls were so excited that I got excited about what we were learning together, for the first time in my life I am happy, and I'm going to stay that way."

Robert, a Caucasian, is 39 and grew up in the city. His father was an alcoholic and was always losing his job, and his mother had a difficult time trying to make ends meet. His parents separated when he was a child. After that, they moved frequently and so, as a child, he was always losing his friends. His mother remarried and Robert felt that he was sidelined from the lives of his family. He tried and failed Grade 10 several times and then left school. Robert is a single dad and he wants a stable home for his two daughters and a stepdaughter. He works long hours and hard days as a construction worker but takes delight each evening reading to his children in English and French. He learned English from playing street hockey. He taught himself music and how to play guitar. Robert is clear that he wants to learn how to make sure his girls do well in school. "There's ways to get your children ready for school but I don't know if I'm doing what will help them most. We read together at night but I think I should be trying to get them into the stories and stuff more, so I fixed it with the boss to get time to go to a program with them, so we're all going to school."

Lori, Marie, and Robert each have regrets about their own childhood circumstances, but they are the ones coming forward with goals and plans for their children's future. These parents have learned to value literacy and they see a value in it beyond their own direct individual experience (Heath, 1991). The *Learning Together* facilitators work with what the families want and there is no attempt to "fix" problems. Indeed, it is our position that these families bring a wealth of experience, knowledge, and motivation to the program. Within this sociocultural perspective, we acknowledge that these families are looking for ways "to support transition between home and school" (Rodriguez-Brown, 2003) as they plan for the future of their children.

Planning for the Future Beyond the Here and Now

The families in our *Learning Together* program declare that there is a "book world" beyond their everyday local literacies and they want it for their children. Much has been written about the importance of breaking with everyday experience in order to see the range of options for living and thinking beyond the here and now (Floden & Buchmann, 1993). All families live at a particular time and in a particular place, "but school and university are places apart where a declared learner is emancipated from the limitations of his [sic] local circumstances and from the wants he may have acquired, and is moved by intimations of what he has never yet dreamed" (Oakeshott, 1989, p. 24). Perhaps without even knowing anything of his views, our families want their children to be successful in school for reasons similar to those of Dewey (1916/1966): It is "the office of the school environment . . . to see to it that each individual gets an opportunity to escape from the limitations of the social group in which he was born, and to come into living contact with a broader environment" (p. 20) and to have choices.

Behind parents' wishes lie certain expectations for learning, and they recognize that they need more than their previous experiences and current knowledge. Tina (Marie's friend) is 31 and grew up in a small town where her mother struggled to make a living because her father died young. Tina felt mixed up and poor, and reports being teased and bullied mercilessly at school. She left school in Grade 8 because she did not have any friends and was frustrated by her failure to learn. She has four children ranging in age from 4 to 13. Tina appears determined to make sure that her youngest does well in school because "I see my other children in school and they can't read, they didn't know where to start when they got to school but my littlest fellow will. Take me, I have a Grade 7 education, I have never read a book in my life, I don't have any real friends or family, just me and the kids and I don't have any book friends. You know book friends can help. I met a woman in family literacy who said her favorite book friend is Margaret [*Are You There, God? It's Me, Margaret*; Blume, 1970]. And she said she reads to get her mind off things and to learn about other people and places. I wants that for myself but I wants it more for my children and if there's just talking in this program, it's no good, we wants to read." Tina recognizes that there is a world in books that she does not know, that there is "book language and book knowledge," and that these expand opportunities. Tina wants to know more about the written register, about how written language is a representation of thought, and about how she can participate more in that world. Tina is back to school now and she says she couldn't do it without a friend. "Without Marie, I never would've gone back to school, without me, she wouldn't've gone, but we got excited together, got to be friends, we are stronger together, and we encourage one another."

Sabrina is 26 and grew up an Iraqi Kurd under strict rule that girls were not permitted to attend school (she did get the equivalent of Grade 3 and then her father tried to help her before he was taken away). Her marriage was arranged at the age of 15 and she has six children. Sabrina wants to complete high school but her main concern right now is her children. "I grew up in a world without books and toys. Why keep books from us? I think because we could learn new things about animals, foods, other people, and places, and because we were not allowed to have them, then we wanted them more. I buy books for my children all the time and we talk about the pictures and my older children read to us. I feel everyday that there is another world in the words that I can't read and it is not a good feeling. I want my children never to feel it, that's why I am here, I want help for my children and for me."

Tina and Sabrina are from two very different cultures, yet they both long to enjoy what Heath (1991) calls "the sense of being literate" and they are dedicated to ensuring that their children are able to partake in a world beyond the here and now. These parents understand that the sense of being literate provides an important challenge to firsthand experience that "limits not only personal understandings but views of the social and political worlds" (Buchmann & Schwille, 1993, p. 26). They want to use their local literacies to engage in the more formal literacies of schooling. Breaks with everyday experience are necessary for all children to think and act with a sense of methods and ideas that reach beyond the immediately given. However, these breaks come at a cost. As Floden and Buchmann (1993) state, "Equalizing opportunities often disconnect individuals from their backgrounds" (p. 48) and increase the distance from that which is deeply personal and cherished. To live is to learn and to learn means to alter, and in so doing, the familiar is changed, as are the interactions between and among families and their children. We see that when the families' own perspectives are taken into account, the gains they perceive justify the opening up of alternative interactions for those who choose to participate in family literacy programs.

CONCLUSION

To return to the beginning of our chapter, we think the conclusion by Yaden and Paratore—"Family literacy is a research diaspora"—is an overstatement. Indeed, there are a number of mistaken assumptions by many educators, social workers, and politicians that family literacy programs will solve educational and social ills despite issues of race and gender. Some mistaken assumptions include pervasive beliefs that there is an absence of literacy practices, a lack of interest in their children, and reports of bad parenting in the homes of the poor and uneducated. Programs built on assumptions that imply families are responsible for their educational and economic circumstances would undoubtedly lead to questionable results. Those who work with families as they struggle for a life of dignity for their children and then for themselves know the fallacy of these assumptions.

We have found large funds of knowledge in families, families who care deeply and profoundly about their children, and families who hold beliefs about how best to help their children with successful schooling. We have presented the lives of five families of diverse backgrounds, and we corroborate the work of Yberra (1999) on Latino life in the United States: "Despite our diversity, we are nonetheless bound by a common search for a better life for ourselves and our children" (p. 84). We advocate a familial perspective in family literacy—a perspective that puts the beliefs, wishes, and desires of the families first.

We have found also that the families in our study articulated clearly what they believe they need for their children, and provided justifications for and offered supportive examples of their experiences to demonstrate those needs. Some in the literacy field argue that the reason these children fail in school is because their language and literacy is different from that of the language patterns and literacy events privileged by the schools and that the schools should change to honor the literacy of the home. The families in our study at no time gave any hint whatsoever that they felt their language and literacy was either deprived or undervalued. Rather, they saw a need to build on it in order to provide alternative experiences and opportunities for their children to acquire basic knowledge about language and literacy. Our families expressed concern that they wanted to move beyond what they were doing at home for their children. In accord with the work of Sénéchal et al. (1998), the families in our study expressed a desire to learn more about, and the ways to engage in, formal literacy experiences wherein the goal is to focus more on the print so that their children would be better prepared to understand and engage in what Snow (1983) calls decontextualized print and Heath (1991) calls the sense of being literate. The families are the insiders in the family literacy debate and they have their beliefs about what they need to help their children. Academic debates by outsiders who claim that family literacy programs privilege school-based literacy rather than home-based literacy are suppressing the very wishes and needs of the insiders. Successful schooling experiences for their children are what most concerns these families. Family literacy programs based on a familial perspective are clearly an important alternative route against the dissenting point of view about families' perceived literacy needs.

We agree with Yaden and Paratore (2003) that literacy is a complex phenomenon. Answers about the efficacy of family literacy programs cannot be obtained through research unless we know what questions to ask. Although quantifiable outcomes for family literacy programs are considered essential, a familial perspective affirms the importance of considering qualitative information provided by the participants. Obtaining information about parents' personal goals, views about program design and content, and perceived benefits is critical to understanding how family literacy programs meet the needs of participants. We contend that families have much to contribute to the success of family literacy programs. Moreover, they are the final arbiters of the success of any program—if they see value in it they will attend whenever possible despite sometimes very difficult and complex daily living circumstances.

There is a growing body of research, as we have outlined, that provides strong support for family participation in literacy programs. The development of programs that support what the families believe they need, in addition to what they do at home, in order to support their children's literacy development may represent a much-needed change in perspective. A familial perspective in family literacy programs may allay the concerns of researchers about replacing the literacy of the home with that of the school. A change in perspective as we have presented here would be a win–win for families, family literacy advocates, and for those concerned about change in the family literacy dynamic. Furthermore, a familial perspective may become the defining feature of successful family literacy programs and inexorably become the keystone to resolution for those on either side of the debate.

To fully advance the familial perspective, research is needed into the ways in which participating in family literacy programs influences the family units. Consideration of the effects on family dynamics, marital relationships, and interactions with older and younger siblings who are not directly involved has been recommended by Wasik et al. (2001). We add to their list the dynamic of the power of friends, as was raised by the families in our study. There is a need to identify specific ways in which family literacy programs can be grounded in the cultures of participating families. We need also to consider potential roles those persons in the family other than a parent or child might play to support family literacy. These and other considerations are essential as we advance research in the area of family literacy and confront the reality of those who ask for help with their children's ABCs.

REFERENCES

Auerbach, E. R. (1989). Towards a socio-contextual approach to family literacy. *Harvard Educational Review, 59*, 165–181.

Auerbach, E. R. (1995). Which way for family literacy: Intervention or empowerment. In L. Morrow (Ed.), *Family literacy connection in schools and communities* (pp. 11–28). Newark, DE: International Reading Association.

Barton, D., & Hamilton, M. (1998). *Local literacies.* London: Routledge.

Blume, J. (1970). *Are you there, God? It's me, Margaret.* New York: Dell.

British Columbia Women's Institute. (1892). *Modern pioneers.* Vancouver, BC: Evergreen Press Limited.

Brizius, J. A., & Foster, S. A. (1993). *Generation to generation: Realizing the promise of family literacy.* Ypsilanti, MI: High/Scope Press.

Brooks, G., Gorman, R., Harman, J., Hutchison, D., & Wilkin, A. (1996). *Family literacy works: The evaluation of the Basic Skills Agency's Demonstration Programmes.* London: The Basic Skills Agency.

Buchmann, M., & Schwille, J. R. (1993). Education, experience, and the paradox of finitude. In M. Buchmann & R. E. Floden (Eds.), *Detachment and concern* (pp. 19–33). New York: Teachers College Press.

DeTemple, J. M. (2001). Parents and children reading books together. In D. K. Dickinson & P. O. Tabors (Eds.), *Beginning literacy with language* (pp. 31–51). Baltimore, MD: Paul H. Brookes.

Dewey, J. (1966). *Democracy and education: An introduction to the philosophy of education.* New York: Free Press. (Original work published 1916)

Durkin, D. (1966). *Children who read early.* New York: Teachers College Press.

Edwards, P. A. (1991). Fostering early literacy through parent coaching. In E. Hiebert (Ed.), *Literacy for a diverse society* (pp. 199–213). New York: Teachers College Press.

Edwards, P. A. (1995). Combining parents' and teachers' thoughts about storybook reading at home and school. In L. Morrow (Ed.), *Family literacy connection in schools and communities* (pp. 54–69). Newark, DE: International Reading Association.

Evans, M. A., Shaw, D., & Bell, M. (2000). Home literacy activities and their influence on early literacy skills. *Canadian Journal of Experimental Psychology, 54*(2), 65–75.

Floden, R. E., & Buchmann, M. (1993). Breaking with everyday experience for guided adventures in learning. In M. Buchmann & R. E. Floden (Eds.), *Detachment and concern* (pp. 34–49). New York: Teachers College Press.

Gadsden, V. L. (2000). Intergenerational literacy within families. In M. L. Kamil, P. B. Mosenthal, P. D. Pearson, & R. Barr (Eds.), *Handbook of reading research* (Vol. III, pp. 871–887). Mahwah, NJ: Lawrence Erlbaum Associates.

Hayden, R., & Phillips, L. M. (2000). *The forecast is good: Report on the formative evaluation of the "Learning Together—Read and write with your child" program.* Ottawa: National Literacy Secretariat.

Heath, S. B. (1983). *Ways with words.* Cambridge: Cambridge University Press.

Heath, S. B. (1991). The sense of being literate: Historical and cross-cultural features. In R. Barr, M. L. Kamil, P. B. Mosenthal, & P. D. Pearson (Eds.), *Handbook of reading research* (Vol. II, pp. 3–25). New York: Longman.

Hendrix, S. (1999). Family literacy education—Panacea or false promise? *Journal of Adult and Adolescent Literacy, 43*(4), 338–346.

Morrow, L. (1989). *Literacy development in the early years.* Englewood Cliffs, NJ: Prentice-Hall.

National Center for Family Literacy. (1991). *The effects of participating in family literacy programs.* Louisville, KY: Author.

Neuman, S. B. (1998). A social-constructivist view of family literacy. In E. G. Sturtevant, J. Dugan, P. Linder, & W. M. Linek (Eds.), *Literacy and community: The twentieth yearbook* (pp. 25–30). Carrollton, GA: The College Reading Association.

Newman, A. P., & Beverstock, C. (1990). *Adult literacy: Contexts and challenges.* Newark, DE: International Reading Association.

Nickse, R. (1989). *The noise of literacy: Overview of intergenerational and family literacy programs* (Report No. CE-053-282). Boston: Boston University Press.

Oakeshott, M. (1989). A place of learning. In T. Fuller (Ed.), *The voice of liberal learning: Michael Oakeshott on education* (pp. 17–42). New Haven, CT: Yale University Press. (Original work published 1975)

Olson, D. R. (1994). *The world on paper.* Cambridge: Cambridge University Press.

Paratore, J. R. (2001). *Opening doors, opening opportunities.* Needham Heights, MA: Allyn & Bacon.

Paratore, J. R. (2002). Family literacy. In B. Guzzetti (Ed.), *Literacy in America: An encyclopedia of history, theory, and practice* (pp. 185–187). Santa Barbara, CA: ABC-CLIO, Inc.

Phillips, L. M. (2002). Making new or making do: Epistemological, normative, and pragmatic aspects of reading a text. In J. Brockmeier, M. Wang, & D. R. Olson (Eds.), *Literacy, narrative, and culture* (pp. 283–300). Surrey, UK: Curzon Press.

Phillips, L. M., Norris, S. P., & Mason, J. M. (1996). Longitudinal effects of early literacy concepts on reading achievement: A kindergarten intervention and five-year follow-up. *Journal of Literacy Research, 28*(1), 173–195.

Purcell-Gates, V. (2000). Family literacy. In M. L. Kamil, P. B. Mosenthal, P. D. Pearson, & R. Barr (Eds.), *Handbook of reading research* (Vol. III, pp. 853–870). Mahwah, NJ: Lawrence Erlbaum Associates.

Purcell-Gates, V., & Dahl, K. (1991). Low SES children's success and failure at early literacy learning in skills based classrooms. *Journal of Reading Behavior, 23*, 1–34.

Rodriguez-Brown, F. V. (2003). Essay Book Review: Reflections on family literacy from a sociocultural perspective. *Reading Research Quarterly, 38*(1), 146–153.

Rodriguez-Brown, F. V., & Meehan, M. A. (1998). Family literacy and adult education: Project FLAME. In M. C. Smith (Ed.), *Literacy for the twenty-first century: Research, policy, practices, and the national adult literacy survey* (pp. 175–193). Westport, CT: Praeger Publishers.

Scarborough, H. S., Dobrich, W., & Hager, M. (1991). Preschool literacy experience and later reading achievement. *Journal of Learning Disabilities, 24*, 508–511.

Sénéchal, M., & LeFevre, J. (2002). Parental involvement in the development of children's reading skill: A five-year longitudinal study. *Child Development, 73*(2), 445–460.

Sénéchal, M., LeFevre, J., Thomas, E., & Daley, K. (1998). Differential effects of home literacy experiences on the development of oral and written language. *Reading Research Quarterly, 33*(1), 96–116.

Sénéchal, M., Thomas, E., & Monker, J. (1995). Individual differences in 4-year-old children's acquisition of vocabulary during storybook reading. *Journal of Educational Psychology, 87*, 218–229.

Snow, C. (1983). Literacy and language: Relationships during the preschool years. *Harvard Educational Review, 53*(2), 165–189.

Sticht, T., & McDonald, B. (1989). *Making the nation smarter: The intergenerational transfer of literacy.* San Diego, CA: Institute for Adult Literacy.

Street, B. V. (1995). *Social literacies.* Essex: Longman.

Sulzby, E., & Teale, W. (1991). Emergent literacy. In R. Barr, M. L. Kamil, P. Mosenthal, & P. D. Pearson (Eds.), *Handbook of reading research* (Vol. II, pp. 727–758). New York: Longman.

Taylor, D. (1982). *Family literacy.* Exeter, NH: Heinemann.

Taylor, D., & Dorsey-Gaines, C. (1988). *Growing up literate: Learning from inner-city families.* Portsmouth, NH: Heinemann.

Teale, W. H. (1986). Home background and young children's literacy development. In W. H. Teale & E. Sulzby (Eds.), *Emergent literacy: Writing and reading* (pp. 173–206). Norwood, NJ: Ablex.

Teale, W. H., & Sulzby, E. (Eds.). (1986). *Emergent literacy: Writing and reading.* Norwood, NJ: Ablex.

Tracey, D. H. (1995). Family literacy: Overview and synthesis of an ERIC search. In E. Hinchman, D. Leu, & C. Linzer (Eds.), *Perspectives on literacy: Research and practice* (pp. 280–288). Forty-fourth Yearbook of the National Reading Conference. Chicago: National Reading Conference.

Wasik, B. H., Dobbins, D. R., & Herrmann, S. (2001). Intergenerational family literacy: Concepts, research, and practice. In S. B. Neuman & D. K. Dickinson (Eds.), *Handbook of early literacy research* (pp. 444–458). New York: The Guilford Press.

Yaden, D. B., Jr., & Paratore, J. R. (2003). Family literacy at the turn of the millennium: The costly future of maintaining the status quo. In J. Flood, D. Lapp, J. Squire, & J. Jensen (Eds.), *Handbook of research on teaching the English language arts* (2nd ed., pp. 532–545). Mahwah, NJ: Lawrence Erlbaum Associates.

Yberra, L. (1999). The family/la familia. In E. J. Olmos, L. Yberra, & M. Monterrey (Eds.), *Americanos: Latino life in the United States/La vida Latina en los Estados Unidos* (p. 84). New York: Little, Brown & Company.

Snapshot 2

VOICES FROM THE FIELD: PRACTITIONER PERSPECTIVES ON ISSUES IN FAMILY LITERACY

Ruth Hayden
Maureen Sanders

The explosion in research investigations on family literacy that has occurred over the past decade attests to the wide interest in this topic from a myriad of perspectives. However, the voice of the family literacy practitioner is less evident within the literature than that of the researcher. Although it is a truism to say that academic researchers conduct their investigations and dialogue with those on the front lines of family literacy, the issues that surround the routines of everyday family literacy practice appear to obtain far less attention, as an avenue for research, than might be warranted. One may ask: What issues are central to the lives of family practitioners? What questions do practitioners have with respect to what issues are explored within the research? The following conversation provides a small window on the concerns that some practitioners consider worthy of investigation.

Scenario

Three family literacy practitioners are attending a conference on family literacy. They have also registered for a presession, full-day workshop on "Issues in Family Literacy," presented by a renowned researcher. One of the tasks asked of participants during the workshop is that they gather in small groups, for about an hour, to address what they consider to be pertinent issues in family literacy, and to report the main points of their discussion to all participants.

Jennifer and Allyson work in a large urban center where the populations with whom they interact are frequently comprised of unemployed, single-parent families. Darlene, on the other hand, works primarily with families scattered across a wide rural area, many of whom are of Aboriginal descent. The three women have decided that each of them will first jot down notes on what she considers to be the most important issues facing her in her practice. Their conversation surrounding those topics ensues.

Allyson: Well, at the risk of sounding like a broken record, one of my top issues is funding. This has always been a concern in the family literacy field and in literacy generally. I recognize that we have come a long way—10 years ago there was virtually no funding for family literacy, and at least now we can get some funding to support programs from year to year. But obtaining funding has become so complex. The amount of paper you have to submit to get even limited financial assistance, like a few thousand dollars, escalates each year. And the application process often changes for no apparent reason. This year I have to submit an on-line application for one funder and it's a terrible process. There are still too many glitches. I keep losing information I have typed in, and it's taking me hours longer than usual to provide the information. And they're asking for way more information, too. I'm not sure why I should I have to be the guinea-pig for something like this. I often wonder who decides what is needed. Certainly not those of us on the front lines of family literacy—we are overwhelmed with the daily demands of our job—offering programs throughout the community, finding suitably trained facilitators, and so on.

Jennifer: I agree with you, Allyson, writing these proposals consumes huge amounts of time, usually my personal time because the grants just don't cover the hours needed to actually apply for them. And at the other end of the process looms my biggest issue—accountability. It seems every time I turn around, I have to justify what I do—to the funders, my board, and the public. I offer two programs to the families in my area, programs like Books for Babies and book sharing for parents and preschoolers. I get funding for these programs from a few funders. But . . . and I hate to say it, the expectations of these agencies goes beyond the imagination. They want goals and objectives and outcomes that are measurable as if they expect these programs to radically change the lives of the families. Each program only lasts a few weeks, or months at the most; so for funders to think that there will be a miraculous shift in the behaviours of participating families is not only ludicrous, it is a waste of my time. I'm not saying we shouldn't be accountable—on the contrary, we need to be answerable for what we do. But the level of accountability is excessive.

Darlene: I know what you mean. And you begin to wonder if anyone actually reads those interminable reports. Interestingly, they all want quantifiable results, but what they remember most when we talk to them are the stories we include in our reports that highlight how programs affect our participants—the qualitative stuff. We know these programs are effective; there is a plethora of research on them but we continually have to reaffirm to our funders that the programs we offer—the same ones as in the research—are valuable to our participants in particular and the community in general. Do any of you know if any research has been done on the influence on future funding as a result of all the massive accountability reports we have to write?

Allyson: The only way we will have true measures of accountability is to do some longitudinal research studies that would be incredibly expensive given the transient nature of many of our participants. Certainly it would be beyond the capabilities of those of us on the front lines, and I have never felt very comfortable in research circles anyway. Without at least a Master's degree, I don't feel I have much credibility doing traditional university research. I was involved in a small participatory research project and it was very interesting, but it took a lot of extra time and I never did manage to write up anything about it. I guess I learned something for myself by doing it, but I don't feel I added to the body of family literacy knowledge very successfully. We need to be able to partner more effectively with researchers, but they also need to understand the reality of our lives, working in jobs with inadequate pay and no benefits. We just can't add more work without compensation for doing it.

Jennifer: Speaking of researchers, I think they spend too much time just talking to each other and writing for each other in academic journals. I've often wondered why they don't get more involved in the popular press—newspapers and magazines, for example. Sometimes major research studies get picked up by the media, but there's a lot that never gets out of the academic setting. Don't you think researchers could have much more of an impact on the general public and could better help to support our work if they would talk about their research more broadly? I would like to see them write in a way that is informative for ordinary people and that helps them understand the importance, for example, of simple early language and literacy activities. Just imagine what a difference it could make if there were regular articles about family literacy, by respected researchers, in Canadian Living or the Edmonton Journal!

Darlene: Well, to switch gears, for me the training of family literacy practitioners is a crucial issue. Those who work in family literacy need to have a thorough understanding of the principles of adult education as well as early childhood development. But finding such people is a bit like looking for the proverbial needle in the haystack. Most of us who are involved in family literacy come from the adult education field, so the whole area of early childhood education is novel and challenging for us. We do now have Foundational Training in Family Literacy, developed and implemented with input from practitioners and academics from across Canada. This training is a weeklong intensive training session in the theory and practice of family literacy. But it is an expensive proposition to send all staff to such a training session—and that brings us back to the issue of funding. I'm sure none of us wants to go there again now.

Jennifer: You know, it's not just the initial training that concerns me; I can sort of manage that. My issue, with respect to training, goes beyond that. I'm thinking of the on-going professional development that is needed in the field—training staff in different program models, training staff how to collect data for funding purposes, training staff in community development, etc., etc. There's a huge push, within the community, to build capacity and sustainability with respect to literacy development. In other words, our staff is supposed to be able to "train" (and I use the word advisedly) other community service providers to be aware of and include family literacy aspects within their own professional practices. My own experience shows me that the majority of community service providers such as nurses, social workers, or licensing staff for child-care workers hold very traditional views for how literacy is learned. In other words, many of them feel that literacy development starts at school age. Their professional practices with families places them in an ideal position to support and/or sustain early literacy development within the home. The issue of how family literacy practitioners might liaise and collaborate with such professionals to build a community mind-set for literacy needs to be more front and center of the whole topic of family literacy. If literacy practitioners are to perform this role, they need greater on-going professional development to ensure that they can show other community professionals how literacy is a key component of healthy families.

Allyson: Good point, Jennifer. I feel this could be a mammoth task, and one that needs greater exploration. The perspective that anyone who can read can teach reading is probably at the core of this desire for capacity building and sustainability. And to add fuel to the fire, we have to be careful that we, as family literacy practitioners, don't buy into the concept of using literacy as a club to solve all the problems of society. The theory for family literacy stands firmly on the base of family strength—what families do well—as opposed to the deficiency model—how we can fix families so they will no longer demand society's financial resources. Family literacy practitioners not only have to help other community service providers recognize literacy development as one component of a healthy family, they also have to ensure a strengths-model perspective as a means to support and extend the current literacy practices of families.

Darlene: There's one issue I would like us to include in our list of issues before we go back to the whole group—something I call the feminization of family literacy. It seems to be a field that primarily attracts women—whether as adult participants in our programs or as program facilitators. I'm wondering why that might be. Are we are only seeing one side of the breadth and depth of family literacy because of the predominance of women within the field?

Jennifer: The part time nature of the work, or the low salaries for practitioners might be causes, but I am sure the issue is much more complex than that. I know there are programs designed to attract men, such as the lads-and-dads programs in Britain, or the family literacy work conducted in prisons. But your point is well taken, Darlene. It's possible the potential richness of family literacy may be wanting because of the lack of male participation at all levels.

Allyson: Perhaps we just don't understand the culture of men's literacy, which would not be surprising given that the whole issue of cultural awareness in general is one that we grapple with in family literacy—recognizing and respecting the family's culture as a resource for literacy development.

Darlene: Well, it looks like our time is up. It's interesting how we all generally listed the same issues. Maybe that is the prime issue—those perennial questions that surface time and time again, regardless of where we work or how long we have practiced in the field. Maybe the next session of the workshop will help us find some realistic solutions to some of our family literacy concerns.

Conclusion

As the preceding conversation demonstrates, the view from the field, with respect to the issues needing attention in the research, does not completely relate with what is currently found in the literature. Practitioners are anxious and troubled by the demands of their work—funding, accountability, training, and the feminization of the domain. In addition, they feel inadequate to conduct research themselves on those topics within the field that disturb them. Furthermore, they believe that the arena for publishing the results on family literacy practice needs to include the popular press. Given these concerns, it appears that greater collaboration and understanding between the research and practitioner communities is necessary so that a more fully formed perspective for family literacy evolves.

Part II

EARLY AND YOUTH LITERACIES

"Down, Up, and Round": Setting Children Up as Readers and Writers in South African Classrooms

Mastin Prinsloo
University of Cape Town

Pippa Stein
University of the Witwatersrand

INTRODUCTION

What are the limits and uses of reading and writing, and how do small children learn about these limits in preschools? How do children learn to attach meaning to signifiers and take meaning from signifiers when they first encounter reading and writing in institutional settings? If the learning of reading and writing are socially contested activities, with boundaries, prohibitions, and procedures set by different theories of reading and different sets of institutional practices, how do children learn about these limits in preschools? What kinds of readers and writers are they set up to become, with what sorts of likely consequences for their later learning?

We reflect on these questions while examining research data from three preschool centres and one Grade 1 class in South Africa that were studied as part of the Children's Early Literacy Learning (CELL) research project recently carried out in the Western Cape, Gauteng, and the Northern Province. The research is an ethnographic-style study of the processes and influences shaping children's early literacy learning in out-of-school and school settings across multiple sites.[1] Working within a social practice account of literacy (Barton, 1994; Barton & Hamilton, 1998; Gee, 1996; Heath, 1983;

---

[1]The researchers and research assistants employed by the CELL project who aided the authors in collecting, transcribing, and translating data at these sites included Jonguxolo Nana, Xolisa Gazula, Pumza Mbembe, and Thandiwe Mkhabela.

Prinsloo & Breier, 1996; Street, 1984, 2001), it focuses on the contextually variable nature of reading and writing in social practice and across cultures. Our research starts with the proposition that the contrast in the culture of literacy use across home and community, on one hand, and school, on the other, is a major reason for variable school achievement. This understanding is critical in our attempts to make schools more accessible to students from diverse social, cultural, and linguistic backgrounds. A significant body of research literature has identified the difference between the language and literacy of school and that of home/community as an important factor in the achievement and nonachievement of students at school (Gee, 1996; Heath, 1983). It has been argued that many of the difficulties students encounter in becoming literate result in part from the misunderstandings that occur when the speaking and communication styles of their community vary from those expected and valued in school settings. Reading and writing also involve specific forms of social languages in order to perform particular functions and produce specific social identities (Gee, 1996).

In this chapter we explore how children come to learn about the limits of reading and writing in school settings. We focus on data collected from three preschool centres situated in and around Khayelitsha in Cape Town in the Western Cape, and a Grade 1 class in a semirural school on the borders of Johannesburg, the industrial centre of the country. Preschool attendance is not compulsory and therefore not subsidised with government funding. As a result, there are many low-budget "educare" and preschool centres operating with very limited public funding, professional training, and support in the urban townships around South Africa. Children at these centres are commonly the children of working class parents, some of them in secure jobs, others without work, living in either township houses or in shacks. The group of children in this study had very similar backgrounds, so the noticeable variations that we point to across the sites were not a function of the differences that children brought to these institutions. The differences were, rather, a result of the way the teachers at each site invented their activity differently. The teachers draw on different notions of what should make up literacy learning and early literacy and what was important for getting children ready for schooling. In the case of the preschools, each centre could be said to be concerned with giving children a preschool package of knowledge that included the alphabet, nursery rhymes, songs, and exercises in "how to listen." However, the substance and social interactions that framed these activities varied so dramatically that the children at each site were undoubtedly taking different orientations to literacy and meaning making resources away with them into the first years of schooling.

We present the case studies of three preschools: Thembani Educare Centre, Sivile Pre-school Centre, and the Paul Fereira Learning Centre. We consider what these comparative case studies have shown in relation to our opening concerns, and then look at one alternative to these models, which is taken from a Grade 1 class at Olifantsvlei Primary School outside Johannesburg, where school is reimagined in different ways. We are not primarily concerned with whether, in any of the examples that we examine, the children were being set up to succeed at school. Our primary concern is more to examine comparatively the particular kinds of orientations to school-based literacy learning that each site is presenting to children. We focus selectively on examples of teaching from each site and selected the data to illustrate what we have identified as telling features of pedagogical orientation in each case.

THEMBANI EDUCARE CENTRE: RECITATION, REPERTOIRE, AND PERFORMANCE

The first school presents one example of a common form of preschool pedagogy, where the focus is on recitation learning. However, the varied and culturally eclectic resources that are drawn on and presented to the children give these practices a particular "local" dimension that we think is worth examining. This Centre, which we call Thembani Educare Centre, is linked to the local Ethiopian church (an Africanised, "Independent" or syncretist Christian church that refigures Christian worship against African religious and cultural practices, including ancestor veneration). Thembani is presently at a donated site in the township, where two makeshift rooms (called *hokkies*) were built with planks, one of which is situated next to the gate facing the street and is used as a kitchen and administration office.

Parents pay R50 per month to leave a child at the Centre, though the Centre's principal/teacher says that only a few manage to pay regularly. A number of children are being raised by their grandparents, who are living on small state pensions. The principal, "Mrs. Sibhene,"[2] sees herself as filling a real need for child-carers in the township. She tells a story about a single mother in Nyanga who left her two children locked inside her house (for their own protection) while she was at work. A fire started inside the house and both children were burned to death. Although this story suggests a rationale for the work she does, it is also evident that child-minding is one of only a few money-earning activities available to women in an area where unemployment is rife.

In qualifying herself to do this work, Mrs. Sibhene did a 2-year, part-time course in preprimary teaching, run at St. Francis, the local adult night school in Langa township, as well as a short course run by a local develop-

---

[2]The names of children and teachers given here, as well as the names of the preschool centres, have been changed to protect the confidentiality of our sources.

ment charity (the Community Chest) where she was shown administrative procedures, including basic bookkeeping. She employs other staff, including another teacher, a caretaker, and a kitchen worker who prepares food for the children.

While she and the other teacher are absent or busy attending to administrative matters such as purchasing food and equipment, the children are often left in the care of the older caretaker at the Centre, Mr. Kutumani. He is an enthusiastic and charismatic teacher, who has not been formally trained as a preschool teacher. He has developed a distinctive teaching style and makes up his own teaching content, which includes a large reservoir of Xhosa-language poems, prayers, and narratives that he teaches to the children. The majority of children speak Xhosa as a home language.

For all three teachers, the curriculum is broken into three key functions: teacher-led direct instruction, characterised by collective rote and chant learning; supervised play time where the children are left to play with each other in the small playground; and eating and drinking times. Explicit pedagogy is exclusively dedicated to chant learning and recitation. The principal and Mr. Kutumani have taught the children to collectively and sometimes individually recite a large and varied body of songs, rhymes, prayers, psalms, poems, and chants in the Xhosa and English languages. We discuss some examples briefly next. We are concerned to identify the distinctiveness of the cultural resources acquired by the children, and the energy and enthusiasm that the children bring to the processes of their acquisition. We are also concerned to identify the limiting effects these processes bring to children's emergent literacy.

Recitation as Pedagogy

Mrs. Sibhene taught the children, whose ages ranged from 4 to 7, to perform the following chant:

Mrs. S:	Lelethu, Lelethu.
Children:	Aksha, kusha dana.
Children and Mrs. S:	Akusha, kusha dana.
Children and Mrs. S:	Hesheshe kakatu ha-ha, hupa, aah hupa le bafana, aah hopa hesheshe hesheshe tamati ha-ha tamati ha-ha, aah hishima fana aah hishuma, aa hishima fana, aah hishima, Aah Yeeee-eeee.

While reciting the made-up sequence of sound-words, the children perform an elaborate "war dance" that involves limited, but precise dance steps and much beating of chests, flexing of muscles, and combative gestures toward an imaginary opponent. At the last line, they leap into the air and scream in unison. This is Mrs. Sibhene's version of the *haka*, the All Blacks' prematch war dance[3] (her own version reconstructed from television), which she has taught the children. It is an imaginative reconstruction of the exotic sounds of the Maori war chant and includes her own made-up words intermixed with arbitrarily inserted Xhosa words such as *tamati* (tomato) and *bafana* and *fana* (boys). In doing the *haka*, the children engage in embodied, performative sign making and learn and use sound patterns that are nonsense sounds but are precise in their sequence, nonetheless. As a prereading activity that is likely to enhance children's phonemic awareness (their sense of the sounds in language, how they are distinctive as well as how they merge and combine), this exercise might be said to be a successful example of "local" pedagogy.

Children learn the chant by doing it collectively, learning from each other, and distributing the knowledge of the sequence among each other, so that they collectively sustain one another in their learning. Chant learning makes complete sense when it is about oral performance, such as learning the *haka*, or choral singing. But it is more problematic when it is the dominant mode for learning (and prelearning) when it comes to reading and writing. The learning task becomes that of successful, collective reproduction of a sequence, not with meaning making or reflexive deployment of these resources in any other way. There is little space for developing meta-awareness of how sounds and letters combine to make particular signs, or for reflexive deployment of these resources in any other way. This point is evident when it comes to chant learning of the alphabet in English, and numbers from one to ten in English and Xhosa. Alphabet and number charts pasted on the walls of the rooms are used to initiate these exchanges, as in the following brief examples:

(Mr. Kutumani, caretaker = Mr. K; Children = C)

Mr. K: Ngubani lo? (*what is this*) (pointing to the number chart).

C: Ngu-one, two, three, . . . (and they continue counting up to ten).

Mr. K: Masibaleni ngesi Xhosa (*Let's count in Xhosa*).

C: Inye, zimbini, zintathu, zine, zintlanu, zintandathu, sixhenxe, etc. (*One, two, three, four, five, six, seven*, etc., up to ten).

Mr. K: Masiphindeni (*let's do it again*).

C: Inye, zimbini, etc. (*one, two*, etc.—to ten).

Mr. K: Siya phaya ke ngoku (*we are going there now*) (he points to the alphabet chart).

---

[3]The All Blacks are New Zealand's national rugby team. The *haka* is their prematch war dance, said to be an old Maori war-song-and-dance that they have adopted. Mrs. S and the children will only have seen it on South African television when the All Blacks play the South African national side.

Mr. K: A for what (pointing at the letter, and its accompanying word and picture).

C: A for apple.

Mr. K: B.

C: B for ball.

Mr. K: C.

C: C for cake.

Mr. K: D.

C: D for doll.

(through the rest of the alphabet, finishing off as follows)

Mr. K: X.

C: X for xylophone.

Mr. K: Y.

C: Y for yacht.

Mr. K: Z.

C: Z for zip.

There is, notably, no attempt to explain the meaning of words or to show the letters of the alphabet at work in any other way than in this list. The children learn and recite these sequences with much enthusiasm and energy, however, the younger children following the older children in getting the words and sequence right. Mr. Kutumani noted, in an aside to the researcher, that the children were doing fine, but were having problems with calling out the words *xylophone* and *yacht*. He had to help them to pronounce those words, he said. Because the task was that of recitation, however, he made no effort to translate or explain these unfamiliar and arguably inappropriate examples. Nor was there any effort to get the children to use these resources in any way besides their recitation as part of a list. Numbers are learnt in a similar fashion:

Mrs. S: Numbers one up to ten.

C: Numbers one up to ten.

Mrs. S: One cloud (reading off the numbers chart on the wall).

C: One cloud.

Mrs. S: Two dinosaurs.

C: Two dinosaurs.

Mrs. S: Three trains.

C: Three trains (and so on).

Individualised pedagogy, when it occurred, was simply about getting the children to recite the sequence on their own, accompanied by threats of sanctions if they made mistakes. In other words, the concept of the "individual" that is at stake here is not a Western idea of an autonomous, creative, personal subject, but rather, the individual as responsible to and controlled by the demands of the larger group or community of which he or she is part. Thus, making sure that individual children get the words and sequences "correct" is in the service of making sure the class as a cohort functions smoothly.

Song and Dance

Although the only modality was that of chant learning, the repertoire of songs, poems, prayers, and rhymes learnt was impressively large and varied, and absorbing for the children. It included traditional English nursery rhymes, Xhosa rhymes, religious hymns, prayers and psalms, Xhosa traditional praise poems, and several of the teachers' own design, drawing from popular and TV culture, like the *haka* described earlier, as well as from religious sources.

English nursery rhymes that the children learnt included such standards as *Wee Willie Winkie* and *Jack and Jill* (which was taught in both English and Xhosa). The children, though, were less comfortable with obscure English-language rhymes such as *Wee Willy Winkie* and mumbled and stumbled their way through the recitation. Words that could be heard were *Willy Winkie*, *town*, and *in the nightgown, window, o'clock*. The teacher would then respond, "Phindani nonke!" (Do it all again). She would get children to perform on their own when they were struggling, as in the following example, while teaching them *Jack and Jill* in the Xhosa language.

Teacher:	Anisonqeni! (You are lazy!).
Teacher:	Yiza. Hamba mboma phaya ukhwaze, Tumi. (Come. Go and stand there and shout, Tumi).
Teacher:	Cula. (Sing).
Tumi:	UJackie noJilly (Jackie and Jilly) Banyuka intaba (They climbed a mountain) Bephethe igongqo lamanzi (Carrying a bucket of water) UJackie wawa (Jackie fell) Waphuka intamo (And broke his/her neck) UJilly waqengqeleka (Jilly rolled down the mountain)

The children's reciting of their learnt repertoire of Xhosa-language and syncretist religious poems was considerably more confident and joyful than both their English language repertoire and other such awkwardly translated nursery rhymes. When they were left to nominate their own songs and chants to perform, it was clear that their favourites were Xhosa-language rhymes. In the next transcript, while Mr. Kutumani is attending

to a crying child, the children carry on with their own selections. This one
is called *Unogwaja* (a rabbit) and is full of sound and action in the Xhosa
original:

Children: Nanku unogwaja (Here is a rabbit.)
                Wandophula (It broke me!)
                Shunqu! (*sound of breaking*)
                Esinqeni (In the waist line.)
                Shunqu! (*the sound that is made by a breaking thing*)
                Esikabani? (Whose waist line?)
                Shunqu! (*the sound that is made by a breaking thing*)
                Joni kabani? (Johnny who?)
                Joni kabani? (Johnny who?)
                Shunqu! (*the sound that is made by a breaking thing*)
                Joni maqanda (Johnny eggs!)
                Shunqu! (*the sound that is made by a breaking thing*)
                Gokwe, Gokwe
                Betha lendoda (Hit this man!)
                Le ndoda (This man!)
                Hayi bantwana (No, children!)
                Bantwana (Children!)
                Phezu kwelwandle! (Over the sea!)

Our last example of a mostly Xhosa-language nonsense-rhyme that the
children greatly enjoyed involved a cue/response chant led by Mrs.
Sibhene. The children particularly delighted in shouting the complex signs
of the dog's name, with its double, clicked consonant sounds:

Mrs. S: Mheyi
Children: Flower
Mrs. S: Mheyi
Children: Flower
Mrs. S: Ndinenja emnyama. (I have a black dog.)
Children: Inamadzedze. (It has fleas.)
Mrs. S: Ndinenja emnyama. (I have a black dog.)
Children: Inamadzedze. (It has fleas.)
Mrs. S: Ngubani igama. (What is its name?)
Children: NguSgxobhagxobha. (It's Sgxobhagxobha.)

This example of a chant dialogue, where the lead singer's line is followed
by a chorused but dialogic response, is a simple example of a distinctive
genre in Xhosa and southern African performed song and poetry.

Religious Recitation

The children were taught to recite a formidable, varied, and often linguistically complex body of prayers, most of them in Xhosa. Having drilled the words for some time, the teachers then simply nominated these prayers and the children collectively took up the cue. For example, their repertoire included most of David's Psalms from the Bible:

Mr. K: amelani siza kwenza indumiso twenty-onenke indumiso 21 (Listen we are going to do Psalm 21. Let's do it all of us.)
C: Ndumiso twenty-one zilumko. (Psalm 21: Song of the wise)
Indumiso ka Davide. (David's psalm.)
Wathi masiye endlwini kaYehova, (Let's go to God's house.)
Inyawo zethu zafika zema, (Our feet came and stood)
Emasangweni akho Yerusalem, (In your gates Jerusalem.)
Yerusalem wena wakhiweyo, (Jerusalem you were built)
Ngokomzi ohlangeneyo wamnye. (Like one house)
Apho zinyuka ziye khona izizwe (Where the nations go.)
Izizwe zikaYehova (God's nations.)
Amen.

Besides this repertoire, the caretaker has taught the children a body of more idiosyncratic poems, many of which draw directly on Africanist Christian poems, associated with the Ethiopian church, that mix prophetic Christianity with images and narrative from African culture. For example, the children learnt and recited a long and complex narrative, undoubtedly sourced from prophetic narratives of the Ethiopian church. The opening lines were as follows:

Vukani kusile magwalandini (Wake up it's the morning you cowards!)
Yabinza inkwenkwezi isixelela (The star told us.)
Labetha ixilongo lisibizela (The trumpet rang calling us.)
Ndithe ndinika ubukumkani (I said I give you the King.)
Ndithe ndinika imfundo (I said I give you education.)
Nayishunqula (You cut it.)
Ndithe ndinika umhlaba (I gave you earth.)
Nawushunqula (And you cut it.)

The children learnt the whole prayer by repeating it line by line after Mr. Kutumani, and practicing it over time.

What do children take away from this preschool when they head off to school? Unlike many schools and preschools, the curriculum is eclectic in blending and mixing knowledge and language resources drawn from diverse cultural and narrative sources and communications media. The teachers have passed on to the children a genuine pleasure in the reproduction of a varied repertoire. But the emphasis on recitation means that the children have not spent a lot of time inventing and creating new meanings around these texts nor gained much experience in simple analysis and synthesis. The texts used in these classrooms are always selected by the teacher, leaving little opportunity for the children to draw on their own stories and available resources. However, these songs, and the children's knowledge of them, could well be seen as a resource that later schoolteachers could draw on. They constitute a potentially rich source of language, image, and metaphor, resources for meaning making that could be creatively deployed. In practice, the power of these resources is often underutilised by schoolteachers who tend to draw on children's repertoire of songs as filler exercises, for quieting down talkative children, or for getting children's attention before moving on to what they see as the real stuff of school learning. It is also likely that the children's skills in recall and reciting word-for-word, developed at preschool level, will stand them in good stead and will be enhanced when they encounter the rote learning and list learning strategies that characterise most learning in nonelite schools in South Africa. It is also possible that the children from Mr. Kutumani's class could be regarded as children who don't have any cultural resources at all to draw on because the resources they are getting in preschool are not conventionally school-like.

It seems that at the Thembani Educare Centre, the teachers' imagining of schooling has distinctive features, and these are communicated directly and indirectly to the children through the kinds of texts and communicative practices that are enacted. It is through these processes that the limits and boundaries around what constitutes "being a reader" and "being a writer" are actually defined. Firstly, there is an expectation that school knowledge is about collectively learned recitation. Although these children have knowledge of the alphabet and nursery rhymes and have learnt "how to listen," it is apparent that the kinds of social interaction that the teachers promoted in this classroom have communicated particular attitudes to the social construction of knowledge as well. The children can be seen to be internalising conceptions of what is relevant, and to be developing habits of engaging mentally. Thus they might perform enthusiastically and well in rote learning exercises and in choral singing activities, but they have probably not been prepared to make and take meaning in the critically reflexive ways that will enable them to make sense of school reading and writing practices in later years. On the other hand, it might be preparing them very well for very traditional school practices.

SIVILE PRE-SCHOOL CENTRE: "READY-MADE CHILDREN"

We now turn, more briefly, to the second preschool, Sivile Pre-school Centre (name changed), which is located elsewhere in Khayelitsha. The learning here is more school-like but undoubtedly more limited in certain ways. We examine here how reading and writing are encountered by small children in ways that are inseparable from the disciplinary practices of the school. We present what might be seen as an extreme case, which illustrates that general point in a telling way.

The Centre is sponsored by the Cape Provincial Administration, which pays teacher salaries. The Centre has around 50 children and fees charged are R60 per month. A school-like hierarchy exists, with a principal, a deputy principal, and two teachers, with small pay differentials (of about R200 per month between the principal and the teachers). A cook is also employed to prepare food daily for the children. There are ongoing tensions between the principal and the teachers over decision making, time keeping, and uses of money. The principal, Mrs. Ngada, says, "I'm confused by my deputy, she doesn't want to understand." She recounts details of various plans for school initiatives, such as organising parents' meetings, that lead to conflicts and mutual hostility among the staff. For example, she says she wanted to employ another teacher. The children at the Centre are divided into three classes, of 2- to 3-year-olds, 3- to 4-year-olds, and 4- to 6-year-olds, each with their own class teacher. She says she has two jobs, teaching and managing the educare centre, and wants to employ a new teacher to take her class. The other teachers objected, arguing that any money that was available should be used to increment their salaries, rather than on a new member of staff.

Despite the openly mercenary attitudes displayed by the teachers on these occasions of conflict, they appear to be confident that they are doing good work. As one of them puts it:

> Do you think the government sees the huge work that we do? We carry these children, teach them to sit, to wee independently, to feed themselves such that we don't teach in January and February. We start in March. For now we are getting them used to our lifestyle here. We take them out, make them happy so that the next day they wake up with interest to come to school. Do you think the government doesn't see this? We prepare these children for Grade One. Grade One teachers take ready-made and prepared children.

Parents also see the Centre as doing good work. One mother, the wife of a policeman, living in Tembani, said, "We decided to take (our child) to the Sivile Educare because it is cheap and ikufuphi and abantwana abaphuma phaya baphuma baclever (*It's nearer and children who come from them are clever*)."

It is the processes of producing "ready-made and prepared children" that we focus on here. We are concerned with how procedures of disciplining are interleaved or folded into children's school-based early engagement with modes of information, whether of inscription and print, visual image, spoken language and gesture. We ask the same questions as in the preceding case study: What conceptions of what is relevant are children being encouraged to internalise? What habits of engaging mentally in relation to literacy are being developed? A poem that the children learn early on at the Centre and repeat often goes as follows:

> Umntwana othand'iindaba mbi, mbi (A child who likes news is bad, bad.)
> Wofika ngapha, ejonga ngapha (She always looks from side to side.)
> Efu'ukuphendula (Wanting to answer.)
> Bantwana abancinci yekani abazali (Young children leave parents alone.)
> Bancokole, bancokole kamnandi (Chat, chat nicely.)

That children take on the ideas, ideology, and messages of such rhymes is apparent in the following exchange, where the children are being disciplined to be less noisy. In the following recorded account, at 9:45 a.m., the children have been told to sleep at their tables while the teachers are busy or out of the room:

Sindiwe (teacher; comes out of the kitchen shouting): Hayi, hayi, hayi! Lala! Lala! (No, no, no! Sleep! Sleep)

(Some children "sleep" and some carry on chatting.)

Sindiwe: Heyi cwaka (Hey quiet!)

Child: Umntwana othand'indaba. (A child who likes news).

The fact that the child is repeating a line from the poem indicates that she knows exactly what the message is meant to be. It is this concern to produce docile and passive children that makes up much of the teachers' concern with getting the children "ready." Pacifying the children with threats of punishment for being noisy was a sustained activity.

The children encountered reading and writing at the Centre against the framing background of these discipline procedures. The regulative procedures and the encounters with print, illustration, and other communicative modalities are folded into each other inseparably:

Nosiseko: Khanize apha phandle. Odwa, Thando, khange nindinike uma-phepha enu. Aba ndibabizayo khange bandimike amaphepha abo. (Come here outside. Odwa, Thando, you did not give me your papers. The children I am calling out are those who did not give me their papers.)

Nosieka (*She hits Khalapha*):   Anuva, uyonqena, yintoni le uyibhale apha? (You don't listen, you are lazy, what have you written here?) (*She hits him again.*) Uyalova wena esikolweni. Ndizakubabetha aba bantu batya ipen. Bazakufa eyonanto. (You are behind at school. I am going to hit those of you who eat pens. The thing is they are going to die.)

(*Later, children start making a noise.*)

Nosiseko (comes back with her stick): Ngubani othethayo? Ngubani othethayo (Who's talking? Who's talking?) (*She hits Paula on the head thrice with a stick and then goes to another group and hits another child.*)

(*Yandisa goes to the researcher to show her a piece of writing.*)

Nosiseko: Hayi sanukumdisturba umisi uyabhala izinto endimthume zona. Nani bhalani ezenu (No, don't disturb the teacher, she's writing things. I have asked her to write. You must also write your things).

(*Again, children are already eating porridge. Sindiwe is serving seconds to the children.*)

Nosiseko: Andifuni mntwana ongxolayo namhlanje. Ndiza kubabetha aba bantwana (I don't want any child who's going to make a noise today. I'm going to hit these children.)

Bantwana, bangaphi abathi abazukungxola. Mabaphakamise isandla. (Children, how many of you say they are not going to make noise? They must raise their hands.) Mabalale bona ndiyazazi mna ukuba ndizakubapha ntoni. Uzakubonakala ngokungalali umntu ongxolayo. (They must sleep. I know what I'm going to give them. A noise maker will be seen by not sleeping.)

(*Thuli raises her hand to show that she is not going to make noise. Children "sleep."*)

The teachers on one occasion showed some concern that they were being recorded during these exchanges, suggesting that they were aware that they were not following the child-centred pedagogy to which they had all been exposed on the Early Learning Resource Unit (ELRU) course they attended. The Early Learning Resource Unit is a local nongovernmental organisation that trains teachers in progressive pedagogy.

Our point that punishment, threats, literacy, and approval are folded into each other as the children encounter them is further illustrated in the exchanges below:

Nosiseko: Yilento yenza ukuba nithule. (This is the thing—referring to the stick in her hand—that makes you quiet.) Ngoku soze ndingakwazi ukunibetha (Now I won't be able to hit you.) Ngoku ndizakuninika amaphepha nibhale. (Now I'm going to give you papers to write.) Paula hlala endaweni yakho.

Thuli: Nizobhala amarhoqololo. (You are going to write squiggles.) Wonke umntu ulifumene iphepha phaya? (Did everyone get the paper over there?)

Children: Yes misi (Yes teacher.)

Nosiseko: Asibhali kwicala elinamagama. (We don't write on the side with words.) Nkwenkwe sukubhala ngapha bhala ngapha. (Nkwenkwe, we don't write on this side, write on this side.) Mamela ke ngoku (Now listen). (*She hits the door with a stick*) bhalani umntu angabhali iphepha lomnye umntu. (Write. A person mustn't write on the other child's paper.) Uba niyangxola andinithandi ukuba aningxoli ndiyanithanda (I don't love you when you make noise, I love you when you don't make noise.)

It would be a distortion to suggest that these exchanges of threats and insistence on passivity were all that characterised the pedagogy of the Centre. It is not all quiet and discipline, in fact, and the children also get space to sing and dance. Here, a teacher teaches the children how to dance, while the other teachers are away. There are two groups of dancers dancing to different songs, both of them *kwaito* (rap) songs that are familiar from the radio and that mix local languages in their lyrics. At present, the following is a very popular song:

Oh ho ho ho city Jehova
It's a fiasco
Pap parapapam
Come on every body
It's a fiasco

However, it is significant that all occasions that included exercises and activities of reading and writing were framed by the coercive disciplinary procedures previously described. Thus the encounters with literacy were also encounters with strict and sometimes painful disciplining of attention and bodies. Such examples of physical punishment and enforced passivity are typical of many preschool and schooling contexts in South Africa that we encountered in our research, and we heard similar accounts from other researchers and teachers. Corporal punishment is outlawed in schools but undoubtedly still occurs with frequency in many schools, where teachers defend it as being "part of our culture." In such contexts, literacy and violence become linked in distressing ways in children's imaginations: The struggle to write becomes associated with negativity, feelings of failure, and pain, and this in itself sets limits around what constitutes "becoming a reader and writer." We heard numerous accounts from university students of damaging early literacy experiences in which punishment was a distinct feature of the teacher's literacy pedagogy, and how hard it was to recover a love of reading and writing from these formative experiences.

In contrast, in the third example, we examine very briefly another representative example of a preschool centre where the teachers actively try to implement progressive pedagogical practices.

PAUL FEREIRA EARLY LEARNING CENTRE:
MAKING SENSE AT SCHOOL

The third preschool is the Paul Fereira Early Learning Centre, named after a man who left money in his will to be used for preschooling in needy areas, and managed by Catholic Welfare Development of the Catholic church. There are about 100 children attending the preschool, from 17 in 1997. There are also six teachers and one caretaker. The Centre, like many others in the area, combines day care and preschool activities. The fees are R100 a month per child, which includes the cost of the food that the children eat at the Centre. Although the preschool is open to anyone in the area, the majority are Black children of Xhosa-speaking origin. The Centre gets its children from Mandalay, Tembani, Bongweni, Luzuko Park, and other parts of Khayelitsha. The Centre also gets children from informal settlement areas of New Rest and Lower Crossroads (just behind Mandalay). These children walk to the centre. Jill Daniels has been the principal ever since the Centre opened. She belongs to the Mitchells Plain Principals Educare forum. Four other preschools in Mandalay belong to the forum, and these five schools work closely with each other, sharing resources when possible.

Of the approximately 100 children attending the Centre, two children are Afrikaans speakers at home. The rest speak Xhosa and English, though all the parents are first-language Xhosa speakers. These children are commonly encouraged to speak English and are spoken to in English by their parents because their parents identify "good English" as being vital for their children's success at school and thereafter. They ask the teachers at the Centre to teach their children in English because they hope to send them later to multiracial English-language schools whose reputations for success are much higher than local township schools. Knowing English makes it easier for the children to cope at those schools. Jill, who speaks only English and Afrikaans but is learning Xhosa, says that some of the children pick English up very quickly.

We identify the pedagogical orientation of Jill and the other teachers and go on to show an example of the data to illustrate our point: The teaching involved communicating to the children a largely internal language and reference system. This framework of attaching meaning selectively to a corpus of signs was a school-based one. The meanings that were attached were often idiosyncratic but the teacher designated them as correct, whereas other possible meanings and associations were excluded. Thus reading and writing were first encountered at school in a framework of more relaxed discipline than in the previous example, but the children were still encouraged to look only for the meaning or association of meaning with symbol that the teacher had in mind.

This point is illustrated briefly in this description exchange, around a lesson on rabbits:

Rabbits are white (or red) and eat carrots (or jam)

Teacher Jill separates a class of 14 children from the other children.

Jill asks children to clap hands. Children clap.

Jill shows a picture of a rabbit (above the picture is written *my pet*).

She asks the children what it is a picture of.

Children say, a rabbit.

Jill asks them to repeat.

The children repeat, a rabbit.

Jill asks children what kind of food the rabbit eats.

Some children shout, "pear!"

Jill says a rabbit eats carrots.

Jill shows them a rabbit from a book that hasn't been coloured in and asks what colour it is.

The children are silent.

Jill tells them that a rabbit is white. She tells the children that they are going to make a garden for their rabbit. It is going to live in the garden.

Jill hands out pieces of blue cardboard with a rabbit drawn in black. She gives them scissors to cut the rabbits from the cardboard. Jill gives them wax crayons including some red crayons, for colouring.

Jill takes two rabbits from the desk and a book. She goes to the children and calls them to sit down. She shows them a rabbit and asks them what it is.

Children shout in unison, rabbit!

Jill asks the children why the rabbit has big eyes.

Loyiso says: To see.

Jill: Rabbit can be in what colour?

Children: White.

Jill: Or?

Children: White or red.

Jill tells children that the two small legs of the rabbit are used to scratch out the carrots.

Jill: Who knows a lion?

Children: Me.

Jill: The lion eats the rabbit and the rabbit eats carrots. A rabbit hops with two small legs, to run away from the lions.

Jill reads from the book: Bunny's mommy, Rabbit, wants Jam.

Jill asks: She wants what?

Children: Jam.

Jill: The mommy gives Bunny money.

Jill: What is Bunny going to do at the shop?

Children: To buy jam.

Jill: Who gave Bunny money?

Children: His mom.

Jill pages through the book (rather fast) and shows them that Bunny goes to the shop, comes back home.

This example shows how the teacher is setting up school knowledge as insulated, impermeable, and disconnected from children's emergent meaning making, language, and literacy resources. The teacher is working with mostly Xhosa-language children, but their substantial language and out-of-school knowledge is excluded—for example, the dramatic Xhosa-language song about a rabbit that we discussed in the first case study could have been used as a resource in this instance. She is telling children what counts as knowledge in school. It is not common sense at all. Despite experiential evidence to the contrary, it has been established that in this setting, that of the schoolroom, rabbits are white and eat carrots. Unfortunately, this construct of situated meaning is not even internally consistent, so although the children learn to use this particular situated meaning of rabbit—white, eats carrots—this knowledge is not consistently reinforced by the teacher. She asks the children what colour rabbits are; they all say "white," but she asks for more ("And?"), whereupon the children throw in the colour red, which they perhaps think is as likely as any colour in this arbitrary social semiotic world. Perhaps the response might be because of the red crayons that were handed out. When the teacher reads from the rabbit book, she subverts her earlier dogma around rabbits' diet. Having said that they eat carrots, she reads the story where the rabbit's mom buys jam, without noticing the contradiction. The story in the book is working with a very different, situated meaning of rabbit from the one that has already been endorsed. In this shift, the teacher has moved from a world of the classroom rabbits to the convention of children's literature where animals are personified as real people, doing people things, wearing clothes, talking, going to the shop, and eating jam. The teacher has so absorbed the logic of this device that she doesn't notice the need to explain that rabbit now means something else and is differently articulated in an alternative system of meaning making.

OLIFANTSVLEI PRIMARY SCHOOL: GETTING EVERYONE ON BOARD

A key issue arising out of the previous examples concerns the ways in which teachers create differing expectations, values, and beliefs about literacy in their classrooms, and the consequences for children's later identities as readers and writers. In this final example, we explore how a

Grade 1 teacher, from a semirural farm school on the edges of Johannesburg, has created a radically different understanding of literacy pedagogy
through her attempts at border crossings across home, school, and community domains.

In 1999, Tshidi Mamabolo joined Olifantsvlei Primary School as an early
years literacy teacher. Olifantsvlei Primary School, established in the 1960s,
is a state school receiving state subsidy. In terms of resources, the school has
electricity and a photocopier, and the Grade 1 and 2 classes have small collections of books in each classroom. The school is situated in farmlands on
the borders of the city of Johannesburg and only serves children from the
densely populated informal settlements or "shacks" that are scattered in between the farmlands. These settlements have electricity but no sanitation or
running water. Many children come from female-headed households, and
some children live in children-headed households, as a result of the HIV/
AIDS pandemic that is affecting entire families. Social security in these families comes from child grants of R140.00 ($20) per month per child and
pensions for those over 60 years. Children who live in these settlements exist on the margins of the society, in situations of childhood adversity, unemployment, and poverty.

When Tshidi Mamabolo started working in this school in 1999, she was
surprised and worried at what she calls "the children's passivity, their lack of
motivation and interest in learning." She decided that it was her fault and
that she needed to transform her literacy pedagogy. Shifting from a
teacher-fronted pedagogy that focused on rote learning, phonics, and
drills, she started to introduce more participatory models in which children's histories, languages, and background knowledges were incorporated into literacy activities. In spite of the fact that the children in this
school are multilingual speakers of several African languages, the school
has chosen a "straight for English" language policy from Grade 1. This
means that English is the language of teaching and learning, and children
acquire initial literacy in English, not in their home language.

In one example of how Tshidi Mamabolo changed her pedagogy, she developed a multilingual project in local storytelling and performance in
which the children produced visual texts, stories, and plays in their home
languages. In one example of an improvised play, a group of 7-year-old girls
created four women characters, named after four of the official South African languages: Ma English [Mother English], MamoSotho [Mother Sotho],
Mam'Xhosa [Mother Xhosa], and MamoZulu [Mother Zulu]. They are all
neighbours. Ma English is a wealthy, arrogant woman who secretly goes to
MamoSotho to ask if she can borrow some sugar. She asks MamoSotho not
to tell anyone that she has come to ask her for sugar. MamoSotho promises
not to do so, but as soon as Ma English has left the house, she runs to
MamoZulu to inform her that Ma English has just gone to someone (she

does not say it was her house) to borrow some sugar. When MamoZulu asks her "Where did she go to?" she says she did not know. She also asks MamoZulu not to tell anyone "the gossip." But as soon as she leaves, MamoZulu runs to Mam'Xhosa to tell her "the same gossip." Mam'Xhosa asks her who gave Ma English the sugar. She replies that she does not know. Mam'Xhosa then runs to MamoSotho to pass on the same gossip! When MamoSotho hears the gossip coming back to her, she goes to assault MamoZulu, shouting, "What did I say to you about that matter between us?" She hits her repeatedly. Then MamoZulu goes to Mam'Xhosa, shouting at her, "What did I say to you about that matter between us?" and assaults her repeatedly. The play ends with the children singing this song:

> Let's stop talking about other people!
> Let's stop talking about other people!

This play can be interpreted at a number of levels. Certainly the children construct it as a moral tale about the evils of gossiping, exhorting their audience to "stop talking about other people." But what do we make of these female characters, all named after national languages? In the performances, each character actually communicated in the language of her name, creating a multilingual polyphonic text in which Ma English spoke English to MamoSotho, who in turn spoke Sotho to MamoZulu, who spoke Zulu to Mam'Xhosa and so on in a predictable chain of oral communication. This play can be read as a powerful symbol of multilingualism at work in South Africa: people living side-by-side using their language resources to successfully communicate the same message. However, the play is also an interesting sociocultural commentary on the power and status of different South African languages. Ma English is a snob, unable to openly ask for sugar from her poorer neighbours. The play is remarkable for the expectations it sets up for the possible downfall of arrogant Ma English, but nothing like that occurs. Ma English gets away with her behaviour, obliviously enjoying her sugar whilst havoc reigns among her neighbours. One moral of the story is that wealth and snobbery get rewarded but gossiping does not!

For 3 years Tshidi Mamabolo experimented with pedagogies that gave her children more agency in her classroom, with very positive results. Children became more assertive and started taking initiatives in relation to the curriculum. In one such example, she informed her class that she would be teaching them about water transport and asked them if they had any ideas about how they might learn about it. Some children suggested that they all bring containers to school the next day, fill them with water, and make paper boats. Such was the nature of the relationship between this teacher and her class.

At the beginning of 2003, Tshidi Mamabolo acquired a new class of Grade 1 children. This year, she noticed high levels of absenteeism in her class. Parents never came to enquire about their children's progress; indeed, they stayed away from the school. She noticed children falling asleep in class early on in the school day. Children were complaining of hunger— the one peanut butter sandwich provided by the school feeding scheme at break made little difference. One day a 7-year-old girl from her class crawled into her classroom, desperately ill. Her mother and father were dead. She lay under a blanket at Tshidi's feet, dying of AIDS.

In April, Tshidi decided that some form of action had to be taken. She decided that a local, classroom-based pedagogical solution was not enough to address the social crisis that surrounded her. In order to "be in" the classroom, she had to "go out" of the classroom. She had to cross the border between the school and children's homes. She negotiated access to each child's home through the child, and on ascertaining that the household was willing to see her, visited each household to hold talks with the family on why their children were frequently absent from school or falling asleep in class. She found neighbours were feeding some children. Others were being kept at home because there was no money for school fees, uniforms, or transport. Parents told her that they were afraid to come to school because, as one parent said, "No one listens to me there." The fundamental problem was not lack of awareness of the importance of education, but unemployment and poverty. All that concerned the families was how to get food on the table. Tshidi returned to her school and decided to focus on food first. She approached the principal and the teachers, who collectively decided to allocate a section of untilled school land to vegetable gardens that parents or households could use as a form of income generation. They formed an organising committee and applied for a grant from local authorities to buy seeds. Local HIV/AIDS Support Campaigns came on board to support the vegetable garden project because it is a means of providing fresh food to HIV sufferers in the local community. At this point, the first crop of vegetables is ready to be harvested.

The seeds have been sown, though whether they are the seeds of literacy or of something else is what we reflect on here. Whilst teachers are obviously not the only agents in this complex construction of what counts as literacy, as presented in the other case studies (or portraits), they are central to its formation in the early years. They are particularly important in contexts where children do not have access to a range of literacy resources in their homes. Street (2001), referring to research on indigenous, non-Western encounters with literacy, talks about the impact of literacy as a form of "taking hold" of literacy. He has suggested in his work on literacy and development that *what gives meaning to literacy* may not, on the surface, be *about literacy*. For Tshidi Mamabolo, taking hold of literacy means, to use her own words, "getting everyone on board." But what does "getting everyone on board" mean in the context of poverty, the HIV/AIDS plague, and no food on the table? Is planting vegetable gardens in the school grounds a form of taking hold of literacy?

We answer "yes" to this question and have referred to Tshidi Mamabolo's story as *the seeds of literacy* in order to signal the different kinds of linkages that are possible in relation to what it means to hold literacy in different contexts. On the surface of things, one could well ask what the planting of vegetables has to do with holding literacy. Tshidi Mamabolo answers, "If the parents are regularly in the school grounds, working in the gardens, it will be easier to talk to them about their children's literacy." Therefore, we argue that the garden project holds literacy at a number of levels:

- It provides a site for parents, their children, and the community to engage materially and intellectually on a regular basis with the concept of "school" and its benefits.
- It provides food for children and families who have none.
- It provides a context in which teachers and parents can meet informally and discussions around children's literacy can begin to take place.
- It opens up the possibility of adult basic education and training classes that can commence on the school site. In other words, it begins to build a community that can organise itself around skills development and education.

The steps this teacher has taken to reconfigure home–school–community relations can be seen as a radical reinvention of the idea of literacy in which literacy comes to mean more than a set of discrete, boundaried classroom practices. Taking hold of literacy means working with local cultural practices and community needs as well as school models in a more local/central mix. Tshidi Mamabolo's initial decision to change her pedagogy by "letting the world in" to her classroom brought the world in, in all its inchoate messiness. In letting the world in, she has not only extended the boundaries of what it means to teach literacy, but she has also extended her own sense of identity as a literacy teacher who, through taking certain forms of action, has changed how others see her and how she sees herself. To be "in the classroom," she understood that she had to be "in the world," but being in the world in the context of social disintegration brought with it an unbounded set of moral and ethical dilemmas that she had to face. Through a reconceptualisation of the whole literacy programme within her specific context, she has creatively engaged with these dilemmas, bringing new meanings to this situation that move beyond autonomous models to more inclusive ecologically based literacy pedagogies. In this classroom, children pick up from their teacher, in a kind of Paulo Freire tradition, that becoming a reader and a writer involves more than "reading the word" but "reading the world" as well (Freire, 1970). Their own literacy development is dependent on a complex set of social and economic relations that involve, among others, parents, community, and school.

CONCLUSION

In each one of the portraits we have drawn of literacy learning in the early years, the teacher has acted on particular understandings of literacy and literacy teaching. These understandings are not uniform or homogeneous, and further research is needed to gain deeper insights into how these understandings are socially and culturally produced. We argue that how these different teachers engage with literacy pedagogy has important consequences for the kinds of readers and writers these children will become, both within school environments and as independent readers outside of school. All the portraits we have shown demonstrate that the pedagogic environment is producing certain kinds of messages around what constitutes literacy. In the first portrait, literacy learning draws on indigenous forms of knowledge and performance, which appear to be highly enjoyable, providing the children with familiar territory that can be traversed with ease. The focus here is on recitation and repetition of teacher-led/initiated songs and hymns, with less emphasis on children's production or reflection on meaning making. In the second portrait, there appears to be a seamless relationship between literacy, discipline, and forms of pain and punishment with very little evidence of pleasure. We find this portrait alarming. In the third portrait, the teacher is introducing the children to mainstream academic literacy through story reading and question and answer on the text, but the world of the text seems remote from the children's life worlds, and there is little opportunity offered for children to draw on their available resources. In the final example, the teacher is attempting to bring the children's life worlds and school worlds together in an ambitious project that moves beyond literacy as basic skills into literacy as a form of reading the world in all its messiness.

Although the intention of this chapter is not to pass high-handed judgments about the literacy pedagogy that we have observed in each one of these sites, given the difficulties in which each teacher is working (large classes, few resources, hungry children), we raise the question of what kind of literacy pedagogies are the most effective in the early years, and most appropriate for the local context. It seems to us that literacy pedagogies that work productively and sensitively with indigenous forms of knowledge, and that draw on children's multiple semiotic resources in combination with other forms of knowledge that are equally important and powerful (for example, forms of academic and critical literacy), might be an important starting point.

REFERENCES

Barton, D. (1994). *Literacy: An introduction to the ecology of written language.* Oxford: Blackwell.
Barton, D., & Hamilton, M. (1998). *Local literacies.* London: Routledge.
Freire, P. (1970). *Pedagogy of the oppressed.* New York: Seabury Press.
Gee, J. (1996). *Social linguistics and literacies: Ideology in discourses* (2nd ed.). London: Falmer Press.
Heath, S. B. (1983). *Ways with words: Language, life and work in communities and classrooms.* Cambridge: Cambridge University Press.
Prinsloo, M., & Breier, M. (Eds.). (1996). *The social uses of literacy: Theory and practice in contemporary South Africa.* Amsterdam & South Africa: John Benjamins & SACHED Books.
Street, B. (1984). *Literacy in theory and practice.* Cambridge: Cambridge University Press.
Street, B. (Ed.). (2001). *Literacy and development.* London: Routledge.

Chapter 7

The Chameleon Character of Multilingual Literacy Portraits: Re-Searching in "Heritage" Language Places and Spaces

Mary H. Maguire
Ann J. Beer
Hourig Attarian
Diane Baygin
Xiao Lan Curdt-Christiansen
Reiko Yoshida
McGill University

ENTERING HERITAGE LANGUAGE PLACES AND SPACES

The portrait of Canada as a welcoming *place* for immigrants can be traced to different immigration waves and political climates. Human geographer Soja's (1996) concept of "third space"—a new space between collectives and individuals and historical periods—offers possibilities for exploring relationships among spaces, identity politics, and heritage languages. To understand children's locations in multiple spaces, we draw on the Lefebvre/ Soja tradition within the theoretical landscape of critical human geography. Relevant here are Lefebvre's (1991) three different kinds of spaces: *espace perçu*—perceived physical space, *espace conçu*—conceived, mental, or imagined space, and *espace vécu*—third space as directly lived through social practices. Conceptualizing children's identity construction as a recursive process necessitates a double perspective—looking at local literacy moments in their daily living and the more global, political discourses in which they may be located. To articulate a vision of diverse spaces where locations of possibility are open for children to "speak" and "be," we draw on Bakhtin's (1990) dialogic concept of self, which creates an active response to the utterances of individuals, their social and temporal worlds. We use *chameleon* as a metaphor to characterize our attempts to draw portraits of multilingual children's literacy practices and identity construction in diverse spaces. We also use it in the postmodern sense to signal the paradoxical, elusive nature of identity in global times as fluid and discursively constructed in ways that are not always visible, easily recognizable, or politically and personally valued. Yon (2000) maintains that diaspora "as a theoretical concept . . . helps us to think about culture and cultural processes as forged through transnational networks and identifications" (pp. 17–18). Braziel and Mannur (2003) argue that "Diaspora remains, above all, a human phenomenon—lived and experienced" (p. 8).

Bourdieu's (1990) concept, "symbolic capital," also offers possibilities for exploring contextual relationships among diasporan spaces, languages, and children's identity politics. Recognizing heritage languages presents challenges to past and present mainstream power and political arrangements and diasporan communities. Immigration patterns have played key roles in framing Canadian and Quebec sociocultural linguistic landscapes. Thus, we juxtapose local literacy moments with global political discourses as a *heuristic* for reflecting on children's "possibilities of selfhood" (Ivanic, 1998). When children speak or write, they engage in dialogues that are situated within multiple power relations and evaluative orientations. They explicitly or implicitly signal their awareness of these relations in their utterances, which are always dialogic and entail some form of answerability that is morally responsive to *others' words.* Hall (2003) argues that "cultural identity is a matter of 'becoming' as well as 'being.' It belongs to the future as much as to the past . . . Cultural identities come from somewhere, have histories" (p. 236).

Consider a map drawn by 6-year-old Karine (Fig. 7.1). Labeling her map "*Le monde entier,*" Karine demonstrates her ability to integrate her different literacies, the geographical spaces past and present, and places she knows including Australia, Armenia, Canada, and Old Montreal—places important to her in June 2001. A home visit revealed that they had received a tablecloth with a map of Australia painted on it and in her *home space,* Karine took great pleasure in discovering different places on it. Armenia is her *homeland.* Canada is where she locates herself in her daily activities. Karine's mother reflects on her daughter's awareness of "different languages" around her in this material space, Deguire Street, located in a transient neighborhood:

> I was staying home with [Karine] her. I always went out or went visiting. Very early she noticed that there were different languages, because with those neighbors, I used to speak different languages than what she knew. And she would ask me "What are those things that I am not understanding?" (Baygin, 2001)

At home, Karine is aware her parents use Western Armenian and Arabic when they do not want the children to understand what they are talking about, and that Arabic is also used in her multilingual neighborhood. Her

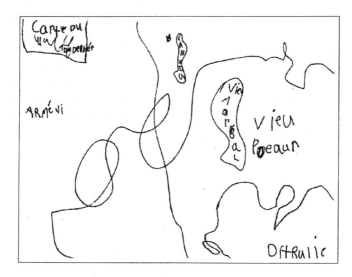

FIG. 7.1.   Le monde entier (The entire world).

map conceptualizes home as a concrete location, a place in a geographic sense and a space circumscribed by her family's personal memories within "the collective space of cultural forms and social relations" (Holland, Lachiotte, Skinner, & Cain, 1998, p. 5). Her map is "a text [that] lives by coming into contact with another text (context). Thus, in every manifestation of the present the individual strives to glimpse a trace of the past, a peak of the present-day or tendency of and appropriation of the future" (Bakhtin, 1984, p. 28).

Holland et al. (1998) argue that identities are "possibilities of mediating agency and the key means through which people care about and care for what is going on around them" (p. 51). Consider Yoyo's and Hanako's comments about belonging and establishing cultural dialogues. Yoyo attends a Saturday Chinese school and Hanako a Japanese Hoshuko. Yoyo's reflections on negotiating multiple languages provide an example of how identities can be constructed, contested, or even resisted in local conversations and elusive moments in different places:

> If I don't speak French at the Zhonguo school, the other children will think that I am stupid or "xin yimin" (new immigrant). It is very bad if they think I am a "xin yimin" because it means that I am poor and don't know anything and don't understand anything. I would try to use my broken French to communicate with other children at (Zhonguo) school although I speak Chinese much better than some kids, but I was afraid to be an outsider, and I didn't want to be an outsider and I didn't want the others to think I was stupid. (Xiao Lan's interview with Yoyo)

A recent immigrant and very competent speaker of Mandarin, Yoyo is concerned about not being recognized as a certain kind of person, a "*xin yimin.*" In this literacy moment, she positions herself between resisting negative representations of self as an "immigrant, other, or outsider" and her educational desire to open a *third space* of strategic engagement with others—her classmates who attend a French school during the week. In an essay entitled *Japanese and I*, Hanako reminisces about Japan and longs for an authentic, perceived, and lived place where "a lot" speak Japanese:

> *I sometimes feel like I want to talk in Japanese with my foreign friends. Even if I went to another country, I don't think I will forget Japanese . . . I still want to go back to Japan. I want to speak Japanese in front of a lot of Japanese people. Especially I want to talk a lot of Japanese in a place like a Japanese train station.* (Ishibashi, 1993, p. 43)

Her image of this place is not Mt. Fuji but a busy Japanese train station. To understand how children engage in the work of identity politics means looking along two axes—locally and globally from different temporal perspectives—past, present, future. Each time zone interlopes on and with another through children's interwoven conversations and intertextual acts of meaning in unexpected ways. When children confront questions such as who they are or where they come from, what languages they speak or prefer to speak in a particular place, they are either tacitly or explicitly asking about their past, present, and future (Appadurai, 2003).

Although the existence of heritage schools is commonplace knowledge, they are invisible within the political and policymaking discourses of schooling. Not withstanding the invisibility of children's perspectives, their self-reflexivity about their language affiliations, allegiances, and identity construction is largely journalistically reported. Our project is located within the nested contexts of power relations that Canadian philosopher Taylor (1994) calls a "politics of recognition" between majority and minority language groups within conflicting political discourses and legislation during different immigration waves. Taking the position that literacy practices are located in sociocultural, historical, and economic forces that are sometimes visible and sometimes invisible, we survey the global linguistic and political discourses in Canada and Quebec. We move to a local urban place, Montreal, a unique location—*espace perçu* for exploring multilingual literacies and identity politics, and *espace conçu* and *espace veçu*—for understanding children's real and imagined worlds.

We use multiple spaces and places as a frame to explore the complexity of multilingual children's literacies, identity politics, and how the politics of place and place making must be historically, locally, and globally situated. Places can be physical territories with clearly defined borders and culturally constructed spaces shaped through intricate networks of social relationships. Multiple spaces, a concept central to cultural studies and human geography, can range from sociocultural locations, to ideological positionings, to geographical imaginings and representations of being and dwelling in the world (Maguire, 2003). What significance do different spaces play in multilingual children's lives, identities, multiple languages, and literate actions? We explore this question in three heritage communities—Armenian, Chinese, and Japanese.

SURVEYING LINGUISTIC LANDSCAPES AND MAPPING POLITICAL DISCOURSES

> Language is like a door, which enables you to learn the world. When you learn one language, you get to know one part of the world. When you learn other languages, you will get an opportunity to know other parts of the world. It is like windows opening up to you one by one, to know other parts of the world. (Curdt-Christiansen, 2003)

The Canadian sociocultural linguistic landscape, frequently framed as a multicultural mosaic in political discourse, recognizes two official languages, English and French, based on the Canadian Charter of Rights (1982) and the Official Languages Act (1969). Within the nested contexts of political discourses about majority/minority languages is the rhetoric of multiculturalism, embedded in a broad framework of laws and policies that support Canada's approach to diversity and embracement of cultural pluralism. In Quebec, the official language is French, based on Bill 101 and the Charter of the French Language (1977). School boards are linguistically organized as either English or French. Since 1974, access to English schools, with their long tradition of French immersion programs, is limited to those children with a parent who has been educated in English. The school day is largely spent in French—a second language for most children and a third or fourth for others. Newcomers must attend French schools (Regulation 85:85.1).

Key legislation pertaining to the language of instruction in Quebec and Canada has been summarized elsewhere (Maguire, 1994; Maguire & Graves, 2001). Although politically mapped in legislative provisions governing language, the sociolinguistic landscapes are neither fixed nor stable. In 1971, Canada was the first country in the world to adopt a multicultural policy that assumes an inclusive citizenship. This policy became the 1988 Multiculturalism Act that promotes the mutual understanding among diverse groups in Canadian society and resulted in the emergence of *heritage* programs as a response to cultural diversity. Ironically, there was little recognition of *heritage* languages in these documents until the 1991 Canadian Heritage Language

Act. The 1997 Canadian Heritage Multiculturalism Program merged multi-cultural education with citizenship education and focused on respect, reality, and diversity with identity, civic participation, and social justice as fundamental goals. This lack of recognition, also apparent in the recent plan for official languages, The New Act (2002), is unsettling as many parents in our family inquiries see the learning of multiple languages as "sociocultural capital" to move across and within more than one language, sociocultural space, and imagined community of practices (Anderson, 1983). Curdt-Christiansen (2003) documented Chinese parents' literacy practices and aspirations. As newcomers who may not speak French but who perceive the social capital of multiple languages, they provide French literacy resources in their homes such as books, videotapes, and private tutoring.

Particularly striking within the contexts of global economies and increasingly diverse, mobile social worlds is the dearth of research on immigrant children's language affiliations and cultural positionings and their families' language polices, literacy practices, and options in language education. Parents must apply for a Certificate of Eligibility if they want their children to attend an English school. In the French system, classes d'accueil (welcome) were set up in the 1980s to help immigrant *allophone* children integrate into Quebec society. Some groups operate trilingual schools such as the Montreal Armenian Jewish Parochial and the Greek schools. Although Canada and Quebec have maintained *heritage* languages either through formal trilingual schools or informal Saturday schools, that *heritage* language schools have remained on the periphery of the national and provincial discourses about multiculturalism, schooling, and education is puzzling. Little has been documented about these spaces, notwithstanding the literacy practices and trajectories within them. Some children attend a trilingual school during the week and a Saturday school; some attend a dual track school and a Saturday school; others attend a dual track school with a cultural enrichment program such as the PELO programs (programmes d'ensignment de langues d'origine) developed for Italian, Portuguese, and Greek children. Just surveying their individual trajectories is much akin to the task of land surveyors mapping uncharted landscapes, let alone understanding what the linguistic landscapes offer to different generations and this generation of children themselves.

QUEBEC/MONTREAL: UNIQUE SPACES
FOR CONSTRUCTING IDENTITIES
AND HERITAGE LITERACIES

Quebec, an official unilingual French province, provides an interesting location for exploring multilingual literacies, identity politics, and diasporan spaces. French is spoken by a large majority of the population. In Montreal, communities with varied histories and immigration patterns speak in languages from all over the world. The nested contexts in Montreal (Maguire, 1994) offer a diversity of places to explore Lefebvre's (1991) triad of spaces in which multilingual learners can live critically between and among cultural and language differences. Having many mixed marriages has created a generation of trilingual or multilingual children—called *Bill 101 children*—who feel comfortable in multiple sociocultural and linguistic worlds. This generation, "young, educated and savvy," value and like being multilingual and multicultural. They "reject the idea of assimilation" (Semenak, 2000, p. A-1). Their language resilience led sociolinguists (Bourhis, 2001), sociologists (Bourdieu, 1990), and philosophers (Taylor, 1994) to speculate that heritage languages have more power and visibility in Montreal than in any other North American city. Although this may or may not always have been or be the case, children's identity constructions are enabled and constrained by their access to and appropriation of multiple literacy practices. Their literate actions must be viewed within the sociolinguistic and political landscapes that encourage or restrict their access to places and their own "social weighing of expressions" in particular spaces (Bakhtin, 1984).

Although the Canadian Education Association (1991) viewed heritage programs as valuable resources of the Canadian multicultural mosaic, they have not been the focus of mainstream theories of and research in second language education. Language choices and identity construction in these multilingual contexts are frequently journalistically reported as multifaceted and changing. A curiosity of the 2001 Canadian census is why immigrants who speak English, not French, are among the growing groups of "newcomers" to Montreal (Heinrich, 2003). This trend contrasts with the exodus out of the province in the mid-1970s when the Parti Quebecois emerged, enacted legislation (Bill 101) that mediated access to English schools, caused disruptions within and/or voluntary displacement of families, and presented new challenges to understanding identity politics in different spaces (Maguire, 2003). Willis (1985) maintains that "the notion of traveling through space is integral to the unfolding of history and the development of the individual's consciousness with regard to the past. The voyage over geographic space is an expanded metaphor for the process of one person's coming to know who she is" (p. 22). Identities are tied to the multidimensional workings of historical, institutional forces and political discourses that influence what Bakhtin (1990) calls one's ideological becoming. His vision of "self-fashioning," which Holland et al. (1998) call the "space of authoring," resonates with the literacy portraits emerging in our inquiry of children's identity construction, identification, and positioning. Yon (2000) maintains that "the passion for identity takes shape as assumptions about sameness or difference between selves and communities are brought into question and people begin to reflect upon who they are or worry about what they are becoming" (p. 2).

Hybrid identities, a common leitmotif in postmodern discourse, may reflect plural language affiliations, inheritances, and cultural allegiances. These in turn reflect individuals' attempts to reconcile the past with their present new cultural environments, different linguistic ecologies, old and new cultural traditions, and ways of being in the world. The complex identity politics some *allophone* children—those who are new arrivals, immigrants, or refugees—engage in as they negotiate language use and multiple social spaces is reflected in this excerpt from Reiko's field notes from her 3-year-old class at the Japanese Language Centre: "*Hiroshi has two names. His mother and everybody else around him (except the people at the language centre) call him Jean-Pierre. So, at the beginning, he did not respond to my calling Hiroshi-kun.*" The New Act (2002) refers to Canadian linguistic duality: "Minority official language communities have always nurtured our linguistic duality and made a strong contribution to our linguistic and cultural diversity . . . (they) are two wonderful wide open windows that give access to the world." Understandably, children's literate actions and life worlds are located in this complex politics of recognition. Quebec refers to the three language groups as *Francophones, Anglophones,* and *Allophones (Others)*—the latter being all those whose home language is neither English nor French. The very naming of linguistic groups as *Allophones* evokes a certain homogeneity of cultural groups as essentialist collective blocs of people who are seemingly different from the mainstream, dominant groups.

Immigrant parents in Quebec confront challenges when deciding on their children's schooling, language, and learning, as do the children in their literate actions. English, French, or a *heritage* language can become the lingua franca—the language of exchange and symbolic capital—in mainstream, heritage schools and playgrounds (Maguire, 1997). Certificates of Eligibility to English schools leave no doubt about immigrant parents' identity in a legal sense. Yet, when their children engage in the work of identity politics, it is often more complex than "belonging" to three legally designated language groups. The children cross back and forth between and among linguistic boundaries in their social interactions, language affiliations, and friendship patterns in Montreal, a city offering social spaces to examine identity politics, language, power, and authority issues. Rampton (1990) distinguishes between language inheritance (maintaining continuity between a closely linked group of people) and language affiliation (connecting groups that are otherwise diverse). These "terms can be used to discuss the position of individuals as well as groups" (p. 100). They enable researchers to move beyond traditional labels such as first or second, or mother tongue language, or majority/minority language groups and to consider Taylor's (1994) provocative questions: Who is seen? What is visible? Who is made visible? Who is made invisible? Who is recognized? Who is not recognized? And how are those who are not recognized then oppressed, excluded, marginalized, and silenced? Although there may be a widespread belief that literacy is desirable for all, the recognition of multilingual literacies problematizes the questions about whose literacy practices are recognized and what literacy practices children value, can access, and perceive they need to succeed in the triad of different spaces they want to negotiate. Diasporan and imagined communities can serve as spaces, real or imagined, for children's complex border crossings, intercultural communication, and appropriation of literacy practices in a globalized world. What is lost and gained in these three diasporan spaces examined here?

A caveat to consider: Wittgenstein (1958) argues that although we think we are tracing the nature of the thing, we are really only tracing the frame through which we view it. Our multilingual research group is a microcosm of the very phenomena—multiliteracies and multilingualism—we are trying to understand. The heritage contexts themselves keep changing as we attempt to engage in discussions about the chameleon meanings of literacy, becoming and being literate, as illustrated in these excerpts from our audiotaped dialogues: Hourig refers to the evolution of literacy within the Armenian context: "*The word literate in Armenian only refers to established writers and authors. . . . There was a political reasoning behind the creation of the alphabet and it really had to do with the preservation of the cultural heritage.*" Diane recalls the differences between printed and cursive handwriting in Armenian; the latter is not taught in schools here: "*When you were my teacher, you came from Armenia and you wrote in a script I couldn't . . . I could not decipher it. I had to sit down with my grandmother and she read it to me.*" Xiao Lan, who grew up during the Chinese Cultural Revolution, insists the meanings of Chinese literacy must be understood within this political context and its historical ties to Confucianism: "*Chinese literacy must be understood within its historical context and ties to Confucianism and the Chinese revolution. Pinyin is now used in Chinese Heritage language schools.*" Reiko's comment challenges the very label and meanings of "heritage language" in discussions of local literacies and historically nuanced meanings of literacies in these different spaces: "*We don't refer to Japanese as a heritage language.*" Family and community discursive literacy practices have been largely invisible to mainstream discourses and communities and even to ourselves when we were designing a project on "heritage schools." What is a heritage language school? Where is a heritage language school? How is a heritage language school? Why is a heritage language school? Who controls the finances, curriculum, and literacy resources of a heritage school?

The label *Heritage Language School* normally refers to the Saturday schools children attend to maintain their languages and cultures. Montreal schools are distinguished by their material building spaces and the community's identity and identification with the Quebec government. Some communities operate trilingual schools that are funded and clearly visible as institutional buildings with identifying logos. The American label *heritage language* refers to non-English languages spoken in the United States. In the Canadian Heritage Languages Institute Act, it means "a language, other than one of the two official languages of Canada, that contributes to the linguistic heritage of Canada." We view *heritage* as the funds of knowledge (Moll & Dworin, 1996) and social capital (Bourdieu, 1990) students from diverse backgrounds bring to different spaces. Arguing that children's positioning is a recursive process that exists in different sociocultural, historical, and political arenas, we turn to the three diasporas—Armenian, Chinese, and Japanese—and examine possibilities for conceptualizing identity and identity politics in these places and spaces.

RECOGNIZING THE ARMENIAN CONTEXT: FROM DIASPORAN SETTLEMENT TO IMAGINED COMMUNITIES

A bubble	Պղպջակ
A bubble tastes like soap gone bad. A bubble smells like honey. A bubble feels like a solid beehive. A bubble looks like a magical flying ball. A bubble sounds like the flight of a delicate butterfly.	Պղպջակը առուած oճառի ճամ ունի: Պղպջակը պատրաստուած մեղրի ճոտ ունի: Պղպջակը կարծր փեթակի մը զգացումը ունի: Պղպջակը կախարդական թոչող զնդակի տեսք ունի: Պղպջակը նուրբ թիթեռնիկի թռիչքին ծախն ունի:

Six-year-old Daron's phrase "A bubble sounds like the flight of a delicate butterfly" is an apt metaphor to enter Armenian diasporan spaces and locate Armenian literacy and identity. Recognized as a diasporic people in the traditional sense of being displaced from their homeland, Armenians' flight to geographical places can be traced back to the 11th century as the "last Armenian kingdom in historic Armenia fell" (Panossian, 2003). While integrating into new countries and spaces, they have maintained their languages, eastern and western dialects, and unique cultural identity as a collective, and created individual identities. The Armenian Apostolic church, its literacy culture, nationalist political ideology of "belonging to one nation," valuing and preserving of sacred manuscripts, has influenced an Armenian collective consciousness, however defined in this postmodern era. The Canadian Armenian community can be traced back to the late 1880s when Armenians immigrated, worked mostly in factories, and sent their earnings back to their country. Labeled as "Asiatics" by the Canadian government in 1908, the most pivotal moment linking Armenian diasporan communities is the 1915 genocide that resulted in persecution, slaughter, and destruction of ancestral villages and homelands. In the 1920s, through the Armenia Relief Association for Canada, the Canadian government admitted 100 Armenian orphans and trained the first group of 50—known as the "Georgetown Boys," who came from the orphanage of Corfu, Greece—in agriculture in the Quebec Eastern Townships. National religious feasts and cultural activities emerged called *hayapahpanoom*, or "the preservation of Armenian identity" (Sanjian, 2001). The Montreal Armenian community has grown since its settlement days of 225 to almost 30,000. Unlike the early generation who came from rural backgrounds, postwar "newcomers" were predominately urban, skilled individuals from countries such as Armenia, Syria, Lebanon, Turkey, Greece, and Iran.

The Armenian community's churches, schools, and community centers play a major role in sustaining "the Armenian heritage" and helping its members integrate into new communities. Such infrastructure organizations and material places provide a public face and offer new imagined spaces for the preservation of an Armenian identity. They combine as material, mental, and lived spaces in different ways for Armenian children. Thus, the concept of diaspora may now be more complex and synonymous with family relationships and socially networked groups than with a particular place or homeland. Shirinian (2000) explains the diaspora–homeland relationship:

> For Diaspora Armenian, the homeland can be lost territory, a historical western Armenian, that is Eastern Anatolia; it can be the short-lived Armenian Republic of 1918–1921; it might be the Soviet Armenia, 1921–1991; it could be the new independent Republic of Armenia, created in 1991 after the dissolution of the Soviet Union; it might be some imagined construct based on some or all of these, or it might be within the boundaries of the Armenian communities in Boston, Detroit, Los Angeles, Montreal, New York, or Toronto. (p. 1)

The vitality of these diasporan communities can be attributed in part to their establishment of heritage language schools. The Montreal schools are places where Armenian youth are provided material and imagined spaces to become "Armenian-Canadian"—individuals with a dual sense of belonging and active members of both heritage and mainstream societies. Central to Armenian identity and literacy practices has been the preservation of the languages and cultural traditions through its classics, poems, and sacred manuscripts and the palpable presence and coexistence of multiple languages and cultures.

Armenian Day Schools and Armenian Literacy

The Armenian day school here, one of three Montreal Armenian schools, operates with a double mission: offering students trilingual literacy practices and knowledge to preserve their heritage language and culture and integrate within the larger mainstream societies. It is an easily recognizable *place*; Armenian is spoken on the playground, heard and represented in classroom interactions and literacy resources. Partially subsidized by the Quebec Ministry of Education, its trilingual program includes French as the language of instruction, Armenian heritage studies (including language arts, history, and religion), and English as a Second Language. Introduction to Armenian literacy begins in kindergarten. French Immersion also begins in kindergarten and English in Grade 1. Noteworthy is the fact that *only* children from the Armenian community attend the school. Many students speak Armenian at home, are enrolled in activities at the Armenian community centre, and are socialized into literacy events in three languages. An Armenian student draws her representation of "Armenian Holy Cross" School (Fig. 7.2) with an identifying logo and the Armenian flag atop and her classroom at 7:30 a.m. (Fig. 7.3). She explains that she gave the school a fictitious name and "there are no children present because it is early in the morning." Although our researchers working within the Armenian community have had different lived experiences in the Armenian diaspora, all have taught at the day school. Arminée attended both the Armenian Saturday and day school and taught at the Saturday school before

FIG. 7.2.   Armenian Holy Cross School.

FIG. 7.3. Armenian Classroom at 7:30 a.m.

teaching at the day school. Diane attended kindergarten at the Armenian day school and the Saturday school while studying in French at a Montreal International school. Arminée and Diane are currently teaching in the school. Hourig grew up and attended an Armenian day school in Lebanon. Having taught at the day school after she moved to Montreal, she is concerned that the Armenian language and literacy will lose its functionality for this generation of children.

Historically, the alphabet dates back to 404–406 AD when Mesrop Mashtots, a court scribe turned priest scholar, created it with 36 letters (Attarian, 2002). The kingdom was partitioned by eastern and western regional powers of the Byzantine and Persian empires. Hourig explains that "both the Armenian king, Vramshapu, as well as the catholicos Sahak Partev, realized that the Armenian language could be the unifying factor needed and asked Mashtots, a revered scholar, to invent the alphabet. Mashtots opened schools with his students to teach and to translate books." Mashtots' students, she further explains, "became equally renowned scholars and opened their own schools." From the 5th century on, books and writing have been closely connected to the preservation of the Armenian language and identity. Armenian genocide survivor narratives "invariably refer to stories of mothers teaching the alphabet to their children by tracing the letters in the desert sands" (Attarian, 2002, pp. 1–2). Hourig comments about the evolving meanings of the word "literacy" in Armenian:

The word "literacy" in Armenian is meant to only signify the elementary deciphering/decoding of the language, nothing more. . . . The word "literate" in Armenian refers specifically to established writers/authors. However, the words "language" and "culture" are always used to talk about the preservation and continuity of the heritage. They are the two ingredients especially important for conserving the Armenian identity, most essentially in the diasporan contexts. Lately, a new word is put more and more into circulation, to indicate the active role of creating and constructing identity, as opposed to the more passive conserving aspect. (Team meeting audio tape, June 2002)

Although there is no recognizable materially bounded Armenian neighborhood, an *espace perçu*, the community has a very strong presence, *espace conçu* largely constructed through its institutions—its churches, schools, and youth organizations. However, the narrow, autonomous view of literacy (Street, 1995) reflected in the school textbooks and literacy practices led Hourig to volunteer her time to conduct and videotape Saturday Fun Writing sessions for a small group of children in the basement of a family friend. This *espace conçu* reconnects to Daron's poem that frames the introduction to this section. Hourig's rationale for creating Armenian literacy practices in an informal place outside the official Saturday or day school can be more fully appreciated when viewed against the larger canvas of the Armenian community as diasporan and discursive literacy practices of the Armenian day school. The next literacy events evoke an appreciation of children's positionings in those elusive moments when they confront the work of identity politics, their creativity and voice in more than one language and dialect. They resonate with Appadurai's (2003) statement about the image, imagined, and imaginary—"These are all terms which direct us to something critical and new in global cultural processes—the imagination as social practice" (p. 30).

> *Daron's Structurings and Images.* Even though Daron went about his usual "structurings" in his poem (in Armenian), in both cases he built them around beautifully created images. He felt at ease with the imagery he created and was very sure of what it was he wanted to convey. In one instance, when he had composed an image using the sense of hearing to describe his subject, he had written that it resembled the sound of "the flight of a delicate butterfly"— *nourp titernigi me trichkin tsayne ouni.* I asked him if he rather meant "delicate flight of a butterfly." He gave me a disapproving look and insisted he knew what he was writing. "Delicate" was to modify "butterfly" and not "flight."

> *Talar Gliding In and Out of Four Languages.* Seven-year-old Talar attended an Armenian heritage language school for a year. Her parents made a decision to pull her out of this setting. She now attends a mainstream French public school. Talar speaks the Eastern dialect of Armenia because both her parents are originally from Armenia. Her father is concerned that she has started to

forget the Armenian alphabet. Even though her parents speak only Armenian at home, Talar prefers to use French. As her paternal grandmother is a Russian speaker, Talar effectively glides in and out of four languages. Before Talar's arrival, the main language of interaction in our small circle was in Western Armenian. Talar's arrival changed the group dynamics naturally. The children immediately started using all the Eastern Armenian they knew.

Diaspora, in its traditional sense of *displacement from homeland as in the diaspora in the Republic of Armenia*, is still central to the discourse on Armenian identity. However, it goes beyond *this place* to *those spaces* inhabited by parents and grandparents in diverse diasporan communities. It takes on more widespread meanings as new technologies such as telephones, jets, fax machines, the Internet, and media expand the possible spaces for diaspora networking, cultural dialogues about belonging, and what it means to be Armenian. Hourig's Saturday literacy sessions provide an *espace perçu*, a material place and *espace vécu*—spaces for children to create poems, stories, and anecdotes and discover their own meanings of Armenianness in their daily lives. Each will imagine the diaspora, construct their visions of homeland, and engage in identity politics in different ways.

UNDERSTANDING A CHINESE CONTEXT: FROM BOUNDED ARCHES TO IMAGINED WORLDS

The Chinese community, estimated to be 42,765 and the fourth largest minority in Montreal, is often perceived as bounded, homogenous, and "Asian looking." Chinese people have scattered around the world as they seek a better life and social justice for themselves and their families. Seven-year-old Amanda is very aware of being Chinese, multilingual, and attending "Chinese School." City-installed golden arches to Chinatown in downtown Montreal lead one to conceptualize this community as fixed, bounded, and a discrete culture. Despite its visible, physical presence as "China Town," there is much heterogeneity within the community that includes several groups, based on different immigration waves and origin of the home country, such as Taiwan, Hong Kong, Singapore, or other countries in southeast Asia. From 1923–1947, through a racial Exclusion Act, immigration from China was prohibited. From 1947–1967, Chinese immigrants who were mainly Cantonese speakers could enter Canada if sponsored by families. In the 1980s, Chinese immigration increased through the federal government's business immigration investment program, attracting immigrants from Hong Kong and Taiwan who speak Mandarin. The Chinese community includes older immigrants and newcomers, Canadian and foreign-born Chinese, Cantonese- and Mandarin-speaking Chinese, investment immigrants and refugee claimants, and immigrants from urban and rural regions.

Chinese Heritage Language, Zhonguo School
and Chinese Literacy

Many Chinese heritage schools, established to maintain Chinese traditions and languages, employ different dialects and phonetic systems (Pinyin or Zhuyinfuhao) as instructional tools for the teaching of either the simplified or the classical Chinese characters. Curdt-Christiansen (2003) describes the seven major dialects as mutually unintelligible: Mandarin, Cantonese, Wu, Xiang, Gan, Kejia, and Min. In 1958, the Chinese government aimed to promote mass education and initiated a language reform by simplifying classical Chinese characters. As immigration from mainland China increases, the community faces changes in the uses of Chinese scripts. Recently, Montreal's newest Chinese language newspaper, Sinoquebec/Chinese, featured some articles in simplified characters rather than the complex characters. In Chinatown, one can see the evolution of written Chinese as an ongoing transformation from the traditional script handed down by parents and grandparents to current reform uses of Chinese script—a literacy evolution influenced by history, politics, and culture, in addition to geography. The demand for schools where parents can send their children for language and cultural education resulted in the development of eight Chinese Heritage Schools in Montreal.

Earlier comments from Yoyo and Zhuzi, next, reflect the diversity among Montreal Chinese children as they negotiate their identities within Chinese and Canadian/Quebec linguistic contexts.

> The studies and lessons at Zhonguo (school) remind me of China. It makes me feel that I am still living there. What I see are people with yellow skin and black hair, what I hear are the familiar sounds of our language. All that happened at Zhonguo (school) reminds me of my classmates and teachers far away in China, my grandparents and the environment I was so familiar with, I miss them. When one day I have the opportunity, I will go back to visit them. (Chinese text by Zhuzi translated from an article in a local Chinese newspaper)

Some children like Zhuzi express strong affiliation to their Chinese grandparents in China and connect to China, its people, culture, and language. Others have difficulty communicating in Chinese with other Chinese children for a number of reasons that can be attributed to either their language loss or dialect differences that their parents and grandparents speak at home. The Zhonguo school, founded in 1994 as a private Saturday school to respond to parents' needs for language affiliation and cultural maintenance, is a discursive space that is autonomous. With no formal connections to the school boards in Quebec or government, or financial funding from the Ministry of Education, it has no recognizable voice in the public discourse of schooling nor recognizable physically bounded space, although it is the largest of the eight schools. Because school officials rent space in a Montreal institution as its location on the weekends for activities, as a discursive place, it has no visible logo that explicitly signals it as a "Chinese school." Of the 1,000 children who are predominately Chinese, 80% come from Mainland China, 10% from Hong Kong, and the remaining 10% come from Taiwan or are Caucasian Canadians who have intermarried. The mission of this school is to create a place where Chinese (Mandarin) is taught and *Pinyin* (Chinese phonetic script) is used to teach simplified Chinese characters, the standard script of China. It offers courses in Mandarin language arts, mathematics, Chinese chess, drawing/painting, national dance, music, and martial arts. English and French courses are also available for newcomers. Most of the teachers were professional teachers in China. There are varied patterns of code switching among the children that seem mostly determined by their socialization, language affiliations, friendship patterns, and family situations. The literacy resources are largely standard textbooks that teach Chinese moral and cultural values and reflect the Chinese national curriculum that many of the children have difficulty engaging with. The literacy teaching methodology is mainly teacher centered. Living in a multicultural/multilingual city with diverse resources, the Zhonguo students appropriate the discourses accessible to them and reveal their identities through their own acts of writing and creation of imagined spaces, as illustrated in Fig. 7.4. Amanda

FIG. 7.4.　Amanda's drawing of herself and friends at Zhonguo School.

offers her commentary on "her Chinese school" and representation of herself and her friends.

Children's appropriation of multilingual literacies can emerge within diasporan or imagined communities. One can look locally at the individual in the social world and imaginatively at the social worlds in an individual's spatial mapping. For example, even though Chinese cultural commodities are available and the Montreal Chinese community has had, since the turn of the century, a well-established public space and face, Beebee reflects on her own identity as "Asian-looking" in relation to other minority children in a culturally diverse school. Her reflections offer an example of the ways in which children's identities are relational in character. Her self-understandings about differences and discrimination have an emotional resonance that impacts on her sense of belonging, socialization, and friendship patterns in her "everyday school" and her other school—"Chinese school":

> I have two schools, one is French and English everyday school Hillrose Academy and the other school is every Saturday Chinese school, Zhonguo school. At my everyday school a boy and I are the only Asian looking people. The rest of them are mainly from Italy or Greece. They look differently from me, they look like Canadians. There are Greek, Italian, Hebrew, and English heritage language classes in the school, but no Chinese or Japanese classes. I do not like my school very much because people make fun of me and call me Chinese girl instead of my name. I try to ignore them. I do not make fun of Italian people because Chloe is my best friend and she is Italian. . . . I don't have as many friends in Zhonguo as in Hillrose, but they are very nice to me. Everybody is Chinese looking with brown eyes and black hair except Xiao An. She is totally blond with very blue eyes. My parents say that they can't believe she is half Chinese. Anyway, she is my best friend in Zhonguo. (Beebee, 9)

Although Hillrose Academy is culturally diverse, Beebee comments on her outsider status in this space. Ironically, her best friend, Xiao An, also attends Zhonguo school. Born in Canada, Xiao An has blond hair and blue eyes; her mother is Chinese and her father is an English-speaking Canadian. A comfortable reader, writer, and speaker in all three languages, she sees herself as a Chinese, White, Canadian with a clear sense of allegiance to her Chinese roots in the following narrative. She deliberately wrote her title, "Chopsticks," in Chinese characters, signaling her Chinese language expertise and connecting readers to her Chinese background through her declarative statement about the lunch she brought to school. The text is also an example of literacy moments that illustrate the complex, contextual worlds of multilingual children, where subtle shifts and slides of meaning collide, occur, and re-occur:

> One day, while I was in 5th grade, I brought chopsticks to school because I had noodles. I found out that the microwave we had in our class was in an-

other class so I had to go to the other class to warm up my noodles. It made me feel weird to walk into a 4th-grade class to warm up noodles. I had to go get their lunch teacher and that meant walking around the class a lot. I hated doing that. When I went back to class and started eating noodles with chopsticks, seven to ten people crowded around my desk looking at me or saying I was weird or asking if I was Chinese. I felt like yelling at them and telling them mind their own bees wax but I didn't say anything. I just kept feeling angry until the teacher came and shooed them away.

An interesting pattern emerges in both culturally diverse mainstream and heritage language schools where some students feel comfortable, welcomed, and able to celebrate their heritage languages, and situations where that is not the case because of either constraining pedagogical approaches, complex cultural negotiations, or discrimination. The imagination and the imaginary must become intertwined social practices and imagined spaces for children to construct their identities and develop their own textual and conceived spaces (Appadurai, 2003). For example, Beebee mixes fantasy and reality as the magic and wizardry of Harry Potter intermingle with Chinese ancestors and her everyday suburban lived experiences as illustrated in excerpts from her story:

Mirror

Hi, my name is Yook-sin-lee, I was given a mirror. At first it looked a normal antique mirror. I got this particularly special mirror from my grandfather the general of the Chinese war.

After I came home from school, I fixed myself a sandwich and stomped up the stairs. I took a bite of my sandwich as I glanced into the mirror and stared in horror; you'd never believe what I saw, a sage running from an evil looking wizard and he ran thorough the mirror and into my room.

"Expelliarmus!" cried the sage and the wizard disappeared into smoke.

"How, what, where, why? How did you do that? Why did you come here?" I asked excitedly.

Afterwards, this sage told me that his world had had an intrusion. The sage looked familiar, but I didn't know from where.

"My name is Chang Yo, I'm the great wizard of Chinta and these invaders are destroying my land, please, pretty please with sugar on top help us!" he hollered sounding like a baby begging for candy. I didn't know what to say so I said I'd think about it. . . . somehow I returned to my own room. Oh great joy! I was home. I looked down and there was the bravery medal. I knew I had brought peace to Chinta.

How multilingual children perceive and choose from or resist the array of mediational means accessible to them, and reveal or conceal their identity is indeed chameleon. The Japanese diaspora provides an interesting example of this chameleon-like stance across generations. The transnational spaces of globalization accessible through the technology of cell phones, digital games, and Walkmans now transcend any particular place for Japanese children and their life worlds in Montreal, in contrast to the discrimination and invisibility that their Japanese ancestors experienced after World War II.

REVEALING JAPANESE CONTEXTS: FROM INTERNMENT AND INVISIBILITY TO GLOBALIZATION AND TRANSNATIONALISM

The Montreal Japanese Language Centre is a material place and social space for developing networks and relationships and socializing children. When Yoshida asked a group of 5-year-olds to draw their Japanese school, many drew portraits of their friends. However, one 5-year-old drew Anpan-man (red-bean man) and Baikin-man (virus-man), a popular Japanese cartoon that represents Japanese cultural mannerisms, morals, and values to children worldwide (Fig. 7.5). However, Japanese literacy and heritage schooling must be located within the different generations of Issei, Nisei, Sansei, and Yonsei—Japanese terms used to describe first-, second-, third-, and fourth-generation Japanese in Canada—and within the dual spaces of the Japanese-born "returnee" children who come to Montreal and eventually return to Japan. These different spaces of "being and speaking Japanese" intersect in the

FIG. 7.5. Drawing of Anpan-man (red bean man).

Montreal Japanese schools. Makabe (1998) examines the different aspirations of the four Canadian Japanese generations: Whereas the Issei strongly identified themselves as Japanese and speakers of Japanese, the Nisei attempted to escape the postwar burden of racism and discrimination by retaining little of their ethnic identity, integrating and becoming "Hakujun-like children" (p. 5). The Sansei and Yonsei generations, who have tended to intermarry, may know little about the diasporan experiences of Japanese immigrants and Japanese-born Canadians after World War II.

The Montreal Japanese community, the smallest of the three communities examined here, is estimated at 2,360. Census 2001 data indicates only 2% of the Canadian population are Japanese. This contrasts with the 23,000 Japanese living mostly in British Columbia in the 1940s, who began to move to Montreal in large numbers in 1942 when the federal government forced their evacuation from west coast communities, interned them in labor camps, and devised a dispersal plan for their homes and assets:

> Their fear of visibly regrouping and of inciting continued racial discrimination was as strong as, and in conflict with, their need for group reassurance and support. . . . Japanese Canadians in Montreal today remain dispersed in terms of the areas they live in, the work they do and the schools they send their children to. They have avoided visible concentration as a collective, hoping to blend in, unnoticed into the larger population. (Bourgault, 1987, p. 24)

Unlike the public face and material *espace perçu* of the Chinese community and *espace conçu* of the Armenian community through its institutional structures, there is no physically demarcated space or identifying markers of "a Japanese community" in Montreal. Until the 1980s, the *espace veçu*, daily lived spaces of Japanese living here, included a strong intergenerational network of people linked through its community-organized social activities such as annual bazaars, church attendance, dinner dances, and picnics. By the Issei generation making themselves less visible as a community as a conscious, strategic choice, many second generation integrated-minded (Nisei) and third generation (Sansei) Japanese Canadians have lost their mother tongue. The history of this dispersed community confounds the definition of Japanese as a heritage language, which is further confounded if we distinguish between Japanese "returnee" children who return to Japan and those who have made or plan to make their home in Canada. After a long invisible presence since World War II, the 1970s saw an influx of Japanese into the city due to booming Japanese and Montreal economies and the opening of two schools, the Montreal Hoshuko School and the Montreal Japanese Language Centre.

The Hoshuko was founded in 1972 in response to demands of Japanese parents living overseas that their children receive Japanese education while living out of Japan. As the number of Japanese people working for Japanese companies in the Quebec region increased, the Montreal *Shokokai* (the Japanese Association of Commerce and Industry), with the support of the Japanese Ministries of Foreign Affairs and Education, supported the Hoshuko. Since its establishment, it has been financially and administratively assisted and managed by the members of the *Shokokai*—the driving cultural and financial force of the school and its mission. Yoshida (2001) identifies two types of families: those whose aspirations are linked to Japan and those whose aims are to integrate into the local environment. Some parents were members of the *Shokokai* (business people who worked for Japanese corporations such as Mitsui, Mitsubishi, and the Bank of Tokyo) and some were academics. Despite differences in the families' approaches toward their children's education, both types of families felt that the Hoshuko was essential for their children's education as "Japanese," however defined. Most Hoshuko steering committee members were also members of the *Shokokai*. Until 1997, the principal of the Japanese Hoshuko was also the president of the *Shokokai*.

The Japanese population increased and decreased in tandem with the development of the Montreal and the Japanese economies during the 1970s and Quebec political legislation in 1977. Reaching its peak in 1989 with 95 students, the goal of the school continued to focus on keeping up with the Japanese school curriculum. The Hoshuko teachers embraced the mission of the school—to teach what students in Japan learn at school—and closely followed the guidelines for the teachers (*kyoiku shido yoryo*) provided by the Japanese Ministry of Education (Ishibashi, 1993). Despite the Japan-centered atmosphere of the Hoshuko since the mid-1980s, Canadian-born children whose parents had emigrated from Japan started to attend the school. This new student population changed the school's cultural portrait as a "Japanese school" and created tensions within this previously clearly defined "Japanese conceived space." In the 1980s, the student population decreased due to the exodus of Japanese (and many other) corporations out of Quebec; ironically, this exodus made the Hoshuko more inclusive. In 2003, the student population is split between Japanese-born and Canadian-born Japanese children. The number of students from mixed marriages has increased, bringing more diversity to the Montreal Hoshuko, which is no longer just an academic *institutional place* to cram Japanese educational materials into students for smooth reentry to another *institutional place*. It has become a *place of* and *space for* intercultural socialization.

Yoshida (2001) documents how the experiences of contemporary young Japanese Canadians in Montreal are quite different from those who experienced internment camps decades ago. An Issei Japanese recalls this dark period in Canadian politics in an interview with Yoshida at the Montreal Japanese Canadian Cultural Centre: "*After the internment (during World War*

II) all Japanese wanted to do was to blend in. They didn't want to stick out at all. That's why they moved here to Montreal and to eastern Canada in general. It was easier to re-begin life again." The Nisei generation largely integrated into Canadian society. The Sansei and Yonsei generation live in seemingly transnational spaces. The new technologies and commodification of Japanese popular culture of cartoons and magazines, electronic media, and television dramas that children can access is changing their evaluative orientations toward their identity and identification with Japan and being Japanese. Pokemon is as popular with Montreal-born Japanese students as with Japanese-born students. In the next literacy moment, an example of identity construction and identification within transnational spaces and the Internet, Masato reveals his chameleon approach to identity.

Masato's Musings: Cyberspace and Transnationalism

Mataso: People often ask me this question. On the Internet, I am always asked, Where are you from? I first say Canada.

RY: Why?

Masato: Why? I wonder why . . . But when I "chat" with the same person for a long time, I will eventually tell this person the truth, that my parents are Japanese.

RY: What do you say?

Masato: Usually, I would say, "To tell you the truth, I was born in Canada, but my parents are from Japan." Then, most of the time, the person would respond saying, "Cool!"

RY: Do you think saying "I am from Canada, but my parents are from Japan" is the same thing as saying "I am Japanese"? Do you think you are Japanese?

Masato: Well, I don't care much about these [identity] issues. But in my class, there are people who like Japanese Anime [Japanese cartoons]. To them, I would say, "Ha, ha, you are from here, and I am from Japan!" Usually, I would say I am from Canada first, but when it is better to say "Japan," I would say that I am Japanese. When I am in Japan and asked to identify myself, I would say I am Japanese. My response would vary depending on where I am . . .

Masato's comments connect back to the two metaphors we used as entry points to this chapter: "politics of recognition" and the "chameleon character of identity construction." Taylor (1994) states "the demand for recognition . . . is given urgency by the supposed links between recognition and identity, where this latter term designates something like a person's understanding of who they are, of their fundamental defining characteristics as a human being" (p. 5). Identity can be a space that may be shared or resisted, material or imagined, constructed from the past or for the future, or simply lived in the present. Yoshida's conversations with the students reveal that their self-identification as Japanese and with Japan is derived from the recognition that they perceive they receive from their classmates at their local schools. She also attributes this positive self-image to the expansion and marketing of Japanese popular culture and commodities, which are easily available, and the Internet, which opens up transnational spaces, virtual attachments, imagined journeys and interactions, and new ways of belonging and being recognized. What does this mean for Japanese literacy?

Historically, literacy has engaged the interests of many Western scholars. Japanese scholars may be reluctant to approach literacy issues that might be attributed to difficulties in defining literacy standards because of the different scripts: *Hiragana* (used mainly for sentence particles, some nouns and verbs and adjective endings), *Katakana* (used for transcribing foreign words), and Chinese characters, *Kanji* (used mainly for nouns and the stems of verbs and adjectives). However, computers and the global Pokemonization of children's cultural artifacts such as video games and transformer toys are the current currency of Japanese culture and the literacies capturing children's imagined spaces. For example, certainly, Doraemon, a popular Manga cartoon, has impacted children's Japanese literacy in Japan and Montreal (Leek, 1997). This blue cat-robot with a four dimensional pocket filled with useful gadgets emerged in the 1970s and expanded to other Asian and Western countries. His traditional gadgets—Dokodeomo Door (Wherever Door) that allows him to go anywhere, the Time Machine that allows him to travel in time, and the Take-copter (a tiny helicopter blade to wear on his head) that allows him to fly—appeal to Japanese and non-Japanese children's imagination, introducing them to a world of multiple literacies as illustrated in Fig. 7.6.

Doraemon projects the image of a reliable friend; born in the 22nd century, his traveling time and space projects occupy children's and adults' imaginative spaces. For example, the Doraemon character Nobita's daily life includes mundane foibles such as being late for school, getting yelled at by the Sensei teacher, or by mother for bad grades or forgetting his books and backpack (Shiraishi, 1997). The characters move back and forth in time, space, and place with an "otherworldliness" that contrasts with the images of internment, redress, resettlement, and relocation of Japanese Canadians after World War II. Doraemon popular culture includes many types of literacies, representations of literacy practices, and travels to past, present, and future places. The portable technology of cell phones, digital games, cameras, Walkman, and the popularity of Mangas thus offer a wide range of goods and services to children. These literacy practices may well displace traditional practices such as family storybook reading and replace familiar literacy tools such as magnetic alphabets, crayons, and pencils. The impact of electronic literacies on children's lit-

FIG. 7.6. Drawing of Doraemon.

eracy practices, ideological knowledge making, identity politics, and cultural positionings is yet to be determined.

REFLECTING ON MULTILINGUALISM AND RE-SEARCHING IN HERITAGE LANGUAGE PLACES AND SPACES

Multilingualism sheds light on multiple literacies and children's identity politics. Multiple places and spaces challenge essentialist and dichotomized concepts of identity and minority/heritage languages. Dialogic perspectives and multiple spaces free children from the idea that collectives or individuals can hold only one perspective at a time (Holland et al., 1998, p. 5). Critical human geographers (Lefebvre, 1991; Soja, 1996) argue for a relational view of space rather than a fixed preexisting space in which things are embedded. Like identities that can be sites of struggle or possibilities for reconstructing selfhood, spaces and places can be contested, resisted, reconceived, and imagined. Lefebvre's triad of spaces—the perceived, the conceived, and the lived spaces—become open texts offering multilingual children differing and multiple possibilities for selfhood and dialogue with others. Space can be a place through which multilingual children speak and can be. Space can be a place to imagine new worlds or remember old ones. Space can be a place through which they reflect on their lived experiences and discover their own spatial possibilities for selfhood and create new landscapes within which they define themselves.

We juxtaposed local, literacy moments that provide insights into children's complex subjectivities and construction of new ways of being within global and political discourses. We explored the roles of heritage languages in framing issues of identity and identification within three diasporic spaces. Cultural geographies of local encounters are mapped within a triad of spaces in which identities are constructed within either collective or individual spaces, real or imagined, shared or resisted, visible or invisible. The chapter's subtitle reflects our team's present living with the uneasy terrains between powerful forms of authority, historical and economic forces, and individual resistance, creativity, and voice in human discourse and identity construction in these heritage language spaces. It draws attention to the self-reflexivity entailed in identity construction among multilingual children and the challenges researchers face working in multilingual contexts and understanding the social capital of multiple literacy practices. As the chameleon portraits of the three diasporan spaces illustrate, each space has a complex, unique development that relates to historical, economic, and political issues in the country or culture of origin during immigration waves and political climates. We evoked a Bakhtinian dialogic view of language as an interpretive lens for understanding the diversity of the Montreal *heritage* spaces in order to illustrate that utterances and texts are always dialogic because they are answerable to others' words in particular times, spaces, and places. However, *that* dialogue entails a form of answerability that is morally responsive to unique others and particular relationships. Indeed, heritage language literacy portraits are not very visible within the hegemonic discourse of second language acquisition research (Maguire & Beer, 2002). Why is that so? And why not? These questions provoke methodological, theoretical, and practical challenges in drawing portraits of heritage language schools, interpreting children's literate actions, and appreciating their life worlds within these spaces.

Life world refers to space(s) for community living where local and specific meanings can be made. *Worlds of literacy* refers to the distinct literacies that exist alongside each other in complex societies (Barton, 2000). Each world has its own literacy practices, historical moments, and key literacy instances that are sometimes taken for granted or go unrecognized. The heritage portraits suggest not only some of the complexities in the work of identity and identification but also the transitions that are taking place within these spaces. They challenge essentialist labels of second language learners and researchers' claims to be able to represent bilingual or multilingual learners independent of their contextualized lived experiences (Maguire, 1999; Maguire & Graves, 2001). Thus, we focused on local portraits and elusive moments when children engage the work of identity, and used a larger canvas to consider the heritage schools as discursive places and spaces with different historical trajectories, diaspora communities of practices, and meanings of literacies. In either mainstream or heritage schools, the playground frequently becomes the space for multilingual children to engage in identity politics. Gee (2001) and Taylor (1994) argue that the kind of person one is recognized as being at a given time and place can change from moment to moment in the interaction and can change from context to context. Luke (2003) argues that "to move forward both in research and policy towards a more inclusive literacy in multilingual societies is a task that will require broader, more complex forms of social science, not reductionist ones" (p. 140).

The multilingual/multicultural character of our research group contributes greatly to the reflective understandings we have constructed to date: (a) *Multiliteracy development is deeply rooted in sociocultural historical, economic, and political forces that are sometimes visible and sometimes invisible*; (b) *becoming and being biliterate or multiliterate is a complex, dynamic relational process*; (c) *the act of finding one's voice can only occur in contexts of equity, justice, and mutual respect and trust*; and (d) *what children experience as literacy practices in communities, classrooms, families, and schools are not neutral, cultural, social, economic, linguistic, political phenomena*. Because multilingual children have a foot in many cultural places and spaces, they do not seem to straddle the stereotypic "two solitudes" linguistic divide between Anglophones and Francophones, mythologized by Canadian writer Hugh MacLennan. Many create multiple spaces for themselves that allow for strategic engagement in social interactions with others in real or imagined spaces. Thus, multilingual children's literacies are imbued with power, ideologies, nuanced cultural meanings, and positionings about identity, both personal and collective. Taking a languages-as-resources orientation, we believe that *heritage* languages should be, but are not necessarily, viewed as sociocultural capital within mainstream society (Cummins, 1996). The dialectic between local and global literacies serves as a reasoning heuristic to confront the ambiguities of multilingual literacies, to make heritage schools more visible in the public discourse of schooling, and to recognize the ways in which power relations constitutes a site's discursive literacy practices and construction of individual, collective, and/or hybrid identities. Whereas the children see the power, potential, and symbolic capital of their multiliterate abilities, their teachers often do not seem to recognize their funds of knowledge. The children frequently reflect on their own sense of self, their insider and outsider status, their sense of belonging, race, and ethnicity as they weave their multiple literacies into their day-to-day activities and construct their identities. Understanding the relationships between individuals, social practices, and political discourses is critical for those in periods of rapid transition. It is especially important for children when different languages and cultures intersect in their classrooms and playground spaces and when these differences go unrecognized and cause disjunctures or even ruptures in their life worlds. Children define their identities by locating themselves in functional material spaces such as schools, relational spaces constructed and negotiated with friends and families. They explore the lived, ethical spaces of their own evaluative orientations and imagined and lived spaces which in turn challenge the very label "heritage/minority language." Above all, they challenge researchers re-searching in multiple places and spaces.

ACKNOWLEDGMENTS

The prime objective of our Heritage Language Research Group is to understand how children from nonmainstream backgrounds, who have diverse school experiences, negotiate their multilingual literacies in multiple spaces. This research was funded by NCTE (National Council of Teachers of English) and SSHRC (Social Sciences and Humanities Research Council of Canada). Members of the Research Group are Professors Ann J. Beer and Mary H. Maguire and graduate students Hourig Attarian, Diane Baygin, Xiao Lan Curdt-Christiansen, Ephie Konidaris, Heekyeong Lee, Arminée Yaghejian, and Reiko Yoshida.

REFERENCES

Anderson, B. (1983). *Imagined communities.* London: Verso.
Appadurai, A. (2003). Disjuncture and difference in the global economy. In J. E. Braziel & A. Mannur (Eds.), *Theorizing diaspora: A reader* (pp. 25–28). Oxford: Blackwell Publishing.
Attarian, H. (2002). *Through the looking glass: A literacy narrative across generations.* Paper presented at the Second University of Vigo International Conference on Bilingualism, Vigo, Spain.
Bakhtin, M. M. (1984). *Problems of Dostoevsky's poetics* (C. Emmerson, Trans.). Minneapolis: University of Minnesota.
Bakhtin, M. M. (1990). Art and answerability. In M. Holquist & V. Viapunov (Eds.), *Art and answerability: Early philosophical essays by M. M. Bakhtin.* Austin, TX: University of Texas Press.
Barton, D. (2000). Foreword. In M. Martin-Jones & K. Jones (Eds.), *Multilingual literacies: Reading and writing different worlds.* Amsterdam, The Netherlands: John Benjamins Publishing.

Baygin, D. (2001). *Thinking, speaking and learning in French literacy development in kindergarten: The case of a heritage language setting.* Paper presented at the Centre d'études éthniques de l'université de Montréal/Centre for Ethnic Studies at the University of Montreal. (CEETUM)

Bourdieu, P. (1990). *In other words: Essays towards a reflexive sociology.* Stanford, CA: Stanford University Press.

Bourgault, E. (Trans.). (1987). *Repartir à zero; Perspectives sur l'experience des Canadiens d'origine japonaise au Quebec* [Perspectives on the Japanese Canadian experience in Quebec]. Japanese Canadian Cultural Centre of Montreal (JCCCM).

Bourhis, R. Y. (2001). Reviewing language shift in Quebec. In J. A. Fishman (Ed.), *Can threatened languages be saved?* (pp. 1001–1141). Clevedon: Multilingual Matters.

Braziel, J. E., & Mannur, A. (Eds.). (2003). *Theorizing diaspora: A reader.* Oxford: Blackwell.

Canadian Education Association. (1991). *Heritage language programs in Canadian school boards.* Toronto: Author.

Cummins, J. (1996). *Negotiating identities: Education for empowerment in a diverse society.* Ontario, CA: California Association for Bilingual Education.

Curdt-Christiansen, X. L. (2003). *Growing up trilingual: Triliteracy practices of immigrant Chinese children in Quebec.* Unpublished doctoral dissertation, McGill University.

Gee, J. (2001). Identity as an analytic lens for research in education. *Review of Research in Education, 25,* 99–126.

Hall, S. (2003). Cultural identity and diaspora. In J. E. Braziel & A. Mannur (Eds.), *Theorizing diaspora: A reader* (pp. 234–246). Oxford: Blackwell.

Heinrich, J. (2003, February 8). "Allo Anglos": Immigrants who favor English are among the fastest growing groups of newcomers to Montreal. *The Montreal Gazette,* p. E1.

Holland, D., Lachiotte, N., Jr., Skinner, D., & Cain, C. (1998). *Agency and identity in cultural worlds.* Cambridge, MA: Harvard University Press.

Ishibashi, T. (1993). *Multiple ways of looking at bilingual children's writing: Case studies of Japanese children learning in an elementary school and their home contexts.* Unpublished manuscript, Faculty of Education Library, McGill University, Montreal.

Ivanic, R. (1998). *Writing and identity: Discoursal construction of identity in academic writing.* Philadelphia: John Benjamins.

Leek, N. (1997). *An introduction to famous Japanese TV and movie characters.* Retrieved August 2003 from http://www.cusd.chicak12.ca.us/librraries/elementary/japan/famousjps.html.

Lefebvre, H. (1991). *The production of space* (D. Nicholson-Smith, Trans.). Cambridge, England: Blackwell.

Luke, A. (2003). Literacy and the other: A sociological approach to literacy research and policy in multilingual societies. *Reading Research Quarterly, 38*(1), 132–141.

Maguire, M. H. (1994). Cultural stances of two Quebec bilingual children informing storytelling. *Comparative Education Review, 38*(1), 144–155.

Maguire, M. H. (1997). Shared and negotiated territories: The socio-cultural embeddedness of children's acts of meaning. In A. Pollard, D. Thiessen, & A. Filer (Eds.), *Children and their curriculum: The perspectives of primary and elementary school children* (pp. 51–80). London: Falmer Press.

Maguire, M. H. (1999). A bilingual child's choices and voices: Lesson in listening, noticing and understanding. In B. Franklin (Ed.), *Reading and writing in more than one language.* TESOL, 115–149.

Maguire, M. H. (2003). *Identity and agency in primary trilingual children's multiple cultural worlds: What role do heritage languages play?* Paper presented at the 4th International Conference on Bilingualism, Tempe, Arizona.

Maguire, M. H., & Beer, A. J. (2002). *Researching multiple literacies in heritage language contexts: Finding that third space.* Paper presented at the Second University of Vigo International Conference on Bilingualism, Vigo, Spain.

Maguire, M. H., & Graves, B. (2001). Speaking personalities in primary children's second language writing. *TESOL Quarterly, 35*(4), 561–593.

Makabe, T. (1998). *The Canadian Sansei.* Toronto, Ontario: University of Toronto Press.

Moll, L. C., & Dworin, J. (1996). Biliteracy development in classrooms: Social dynamics and cultural possibilities. In D. Hicks (Ed.), *Discourse, learning, and schooling* (pp. 221–245). Cambridge: Cambridge University Press.

Panossian, R. (2003). *The Armenian diaspora today: Lobby, politics, and identity.* Paper presented at the World Congress of Basque Centres of Clubs, Victoria-Gasteiz, Spain.

Rampton, M. B. H. (1990). Displacing the "native speaker" expertise, affiliation, and inheritance. *ELT Journal, 44*(2), 97–101.

Sanjian, A. (2001, Spring/Summer). The Armenian minority experience in the modern Arab world. *Bulletin of the Royal Institute for Inter-Faith Studies, 3*(1), 149–179.

Semenak, S. (2000, February 12). Young allophones proud of their roots. *The Montreal Gazette,* pp. A 1–2.

Shiraishi, S. S. (1997). Japan's soft power Doraemon goes overseas. In P. J. Katzenstein & T. Shiraishi (Eds.), *Network power: Japan and Asia* (pp. 234–272). Ithaca, NY: Cornell University Press.

Shirinian, L. (2000). *Writing and memory: The search for home in Armenian diaspora literature as cultural practice.* Kingston, Ontario: Blue Heron Press.

Soja, E. (1996). *Thirdspace: Journeys to Los Angeles and other real and imagined places.* Oxford: Blackwell.

Street, B. (1995). *Social literacies: Critical approaches to literacy in development, ethnography and education.* London: Longman.

The New Act. (2002). *The new momentum for Canada's linguistic duality: The action plan for official languages.* Ottawa, Ontario: Government of Canada.

Taylor, C. (1994). *Multiculturalism: Examining the politics of recognition.* Princeton, NJ: Princeton University Press.

Willis, S. (1985). Black women writers take a critical perspective. In G. Greene & C. Khan (Eds.), *Making a difference: Feminist literacy criticism* (pp. 21–37). New York: Methuen.

Wittgenstein, L. (1958). *Philosophical investigations.* Oxford University Press.

Yon, D. A. (2000). *Elusive culture: Schooling, race and identity in global times.* New York: State University of New York Press.

Yoshida, R. (2001). *Political economy, transnationalism, and identity: Students at the Montreal Hoshuko.* Unpublished master's thesis, McGill University, Montreal.

Chapter 8

Multiple Literacies:
An Alternative *OR* Beyond Freire

Diana Masny
University of Ottawa

Literacy, like an ever-changing chameleon camouflaged within different worldviews, is an ever-becoming controversial term. What counts as literacy, who counts, who does the counting, and what it means to be literate has created much debate. The term *literacy* has been used as a political as well as an economic yardstick of the wealth of a nation. From a Eurocentric perspective, literacy and its Westernized forms have become tied to measures of a "developing nation." Enormous amounts of resources have been poured into literacy projects. In the end, literacy and the uses to which literacy have been put become highly contested.

In some contexts, literacy has a fixed determinate definition and has universal truth value. This conceptualization of literacy has been questioned. In other contexts, literacy is used in different ways, not only across disciplines but also within disciplines. There is a proliferation of meanings assigned to literacy taken up by many disciplines: applied linguistics, psycholinguistics, anthropology, sociology, and critical pedagogy, just to name a few. As a result, there is considerable debate and chaos (*chaos* is a healthy term in a postmodern world) with regard to multiple meanings assigned to the term *literacy*.

The use of the term *multiple* brings up the issue of paradigms. For many years, if not decades, the study of/on literacy has often been placed in a binary mode juxtaposed with the term *ILL*iteracy. The latter, in and of itself, is a controversial term. One very important paradigmatic approach to the study of literacy was, and to some extent still is, fed by a postpositivist worldview. This worldview, which is often referred to as the received view, has gained tremendous legitimacy. Postpositivism derives its traditions from the natural sciences with its desires for replication, laboratory-like controls, generalizable results, and universal appeal.

Applying the term multiple signals a movement away from the binary worldview and a greater openness to more social and value-laden notions of literacy (Lankshear & McLaren, 1993; Luke, 1991; Masny & Ghahremani-Ghajar, 1999). The proliferation of meanings assigned to literacy calls for an examination of conceptual frameworks that situate literacy. Conceptual frameworks cannot be created without understanding the paradigmatic contexts within which frameworks are designed. I understand paradigm as a worldview, a relationship between the knower (the individual), forms of knowledge, and how these intersect in space and time. Because of the proliferation of paradigms, it becomes important to critically explore paradigms from which conceptual frameworks are derived and also to understand how literacy is positioned conceptually within these frameworks. Such understandings can only enrich our knowledge of literacies.

The conceptual framework of multiple literacies retained in this chapter is presented later on. At this time, a brief introduction to the concept of literacies is warranted. Literacies are a social construct. As such, literacies are context-specific. They are operationalized or actualized in situ. They take on meaning according to the way a sociocultural group appropriates them. Literacies of a social group are taken up as visual, oral, and written. They constitute texts, in a broad sense, that interweave with religion, gender, race, ideology, and power. In this way, all literacies are value-laden. No matter what the conceptualization retained, none are value neutral.

In a postmodern world, an individual engages literacies as she or he reads the world, reads the word, and reads herself or himself. Accordingly, when an individual talks, reads, writes, and values, construction of meaning takes place within a particular context. This act of meaning construction that qualifies as literate is not only culturally driven but also is shaped by sociopolitical and sociohistorical productions of a society and its institutions.

Thus, in this chapter, I foreground the context I have been working in as I began documenting my work on literacy. Most of my research is situated in minority language education in Canada, in particular, French language education. It is an entry point that allows me to gain a greater understanding of literacy, to broaden possibilities for forms of literacy, and to revisit a relationship between literacy and reading and between literacy and text. When I refer to moving away from and engaging different and differing views of literacy, reading, and text, I compare these complex relationships between and among literacies to the many and multifaceted ways a crystalline catches light depending on the way it is viewed.

The first part of this chapter is devoted to a multiple literacies model that has been adapted to respond to the challenges facing minority language communities. The model is based on a conceptual framework of multiple literacies presented in this chapter. The second part takes a closer look at the concept of literacy as I assign meanings to literacy, reading, and text within this conceptual framework. Situated within a postmodern world, the framework and the concepts retained are a constant "becoming," not fixed. I conclude with an understanding that literacy can take on multiple perspectives, one of which is linked to power. In the case of minority language communities, I argue for resonance and dissonance that connect power, literacy, and minority language education.

This chapter serves as an entry point to provoke thought and reflection on the process of becoming by engaging texts and reading the world, the word, and oneself. Although many of the terms are familiar, they take on meaning once situated in a particular conceptual framework. Perhaps, in a Derridean way (Derrida, 1976), thought and reflection may bring on moments of doubt or questioning and thus create that space, that opening for what is yet to become.

MINORITY LANGUAGE EDUCATION

For over a decade, I have been involved with French minority communities in Canada. I have studied young children's language use in a school context. During that time, it was inevitable to move toward studying oral language, reading, and writing as contested knowledges involved in power relationships (Masny, 1995). In linguistic communities that cohabit, power relationships are inherent. It soon became very apparent that language, literacy, identity, and power were intertwined. What were also revealing were the tensions that arose between linguistics communities. Just as one might consider exclusionary practices across communities, one also found such practices within communities. Within French minority communities, there are tensions and struggles. Marginalization occurs from within as well as from without (Masny, 1996).

The Canadian Charter of Human Rights in 1982 provided, in law, access for minority language communities to their own educational system. Shortly after, governance of French language education was created by, for, and with French communities. District school boards were established. French was the sole language of instruction. Children were admitted to French school based on Section 23 of the Canadian Charter of Human Rights.[1] To this day, governance persists as a judicial issue, as there are still cases pending before the Su-

---

[1]According to Section 23 of the Canadian Charter of Human Rights, Canadian citizens have the right to have their children educated in French if any of the following three situations apply: (a) if their first language is French, (b) if they received their own primary education in Canada in French, or (c) if they have a child who has received or is receiving his or her education in French in Canada. In Québec, where most people speak French, Canadian

preme Court of Canada regarding the interpretations of the right of French
language communities to French language education.

These judicial contestations as well as victories have brought many communities together in matters of education (Masny, 1998). One of their
goals is the development of an educational project that would affirm the
"linguistic, cultural and social actualization" of French. I participated in
one of these projects at the invitation of the Alberta government, the
French language education department. The meaning assigned to the term
actualization in government policy documents refers to the development of
an educational project aimed at promoting French language/culture in
school and in the community, and improving academic achievement. A major goal of this project is to support French minority schools, for they are
perhaps the most significant sites to promote French language/culture in
partnership with home and community.

Based on earlier work (Masny, 1995), I thought about literacies interacting in a transactional mode, interweaving and constantly in the process of
meaning construction. In Masny (1997), I elaborated a conceptual framework of multiple literacies that was adapted as a literacies model for the actualization of French so that through its educational system, Alberta's
French language community could thrive. The rationale for adopting a curriculum that took up multiple literacies was that, at the time, the curriculum promoted mostly school-based literacy and provided little opportunities for legitimating other literacies.

The educational project for minority language communities required
that aspects of home and community be validated in school. The school is
considered the most significant site for the promotion of French language/
culture. French media (newspapers, magazines, and entertainment) in the
community are at a premium. Moreover, in only a minority of homes will
you find both parents speaking French with their children. Most times,
both languages (French and English) are spoken. Sometimes, no French is
spoken at all. As rights holders of Section 23, these parents have the right to
send their children to French language schools. Increasingly, children
come to school knowing little or no French. Although the school has a mission to educate the children to succeed academically, the school is also an

citizens have the right to have their children educated in English: (a) if they received their
own primary instruction in Canada in English, or (b) if they have a child who has received or is
receiving his or her education in English in Canada. According to Section 59 of the *Constitu-
tion Act, 1982*, the right of persons whose first language is English, who wish to have their
children receive English-language instruction, does not apply in Québec until permitted by
the legislative assembly or government of Québec. In all cases, the right to receive an education in a minority language applies only when there is a sufficient number of eligible children to justify providing schooling in that language. Where those numbers do exist, governments must provide the necessary facilities (see http://www.pch.gc.ca/progs/pdp-hrp/
canada/guide/minority_e.cfm).

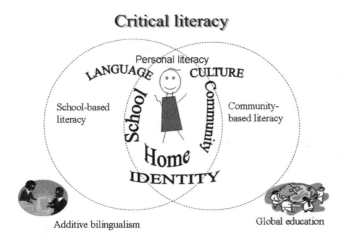

FIG. 8.1.   Multiple literacies: A conceptual framework.

integral part of a community. As such, the school aims to foster in children a sense of community membership. In order to do so, children come to school at an early age, hence the importance of preschool. In most district school boards, preschool education—that is, full-time junior and senior kindergarten—has become an educational priority. The kindergarten period, combined with day care service in the school, has taken on cultural and linguistic capital as children engage in forms of literacies.

Figure 8.1 is an adaptation of the multiple literacies model that is now part of Alberta French language education at the preschool level (Ministry of Education of Alberta, 1999). This model has applications that reach beyond the scope of the present context because it promotes personal, school-based, community, and home literacies and foregrounds critical literacies. In addition, this framework has incorporated aspects of global education and additive bilingualism. I explain each one in the next section.

MULTIPLE LITERACIES

In this conceptual framework, the individual is reading the world, the word, and self in the context of the home, school, and community (local, national, and international). This entails, on the part of the individual, a personal as well as a critical reading.

Personal Literacy

This framework for multiple literacies corresponds to a worldview in which the individual is immersed in different societal settings (school, home, and community) shaped by social, political, and historical contexts within that

society. Personal literacy focuses on reading oneself as one reads the world
and the word. It is within that perspective that personal literacy contributes
to the shaping of one's worldview. It is a way of "being" based on construction of meaning that is always in movement, always in transition. When personal literacy contributes to a way of becoming, it involves fluidness and
ruptures within and across differing literacies. One who reads the world
and the word is in a process of becoming; that is, the person creates and
gives meaning to that process of becoming in relation to texts. Text is assigned a broad meaning to include visual, oral, written, and possibly tactile
forms (Masny, 2001b).

Critical Literacy

No reading of the world, the word, or oneself could take place in any significant manner without a critical reading that calls on reflections (of
texts). For many researchers, the work of Freire (Freire & Macedo, 1987)
comes to mind when referring to reading the world and the word. His
work has inspired many researchers. As well, there have been conceptual
frameworks that are linked to critical literacy, such as critical theory and
critical feminist theory.

The concept of critical literacy espoused by Freire is paradigm specific.
The conceptual framework is situated within modernity. His theory of critical literacy is a theory of practice that serves to liberate and transform individuals, a sense of betterment of the human condition of the individual.
Central to Freire's notion of critical literacy is that socio-economic structures are poised to mainstream *OR* marginalize individuals. In creating
links with critical theory, Freire's concept of critical literacy creates a context for conscious examination of power relationship based on historical,
political, and social conditions at a particular time and space (within a particular community).

Moving beyond Freire in this chapter signals that while the term *critical
literacy* is used, the concept is related to another paradigm, that of postmodernism. Social, political, and historical conditions inform and shape a
reading of the word, world, and self. When doubt and questioning arise in/
through reading the word, world, and self, so does consciousness. Contrary
to Freire, where there is a sense of finality, that critical reading that fosters
transformation and emancipation, the present framework that incorporates critical literacy acknowledges that transformation is taking place.
What remains to be seen is how the transformations happen, how they get
taken up. That is the subject of the next paragraph. An example is provided
in the section that focuses on a conceptualization of literacy.

The meaning of critical literacy retained in this article is likened to a personal journey. One entry point on this journey is that literacies are value-

laden and linked to power. When reading the world and the word in a critical way, there is consciousness that social, cultural, economic, historical, and political values are attached to literacies. At issue is the question of which literacies link to which values and in what context. A second entry point is reading oneself. This occurs in school, home, and community. Let us consider the school. The school can be a space for social justice. It can also be a space for social control and normalization. There is the expectation that children in school will display school-based literacies, often considered literacies of normalization. The power of normalization can seriously challenge an individual's reading of self in reading the world and the word in school. When tensions arise or, as Dufresne (2002) states, when worldviews collide in the individual, transformations take place. The individual seeks stability in the midst of chaos. The questions remain: Whose norm is he or she seeking? A personal norm? A school norm? A community norm? The individual has moved. That is about all that can be ascertained. What reading of self goes on cannot be predicted.

Community Literacy

According to Masny (1997), community-based literacy refers to an individual's reading of literate practices of a community. In the French-minority context presented earlier, the school is a significant site and quite often the hub of the community. Community-based literacies, because they appear not to have the same legitimacy as school-based literacies, are often marginalized and called on in contexts outside the classroom. There are other ways of reading community literacy. One example that comes to mind is the ways of "being" that a farmer refers to when explaining his farming practices and the instruments he uses for his farming practices. How he talks about this is a form of community literacy. These practices are linked to what Fasheh (1990) uncovered when he acquired a postgraduate degree and was returning to his native country to teach mathematics at the university. One day, he observed his mother doing calculations while cutting up a pattern to sew a dress. Her ways of calculation were considered not scientific, at least not according to Fasheh's ways of calculation that earned him his academic degree. Such experiences created an opening, a space for questioning, and challenged his worldviews that moved him to take up his mother's community-based literacy. His desire then became to legitimate such forms of literacy within the community school.

Although the school might be a site for control and normalization, as well as a site for transformation of society, these cannot occur without a partnership between home, school, and community. In this manner, an individual's reading of the world, the word, and self in the context of home, school, and community creates possibilities to construct and reconstruct his or her way of being. If incorporating literate ways from the home and community does not take place in school, it will be impossible for individuals to develop community membership.

School-Based Literacy

According to Masny (2001b), school-based literacy refers to the process of interpretation and communication in reading the world, the word, and self in the context of school. It also includes social adaptation to the school milieu, its rites and rituals. School-based literacy emphasizes conceptual readings that are critical to school success. Such literacies are mathematics, science, social sciences, technologies, and multimedia. Although these literacies are important for school membership, they cannot be devoid of links or partnerships with home and community.

Additive Bilingualism

Although this concept is often linked to social psychology, it is not without its detractors. When two language communities cohabit in a particular context, a power relationship is also part of the configuration. In the Canadian context, English has greater visibility and presence. As a result, it becomes very challenging for minority communities to promote French language/culture when cohabiting with English. Therefore, some would state that by promoting two languages, there is the risk of contributing to what is known as *subtractive bilingualism*. However, it must be recognized that children and, increasingly, adults from French minority communities consider themselves to be bilingual and would name themselves as bilinguals. This has created tensions within minority communities. For instance, the educational system of many minority communities imposes norms of French mother tongue programs as if the communities were in a French majority context such as in the province of Quebec. In the latter context, an individual's reading of the world, the word, and oneself is considerably different. *Additive bilingualism* has been introduced here to acknowledge the bilinguality of individuals and to ensure that measures are in place so that individuals achieve high levels of competence in French and in English. Individuals often have high levels of competence in English. To provide alternatives, partnerships between home, school, and community become the most important catalyst in helping members of a minority community to achieve greater levels of competence in French. In order to maintain a high level of competence in French, the framework incorporates additive bilingualism. Otherwise, the silencing surrounding the nature of bilingualism would bring forth its subtractive nature.

Global Education

The impact of global economic, political, social, and cultural movements has left its imprint on education. Global education refers to diversity that includes pluralism, feminism, community, citizenship, identity, and popular culture (Burbules & Torres, 2000). Globalization can be considered a worldview that reconfigures education (curriculum, pedagogy, teaching, learning) in specific contexts (Dufresne, 2001). A postmodern globalized world is one in which we situate ourselves in nonlinear time and space, one that favors high levels of technology, and one in which English has become the privileged language. In all of this, minority communities must situate themselves and consider the tensions between local, traditional, and contemporary values as well as social and cultural capital that globalization engenders. It obliges us to examine closely the boundaries between minority, majority, and local, national, and international. It also entails a decentering and reconfiguration of worldviews. What is at stake, and the differing perspectives within a minority community, are significant.

Global education in this framework offers multiple perspectives. There is the almost inevitable force of globalization on all communities. It would seem important in French minority communities to establish community membership with similar communities across the globe. At this time, students rarely socially read themselves as Francophones outside their community. It is very localized because their experiences of reading the world and the word occur in French mainly in school. The values that their literacies might have do not extend beyond the community unless students engage in global education. Globalization and new technologies can be interpreted as an extension of social and cultural capital in French minority communities. It also becomes a way of critically reading citizenry, democracy, the environment, and international understandings (Lessard, Desroches, & Ferrer, 1997). This signals that a minority community should seek ongoing creation moving away from imposed norms from outside.

Global education is also a way to counter the power of global English. For a long time, print, TV, and radio were the main media sources in French and were not easily available in most remote communities. The power of English is insidious. With the new technologies, individuals in minority communities can engage in different readings of the world, the word, and themselves, extending their power as one of becoming.

Globalization does not go on unproblematically, however. A highly technological society places significant value on knowledge. This focus on forms of knowledge has transformed knowledge forms into economic leverage, and that, in turn, has resulted in the commodification of knowledge (Masny, 2001a). Combined with the surge of the Internet and information technology, Westernized societies have become information-based, information that is fragmented and decentered. Accordingly, it becomes all the more important to read the world, the word, and self through a critical reading, especially as a member in a minority community.

LITERACIES: A CONCEPTUALIZATION

In presenting the various aspects that shape a multiple literacies framework, the word *literacies* requires conceptualization. Earlier in this chapter, I assigned meaning to the word literacy without necessarily going in depth into the conceptual framework. A concept is operationalized only when it is situated in a conceptual framework and in relation to other concepts as well. In this section, I elaborate on the conceptual framework.

Literacy as a social construct consists of words, gestures, attitudes, ways of speaking, writing, valuing, a way of "being" in the world. Literacies are value-laden, interwoven with gender, race, religion, ideology, and power. When a person talks or reads, she or he constructs meaning in a particular context. More precisely, this act of meaning construction that qualifies as "literacy" is subject to cultural, sociopolitical, and sociocultural interpretations within that society and of its institutions. The meaning of literacy is actualized according to a particular context in the time and space in which it operates (Masny, 2002).

According to this framework, literacies can be considered as a reading of texts embedded in personal and social language practices in diverse situations. Text is assigned a very broad meaning. In addition, there are social, cultural, historical, and political implications embedded in reading.

A person is a text in continuous becoming. Reading the world and the word through text influences the text that a person continually becomes (Dufresne & Masny, 2001). To illustrate this, I take an example from Dufresne (2002). This study took place in an immersion class as learners were confronted with their own errors and error correction in the second language, French. A Grade 4 student, Bruno (a pseudonym), could not accept that in French he could not say twelve o'clock (*douze heures*). The teacher told him that his response was incorrect. The correct form was midnight (*minuit*). Despite the fact that Bruno acknowledged, noticed, and was made aware that the correct form was *minuit*, he was not willing to let go of *douze heures*. Both knowledge forms were, in his view, correct. In his first interview, when he stated his position about mistakes, he said that he was willing to accept that he would make mistakes. He was learning a new language. This first interview is different from the second. In the second interview, Bruno did not want to acknowledge a mistake. He maintained that there was no difference between midnight/*minuit* and twelve o'clock/*douze heures*. Are challenges to his knowledge formation also challenging his being?

In the previous example, there are several literacies operating. In reading the word and the world in a school context, Bruno is also linking with a powerful text, that of the teacher, that of the norm. How does he attempt a reading of self, of these differing literacies? His response to the teacher's correction of the form twelve o'clock is an indication. Moreover, in reading the world and the word through text, (for example, the two interviews reported here), Bruno's reading of self is that of engaging a text and meaning construction of who he is, what he knows, and the relationship between the two. Is his response to both forms part of the continuous becoming, the between-ness, the opening as part of the process of being?

Dufresne (2002), in citing Masny (2001a), refers to reading oneself, one of the literacies in "relation to text as an attempt to tame the uncontrollable and fashion a way of 'being' and to reject the tenets of structuralism" (p. 134). Affirming literacies as multiple is also acknowledging the plurality of and intersecting worldviews, the different and contradictory ways of meaning and experiences that flow in the process of being, that is, becoming.

This process also points to important connections between literacies and identity. Different readings in different situations become the conditions of identity. In other words, the experiences of difference construct identity. According to Parker (1997), "Unless we can articulate and understand our distinctiveness, we cannot conceptualize, identify or defend identity because simply, we have none" (p. 157). We seek to construct identity out of experiences of difference.

Experiences of difference can be about experiences in reading critically. Reading critically in reading the world, the word, and self in postmodern times signals reading critically differing (multiple and contradictory) literacies. At the same time, reading critically creates opportunities for questioning. Questioning points to a sense of between-ness, an indication that a space is opening. With that opening, questioning is seeking difference.

Questioning while reading critically can also extend to reflective experiences. That space or between-ness produces possibilities for engaging reflections. Reflections intend to provoke thought within a process of becoming. Questioning and reflections tie into multiple literacies and the conceptual framework retained, the desire to become in fragmented and contradictory constructions of meaning. Multiple literacies create readings that expose the complexity of becoming. This has significant implications for education and construction of knowledge in postmodern societies.

REFLECTIONS

The impact of globalization is one where social, cultural, and geographical constraints give way to the economic market of globalization. Reading the world, the word, and self, the literacies that are a way of being can raise consciousness of the effects of globalization.

In a postmodern era of globalization, Dufresne (2001) states, just as in chess playing, "Processes and strategies used by governments, nations, states and communities differ based on their ways of 'being,' their literacies, their ability to *read* market goals for the present and the future" (p. 5). In linking conceptually with Derrida, societies evolve between what is and what is yet to come and are heavily influenced by (or in partnership with) industry and an uncertain future.

With the information highway and hypertext, knowledge forms are constantly changing, transforming, and, in the process, becoming. Knowledge forms are viewed as merchandise in our economic market. Those who control the information highway constantly transform power, value, and capital attached to knowledge forms according to supply and demand.

Faced with uncertainty and nonlinearity in the world, there seems to be a desire to establish stability. In a similar manner, an individual's way of being will be uncertain as displacement of one's way of being is continuous when faced with information that is fragmented and decentered. Dufresne (2001) acknowledges that Western society is information-based, and it is constantly changing and constantly becoming. The onus, then, is on the individual, not to establish the veracity of the information but to engage in a power relationship with the information. Adopting a critical reading as part of the process of meaning construction in reading the world, the word, and self, multiple literacies as a way of being can be taken up as a way of becoming in a postmodern society.

What links could there be between a minority community and multiple literacies in a postmodern era of globalization? In large part, it might have to do with the particular context of a minority community and the assigning of value-laden meaning to literacies within that community (Masny & Dufresne, in press). Minority communities are often constructed in relation to majority communities. Minority communities could read critically the extent of imposition of the community's way of becoming according to a majority. A minority is about being different. If a postmodern globalized world is about chaos, nonlinearity, and fragmentation, then minority communities could create and transform. With globalization, multiplicities and difference are visible. Accordingly, affirming literacies as multiple creates an opening that connects with questioning, difference, reflections, possibly, about who we are, but more importantly about what we have yet to become.

This chapter is intended to provoke thought about multiple literacies that conceptually involve reading the world, the word, and self in postmodern times. According to Lather (2000), to provoke thought is to trouble the boundaries, ways of being conceptualized as multiple literacies and linked to nonlinear, indeterminate knowledge forms. In a minority language community, troubling the boundaries can be challenging, uncoupling concepts and taken-for-granted assumptions. From a normalized position, a community gains legitimacy based on power of language, numbers, history, culture, economy, geography, or any combination thereof. Globalization and the techno-information highway are invasive and challenge the singularity of a minority community and its values. Difference and plurality trouble the boundaries of community and of self. Reading critically the world, the word, and self entails continuously seeking differing and different literacies as a way of being in the world and part of a process of becoming.

ACKNOWLEDGMENTS

I thank Dr. Thérèse Dufresne, Anne-Marie Caron-Réaume, and Mary Lou Soutar-Hynes for their support. Their helpful comments are not necessarily an endorsement of the views proposed by the author.

REFERENCES

Burbules, N. C., & Torres, C. A. (2000). Globalization and education. In N. C. Burbules & C. A. Torres (Dir.), *Globalization and education: Critical perspectives* (pp. 1–23). New York: Routledge.

Derrida, J. (1976). *Of grammatology* (G. C. Spivak, Trans.). Baltimore, MD: Johns Hopkins University Press.

Dufresne, T. (2001). Le poststructuralisme: un défi à la mondialisation des savoirs [Poststructuralism: A challenge to globalization of knowledge]. In L. Corriveau & W. Tulasiewicz (Eds.), *Mondialisation, politiques et pratiques de recherche* (pp. 53–68). Sherbrooke, Québec: les Éditions du CRP.

Dufresne, T. (2002). *Through a lens of difference OR when worlds collide: A poststructural study on error correction and focus-on-form in language and second language learning.* Doctoral dissertation, University of Ottawa, Ottawa, ON.

Dufresne, T., & Masny, D. (2001, June). *The makings of minority education: The Québec educational curriculum reforms.* Paper presented at the annual meeting of the Canadian Society and Studies in Education (CSSE), Canadian Humanities and Social Science Congress, Laval University, Québec City, Québec.

Fasheh, M. (1990). Community education: To reclaim and transform what has been made invisible. *Harvard Educational Review, 60*(1), 19–35.

Freire, P., & Macedo, D. (1987). *Literacy.* Westport, CT: Bergin & Garvey.

Lankshear, C., & McLaren, P. (1993). *Critical literacy: Politics, praxis, and the postmodern.* Albany: State University of New York Press.

Lather, P. (2000). Drawing the line at angels: Working the ruins of feminist ethnography. In E. St. Pierre & W. Pillow (Eds.), *Working the ruins: Feminist poststructural theory and methods in education* (pp. 284–312). New York: Routledge.

Lessard, C., Desroches, F., & Ferrer, C. (1997). Pour un monde démocratique: l'éducation dans une perspective planétaire [Toward a democratic world: Global education]. *Revue des sciences de l'éducation, XXIII*(1), 3–7.

Luke, A. (1991). Literacies as social practice. *English Education, 23*(3), 131–137.

Masny, D. (1995). Literacy development in young children. *Interaction, 6*(1), 21–24. Available: http://www.cfc-efc.ca/docs/cccf/00000049.htm

Masny, D. (1996). Meta-knowledge, critical literacy and minority language education. *Language, Culture and Curriculum, 9*(3), 260–279.

Masny, D. (1997). *Le projet d'actualisation linguistique, culturelle et sociale français langue première: cadre conceptuel* [The linguistic, cultural and socialization project for French mother tongue: Conceptual framework]. Edmonton: Alberta Education, la Direction de l'éducation française.

Masny, D. (1998). *Pour une éducation de qualité et une culture de la différence* [Toward quality education and a culture of difference]. Edmonton: Alberta Education, la Direction de l'éducation française.

Masny, D. (2001a). Les littératies et la mondialisation des savoirs [Literacies and the globalization of knowledge]. In L. Corriveau & W. Tulaskiwicz (Eds.), *Mondialisation, politiques et pratiques de recherche* (pp. 69–78). Sherbrooke, Québec: les Éditions du CRP.

Masny, D. (2001b). Vers une pédagogie axée sur les littératies [Toward a pedagogy of literacies]. In D. Masny (Ed.), *La culture de l'écrit: les défis à l'école et au foyer* (pp. 11–22). Montreal, Québec: les Editions Logiques.

Masny, D. (2002). Les littératies: un tournant dans la pensée et une façon d'être [Literacies: A way of being *OR* an alternative way of thinking]. In R. Allard (Ed.), *Actes du colloque pancanadien sur la recherche en éducation en milieu francophone minoritaire: bilan et perspectives.* University of Moncton, Moncton, New Brunswick. Center for research and development in education. Available at http://www.acelf.ca/liens/crde/articles/14-masny.html

Masny, D., & Dufresne, T. (in press). La littératie critique: les enjeux de la réussite d'une école exemplaire et les réformes en éducation [Critical literacy: What's at stake in the success of an exemplary school in the context of educational reforms]. In J. C. Boyer (Ed.), *Entre le savoir intuitif et la littératie critique: enjeux épistémologiques et praxéologiques.* Montreal, Québec: les Éditions Logiques.

Masny, D., & Ghahremani-Ghajar, S.-S. (1999). Weaving multiple literacies: Somali children and their teachers in the context of school culture. *Language, Culture and Curriculum, 12*(1), 72–93.

Ministry of Education of Alberta. (1999). *Programme d'éducation de maternelle français langue première* [Kindergarten programme of studies, French, mother tongue]. Edmonton, Alberta: Direction de l'éducation française. http://www.learning.gov.ab.ca/french/programs.asp

Parker, S. (1997). *Reflective teaching in a postmodern world.* Buckingham, UK: Open University Press.

Chapter 9

The Portrayal of Self in Children's Drawings of Home, School, and Community Literacies

Maureen Kendrick
University of British Columbia

Roberta McKay
University of Alberta

Lyndsay Moffatt
University of British Columbia

In this chapter, we examine children's images of literacy as a window on their constructions of self. In the last decade, research concerning social identity and literacy practices suggests that students' ideas of how reading and writing relate to various social identities may be highly significant in their participation and nonparticipation in school-based literacy (see, e.g., Cherland, 1994; Davies, 1993; Martino, 1995). The multiplicity of communication channels, in combination with increasing cultural and linguistic diversity in the world, make it critical to view students' constructions of literacy in the broadest possible sense. Moreover, given that early experiences with literacy often lead students to form specific learner identities, understanding how young children construct self in relation to literacy is of particular concern. However, as noted by researchers such as Mirzoeff (1999), Pahl (2003), and Stein (2003), it is often difficult to elicit young children's ideas and conceptualisations about complex topics by using traditional modes of inquiry such as talk or writing. In conducting research on children's images of literacy, Kendrick and McKay (see, e.g., McKay & Kendrick, 2001; Kendrick & McKay, 2002, 2004) designed a unique research method that uses drawings as a tool for understanding how children think about literacy in their lives. The inspiration for this research comes from literacy researchers such as Britton, Halliday, Harste, Goodman, and Freire, whose work was grounded in valuing what learners know.

THEORETICAL FRAMEWORK

A Multimodal Perspective

In this research, we adopt a multimodal perspective, which assumes that "meanings are made, distributed, received, interpreted and remade in interpretation through many representational and communicative modes—not just through language" (Kress & Jewitt, 2003, p. 1). Rather than viewing modes of communication other than speech and writing as "add-ons" in theories of learning, a multimodal approach begins from a theoretical position that treats all communicative modes as potentially equal modes for learning. In adopting this perspective, we assume that language is partial, that any communicative event involves simultaneous modes, and that meaning is communicated in different ways by images, gestures, and speech (Kress & Jewitt, 2003).

We view children as sign makers who use the resources available to them in their specific sociocultural environment. Here we draw on social semiotics, which, according to Kress and van Leeuwen (1996), is an attempt to explain and understand how signs are used to "produce and communicate meanings in specific social settings be they 'micro' settings such as the family or settings in which the sign making is well institutionalized and hemmed in by habits, conventions and rules" (p. 264). The signs the children create in their drawings simultaneously communicate the here and now of a social context while representing the resources children have "to hand" from the world around them (Kress, 1997). The sign's intrinsic meanings are not arbitrary but, rather, represent what is central to the sign maker at that particular moment (Kress & Jewitt, 2003). The meanings also reflect reality as imagined by the sign maker and influenced by his or her beliefs, values, and biases. In this way, the drawings offer insights into who the child is, including individual intentions, as well as cultural, societal, and environmental conditions surrounding the making of the drawing.

We argue that although data such as children's drawings seldom feature in the analysis and discussion of learning, they may be a rich source of information for researchers and educators interested in examining what children know and understand about literacy and learning. Drawing as a mode of representation is a valuable tool for collecting information about children's ideas and conceptualisations in part because in most circumstances, drawing frees children to show their real-world abilities. Drawings are forms of iconic representation that reflect the distinctive features of the represented experience (Bruner, 1964); they are graphic images that represent what children know, not what they see (Piaget, 1969). Vygotsky's (1978) notion of multimodality centred on drawing as an internal representation of story, a way of knowing, and a graphic speech critical to young children's concept development. Unlike many language-based activities, drawing provides children with a wide range of possibilities for constructing meaning where the possibilities have not been predetermined by the education system (see, e.g., Kress, 2000b).

Learning and Literacy

We also draw on the sociocultural work of literacy researchers such as Heath (1983) and Barton and Hamilton (2000), and the critical literacy work of Lave and Wenger (1991), Luke (1997), and Norton and Toohey (2003), who view students' literacy practices within the local and larger contexts in which they live and learn. This perspective draws attention to the importance of students' *communities of practice* (i.e., the communities to which they belong) and *imagined communities* (i.e., the communities to which they hope to belong) in understanding how and why they engage or do not engage with particular language and literacy practices (Norton, 2000; Toohey, 2000; Wenger, 1998). Wenger (1998) suggests that engagement with community practices is not the only way in which we belong to communities; an equally important sense of community is derived from imagination, "a process of expanding oneself by transcending our time and space and creating new images of the world and ourselves" (p. 176). From this viewpoint, learning is much more than a cognitive process of acquiring particular sets of skills and knowledge; it is an integral part of changing patterns of participation in various communities with shared practices (Lave & Wenger, 1991). Literacy and language are viewed as practices that construct, and are constructed by, "the ways language learners understand themselves, their social surroundings, their histories, and their possibilities for the future" (Norton & Toohey, 2003, p. 1). We contend that how children portray their literacy practices in relation to their own identities as readers and writers is an integral part of their communities of practice, whether real or imagined.

ELICITING CHILDREN'S IMAGES OF LITERACY

This study involved one elementary school located in a western Canadian city. In this chapter, we focus on the 162 students in Grades 1 to 6, which included 83 boys and 79 girls. The students were from a variety of social, cultural, and linguistic backgrounds. The school was located in a middle socioeconomic neighbourhood and included speakers of Mandarin, Cantonese, Vietnamese, Spanish, and Polish.

The students met in groups with two of the researchers (Kendrick and McKay) for approximately 60 minutes to draw pictures of, and discuss their ideas about, literacy in their lives. The groups ranged in size from 4 to 22 children, with the average group size being 17 children. Because our goal was to explore children's images and ideas as evident in their drawings, the following questions were used to guide the discussions rather than rigidly format them. The discussions served primarily as a predrawing activity. The directions for the drawing task (Question 6) were deliberately left open-ended and did not specify who or what should be in the drawing or where it might take place.

1. What kind of reading/writing do you do in school/outside of school?
2. Why do you read/write in school/outside of school?
3. Where do you read/write in school/outside of school?
4. How is reading/writing in school both similar and different from reading/writing outside of school?
5. How do you think you will use reading/writing in the future, as you grow older?
6. Draw a picture of reading or writing. It can be a picture of reading or writing that you do at home or at school. It can be a picture of reading or writing that you do now or that you think you might do when you're older.

Following the discussion and drawing session, we asked the students to provide an explanation about their drawings. Older students wrote explanations, whereas younger students dictated to their teacher or one of the researchers. The explanations were used to verify and deepen our interpretations of the content and meaning of the drawings (i.e., who and what was in the drawings, when and where the literacy event or activity took place, why the children chose to draw what they did). Because this study focuses on the portrayal of self, only those students who drew themselves or who referred to self in discussing their drawings are included in the analysis (112 of 162 participants = 69%). Each of the drawings represents one particular "snapshot" of a student's construction of literacy. We expect that given additional opportunities to draw reading and writing, the children would produce a broad range (i.e., a series of snapshots) of literacy identities and literacy practices that reflect who they are as readers and writers.

Analyzing the Drawings

Drawings as a data source are relatively easy to collect; they are, however, considerably more difficult to analyze because of the complexity, richness, simultaneity, and multilayering of images and meaning. Rose (2001) asserts, "Interpreting images is just that, interpretation, not the discovery of their 'truth' " (p. 2). She suggests that although an explicit methodology is essential to justify the researcher's interpretation of the visual, interpretation is largely dependent on a passionate engagement with what is seen. We view the drawings as snapshots that represent moments in these children's literacy histories. These snapshots are windows on the children's literacy practices at particular moments in time and place, and reflect the sociocultural context in which the children live. The identities embedded in these literacy practices, which we consider to be an integral part of their larger constructions of self, are the focus of our analysis.

We analyzed the drawings using an extensive, interactive process that involved moving back and forth between the *content* of the drawings and the *meaning* evident in the children's descriptions of what they drew (Rose, 2001). In this initial stage of analysis, categories that reflected the students' constructions of literacy and of themselves were developed. Two of the authors (Kendrick and Moffatt) worked independently to code the content of the images according to five broad categories: *Domain* (e.g., home, school, work, etc.); *Literacy practices* (e.g., reading a novel, writing a story, reading fiction, writing on the computer); *Social identities portrayed* (e.g., self as reader, self as comic writer, self as artist, father as office worker, mother as teacher); *Style/type of text produced* (e.g., comics, diary pages); and *Style/type of text referred to* (e.g., storybooks, novels, e-mail).

Following this initial coding, we focussed more specifically on depictions and descriptions of self in relation to literacy practices. The following categories were used in the final analysis of the images: *self as reader/writer, self as reluctant reader/writer*, and *self as future or potential reader/writer*. The code *self as reader* was used whenever a child described himself or herself as engaged in reading. For example, in describing his picture, Sebastian (Grade 1) told us, "This is me getting a book in the sunshine. I am taking the book home to read it to my mom and dad." *Self as writer* was used similarly in the following instance: "This is me writing in my house. I am having fun. I am writing about Cinderella. I am writing on the computer" (Mitchel, Grade 2). Literacy practices portrayed in the drawings were also coded as writing when students gave explanations such as "working on the computer," "doing homework," "doing math," or "doing paperwork." The code *self as future/potential reader/writer* was used when students described themselves reading or writing at some point in the future, as in depictions of themselves reading or writing as teenagers or in work roles as adults. *Self as reluctant reader/writer* was used whenever a child made mention of the fact that he or she did not like reading and/or writing. More passive displays of reluctance to engage in reading or writing, such as TJ (Grade 1), who drew a picture of his mother reading while he was outside playing, were also coded using this category. In the following sections, a sampling of the drawings for each of the categories are described and analysed to provide a sense of the range of ways in which children use drawing to articulate how they see themselves as readers and writers, now and in the future.

THE PORTRAYAL OF SELF IN CHILDREN'S DRAWINGS OF LITERACY

Diverse Portraits of Readers and Writers

The multiplicity of ways in which these students use literacy was evident in the broad array of contexts and activities in which they pictured themselves as readers and writers. Across the six grades, 53% of the children portrayed literacy at home, 30% portrayed literacy at school, and 46% portrayed literacy in community contexts, including workplace and play settings (e.g., community libraries, office buildings, sports facilities). Although no predominant differences were evident in the ways in which boys and girls represented literacy contexts, Grade 4 shows a marked increase in the number of community/work-related contexts, with almost 60% of this total being portrayed by boys.

Readers. As readers, the children drew themselves reading picture books, comic books, novels, "how to books," TV guides, newspapers, and more. Cole, for instance, portrayed himself reading a book about Poké-mon, a cartoon character popular among his 5- and 6-year-old peers. Alex, in Grade 2, appeared to have similar reading interests. He drew a picture of himself reaching under his bed for a comic book. Kara, also in Grade 2, depicted herself "reading the book instructions to show you how to tap dance." Another Grade 2 boy, Matthew, drew himself engaged in the dual roles of "reading and watching TV," which is a habit of many readers, young and old alike. Aimen, a boy in Grade 3, drew a picture of "reading a newspaper in the sports section," whereas Brittney, his classmate, portrayed her "mom writing and reading at school (she's a teacher)," and herself "reading on my bed at home." Jodi, another Grade 3 student, drew a picture of herself "reading about puppies in the library (puppy care)." Graeme's picture reflects his diverse interests, which include reading a "human body book and writing on the computer at home." Anita, in Grade 5, likes "reading for relaxation," and she has drawn herself reading *Harry Potter* in bed. In her picture (see Fig. 9.1), she looks deeply engrossed in her book. The majority of these reading practices reflect the kinds of out-of-school reader identities that these students have taken up.

Writers. The students' repertoires as writers included, among other things, writing stories, doing homework, sending e-mail messages, working on the computer, keeping journals, and recording sports scores. Some ex-

FIG. 9.1.   Anita (Grade 5).

amples of how the students saw themselves as writers include Matthew, in Grade 5, who illustrated a memory from the past: "This is me writing my very first book/story at school," and Janette, also in Grade 5, gave this explanation for her picture: "I drew a map because I was once reading about a map in a magazine and I got the idea to write a story about that article. And I just thought about that story when [you] told me to think about writing." In Derek's picture (see Fig. 9.2), he drew himself balancing on top of a dinosaur. The style of the picture is similar to what has been referred to in children's literature as postmodern because the illustrations appear to con-

FIG. 9.2.   Derek (Grade 1).

tinue beyond the pages of the book (Goldstone, 1999). Characters, for example, may appear to leap off or onto the page and in so doing, interrupting the storyline (see, e.g., *The Three Pigs* by David Wiesner). As Derek explained, "I was writing a Jack and the Beanstalk story. Then the dinosaur barged in and the lava started coming down. I was standing on the dinosaur and I looked up and saw the lava." It is as though the dinosaur suddenly intervenes in the tranquil scene where Derek is writing a story about the Jack and the Beanstalk, which adds to the picture a level of instability, excitement, and adventure that would not have existed with the story writing alone. The writer identities evident in these examples and across the grades reflect the range of purposes these students have for writing both inside and outside school.

Hybrid Texts and Multiple Literacies.   One of the most interesting aspects of the ways in which these children portrayed literacy was their use of computers and other technologies for their own purposes as readers and writers. One example is Nathan, who was in Grade 2. He drew a picture of himself reading a diary that he wrote on his computer (see Fig. 9.3): "I have a game boy. I have a play station." Computers and computer games in particular appeared to figure prominently in how he viewed himself as a reader and writer. His classmate, John, also depicted himself writing in a diary (see Fig. 9.4): "I like my game boy and I like playing it. I like playing soccer. I got a new fire pit [computer game] an Im 2 fire in it. I have a desk and a pes off paper and I am riten abt the weekn." Although both boys portray writing about computer games in their diaries, one boy uses a computer for writing whereas the other uses pen and paper. These hybrid texts that they create

FIG. 9.3.   Nathan (Grade 2).

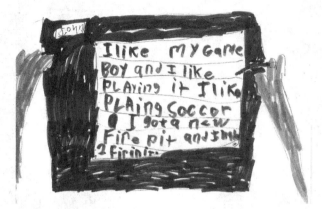

FIG. 9.4. John (Grade 2).

of words and images exemplify the multiple sign systems young children use to communicate. David, a Grade 4 student, uses computers to write letters to his grandfather: "This is me on the com.writing a story to my Grampa. He lives in England. This is at home." One cannot help but notice the resemblance between the way he has abbreviated computer writing as "com.writing" and the format used for web site addresses. Kimberly, also in Grade 4, had another purpose for using the computer. She drew a picture of herself "on the computer drawing a picture and writing about it."

Childhood cultures are comprised of a range of symbols, textual practices, and communicative media. An interweaving of these modes of communication in the drawings epitomized the multiple literacies in these children's lives. Katelyn's picture (see Fig. 9.5) depicts the multiple purposes for and ways in which she uses reading and writing in her daily life:

> I drew things that I use for reading and writing. I drew things like my bed with my book on it because I read in bed every night. I also drew a computer because I like to write stories and play games. I also have a letter I worte to my cousin. I also drew a Harry Potter book because I like to read them. (Katelyn, Grade 4)

Amber's drawing similarly illuminates the multiple tools and texts she uses for reading and writing (see Fig. 9.6), which she described in the following way:

> This is a picture about reading and writing the first picture at the top on the left hand corner is a score bord and I am putting scors that the kisd get in gymnastics and the one beside it in the right hand corner is me doing a spelling test. The one under neth is my reading clender and the one under neth the gymnasticks scorbord is a book report a school we have to do one every

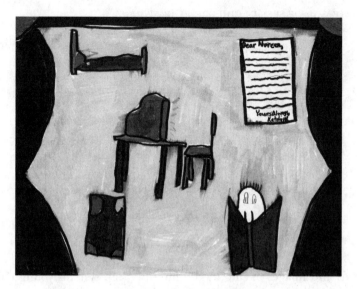

FIG. 9.5. Katelyn (Grade 4).

FIG. 9.6. Amber (Grade 3).

month. The one becid it is a book I took out of the scool library. The one under neth the book report is a time test at scool we do them abt and we are
timed for 2 minutes. The one beside it is a picture for what I wrote for when I
go to disny land and what I am going to do when I go there in order. (Amber,
Grade 3)

A final example is Lyndsay's drawing, which includes three written genres:
story writing on the computer, keeping a diary, and corresponding by e-
mail: "In my picture I drew my computer. On my computer I wrote a story. I
also drew my diary on a puffy couch. In my scene I just left the room. I was e-
mailing my cousin on the computer."

The students' depictions of literacy can be interpreted as a reflection of
their diverse communities of practice, their awareness of the variety of
forms and functions of reading and writing in their daily lives, and their
wide range of interests as readers and writers. That they included images of
computers and other technology in their literacy pictures is evidence of
their knowledge of the broad landscape of literacy in the world today. Their
drawings also provide confirmation that they see themselves as readers and
writers well beyond the walls of the classroom. These children have at their
disposal communicative potentials that open possibilities for them to invent and combine literacies that will allow them to achieve particular goals
in their personal and social lives such as creating images and texts on the
computer, sending e-mail letters to relatives, and writing stories to entertain
themselves and others. Given that these students made particular choices
about what to include in their drawings, and made specific references to
self, we interpret this as a window on the kinds of literacies they choose to
engage in at home, at school, and in their communities. The drawings also
provide a window on their visual and hybrid literacies (i.e., combinations of
words and images), multiple literacies, and multiple modes of meaning
making, all of which, Nixon (2001) argues, significantly broaden our understanding of what children can actually achieve as readers and writers.

Portraits of Imagined Literacies

Numerous children also depicted themselves as engaged in literate activities they envisioned doing sometime in the future as teenagers or adults.
Jalessa, a Grade 1 student, imagined herself as a camp counselor: "This is
me when I am grown up. We are at camp. I am reading a book about camp-
ing to kids around the campfire." Zack, her classmate, drew a picture of
himself signing autographs as a famous hockey player (see Fig. 9.7). Dean-
na, who is in Grade 2, imagined what it might be like to visit a public library:
"I drew a picture of a public library. I have never been to a public library but
maybe I probably will." Her classmate, Meyna, showed herself as a science

FIG. 9.7.   Zack (Grade 1).

teacher: "I am a teacher. We are outside. I am teaching about science—how the stars grow and shine," she explained.

Several of the Grade 3 students also imagined how they might use literacy in the future. For instance, Bryan, who identified strongly with his father, saw himself following the same career path: "This is my dad—me in the future," he described. "He builds towers safety comes first." The figure in the drawing is transported across time from present into future, from father into son. Jennifer drew a picture of herself writing a children's story: "I'm writing it in my house and I'm a grown up," she told us. Ricky, a boy in Grade 4, wrote this description for his drawing: "This is me when I'm a gronup. I'm righting to my family. Writing to family in Dawson Creek." His classmate, Jordan, showed how he might use reading and writing in his future role as a "Chefboy" who makes pizzas. One of the Grade 6 girls, Chelsey, drew herself as a news anchorwoman with documents in hand, reading the news (see Fig. 9.8). Dayna, also in Grade 6, illustrated a doctor's note she might write in the future (see Fig. 9.9): "You have my permission to take 1 month off work to rest your back so it will hopefully get better. I'm going to put you on asperns 2 times a day to help reduce the pain." The language she uses in her prescription (e.g., 'you have my permission,' 'rest your back,' and 'help reduce the pain') provides a strong evidence of her knowledge of medical discourse.

These imagined literacies, whether they belong to communities that exist only in the learners' imaginations or communities they encounter in

ᴗeir daily lives, have considerable potential to influence learners' current
ᴄtions and investment in particular kinds of reading and writing practices
ᴋanno & Norton, 2003). Imagined communities present new possibilities
ᴏr self; moreover, an imagined identity envisioned within an imagined
ᴄommunity can significantly influence the kinds of choices learners make
ᴀbout educational practices (Kanno & Norton, 2003). Because students' vi-
ᴀions of the future can be linked to their current actions and sense of self,
ᴛhe imagined literacies that these learners portray may be particularly re-
ᴇealing in terms of understanding students' willingness to engage in partic-
ᴜlar kinds of literacy practices in contexts such as school. These imagined
ᴀiteracies, although currently beyond the abilities of these students, may
ᴠery well provide a reason and motivation for what they do in the present.
As Kanno and Norton (2003) explain, "Our identities . . . must be understood not only in terms of our investment in the 'real' world but also in
terms of our investment in *possible* worlds" (p. 248).

Portraits of Reluctant Readers and Writers

Drawings that portrayed self as reluctant to engage in reading and/or writing were almost exclusively the domain of Grade 5 boys, with only a few exceptions. For example, Nikola, a Grade 5 boy, told us: "My picture is about
sports because I am not really into reading and writing" (see Fig. 9.10).
More passive displays of reluctance to read or write were also coded using
this category. For example, Sean, also a Grade 5 boy, told us, "I drew about
sports and I couldn't think about reading and writing." Sean's classmate
Dylan's picture shows a buck hanging upside down with blood dripping

FIG. 9.10.   Nicola (Grade 5).

FIG. 9.8. Chelsey (Grade 6).

FIG. 9.9. Dayna (Grade 6).

from his head (see Fig. 9.11). Dylan, with rifle in hand, is standing beside the dead animal. In a caption on the back of his picture, he writes, "I shot my first buck with a doble barel shotgut. It is at my grapernts farm. My dad Helped me." He later explained that the picture was about "something else that I *wanna* put down but we're not allowed." Specifically, the drawing is about hunting, a topic that his teacher does not allow him to write about in school because, according to Dylan, "She just wants us to write about sunny days and stuff like that" (for a more detailed discussion of Dylan, see Kendrick & McKay, 2002).

Four other students, who were not Grade 5 boys, also appeared to present themselves as reluctant readers or writers. Taylor, a Grade 4 boy, described his picture this way (see Fig. 9.12): "Me at school doing novel study questions. I don't really like to do. You have to look in the book a lot. Read between the lines to find the answer." Tyson, a boy in Grade 6, appeared to be both a reader and a reluctant reader: "I drew captain underpants as I enjoy reading funny books, especially captain underpants. I drew it because it is *the only books* I look [at]." Although he affirmed himself as a reader, he also asserted that he did not like reading anything *except* Captain Underpants. We therefore coded his portrayal of self in the drawing as both reader and a reluctant reader because he sees himself as a reader of Captain Underpants books, but not a reader of other types of books. Our youngest example of self as a reluctant reader/writer is TJ, who described his picture this way: "My mom is reading a book in the house. I am playing outside watching the bird." In this drawing, TJ clearly positions his mother as a reader, but not himself. In examining what is present in the drawings, it is equally important to identify what is absent. Markedly absent from this collection of drawings are portrayals of girls as reluctant readers or writers. The only exception was Stacey, a Grade 6 girl, who drew a picture of a girl

FIG. 9.11. Dylan (Grade 5).

 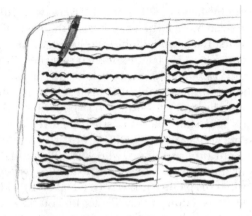

FIG. 9.12.   Taylor (Grade 4).

standing beside her bed not appearing to be engaged in any particular literacy practice. When asked to explain the picture, Stacey said it was a self-portrait and that "She can't stop thinking about Billy Abbot [from the soap opera *The Young and the Restless*], a boy she likes."

We use the term *reluctance* to highlight that not all students identify themselves as readers and writers, particularly in school contexts. Goffman (1961) describes this notion of reluctance as "resistance," which refers to an attempt by an individual to "keep some distance, some elbow room, between himself [herself] and that with which others assume he [she] should be identified" (p. 319). As evident in this collection of drawings, resistance of this nature may be especially attractive to boys who see "good studenthood" as "acquiescent, unmasculine, a denial of who they are and want to be" (Newkirk, 2000, p. 299). Why Stacey distances herself from literacy practices in her picture may be much more complicated. As Goffman (1959) emphasizes, "We do not have a self that we selectively present, hiding x, revealing y. Rather the sense we have of being 'self' is rooted in a sense of competence primarily, but not exclusively, in social interaction" (p. 5). This "sense" is one of effectiveness, the robust feeling that we possess a repertoire of performances so natural that they cease to feel like performances at all (Newkirk, 2000). In other words, our competence as social beings comes, in large measure, from successfully internalising the idealized models of who we should be.

IMAGES OF LITERACY IDENTITIES

Increasingly, meaning is made through multimodal ways in which written language and linguistic modes "are part and parcel of visual, audio, and spatial patterns of meaning [. . .]. When technologies of meaning are changing so rapidly, there cannot be one set of standards or skills that constitute the ends of literacy learning, however taught" (Cope, Kalantzis, & The New London Group, 2000, p. 6). Yet, the development of teaching and research methods that utilize visual forms of representation as a means of examining what children know and understand about a particular topic remains largely unexplored in the field of literacy. Moreover, the idea that the world cannot be represented through modes other than the abstractions of language remains largely unchallenged.

In the same way that Hamilton (2000) showed how visual data such as photographs can be used to focus and extend knowledge of literacy as social practice by more closely identifying the elements of literacy practices, and by challenging and elaborating the underlying concepts of practice and event, so too can children's drawings be used to extend knowledge of their literacy practices and learning. The drawings represent "snapshots" of the literacy identities embedded in the literacy events and practices portrayed by these students. They depict themselves as readers of popular culture books such as Pokemon, Harry Potter, and Captain Underpants, pet care books, and newspapers; they picture themselves as writers of map stories, fairy tales, sports scores, e-mail, computer diaries, stories, and games; and they imagine themselves as teachers, hockey players, doctors, camp counsellors, news anchorwomen, children's literature writers, and office tower builders. How these children picture themselves in relation to literacy reveals their willingness to engage in particular kinds of literacy practices. The images, however, also make known children who, at particular times and places, may be reluctant to engage in reading and writing. Instead of identifying with readers and writers, some of the children in this study depicted themselves as athletes, hunters, or bird watchers because they are "not really into reading and writing."

Over the past 5 years, we have collected over 400 children's drawings about reading and writing. In the process, we discovered that these visual images have considerable potential for enhancing understanding of children's literacy learning and engagement. The drawings provide a "sideways glance" (Schwartzman, 1976) at children's complex and sometimes hidden literacies because they make visible that which is not directly available through language-dependent modes alone. As Kress (2000a) explains, drawings show an astonishing conceptual understanding and imagination that cannot be expressed through language, even language in narrative format. The children's ability to communicate their literacy knowledge and understandings through drawing—to make the invisible visible—exemplifies Eisner's (1985) notion that becoming literate means more than being able to read, write, or code—it means acquiring the ability to use a variety of representative forms for conceptualising and expressing meaning.

Our examination of the drawings as evidence of children's literacy knowledge takes into account that "each and every literacy transaction is a moment of self-definition in which people take action within and upon their relations with other people" (Solsken, 1993, p. 8). How the students in this study take up particular literacy practices is directly connected to their own histories, which are vividly communicated in their visual images of literacy. The portrayal of self in each of the drawings can be directly linked to the children's own literacy experiences, inside and outside school. What gives meaning to the literacy events portrayed in the drawings is not literacy for the sake of literacy, but rather literacy for a plethora of other purposes that relate to children's own interests, identities, and desires.

Our interpretation of the drawings is intended to raise important questions about the complex nature of literacy and identity in students' lives, and the need for alternative means of assessing what children know and understand. In this study, the children's visual representations of literacy serve to emphasize that their constructions of literacy and self are multidimensional and inextricably embedded within and diffused across the many contexts that constitute the broader social world. Because the drawings open up possibilities for questions about what these students know about literacy beyond what they can express through language, they allow us to better see the accomplishments and struggles of individual children. From this viewpoint, however, we are also left wondering about the students who did not portray themselves or describe themselves as actively engaged in reading or writing (31% of the participants). What these students can tell us about their constructions of literacy and its relationship to self remains a topic for further research.

REFERENCES

Barton, D., & Hamilton, M. (2000). Literacy practices. In D. Barton, M. Hamilton, & R. Ivanič (Eds.), *Situated literacies: Reading and writing in context* (pp. 7–15). London: Routledge.

Bruner, J. S. (1964). The course of cognitive growth. *American Psychologist, 19*, 1–15.

Cherland, M. R. (1994). *Private practices: Girls reading fiction and constructing identity.* Bristol, PA: Taylor & Francis.

Cope, B., Kalantzis, M., & The New London Group. (2000). *Multiliteracies: Literacy learning and the design of social futures.* London: Routledge.

Davies, B. (1993). Beyond dualism and towards multiple subjectivities. In L. Christian-Smith (Ed.), *Texts of desire: Essays on fiction, femininity, and schooling* (pp. 145–173). London: Falmer.

Eisner, E. W. (1985). *The art of educational evaluation: A personal view.* London: Falmer Press.

Goffman, E. (1959). *The presentation of self in everyday life.* New York: Doubleday.

Goffman, E. (1961). *Asylums: Essays on social situations of mental patients and other inmates.* New York: Anchor.

Goldstone, B. (1999). Brave new worlds: The changing image of the picture book. *New Advocate, 12*, 331–343.

Hamilton, M. (2000). Expanding the new literacy studies: Using photographs to explore literacy as social practice. In D. Barton, M. Hamilton, & R. Ivanič (Eds.), *Situated literacies: Reading and writing in context* (pp. 16–34). London: Sage.

Heath, S. B. (1983). *Ways with words: Language, life, and work in communities and classroom.* Cambridge: Cambridge University Press.

Kanno, Y., & Norton, B. (2003). Imagined communities and educational possibilities: Introduction. *Journal of Language, Identity, and Education, 2*(4), 241–249.

Kendrick, M., & McKay, R. (2002). Uncovering literacy narratives through children's drawings: An illustrative example. *Canadian Journal of Education, 27*(1), 45–60.

Kendrick, M., & McKay, R. (2004). Drawing as an alternative way of understanding young children's constructions of literacy. *Journal of Early Childhood Literacy, 4*(1), 109–128.

Kress, G. (1997). *Before writing: Rethinking the paths to literacy.* London: Routledge.

Kress, G. (2000a). Multimodality. In B. Cope & M. Kalantzis (Eds.), *Multiliteracies: Literacy learning and the design of social futures* (pp. 182–202). London: Routledge.

Kress, G. (2000b). "You've just got to learn how to see": Curriculum subjects, young people and schooled engagement with the world. *Linguistics and Education, 11*(4), 401–415.

Kress, G., & Jewitt, C. (2003). Introduction. In C. Jewitt & G. Kress (Eds.), *Multimodal literacy* (pp. 1–18). New York: Peter Lang.

Kress, G., & van Leeuwen, T. (1996). *Reading images: The grammar of visual design.* London: Routledge.

Lave, J., & Wenger, E. (1991). *Situated learning: Legitimate peripheral participation.* Cambridge, England: Cambridge University Press.

Luke, A. (1997). Critical approaches to literacy. In V. Edwards & D. Corson (Eds.), *Encyclopedia of language and education: Volume 2, Literacy* (pp. 50–57). Boston: Kluwer.

Martino, W. (1995). Boys and literacy: Exploring the construction of hegemonic masculinities and the formation of literate capacities for boys in the English classroom. *English in Australia, 112,* 11–24.

McKay, R., & Kendrick, M. (2001). Children draw their images of reading and writing. *Language Arts, 78,* 529–533.

Mirzoeff, N. (1999). *An introduction to visual culture.* London: Routledge.

Newkirk, T. (2000). Misreading masculinity: Speculations on the great gender gap in writing. *Language Arts, 77,* 294–300.

Nixon, H. (2001, December). *"Slow and steady—not enough pace!": The absence of the visual in valued middle primary literate competencies.* Paper presented the Australian Association for Research in Education National Conference, Fremantle, Australia.

Norton, B. (2000). *Identity and language learning: Gender, ethnicity, and educational change.* England: Pearson Education.

Norton, B., & Toohey, K. (2003). Introduction. In B. Norton & K. Toohey (Eds.), *Critical pedagogies and language learning* (pp. 1–17). Cambridge, England: Cambridge University Press.

Pahl, K. (2003). Children's text-making at home: Transforming meaning across modes. In C. Jewitt & G. Kress (Eds.), *Multimodal literacy* (pp. 139–154). New York: Peter Lang.

Piaget, J. (1969). *The mechanisms of perception.* London: Routledge & K. Paul.

Rose, G. (2001). *Visual methodologies.* London: Sage.

Schwartzman, H. (1976). Children's play: A sideways glance at make-believe. In D. F. Lancy & B. A. Tindall (Eds.), *The study of play: Problems and prospects* (pp. 208–215). New York: Leisure Press.

Solsken, J. W. (1993). *Literacy, gender, and work in families and in schools.* Norwood, NJ: Ablex.

Stein, P. (2003). Representation, rights, and resources: Multimodal pedagogies in the language and literacy classroom. In B. Norton & K. Toohey (Eds.), *Critical pedagogies and language learning* (pp. 95–115). Cambridge: Cambridge University Press.

Toohey, K. (2000). *Learning English at school: Identity, social relations and classroom practice.* Clevedon, England: Multilingual Matters.

Vygotsky, L. (1978). *Mind in society: The development of higher psychological processes.* Cambridge, MA: Harvard University Press.

Wenger, E. (1998). *Communities of practice: Learning, meaning, and identity.* Cambridge, England: Cambridge University Press.

Wiesner, D. (2000). *The three pigs.* New York: Clarion Books.

Chapter 10

Things Thicker Than Words: Portraits of Youth Multiple Literacies in an Alternative Secondary Program

Theresa Rogers
University of British Columbia

Andrew Schofield
Surrey School District, British Columbia

This chapter explores the use of multimedia in an alternative secondary program to engage students in multiliteracy projects that traverse their in-school and out-of-school lives and literacy practices. One student is JJ, a secondary student who had effectively dropped out of regular school, where he was considered "too disruptive." He joined the alternative Youth Literacy Program where, after being introduced to Octavio Paz's short story "The Blue Bouquet," he made a short film of the story (described later). Shortly thereafter, JJ went into hiding in downtown Vancouver, British Columbia to escape the consequences of an unpaid drug debt. Two weeks later, he came back to school, beaten up but alive, and returned to his schoolwork, writing prolifically. What might account for this transformation from a student who actively resisted school and "school literacies" to one who now engages with his schoolwork?

YOUTH LIVES AND LITERACIES

We begin our collaborative (teacher/researcher) exploration of this question through an examination of current understandings of youth literacies in and out of schools. Theresa, a faculty member at the University of British Columbia, and Andrew, the Youth Literacy Program teacher, have been working together to create and investigate practices that support the literacy development of students who have not found success in traditional secondary school contexts.

In a comprehensive review of research on out-of-school literacies, Hull and Schultz (2001) point out that there has been considerable work in the last 20 years, documenting out-of-school performances of children and youth, that draws on theoretical work in ethnography (e.g., Heath, 1983), Vygotskian and activity theory (e.g., Scribner & Cole, 1981), and the New Literacy Studies (Gee, 1996; Street, 1995), including the more recent conceptualization of multiliteracies (New London Group, 1996, 2000). Hull and Schultz (2001) argue that research associated with the New Literacy Studies in particular has "unabashedly valued out of school literacy practices" (p. 589); they call for more research that examines the relationship of in-school and out-of-school literacies, arguing that "we ignore at students' peril the close connections that exist between economic change, the material conditions of people's lives, and literacy and literacy learning" (p. 598).

At the same time, we are witnessing increased calls for making classrooms places in which hybrid and unsanctioned youth literacies can be integrated in ways that preserve their power and creativity; that is, places that allow literacy practices to travel across institutional boundaries (e.g., Leander, 2003; Moje, 2000; Weinstein, 2002). Moje (2000) for instance, argues against either vilifying or romanticizing unsanctioned youth literacy practices, but instead acknowledging their potential power to help students use their metalinguistic and metadiscursive knowledge to reconstruct the dominant stories around them.

How can we support the creation of *social spaces* within the school curriculum in which students can narrate their lives and stories in ways that do not simply reproduce, but begin to recreate and even critique, dominant discourses? Space in this sense can be seen as a social product, rather than a physical place. As Soja (1989) points out, what we call "place" might appear initially as a physical husk—a disused parking lot, or a classroom—but "the organization and meaning of space is a product of social translation, transformation, and experience" so that knowing oneself is "an exercise in mapping where one stands" (Keith & Pile, 1993, p. 26). In our work in an alternative youth literacy program for students who have a fragile relationship with schooling, we have been exploring these intersections between students' production of social spaces in their lives and multiple literacies. In order to support students' literacy development, we draw on students' biographies, imaginations, and desire to produce, narrate, and translate their stories in spaces that traverse the perceived boundaries of their lives and literacies. This work rests on notions of literacy that have emerged in the areas of social literacies and multiliteracies, as well as work in youth or adolescent literacy.

SOCIAL LITERACIES, MULTILITERACIES, AND YOUTH LITERACIES

Literacy has traditionally been understood as reading and writing, and much literacy analysis has focused on texts and processes of academic literacy acquisition. However, more recently there has been a focus on social literacies (Street, 1995) or literacy practices as the "general cultural ways of utilizing written language" (Barton & Hamilton, 2000, p. 7). Social literacy perspectives view literacy as "situated" rather than "autonomous," and the researcher's "interest is in social practices in which literacy has a role" (Barton & Hamilton, 2000, p. 7). The object of analysis, then, shifts from approaches to teaching reading to an examination of the diverse practices of literacy—the texts of daily, personal life: ". . . *literacy is best understood as a set of social practices; these are observable in events which are mediated by written texts*" (Barton & Hamilton, 2000, p. 9; italics in original). It is important to note that, for social literacy theorists, texts used in daily life do not assume an autonomous life of their own; instead, material practice remains central in examining how texts fit into the practices of people's lives, and how they are used.

The social literacies perspective marks a growing shift in the conception of literacy from identifying literacy as located in individuals to examining ways in which people in groups use literacy. This perspective draws on decades of rich work in ethnography, sociolinguistic research, and cultural studies, and opens up fruitful avenues of research (Barton, Hamilton, & Ivanic, 2000) and practice, confirming what many teachers understand, at least implicitly: that literacy is learned not only inside the classroom, and that school curricula focused on a prescribed range of literacy practices are restrictive.

Multiliteracy theory is structured around three intersecting theses: one, that in "late capitalist countries," work lives and modes of work organization are changing; two, the nature of citizenship is changing with the retreat of the welfare state; and three, subcultural differences (of gender, ethnicity, generation, and sexual orientation) are becoming "more and more significant" (New London Group, 2000, p. 15), giving rise to multilayered and multiple life-worlds (p. 17). Paralleling these changes is change in "the languages needed to make meaning" (p. 10) of our social, cultural, work, and personal lives.

Multiliteracy theorists (cf. Cope & Kalantzis, 2000), as semioticians, arts in education proponents, and hypermedia researchers before them, expand the notion of texts and literacy to include "multimodal" forms of representation and meaning making, arguing that "literacy pedagogy must now account for the burgeoning variety of text forms associated with information and multimedia technologies" (New London Group, 2000, p. 9). Consequently, schools need to accommodate these changes by, for example, designing curricula to "mesh with different subjectivities, and with their attendant languages, discourses, and registers, and use these as a resource for learning" (p. 18). In addition, they argue, "learning processes need to recruit, rather than attempt to erase, the different subjectivities, interests, intentions, commitments, and purposes that students bring to learning" (p. 18).

"Multiliteracy" perspectives, in particular, emphasizes situated learning, explicit scaffolding of language and literacy patterns, a critical framing of those practices in the overall system of knowledge and social relations, and the uses of language and literacy to transform and consume knowledge in new contexts (Gee, 2000; New London Group, 1996). These formulations include, among other aspects, the essential tenets of progressive pedagogy—specifically, the design of learning to intersect as closely as possible with the life-worlds of our students, and the assumed importance of teaching from "where the student is," as well as an emphasis on critical pedagogical practices (e.g., Freire, 1978; Freire & Macedo, 1987).

These social literacy (Barton, 1994; Street, 1995) and multiliteracy theories (Cope & Kalantzis, 2000) are powerful and important reminders that literacy practices are varied and situated across different media, and that school-based literacy practices need to be inclusive of a broad range of students, cultures, and text formats. From this perspective, traditional school literacy practices are critiqued as situated cultural practices that privilege particular kinds of written processes and products, which are limited forms of representation in a broader possible array of cultural expression or multiliterate activity (Cope & Kazantlis, 2000). The "New Basic Project" of Queensland, Australia, for instance, calls for new uses of communications media in new multiliteracy pedagogy that blends old and new technologies that incorporate arts, sound, and print and encourages the presentation of self across a range of media (see http://education.qld.gov.au/corporate/newbasics/html/curric-org/comm.html).

Although multiliteracy theory has become a powerful influence in the field of literacy studies, The New London Group (1996) describes their pedagogical model as "highly provisional" and yet to be widely developed and evaluated. Nevertheless, with the insights of social and multiliteracy theories in mind, we have attempted, in our work, to "rethink what we are teaching, and . . . what new learning needs literacy pedagogy might now address" (New London Group, 2000, p. 10).

Our experiences in the Youth Literacy Program support the hypothesis that emphasizing *only* print texts and "school" literacies, and neglecting the range of artistic expression, popular cultural influences, and multimedia savvy that they bring, simply pushes students further toward the margins of the classroom and our society. To address this marginalization, we have come to rely on rearticulating school texts into the narratives and biographies, the stories, of the student's lives. As O'Brien (1998) points out, for adolescents who struggle with literacy and have been alienated from traditional secondary schools, issues of biography, resistance, and school literacy practices necessarily foreground any approach to curricular innovation. We feel that multiliteracy theory and adolescent literacy practices sometimes underemphasize key components: the dimensions of biography (cf. Fine, 1994), creativity and imagination (Egan, 1997; Searle, 1998), and identity and storytelling (Dyson, 1997; Eisenhart, 1995; Harre, 1998; Holland, Skinner, Lachiotte, & Cain, 1998), that can, at times, lessen or integrate resistances to schooling (see Schofield & Rogers, 2004).

YOUTH LITERACIES AND PEDAGOGIES AS SPATIAL TOURS

Our definition of youth multiple literacies and youth literacy pedagogy, then, moves away from the emphasis on print alone toward a braiding of multimodal texts into narratives—stories constructed on the playing fields of curriculum—that draw on adolescent biographies, imaginations, and their multiple and hybrid identities (McCarthey & Moje, 2002). As Cope and Kalantzis argue (2000), transformed practice begins with the situated lives of learners and the multiple layers of their identities.

We extend this idea by drawing on Harre's (1998) insight that our lives, in addition to a sequence of events and experiences, are "a story which I tell myself and which is forever being updated and revised" (p. 138). In this retelling of our biography, Ricoeur (1984) observes that we choose to recall and retell events depending on who we currently see ourselves to be; we do not recall an empirical reality but rather we reread past experiences. Thus biography and the narratives that we retell to form that biography vary with context and audience; as our lives are "lived and told with others, autobiographical story telling, like all forms of memory work, is essentially social, produced dialogically" (Harre, 1998, p. 146).

We view (auto)biography as a rich and immediate source of multiple literacy practice, constituting the stories youth tell to improvise and project their multiple identities in the flow of social and cultural spaces (Eisenhart, 1995; Holland et al., 1998), relying on imaginatively integrated readings and retellings of their material lives (Bruner, 1987; Whitty, 2002). Youth literacy pedagogy, as we define it, includes this understanding of youth as engaging in a play of (auto)biography, resistance, and imagination within the context of curricular content and the institutional norms of schooling (Alvermann, 2001; Fine, 1994; Gee, 2000; McCarthey & Moje, 2002).

As illustrated later, the students in our youth literacy program integrate their biographies and imaginations in conjunction with developing their multimodal narratives, and we begin to see how the narrative "tours" (de Certeau, 1984) they produce intersect their in- and out-of-school lives and literacies. As de Certeau (1984) argues, every story is a travel story and therefore a spatial practice. In creating new, socially produced narrative spaces, the students draw on the real and imagined spaces that they inhabit and traverse in their everyday lives to articulate, reimagine, resist, and critique their experiences and identities.

Our definition of youth literacy includes the integration of these elaborate(d) understandings of youth identity within a literacy framework that, where possible, draws on available technologies and skills to facilitate learning. Seen in this way, pedagogy becomes a complex exploration of visual and spatial practice that draws on autobiography and imagination to create socially produced spaces or narrative tours of their lives and experiences. In the next part of the chapter, to capture the complexity of such youth literacy practices and to bring our argument to life, we draw on the student's filmed narratives, their writings, and our field notes and observations of ongoing teaching (since April of 2001) with "at risk" designated students enrolled in a Youth Literacy program.[1]

PORTRAITS OF YOUTH MULTIPLE LITERACIES

The classroom context: In an interview digitally videotaped and edited by a peer, a student, Kuresh, commented, "The classroom's not like a normal classroom. It's more like a home, a church almost. We're more of a community" (Interview, 18 April 2003). A sense of community does not come easily in Kuresh's world: The school's local environment is predominantly low-income and has a reputation for its high crime rate ("War on Crime," 2003) and litany of social problems ("Fourth Violent Attack," 2003; "Voices," 2003).

The classroom and Youth Literacy Program that Kuresh refers to, and on which this chapter is based, is located in a Learning Centre, one of 125 public schools in the largest school district in British Columbia and one of the fastest growing in Canada. Within the district, Learning Centres provide fo-

---

[1]This chapter is based on a 2-year intensive collaborative case study of the Youth Literacy Program. Data sources include samples of student work, teacher and researcher journal entries, teacher and student records, digitally videotaped classroom recordings, formal and informal assessments, and annual student interview transcripts.

cused support for predominantly "at risk" designated students[2] as they work toward earning their grade 12 graduation certificates.

Over 7% of Learning Centre students live independently (generally, on the street) at some point in the school year. On average, four students each month are entering or being discharged from a local Youth Detention Centre, and over half of the students experience violence as part of their daily lives, either at home or on the streets. Over 60% of the students indicated that a Sky Train station was a focal point for their social interaction, a station plagued with problems related to youth crime, drugs, and violence (Canadian Centre for Education Alternatives [CCEA], 1999, p. 2). In a random survey conducted by a literacy class student, 64% of the Learning Centre's morning student group had not eaten breakfast, and had not eaten any food by 11:00 a.m.

Principals in the school district annually identify students who, in addition to their at risk designation, have low literacy and numeracy scores on provincial standardized assessment tests. These students are referred to the Learning Centre's Youth Literacy Program. For example, in provincial standardized assessment tests, students in the literacy program are often five grades below average in reading comprehension and six grades below average for numeracy.

The Youth Literacy Program accommodates approximately 32 students (whose ages range from 15 to 20 years), about 75% boys and 25% girls, who are divided into morning and afternoon class sessions. The blend of students, with a range of literacy and numeracy levels and diverse life experiences, are enrolled and placed in the classroom on a full-time basis. When students leave the program and The Learning Centre, new students are accepted. Continuous entry and departure, and the particularities of each student's life, call for a flexible teaching process that includes individualized, group, and peer literacy support and instruction.

The Youth Literacy Program goes beyond traditional literacies by integrating imagination, the material contexts of the students' lives, the readings and rereadings of their own biographies, traditional print-based literacies, and opportunities for students to express themselves across multiple literacies while working through the district mandated curricula toward a diploma.

Video Narratives: Ancestral Drumming, Blue Bouquets, and Chili Chicken

As part of the school/university collaboration, a multimedia (digital video, I-movies, CD compositions) unit was introduced into the Youth Literacy

---

[2]District counselors, learning and behavior psychologists, and principals make the "at risk" designations. Moderate (classified "323") and severe (classified "333") designations are made. "323s" are students with behavior "difficulties"; "333s" are students with criminal records or substance abuse histories.

Program. In Year 1 of the project, a group of students came to the university's education multimedia lab to participate. The unit integrated digital video and CD technology into the literacy program and encouraged the development of language and literacy skills through various multimedia projects. They were assisted by two university teachers who taught them various technological skills, and for one session, a filmmaker worked with them. Drawing from popular cultural artifacts, short stories, and/or their own creative work, students developed storyboards and composed, danced, acted, filmed, and edited their work. Finished projects included a video exploring peer pressure among girls, a video of an artist's portfolio of drawings that accompany an original mythological story, original poetry set to student-composed music, a video interview with a First Nation's student exploring his culture and worldview, a dance video, and a video showcasing snowboarding and skateboarding in an urban environment (view a sample of these videos at newtonliteracies.ca). During the second year of our collaboration, we brought this technology into the school site so that more students could participate, and to fully integrate the multimedia technology into the curriculum. The students taught each other the skills of filming and editing videos. This integration includes engaging students into the life of the classroom, into particular subject areas such as English, science, and film and TV, as well as engaging them in themes that Andrew introduces across the curriculum, such as First Nations studies.

Three student videos described here provide a sampling of the work of the students during Year 2: one is a film of a group of students, a research assistant, and a youth worker engaged in an aboriginal drum-making activity; one is a filmed reinterpretation of a short story by Octavio Paz; and one is a display of a student's interest in cooking that incorporates his family and cultural background.

Ancestral Drumming. The first video narrative is the filming of a drum-making workshop run by the school's Aboriginal Support worker in the literacy classroom. Several of the Youth Literacy students are First Nations. The workshop offered avenues to explore student narratives in a context less formal than that typically offered in the classroom setting. Although the workshops are traditionally attended by First Nations students, one non-Aboriginal student, Scott, asked if he could film the process of making a drum, and produce a documentary of the event. Two narratives intersect here: The first is that of the First Nations students who were provided an opportunity to share their knowledge in a way that displayed it as valuable and important; the second is Scott's narrative. As he says in Snapshot 3 (see p. 221), "I was trying to understand other people's existence through my eyes."

After a discussion regarding the spiritual importance of drum making to Aboriginal peoples and the need for sensitivity, respect, and understanding when filming sacred cultural processes, the workshop commenced. Scott

FIG. 10.1.   Cutting the hide. From "Drum-Making" by S. Moloney. Photograph by Andrew Schofield.

used two digital video cameras to film the 4-hour workshop (see Fig. 10.1).
In addition to these 8 hours of footage, Scott also interviewed the Aboriginal support worker, who pointed out specific technical and spiritual aspects
of the workshop. For example, he pointed out that the slow, unhurried
process of drum making was considered of secondary importance to the
equally leisurely discussion that occurred in the group as they made their
drums. During this time, the students and adults quietly spoke and listened
to each other, occasionally pausing to pass a thread of leather or to braid a
thong, telling stories about their lives, backgrounds and dreams.

   To capture the mood of the workshop, Scott decided to "erase" (extract)
all sound from his film and use only recordings of First Nations music as his
sound track. As he describes it, "Words. . .can be twisted and misinterpreted.
I wanted to capture things that are thicker and more important that words."
He then edited his film into a 9-minute documentary, constructing a narrative sequence that shows the process of drum making; but also, through his
use of music, extreme close-up shots, montage, and cross-overlay of the process, he creates a moving piece of filmmaking that captures teaching and
learning in a social and cultural context that crosses several traditional
boundaries between school and nonschool learning. In addition, the development of this video provided Scott, a talented poet who was at one time at
risk for leaving school (see Snapshot 3), an opportunity to recreate his own
story while witnessing the practices of a parallel culture, providing a rich and
imaginatively represented narrative tour of his own experience.

The Blue Bouquet. The second video narrative was engendered by a process of reading and writing that culminated with a student, JJ (described in the opening of this chapter), transforming Octavio Paz's short story "The Blue Bouquet" into a 1-minute digital video. "The Blue Bouquet" is a very short, haunting story of a man who is victimized by a stranger who wants to present "a bouquet of blue eyes" to win his girlfriend (see Fig. 10.2). In his artist's statement, JJ simply said he really liked the story and decided to make a film about it. He also decided to set his film in a disused underground parking lot, where the local market once was, located across from the school: "It seems like a place where crime takes place." After developing his storyboard and deciding on the thematic elements of the story that he wished to highlight—with an emphasis on the role of observers, perpetrators ('the mugger"), and victims—JJ's challenges began. First, he had to negotiate with peers to agree to be in his film, and to learn their lines. He then had to approach a support worker and ask her to accompany the students to the set, and seek permission from the school's principal (who became the "observer" in the film) to allow the filming to proceed. Once these tasks were attended to, JJ had to coordinate students, camera availability, additional props, and the support worker to allow the filming to proceed.

JJ's initial film footage includes scenes in which the victim leaves school for a walk and is mugged in the abandoned building saturated with colorful graffiti. When he began to edit, JJ realized that he would need to retake some of his shots, and that by changing the camera angle and shot type he could achieve different effects and highlight different aspects of Paz's story.

FIG. 10.2. "But I have brown eyes . . .". From "The Blue Bouquet" by JJ. Photograph by Andrew Schofield.

For example, in the final video the mugging scene is exaggerated by the quick, repetitive shots of the mugging and the request for "blue eyes" and the close-up of the victim's brown eyes. In his "artist's statement" written about this video at the end-of-year gallery, JJ points out that it is important for viewers to look at that scene.

Finally, JJ downloaded and extracted a short soundscape of contemporary rap (Xzibit/Nate Dogg, "Multiply") that introduces and concludes his film. JJ worked assiduously on the project. He was passionate, excited, and occasionally frustrated during the hours that he edited and re-edited his film, showing that he could be totally immersed in "schoolwork," and that it could be challenging and rewarding. This project gave JJ the opportunity to draw on his own experiences and familiar nonschool places and music to translate a powerful and classic short story into a new setting that represents one aspect of his contemporary material life. In a short video, he has transformed the story into his own narrative tour that crosses imagined boundaries of in- and out-of-school lives, so that school becomes less a site of resistance than a site of engagement with multiple forms of literacy.

Chili Chicken.   During an early teacher–student interview, Kurin indicated to Andrew his desire to "become a chef" (K, personal communication, 12 December 2002). His subsequent writing explored the influences on his cooking—his grandparents living in Northern India, their village life, and his father's restaurant in Surrey, BC where he has cooked for 8 years. In another activity, Kurin identified and chose his favourite recipe, and wrote a story that included the recipe. Finally, Kurin imagined himself as a TV cooking show host, presenting his recipe. Over 2 weeks, Kurin identified his camera operator and briefed him about his required camera angles and shots. Andrew and Kurin discussed the importance of shot sequence and different approaches to sustaining viewer interest. Kurin decided to prepare several ingredients beforehand and develop a shot sequence that could be filmed within the 90-minute timeframe that he had access to the camera. Kurin's 10-minute "cookumentary" begins with him proudly looking into the camera and saying: "Hi. My name is Kurin and I am going to show you how to make spicy Chili Chicken."

To complete his narrative, Kurin drew on several aspects of his life and literacies: his home, the memory of his grandparents, remixed Punjabi music that he uses at various points of the film, and the various technical skills of filmmaking. The completed video was one end product; another was a basin of cooked Chili Chicken that Kurin shared with students, teachers, and support workers. Again, we saw the transformation of a student from the margins into the center of school life by narrating a new space for himself that was imagined to life through a narrative tour of his cultural and material life out of school.

While students in the program are encouraged to find their own paths to literacy, drawing on lives in and out of school, more traditional school literacies slip in and out of the learning process. The students' work illustrates the range of possible literacies that can be drawn on and that intersect with school literacies. The motivation for the students to participate in the multimedia projects is derived from two sources. One, their work has a simple instrumental value: Completing work leads to completing graduation course requirements. A second source of motivation is social: The students' class work is oriented toward broader social purposes that echo the students' material lives—their homes, the street, the mall, work.

Kurin is creating a narrative in which he constructs his identity as a developing chef; Scott is creating narratives that interrogate his connection to society; JJ is creating hybrid narratives (a class short story/his understanding of victimization) that begin to explore the assumed romance of street life. Video work is important here because the students discuss camera angles, shot sequence, and lighting and sound, negotiate access times to the camera, and establish partnerships and production teams. This social aspect to literacy learning includes laughter, anxiety, patience, betrayal, and disappointment—such as when students don't show up to act a scene, when footage is lost or deleted, or when a planned script fails technologically.

RECONCEPTUALIZING YOUTH MULTIPLE LITERACIES AS IMAGINATIVE, BIOGRAPHICAL SPATIAL PRACTICES

If we reconceptualize literacy as a set of imaginative and material social practices (Archer, 2001; Dallow, 2001), the assumed dichotomy of in- and out-of-school literacies comes into question. We work with the literacies of youth by finding ways of valuing their reading and writing across school boundaries, or within the interstices of those boundaries, and extending their narratives to include wider and wider horizons of experience. And while we recognize that there are powerful templates, often associated with youth masculinities (cf. Imms, 2000; Martino, 2000), such as racism, homophobia, nationalism, and the edification of street life, violence, and warfare, that are used to structure an individual's self and worldview, these discourses take effect materially, at particular times and in particular places, among particular individuals. Expressing themselves through multimedia narratives provides an opportunity for students to display, reflect on, and reinterpret these identities and experiences. As Munt (2002) points out, "The bounded self has to manage intelligibility of itself through time, and it achieves this through narrative, through becoming the 'hero' of its own story . . . Techniques of the self, such as writing, render the self visible and plausible to itself and to others" (p. 8).

The ways these emergent narratives or identity texts are fundamentally imbricated within the spaces of the students' lives can be seen in another of JJ's videos. Figure 10.3 is a still photo taken from a second video by JJ that explores graffiti art and further illustrates the intersection of space and biography in the lives and literacies of the students. In this film, JJ interviews another student who is a graffiti artist. As the graffiti artist explains, "I do this form of art because it lets me show what I am like . . . it's a form of art that makes everything look better in a ghetto place. Graffiti art just adds color to everything around you." As the soundscape to his film, JJ again used rap music (Tupac's "Thugs Mansion"), which contains the refrain "ain't no place for me." He pointed out in his artist's statement the importance of the site where the interview took place, underlining the broader themes that he is reaching toward: the marginalization of the art form and the liminal or marginal spaces of young people's lives. These identity themes are bound up in space; knowledge, power, and space/place intertwine to frame our social practices (Lefebvre, 1974; Soja, 1989), practices that in this case entail attending school and learning to narrate and reflect on their lives through language, art, print, and multimedia.

Identity and space, from this point of view, are mutually constituted and constituting, both medium and outcome (Giddens, 1979). These narrative artifacts are also socially produced spaces that represent the interstices of students' in- and out-of-school lives. We contend that in- and out-of-school "spaces" meet in the imaginatively produced in-between spaces of these stu-

FIG. 10.3.   Students arrive. From "Graffiti Artist Interview" by JJ. Photograph by Andrew Schofield.

dent narratives. As our portraits of youth multiple literacies illustrate, there can be a constant imaginative interplay across these spatial boundaries.

In our work with these students, we are reconceptualizing youth literacy as including these imaginative and fluid visual and spatial practices that help students integrate their biographies in ways that cross the perceived disjuncture between their in- and out-of-school lives. Viewing literacy practices in this way provides a new lens for thinking about the ways in which multimodal narratives become spatial tours (de Certeau, 1984) of student's biographies and identities, their imaginations, and their multiple literacies.

IMPLICATIONS OF RECONCEPTUALIZING YOUTH LITERACIES

As we illustrated in the opening passage of this chapter, many of the students we work with have fragile relationships to schooling. Many have been previously alienated from traditional schooling and programming or may not see the value of continuing their education; our primary goal, therefore, is to keep as many students as possible engaged in school long enough to earn a diploma. Fortunately, the context of the Learning Centre that houses the Youth Literacy Program allows the flexibility to introduce innovations such as these within the provincial guidelines and district-developed Learning Centre curricula. We note that most traditional secondary schools do not provide programming that engages struggling students in curricular projects that allow them to creatively draw on the material contexts of their lives and their multiple literacies to narrate their stories. Many innovative multimedia programs exist on the borders of school life, in literacy labs or after-school programs, but not as a central aspect of academic subjects. For this to change, schools will have to embrace the notion that learning spaces that focus on new media and new literacies should be at the center of schooling (Hull, 2003).

At the same time, new forms of evaluation will have to be developed. For instance, in our work, we developed portfolio guidelines for evaluating multimedia work that have expansive and generous enough criteria to value the various accomplishments they represent. These guidelines include criteria that emphasize the *genesis* of the projects, including biographical, imaginative sources of storytelling, the integration and transformations of texts across media and genres, the flexible use of various print and media tools; the links across students' out-of-school literacies (including cultural resources) and their in-school literacies; and their ability to create and critique their own and others' imaginative representations.

If we are to take seriously the calls for new literacy pedagogies that take into account the burgeoning variety of text forms, the changing nature of work lives and organization, and draw on the resources of the various subjectivities of students (New London Group, 2000, p. 9), we will have to redesign our curricula in ways that are rich and inclusive for all students.

REFERENCES

Alvermann, D. (2001). Reading adolescents' reading identities: Looking back to see ahead. *Journal of Adolescent and Adult Literacy, 44*(8), 676–690.

Archer, M. (2001). *Being human: The problem of agency.* New York: Cambridge University Press.

Barton, D. (1994). *Literacy: An introduction to the ecology of written language.* Oxford: Basil Blackwell.

Barton, D., & Hamilton, M. (2000). Literacy practices. In D. Barton, M. Hamilton, & R. Ivanic (Eds.), *Situated literacies: Reading and writing in context* (pp. 7–15). London: Routledge.

Barton, D., Hamilton, M., & Ivanic, R. (Eds.). (2000). *Situated literacies: Reading and writing in context.* London: Routledge.

Bruner, J. (1987). Life as narrative. *Social Research, 54,* 11–32.

Canadian Centre for Education Alternatives (CCEA). (1999). *Peer to Peer Literacy Corps: Stage 3.* Funding documentation prepared for Ministry of Advanced Education, Training and Technology. Province of British Columbia. Vancouver: Author.

Cope, B., & Kalantzis, M. (2000). Introduction. *Multiliteracies: Literacy learning and the design of social futures.* London: Routledge.

Dallow, P. (2001). The space of information: Digital media as simulation of the analogical mind. In S. Munt (Ed.), *Technospaces* (pp. 57–70). New York: Continuum.

de Certeau, M. (1984). *The practice of everyday life.* Berkeley, CA: University of California Press.

Dyson, A. H. (1997). *Writing superheroes: Contemporary childhood, popular culture and classroom literacy.* New York: Teachers College Press.

Egan, K. (1997). *The educated mind: How cognitive tools shape our understanding.* Chicago, IL: The University of Chicago Press.

Eisenhart, M. (1995). The fax, the jazz player, and the self-story teller: How *do* people organize culture? *Anthropology and Education Quarterly, 26,* 3–26.

Fine, M. (1994). Working the hyphens: Reinventing self and other in qualitative research. In N. K. Denzin & Y. S. Lincoln (Eds.), *Handbook of Qualitative Research* (pp. 70–82). Thousand Oaks, CA: Sage.

Fourth violent attack in a week: Two more Whalley homes fall prey to invaders. (2003, January 29). *Surrey Leader,* p. 1.

Freire, P. (1978). *Pedagogy in process: The letters to Guinea-Bissau.* London: Writers and Readers Publishing Cooperative.

Freire, P., & Macedo, D. (1987). *Literacy: Reading the word and the world.* London: Routledge.

Gee, J. (1996). *Social linguistics and literacies: Ideology in discourses* (2nd ed.). London: Falmer Press.

Gee, J. (2000). New people in new worlds: Networks, the new capitalism and schools. In B. Cope & M. Kalantzis (Eds.), *Multiliteracies: Literacy learning and the design of social futures* (pp. 43–48). London: Routledge.

Giddens, A. (1979). *Central problems in social theory.* Berkeley: University of California.

Harre, R. (1998). *The singular self.* London: Sage.

Heath, S. B. (1983). *Ways with words.* New York: Cambridge University Press.

Holland, D., Skinner, D., Lachiotte, W., & Cain, C. (2001). *Identity and agency in cultural worlds.* Cambridge, MA: Harvard University Press.

Hull, G. (2003). Youth culture and digital media: New literacies for new times. *Research in the Teaching of English, 38*(2), 229–233.

Hull, G., & Schultz, K. (2001). Literacy and learning out of school: A review of theory and research. *Review of Educational Research, 71*(4), 575–611.

Imms, M. (2000). Multiple masculinities and the schooling of boys. *Canadian Journal of Education, 25*(2), 152–165.

Keith, M., & Pile, S. (Eds.). (1993). *Place and the politics of identity.* London: Routledge.

Leander, K. M. (2003). Writing travelers' tales on new literacyscapes. *Reading Research Quarterly, 38*(3), 392–397.

Lefebvre, H. (1974). *The production of space.* Oxford: Blackwell.

Martino, W. (2000). Mucking around in class, giving crap, and acting cool: Adolescent boys enacting masculinities at school. *Canadian Journal of Education, 25*(2), 102–112.

McCarthey, S. J., & Moje, E. (2002). Conversations: Identity matters. *Reading Research Quarterly, 27*(2), 228–238.

Moje, E. (2000). "To be part of the story": The literacy practices of gangsta adolescents. *Teachers College Record, 102*(3), 51, 651–691.

Munt, S. (2002). Framing intelligibility, identity, and selfhood: A reconsideration of spatio-temporal models. *Reconstruction, 2*(3), 1–14.

New London Group. (1996). A pedagogy of multiliteracies: Designing social futures. *Harvard Educational Review, 66*(1), 60–92.

New London Group. (2000). A pedagogy of multiliteracies. In B. Cope & M. Kalantzis (Eds.), *Multiliteracies: Literacy learning and the design of social futures* (pp. 9–37). London: Routledge.

O'Brien, D. (1998). Multiple literacies in a high school program for "At Risk" adolescents. In D. Alvermann, K. Hinchman, D. Moore, S. Phelps, & D. Waff (Eds.), *Reconceptualizing the literacies in adolescents' lives* (pp. 27–50). London: Lawrence Erlbaum Associates.

Ricoeur, P. (1984). *Time and narrative* (K. McLaughlin & D. Pellauer, Trans.). Chicago: University of Chicago Press.

Schofield, A., & Rogers, T. (2004). At play in fields of ideas: Teaching, curriculum, and lives and multiple literacies of youth. *Journal of Adolescent and Adult Literacy, 48*(3), 238–248.

Searle, C. (1998). *None but our words. Critical literacy in classroom and community.* Philadelphia, PA: Open University Press.

Scribner, S., & Cole, M. (1981). *The psychology of literacy.* Cambridge, MA: Harvard University Press.

Soja, E. (1989). *Postmodern geographies: The reassertion of space in critical social theory.* London: Verso.

Street, B. (1995). *Social literacies: Critical approaches to literacy in development, ethnography and education.* New York: Longman.

Voices form Whalley's Ground Zero: Residents talk about the hazards of living at the epicenter of drugs and crime. (2003, January 30). *The Vancouver Sun,* pp. A1, B4.

War on crime in Whalley heats up. (2003, January 28). *The Vancouver Sun,* p. B1.

Weinstein, S. (2002). The writing on the wall: Attending to self-motivated student literacies. *English Education, 35*(1), 21–45.

Whitty, M. (2002). Possible selves: An exploration of the utility of a narrative approach. *Identity: An International Journal of Theory and Research, 2*(3), 211–228.

Snapshot 3

A SMALL PIECE OF THE TRUTH

Scott Moloney
Newton Learning Centre

When I came to this school, I believed that school was for people who could not survive on the street. Then I realized that no one survives on the street, so I thought I would give school a try again. When I got here, I was put into a room and handed bookwork. I thought, "Great, just another school." Then I met Andrew, my teacher, in the literacy programme. He showed me that learning isn't as boring as I thought, but I still had doubts. When we went to UBC for the multimedia unit where I turned one of my poems into a CD, and worked on some videos, I sat back and thought, "There is so much more to school than just the building."

I was always the kind of kid who skipped class to make money because school does not make you money. But when I got into my groove at school, I was mad when I had to stay home because I wanted to see what I could do. I never thought I would get the opportunity I have now, and I know for a fact that I would not get the same chance in a regular school. We found out we did pretty well with what I call the "UBC" mission.

A local grant foundation and our partnership with UBC hooked us up with some money and the journey began. I had my best teacher at my side, the camera in my hand, and was staring the world in the face. It was a slow process finding myself and the spot where the camera and I fit together, but when I did . . . watch out, because here comes Scotty. I found it easy to get footage just because I like real film, not acting. In some films it's okay to have acting, but not in mine. I look for spontaneous real action.

I've always had one foot in the street and the other foot floating in the clouds. I did my own thing by working away, making films that I could express myself with any way I could. For instance, my "Belgium" film [made for an academic conference presentation] shows what's going on with kids today. Then one day a younger guy in my class asked for help and I found another way to work with the camera—by teaching my peers. I don't know what it is or what got me so hooked on filming. All I know is that when I am filming, I am so happy. Even with the hardest, most frustrating problem, I still love it.

In my work I try to understand myself through my own words and through my thoughts, but I can't always show these thoughts or what should be done. For instance, in my Belgium film and my film about drum making, you can see what people have in their lives and, through seeing their lives, maybe you can understand them. In the Belgium film, I tried to show what kids have to grow up with. I did this by interviewing students and doing free filming on streets in my city. It's a film about daily lives captured in a video collage. So through "blind eyes" (the camera) I see the truth of humanity—that there are people stuck on the streets because uncaring citizens don't understand homelessness and poverty.

In the drum-making film [described in Rogers and Schofield, chapter 10, this volume], I was trying to understand other people's existence through my eyes. I don't believe in "culture"—that leads to stereotypes. I was looking at the people and trying to understand them through my experience and my eyes. In that film, I also took out all dialogue, replacing it with a different soundtrack. I did that because words can show the good and the bad, they can be twisted and misinterpreted. While words can show how people reflect themselves, we don't always need words to show ourselves. And people also sometimes hear things differently, based on their lives and experiences. So I erased the words because I wanted to capture things that were thicker and more important than words.

I only have a small piece of the truth. The best way I have it is through the people around me slowly making my piece of the truth larger and more power-ful, which will take me through the valleys of life. With all my films, I try to cap-ture my feelings and thoughts and, if done properly, you get your piece of the truth. I don't have a fear of speaking about what needs to be said. This gift I give to myself is a way of life, all that I need to succeed. My poem is another way of saying this:

WHAT WE NEED TO SUCCEED

In life you don't always get a fair chance
because it's never given to you
You have to earn what you get
In life an opportunity is a mind in motion,
and a mind could be you?
or me?
Whoever it is
is true to the thought
and true to the mind
because blood bleeds thickest from the heart,
but truest from the mind.
In all our glory
we still hate the work,
the work of a savior
or the work of the slave.
Through our thoughts we get better
but through our thoughts we get worse to ourselves.
People are stupid,
but a person is very smart
And through our stupidity
we find the means of thought and mind

The brain is a muscle of mush
but a mind is a mountain of successes
And through our thoughts
we learn
what we need to succeed.

Chapter 11

A Portrait of Literacy From the Youth Millennium Project

Bonny Norton
University of British Columbia

> *If I like a photograph, if it disturbs me, I linger over it. What am I doing the whole time I remain with it? I look at it, I scrutinize it, as if I wanted to know more about the thing or the person it represents.*
>
> —Barthes (1981, p. 99)

225

CLOSE-UP

There are 12 children in the photograph, most of them standing around a large wooden desk. The smallest child, a girl, is sitting down, looking directly at the camera. Behind her is a teacher, standing protectively, her attention diverted away from the camera. She is wearing a beautiful blue and yellow shalwar kameez—a long shirt over loose trousers—with a scarf draped over her shoulders. On the one side of the desk, a group of girls and boys in school uniforms, ranging in age from about 11 to 14, stand close together. They are smiling at the younger children, all girls, on the opposite side of the desk. The girls are wearing brightly colored floral dresses, and one is smiling shyly at the older children. Books, pens, and pencils lie scattered on the table. On the walls are colorful letters of the English alphabet, pictures of fruits and vegetables, and a drawing of a tree, with the title "GREEN DAY Tree" in large letters above it. There is also a drawing of a hand, with the letters a, e, i, o, u, on each of the fingers, the word "VOWELS" serving as the title of the drawing.

This photograph is a portrait of literacy: students, teacher, desk, pens, papers, books, posters. What distinguishes it from many other familiar portraits of literacy, however, is the unique story that frames it. The story of this photograph serves as the substance of this chapter.

ZOOMING OUT

This photograph was taken in June 2001. The location is an orphanage for Afghan children in the teeming city of Karachi, Pakistan. The girls in the floral dresses are young Afghan orphans; the children on the left side of the photograph are visitors from Model Elementary School in Karachi. The visiting students are participating in the global Youth Millennium Project (YMP) of the University of British Columbia (UBC), Canada. Referring to themselves as "The Reformers," the children at Model Elementary have chosen to implement a project that they have called Literacy for All, in which they are supporting the young girls depicted in the photograph. The Reformers describe the project as follows:

> We have collected books (story and reference) and stationery items to give as gifts to underprivileged youth, as a move to help them read and write. We have selected a nearby orphanage which looks after 25 children of ages 3–13 of "Afghan War Refugees" to give away all our collection. Our action plan was very exciting and completed in three months. This project was part of our English and Social Studies curriculum of the first term. We have carried out many interesting activities during this project.

In their June 2001 report to coordinators of the YMP at UBC, the students outlined how they planned to extend their Literacy for All project in September, 2001:

> Our next YMP action plan is an extension of this plan during which we have focused on literacy. But this time, we plan to organize English speaking classes for the same group of children in the "Afghan orphanage." We will conduct at 15 classes of 2 hours each during which we will teach these students simple English phrases, used for daily life communication. We will take up this project 2nd Term beginning September 2001.

The children's extension of their YMP project never took place. Since 9/11, when the United States of America was attacked and an international force retaliated against Pakistan's neighbouring country, Afghanistan, students at Model Elementary have seen refugees pouring into the city of Karachi; they have experienced temporary school closures; and they have witnessed a region in turmoil. The story of their Literacy for All YMP project needs to be told. It not only represents a moment of hope in a time of despair, but provides important insights into the students' perceptions of literacy and their investment in the English language.

THE RESEARCH FILTER

In October 2000, I had the good fortune to visit Model Elementary School while participating in the annual SPELT (Society of Pakistan English Language Teachers) conference of Pakistan's English language educators. I was excited to find that there was much interest in implementing YMP in this school, and considered myself ideally placed to conduct research on the ways in which students responded to this social action opportunity. The research study was thus conducted concurrently with the implementation of the YMP. The first stage of the study (March–June, 2001) included 40 male and 40 female students of approximately 12 to 13 years of age, whereas the second stage of the research (October–December, 2001) included 26 students, 13 girls and 13 boys from the larger sample. The research sample also included four teachers of language and social studies, as well as the head of the language department and the head of social studies. Methods of data collection in the first stage of the research included completion of a questionnaire by students and participating teachers, and on-site observation of classrooms.

It was the data collected in the second stage of the research (October–December 2001) that gave particular insight into the students' conceptions of literacy and the English language. I addressed the following two questions to 26 students (13 girls and 13 boys) in an e-mail exchange in October 2001:

> Question 1: I think it is very interesting that although you had considered a number of action plans dealing with social issues, the one that you decided to implement was about literacy. I have no doubt that your efforts to help the Afghan refugee children in your community were very welcome. I have a number of questions about this project. Why did you decide to focus on literacy? Why do you think literacy is important? How can children become literate?

> Question 2: You said in your student report that your next step would be to help the Afghan children learn some simple English phrases. Why did you choose this as the next step?

After providing a theoretical frame to the research, the photograph and the Literacy for All project are analysed through three lenses. "The Lens of Social Action" addresses the genesis of the Literacy for All project, the expectations of stakeholders, and the conditions that needed to be in place for it to succeed. "The Lens of Literacy" addresses why the students chose to focus on literacy as an action plan, and what their conceptions of literacy were. "The Lens of English" addresses why the children chose English as the language they hoped to teach the Afghan refugee children, and how their investments in English were socially and historically constructed. Drawing on earlier work (Norton, 2000), I use the notion of "investment" to reference a learner's desire to learn a language in the context of shifting identities and unequal relations of power.

THE THEORETICAL FRAME

The theoretical framing of this discussion draws on work in social and critical literacy (Barton & Hamilton, 1998; Cope, Kalantzis, & New London Group, 2000; Freire, 1970; Heath, 1983; Kendrick, 2003; Luke, 2003; New London Group, 1996; Norton & Toohey, 2004). As these researchers note, educators who are interested in critical literacy are interested in literacy as a site of struggle, negotiation, and change. Whereas earlier psychological perspectives conceived of literacy as the acquisition of particular behaviors, cognitive strategies, and linguistic processing skills, more recent insights from ethnography, cultural studies, and feminist theory have led to increasing recognition that literacy is not only a skill to be learned, but a practice that is socially constructed and locally negotiated. In this view, literacy is best understood in the context of larger institutional practices—whether in the home, the school, the community, or the larger society. These institutional practices, in turn, must be understood with reference to frequently inequitable access to social, economic, and political power.

THE LENS OF SOCIAL ACTION

The Literacy for All project was developed in the context of the students' involvement in the YMP (www.ympworld.org), a global initiative of UBC. YMP was motivated by research that suggests that youth often feel powerless in the face of global events, believing that they have little contribution to make to social change. It began in 1999 and currently comprises over 10,000 young people in 80 countries internationally. The goal of YMP is to provide youth with the opportunity to build self-confidence and community by creating a local plan of action that addresses a larger social issue. Local plans of action can be large or small, and include groups of students approximately 11 to 14 years of age. Schools learn of the project via diverse means. In Sri Lanka, for example, UNICEF in Colombo distributed information about the project to high school principals, some of whom passed on the message to the United Nations clubs in their schools. If there is interest in the project, schools register with the YMP at UBC, and are linked with three other schools internationally. At the conclusion of the project, students submit reports on their activities to a YMP coordinator at UBC. Thus the YMP seeks to encourage community building within and across national boundaries.

Language and social studies teachers at Model Elementary were interested in the YMP because proficiency in English communication is one of the most important academic goals for most students in Pakistan, particularly for those residing in urban areas. Involvement in the YMP offered an opportunity for language learning as well as engagement in both the local and global community. It presented an opportunity to achieve mastery over English beyond use of conventions and decoding of text, and it provided an interesting dimension to existing English language and social studies curricula. Furthermore, YMP offered the possibility for innovation in classroom practices. In Model Elementary, the pedagogy of language and social studies is highly structured, with tests and examinations a central focus of the curriculum. By involving students in YMP, the Grade 8 teachers were hoping to bring about pedagogical change and to create the conditions for active engagement in learning. The teachers were enthusiastic about incorporating a more dialogue-based pedagogy into their classrooms.

The students who participated in the YMP project were mostly second, and in some cases third, language speakers of English. Urdu enjoys the status of the "national language" as well as the *lingua franca* in Pakistan, and almost all the students at Model Elementary are comfortable in communicating in Urdu orally. At home, the majority of students speak two or more languages, including Urdu, English, and one of the regional languages. Nevertheless, English is the medium of instruction in Model Elementary, and having command over written and spoken English promotes social and economic success in Pakistani society.

A day before the first discussion of the YMP project in spring 2001, teachers encouraged students to listen to national and international news on television and to read a few newspaper articles. The next day, there was much animated discussion on local and global issues. The first impressions students had in identifying social problems were of distress: "I never realised there are so many problems around us," said one of the Reformers. "I thought a lot about the 'poor children' and the 'homeless' ones even after the discussion was over and when I was at home," said another. "We were extremely confused when we went on talking and discussing about so many problems in the society, we thought it's a bad world and scary too," said a third.

The YMP provided an opportunity for students to improve their understanding of political and democratic processes. After expressing concern about social conditions both locally and globally, students focussed their attention on how they could address the inequities they had identified. Some, in despair, looked for magical solutions: As one said, "How come I never knew of anything like this before. I wish I have magic wand to put every thing straight." For most students, however, it was through debate and discussion that they seemed to regain some confidence. As one said, "Our group members and teachers asked each other what can be done and from here we actually felt better that something can be done." Through their local action plans, students considered themselves capable of making a difference to their community and were eager to do something beyond chalk and talk. As one of the teachers commented, "By identifying the global issues, their minds opened from self to society, to other communities, from their country to other countries of the world."

Although the Reformers had identified different action plans, the one they decided to implement in the first stage of the project was a literacy program for Afghan refugee children in a local orphanage. Because these children lacked school supplies and resources, the Reformers planned to collect storybooks, reading materials, and stationery items appropriate for children aged 3 to 13. The texts they chose were all in English. Their slogan was a *"a pencil a person."* The students' idea was that if each person on the larger school campus of Model Elementary donated a pencil, they could collect hundreds of pencils that would make a great difference to the Afghan children. In order to achieve this objective, the students undertook the following activities in April and May, 2001:

- The students designed and displayed posters and memos to publicise their cause and draw the attention of other classes in the school. They invited all students to donate books, stationery, and pencils.
- Pairs of students gave talks in the staff room, principal's office, and in all other sections of the school.
- Students collected, sorted, categorized, and packed the collected books and supplies for distribution.
- The Reformers then delivered the packages to the orphanage and interacted with the Afghan children and their teachers—a visit captured in the photograph described earlier.

During their involvement in YMP, students encountered learning opportunities that gave them the opportunity to critically reflect on social issues both locally and globally. One enthusiastic youth responded, "Despite it created some problems, action planning was the most interesting part of the project. This type of project work can give us more information, involve us mentally and physically in action planning." Most of the students said that they were shocked to find that there are so many problems in the world that need attention, and that YMP made them more aware of the world and their immediate environment. As one said, "We got an opportunity to become aware of local and global issues and to think how to solve them." Although the students recognized that they "cannot solve the problems completely," they felt sufficiently confident to begin addressing the problems they had identified. With reference to the Afghan children, in particular, one student noted, "I liked going out of the school to make presentations and to the orphanage," while another observed, "We expect that by providing education to others, we can improve our environment and community."

THE LENS OF LITERACY

The photograph I described depicts a literacy classroom where there are posters, pencils, desks, and chairs. The students at Model Elementary were committed to the notion that all children should have access to literacy, and had many insights about the importance of literacy in the wider community. Significantly, the students held the view that literacy is not only about reading and writing, but about education more broadly. "The word literate is known as to educate," said Samira, while Salma, similarly, noted that "The worldly meaning of literacy is educated or having education." Other students, however, extended this view to include the notion that a literate person has greater ability to reason than one who is illiterate. Shahid, for example, noted that a literate person "can make better decisions" than an illiterate person, while Kamran said that "If we are not literate we cannot do any work with thinking." The comment by Fariha perhaps summarizes best the views of many of the students:

> Literacy is very important because education gives understanding to people. The thinking of an educated person is different and he thinks properly about his country and people. An uneducated person thinks differently. He thinks of taking revenge and fighting with their enemies, but an educated person wants to solve big problems and settle their dispute of territories by arranging dialogues. They realize and analyze the situation and an illiterate person does not have this ability.

While many students focused on the meaning of literacy for individual members of a community, other students focused on the importance of literacy for the development of a nation. "Literacy plays a vital role in the progress of a country," said Saman, whereas Nida noted passionately that "without education our beloved country Pakistan cannot develop." Indeed, Samira was of the opinion that "the person who is illiterate doesn't have any respect for his own country." The development of a country, students noted, lies in the education of children, "the stars of their countries." Thus, an investment in the education of children is an investment in the future.

Many students attributed the disparity between developed and developing countries to literacy practices, noting, in particular, the literacy challenges that Pakistan faces: "The literacy rate in our country is much less than well-developed countries," said Rubina. Others made the case that high levels of literacy give a country a competitive edge in international politics. Shahid, for example, noted, "If a nation didn't raise its literacy it can't compete with other nations and it can't maintain independence." Many students agreed that developed countries are powerful because people in developed countries are literate. As Ahmed said, "We know that in developed countries everyone is educated and goes to school. That is why they are rich and have no problems."

Students recognized, however, that resources—what Nida called "funds and donations"—are needed to promote literacy in a country, and they offered many suggestions as to how resources could be shared to promote literacy in the broader society. "The most important thing," said Javed, "is that the people who are already literate should give free tuition and support to poor people." Fariha, similarly, noted that if children are unable to pay school fees, "we can educate them by opening schools in which they will not have to pay the fees." Tahira reported on a conversation she had with a person she called a "childlabour," who had requested the provision of night school:

I spoke to a childlabour about education. They said that their parents are not able to earn enough in order to survive: . . . "If any one will open night school for us we will get education, because we are not free in the morning and afternoon."

In his recent work on literacy and development, Street (2001) makes the case that if literacy projects and programs are to be effective in diverse regions of the world, researchers need to understand the uses and meanings of literacy practices to local people themselves. In the developing world, in particular, he notes that development workers need to understand what counts as learning and education, and who has the right to define what education is. His own research in Iran provides convincing evidence that people perceived to be " 'illiterate' backward villagers" (p. 6) are engaged in diverse literacy practices, whether in traditional Quaranic schools or in the local fruit market. The consequences of ignoring or negating local experiences can have dire consequences. As Street notes:

> Even though in the long run many local people do want to change their literacy practices and take on board some of those associated with Western or urban society, a crude imposition of the latter that marginalizes and denies local experience is likely to alienate even those who were initially motivated. (p. 7)

It is interesting to note to what extent the students' perceptions of literacy are consistent with current conceptions of literacy in Western academia. Like many contemporary theorists of literacy (Barton & Hamilton, 1998; Cope et al., 2000; Heath, 1983; Luke, 2003), the students take the position that literacy requires more than an understanding of isolated symbols and discrete texts; they perceive literacy as associated with social and educational practices. Furthermore, like Street (2001), they recognize that "the ways in which people address reading and writing are themselves rooted in conceptions of knowledge, identity, being" (p. 7).

In this regard, Samina's view that "the person who is illiterate doesn't have any respect for his own country" requires further analysis. Given Anderson's (1991) conception of the nation as an "imagined community" (p. 6) in which members of even the smallest nation don't meet or know most of the members of the nation, it is intriguing to consider the ways in which literacy practices, in general, and education, more specifically, serve to "invent" the nation. Indeed, Anderson makes the point that "print-capitalism . . . made it possible for rapidly growing numbers of people to think about themselves, and to relate themselves to others, in profoundly new ways" (p. 36). The data support the view that literacy is associated with nation building, and that students were acutely aware that the very idea of "beloved Pakistan" was constructed through literacy practices in schools and in the wider community.

Significantly, however, students were also eager to use literacy to build relationships across nations, and imagined a global community in which nations can relate to one another on more equitable terms than currently exists. In this view, literacy would not only develop Pakistan, but enable Pakistan to connect more democratically with other nations, thereby promoting greater international stability and reducing the isolation of Pakistan. Such views suggest that the relationship between literacy and community building is perhaps even more profound than Anderson has predicted, transcending national boundaries, and emerging in a variety of ways.

THE LENS OF ENGLISH

Notwithstanding the native language of the Afghan children, English is the dominant language in the photograph: The walls are covered with colorful letters of the English language; the posters are titled in English; a drawing of a hand signals the 5 vowels of the English language. The photograph provides support for the students' decision to teach the Afghan children "some simple English phrases." Like notions of literacy, these students' responses to the importance of English were complex and can be summarized in a number of related themes about the perceived usefulness of English, both locally and internationally.

Students at Model Elementary were motivated by the belief that English is an international language and the language of science, technology, and the media. As Shahida said, "The English language is an international language spoken all over the world and it is the language of science. Therefore to promote their education and awareness with modern technologies, it is important to teach them English."

Students noted further that knowledge of English would enable the Afghan children to communicate directly with people all over the world, without the help of translators, and to explain to the wider community how much they had suffered. As Fariha noted, "English is the language spoken commonly. This language is understood throughout the world. If the Afghan children learn English, know English, speak English, they will be able to discuss their problems with the people of the world."

Students such as Jamshed also noted that English serves as a common language not only across nations, but within nations: "We choose this as our next step because English is the international and global media language and most of the Afghan immigrants do not know English and have no particular language to communicate with local people. Therefore we choose this as the next step so they can communicate with local people." Furthermore, it is knowledge of English, students believed, that would redress imbalances between developed and developing nations. As Salma said, "The world is not at all really aware of the problems faced by the people living not only in third world countries but also in far away nations due to lack of knowledge about their culture, and about their language."

Finally, many students noted that knowledge of English gives people access to resources that will give them greater opportunity in life. Fariha noted, for example, that with English, "Afghan children will be able to get admission in schools." Furthermore, knowledge of English would help the Afghan children develop their country when they return to Afghanistan. "If every citizen of the nation could take one step towards their betterment, they could follow the path of knowledge and success instead of the gun," said Zaib.

With only a few exceptions, the students demonstrated little ambivalence toward the English language and perceived it as an important tool for social, economic, and political advancement, within Pakistan as well as the international community. When students were pressed to consider whether the spread of English had any negative consequences, only two students noted that a country's native languages could be compromised, and only one noted that the spread of English would be accompanied by the spread of Western culture, "a bad sign." Such a positive evaluation of English needs to be understood against the backdrop of a substantial body of literature that suggests the spread of English is a form of Western imperialism, implicated in the loss of local and minority languages (Pennycook, 1998; Phillipson, 1992; Skutnabb-Kangas, 2000; Tollefson, 1991). An emerging body of research by scholars such as Canagarajah (1999), May (2001), and Brutt-Griffler (2002), takes up the challenge of earlier studies and helps to explain the students' investments in English.

In his seminal work, *Resisting Linguistic Imperialism* (1999), Canagarajah provides a number of important insights about the experiences of students living in what are sometimes called "periphery" communities—postcolonial communities that speak English as the first or dominant language, or have acquired English alongside one or more local languages. Such countries include India, Pakistan, Malaysia, Barbados, and Nigeria. Drawing on the work of postcolonial scholars such as hooks (1989, 1990) and Said (1979, 1993), Canagarajah (1999) argues that a particular "politics of location" (hooks, 1989) provides for a different understanding of the spread of English than that dominant in Western academia: "Just as center resistance is grounded in the social practice and cultural concerns of center communities, periphery thinking has to be shaped by its own location" (p. 35). He suggests that a number of Western academics who have investigated the effects of the global spread of English have been paralyzed by dichotomizing perspectives that frame debates about English—arguing for and against

English; for and against the vernacular (p. 3). He suggests, in contrast, that people can engage favorably with both English and the vernacular, and that people in marginalized communities have the human agency to think critically about their options and to work out ideological alternatives that promote their own empowerment. Furthermore, in arguing for what he calls the "resistance perspective," Canagarajah makes the case that both English and vernacular languages are sufficiently heterogeneous for diverse groups to make them serve their own purposes, and enable subjects to rise above their domination (p. 2).

May (2001), like Canagarajah (1999), argues that debates on the spread of English should be centrally concerned with the extent to which English is promoted at the expense of other languages in the public realm. By way of example, May cites the case of the English-only movement in the United States, which he describes as a deliberate attempt to marginalize other languages in the country. My research suggests that the students at Model Elementary, although being favorably disposed toward English, still had high regard for Urdu, and had no difficulty code-switching between Urdu and English as the need arose. Brutt-Griffler (2002), furthermore, makes the case that those who equate the spread of English with linguistic imperialism may overlook what she understands as a more essential element, which is the desire of diverse nations to link to the world at large. This desire, she suggests, should not be confused with attempts to link with the United States or the United Kingdom exclusively.

Clearly, the persistence of English in Pakistan is partly explained by Pakistan's geopolitical isolation. Pakistanis, like the Tamils in Canagarajah's (1999) study, have struggled for international connection and recognition, and have used English to reach out to international media, connect with the diaspora community, and communicate with hotlines and electronic mail. Pakistanis, like Tamils, have a powerful neighbor, India, that is not sympathetic to its interests; it has another neighbor, Afghanistan, that has been politically unstable for decades; and it has a government that has been struggling for legitimacy in a skeptical international community. Under these conditions, English provides Pakistanis with the opportunity to remain socially, economically, and politically connected—not only to the United States and United Kingdom but to the wider international community. The Model Elementary students in the photograph wanted to encourage the young girls in floral dresses to become global citizens.

A WIDE-ANGLE LENS

The photograph described at the beginning of this chapter, and the Literacy for All project, are best understood within the context of social and political instability, both nationally and internationally. The students at Model

Elementary valued their involvement in the YMP, but realized that they could not address all social problems. They appreciated being literate, but recognized that literacy is a privilege. They saw themselves as part of a larger community of English speakers, but acknowledged Pakistan's marginal status in the international community. The struggle for literacy, access to English, and educational change can be seen as interdependent, reflecting the desire of students in a postcolonial world to engage with the international community from a position of strength rather than weakness. I sought to understand the students' investments in English from a geopolitical and historical perspective, and suggested that the appropriation of English does not necessarily compromise identities structured on the grounds of linguistic or religious affiliation. The data suggest that English and the vernacular can coexist in mutually productive ways and that the "politics of location" (Canagarajah, 1999) has great explanatory value.

Furthermore, like Canagarajah (1999) and Luke (2004), I take the position that if we wish to understand the meaning of literacy in the students' lives, we cannot ignore the imperatives of the material world and the ways in which resources are distributed—not only nationally, but internationally. Canagarajah (1999) makes a compelling case that in periphery contexts in which there is a daily struggle for food, clothing, shelter, and safety, "a diet of linguistic guerilla warfare, textual resistance, and micro-politics will not suffice" (p. 34). Luke (2004), similarly, argues that while we as educators might debate the meaning of critical literacy, we may not do justice to the lived experiences of physical and material deprivation in diverse communities throughout the globe. The students in the study made frequent reference to the relationship between literacy, the distribution of resources, and international inequities. For these students, a community that is literate and skilled in English is also a community that has food, shelter, and peace.

However, it is of some concern that students might, in fact, overestimate the benefits that can accrue from the development of literacy and the spread of English. Ahmed's assessment, for example, that people who are educated "are rich and have no problems" may lead to a crisis of expectations. Furthermore, May (2001) makes a convincing argument that there is no necessary relationship between the adoption of English by developing countries and greater economic well-being. Of even more concern is the ways in which pedagogical and social practices may be serving, perhaps inadvertently, to reinforce the view held by the students that people who are literate are more rational and intellectually able than those who are not literate. If students in Pakistan, and perhaps in other parts of the world, equate literacy with rationality and intellectual ability, while at the same time embracing English as *the* international language of science, media, and technology, is there a danger that they may consider people who are literate in English as more rational and intellectually able than those who are not? Such a question requires greater depth of focus.

ACKNOWLEDGMENTS

I thank students and teachers of Model Elementary School who generously participated in this study. I also thank Farah Kamal for helping to collect some of the data used in the study. I gratefully acknowledge the financial support of the Social Sciences and Research Council of Canada.

This chapter is a modified and extended version of Norton and Kamal, 2003.

REFERENCES

Anderson, B. (1991). *Imagined communities: Reflections on the origins and spread of nationalism* (Rev. ed.). London: Verso.

Barthes, R. (1981). *Camera lucida: Reflections on photography.* (R. Howard, Trans.). Farrar, Straus & Giroux.

Barton, D., & Hamilton, M. (1998). *Local literacies: Reading and writing in one community.* London: Routledge.

Brutt-Griffler, J. (2002). *World English: A study of its development.* Clevedon, England: Multilingual Matters.

Canagarajah, A. S. (1999). *Resisting linguistic imperialism in English teaching.* Oxford: Oxford University Press.

Cope, B., Kalantzis, M., & New London Group (2000). *Multiliteracies: Literacy learning and the design of social futures.* London: Routledge.

Freire, P. (1970). *Pedagogy of the oppressed.* New York: Seabury Press.

Heath, S. B. (1983). *Ways with words: Language, life, and work in communities and classrooms.* New York: Cambridge University Press.

hooks, b. (1989). *Talking back: Thinking feminist, thinking black.* Boston: South End Press.

hooks, b. (1990). *Yearning: Race, gender, and cultural politics.* Boston: South End Press.

Kendrick, M. (2003). *Converging worlds: Play, literacy, and culture in early childhood.* Bern: Peter Lang Publishing.

Luke, A. (2003). Literacy and the other: A sociological approach to literacy research and policy in multilingual societies. *Reading Research Quarterly, 38*(1), 132–141.

Luke, A. (2004). Two takes on the critical. In B. Norton & K. Toohey (Eds.), *Critical pedagogies and language learning* (pp. 21–29). Cambridge: Cambridge University Press.

May, S. (2001). *Language and minority rights: Ethnicity, nationalism and the politics of language.* Harlow, England: Pearson Education.

New London Group (1996). A pedagogy of multiliteracies: Designing social futures. *Harvard Educational Review, 66*(1), 60–92.

Norton, B. (2000). *Identity and language learning: Gender, ethnicity, and educational change.* Harlow, England: Longman/Pearson Education.

Norton, B., & Kamal, F. (2003). The imagined communities of Pakistani English language learners. *Journal of Language, Identity, and Education, 2*(4), 301–317.

Norton, B., & Toohey, K. (Eds.). (2004). *Critical pedagogies and language learning.* Cambridge: Cambridge University Press.

Pennycook, A. (1998). *English and the discourses of colonialism.* London: Routledge.

Phillipson, R. (1992). *Linguistic imperialism.* Oxford, England: Oxford University Press.

Said, E. (1979). *Orientalism.* New York: Random House.

Said, E. (1993). *Culture and imperialism.* New York: Alfred Knopf.

Skutnabb-Kangas, T. (2000). *Linguistic genocide in education—or worldwide diversity and human rights?* Mahwah, NJ: Lawrence Erlbaum Associates.

Street, B. (2001). *Literacy and development.* London: Routledge.

Tollefson, J. (1991). *Planning language, planning inequality: Language policy in the community.* London: Longman.

Part III

COMMUNITY AND ADULT LITERACIES

Chapter 12

To "Know Papers": Aboriginal Perspectives on Literacy

Jan Hare
University of British Columbia

In a conversation with her grandfather, a young Saulteaux woman posed to her grandfather the question, "What do you think Native students and educators ought to know about Native education?"[1] Her grandfather, a respected Saulteaux Elder, Alfred Manitopeyes of the Muskcowekwun Band in southern Saskatchewan, Canada, did not offer a straight or direct answer to her question. Rather, he took her through a series of stories that demonstrate what the young can learn from "good talking" and "good walking." Within Aboriginal[2] traditions of storytelling, she must then apply these stories to her original question. It becomes clear to the young woman that "good walks and talks" are ways in which Aboriginal knowledge is created and passed on in the learning process.

His "stories" further conceptualize understandings of education for Aboriginal people. He describes education as a balancing act between the "whiteman's" teachings and traditional teachings of the Saulteaux. The fo-

---

[1]This conversation is drawn from Akan (1999). The Saulteaux are part of the Algonquin linguistic speaking group, one of 11 language groups in Canada. They have also been referred to as Ojibwe or Chippewa and were originally located at Sault Ste. Marie at Lake Superior and in northern Michigan and much of the Great Lakes regions.

[2]Aboriginal is inclusive of First Nations, Metis, and Inuit people of Canada. Although I use Aboriginal as an inclusive term, many Aboriginal people refer to themselves individually by their land base. For example, I, the author of this chapter, am Anishinaabe of the M'Chigeeng First Nation. The United States refers to North American Indians as Native Americans or American Indians. In a global context, I refer to the First Peoples of their land as Indigenous.

cus of the "whiteman's" teachings was print literacy, or to "know papers," as his term for it is translated from the Saulteaux. Elder Alfred Manitopeyes sees the conventions of Western modes of communication, which give primacy to print and legitimize the dominant languages, as no more than "pacoosewaywin" or a "borrowed cultural product." Aboriginal people were very aware of the changing world, and Western literacy was seen to offer a gateway, indeed *the* gateway, to the newcomer's world. To learn to "know papers" in this way was recognized by many Aboriginals as offering their people new opportunities, although the cost of such lessons was far more than we, as Aboriginal people, could ever have expected.

In this chapter, I draw on the narratives of elderly Aboriginal men and women, which I gathered in an Anishinaabe[3] community on Manitoulin Island in northern Ontario, Canada. They illustrate how Aboriginal people have constructed multiple meanings for literacy that are not only based on print literacy and now-dominant languages, but also draw on Aboriginal ways of knowing that incorporate the cultural practices by which Aboriginal peoples live and make sense of the world. This Aboriginal approach to a broader concept of literacy, I contend, is firmly rooted in place and community and, as such, has been disrupted and marginalized by a singular educational focus on conventional forms of Western literacy, resulting in home-and-school breakdowns for Aboriginal peoples. After centuries of government policies and educational practices that would supplant Aboriginal literacies with this Western approach to literacy, it is now time to realize the educational value of Aboriginal ways of knowing and learning through "good talks" and "good walks," as suggested by our Saulteaux Elder, and to see how the privilege and pain of the Aboriginal experience of schooling gives rise to a helpful critique of Western literacy and its limits.

INSCRIBING MEANING ON LANDSCAPES

Reflecting on the their earliest childhood memories with their families, their encounter with formal education, and their life in this Anishinaabe community, this elderly group of Anishinaabe, ranging in age from 62 to 82, reveals the functions and uses of Western and Aboriginal literacy in their lives. Like most Aboriginal people born in the early 1900s, the lives of these men and women were closely rooted on the land. They lived with their families, some in large extended networks, and traveled seasonally around Manitoulin Island trapping, hunting, and fishing, and gathering

---

[3]This work is drawn from Hare (2001). The Anishinaabe are commonly known as the Ojibwe and belong to the Algonquin language speaking group. The term means "man lowered from above."

plants and berries that would be preserved for winter months. Though treaties eventually restricted them to a fixed land base and they turned to more agricultural pursuits or worked in the bush to clear, cut, and sell timber, their relationship to the land remained strong as they continued with traditional subsistence activities. The nature of their literacy, I contend, was a matter of learning to read symbols and inscribe meanings across landscapes within the family, which served as the primary medium of cultural continuity and the context for their literacy experiences.

The seven men and women recalled their childhood days as a family time closely interwoven to the themes of the land and seasons. You can hear this, for example, in the way one elderly woman, Irma, born in 1918, describes her early days of berry picking: "You were out all day with your family. I picked berries, strawberries, raspberries, blueberries, cranberries. I was always berry picking. Then I had to bring them home. And we had to can them. Make preserves. I was always making preserves or jam." Another Anishinaabe woman, too, remembers the "old folk" watching for the ripening berries, which would draw them across the countryside harvesting a winter's supply of fruit: "The old folks used to do it. And when they go picking, they see the strawberries are ripening, they go and pick them. The same with everything, blueberries. They used to go out to the north shore to pick blueberries and low bush cranberries and they would do us all winter." Joan, the eldest of the participants for this study at 82 years of age, spoke in Anishinaabe about following her mom and dad and aunties as they traveled about the island for fish and berries, watching and listening to them, for they knew when it was time to be out on the water fishing, setting snares, or when the geese or partridge would be making their return. Having occupied this territory their entire lives, they knew the land and the waterways. Joan spoke little English, having received very little formal schooling; she neither read nor wrote the English language. Her conversations, translated by her son, revealed only the activities she engaged in with her family and centered on how they survived on the land. Knowing the landscapes, the seasons, animal behaviors and cycles, and weather patterns ensured the survival of these Anishinaabe.

Many aspects of Aboriginal life were associated with seasonal activities, even as families moved to more sedentary lifestyles. Ned, born in 1927, gives a vivid sense of what had to be done season by season, on the farm and off, to keep the family going:

> Fish in the fall. Put fish away for the winter. In the winter pulp. Feed the cattle. Pulp some more. We used to put apples away. Everything we'd put away for the winter. We used to have a big root cellar. Everything would be in there, cabbage, carrots, apples, potatoes. Yeah. We would keep them in the root cellar until. . . . Hog or cow. You have your meat . . . In the spring we'd start getting ready for planting. Well, maple syrup first. We make maple syrup; we'd

start about March making maple syrup. We would tap trees, haul sap, boil it down, haul sapping in, and empty the pails . . . I just followed my Dad. My Dad was there. We did it together, everything was together. The whole family was involved.

When asked how he knew it was time to start the maple syrup, Ned explained it in a way that captures both the difficult and obvious lessons that had to be learned in living on the land: "When the weather gets, well, just watch the weather. When the weather gets warm. You tap the trees, then if it runs, then it runs. If it doesn't run, then it don't run." For the young who went along with family, it was all very much a sense of learning to read where, when, and how to live on the land, with the benefits both immediate and long term, both personal and communal.

Making meaning of seasons, land and weather patterns, animal migrations, and changing plant life framed the Aboriginal experience of survival, and this knowledge was transmitted from one generation to the other. The experiences shared by these Anishinaabe elders resonate with the experiences of Aboriginal people across Canada whose relationship with the land formed their spiritual, social, and economic base. For example, Dr. Shirley Sterling, a Nlakapamux educator, recalls one of the many stories her mother shared with her about her grandmothers, Quaslemetko and Yetko, who taught Shirley's mother how to read the environment around her. Shirley shares:

> Yetko was an herbalist, a gatherer of medicine tea and medicine food. A gentle, kind-hearted woman who laughed a lot, she packed food and camping gear and took my mother, and sometimes my mother's sister, Theresa, into the mountains or down to the Coldwater River on horseback . . . There they gathered berries. Once, they made a small red willow fish trap . . . Yetko explained things to the girls as they went along; what the deer root looks like when it's ready to pick; why trout like to rest in fish traps; which medicine plants to use for headache, for woman trouble, for fever, for rashes, wounds, bee sting, for birth control. (Sterling, 1995, pp. 115–116)

The book, *In the Words of Elders*, which describes Aboriginal cultural thought from perspectives of Elders across Canada, speaks to the Aboriginal people's intimate relationship with the land. In the Northwest Territories, George Blondin, of Slavey and Dogrib descent, born in 1922, grew up on the land and knows well the traditional ways of the Dene people. Reflecting on concepts of time and how his people lived, he tells:

> They moved around by the seasons. They go by animals, eggs of ducks, in the fall the caribou and moose are fat, it is a good time to get food. The Elders and hunters go hunting when the animals are fat, they save the fat, dried

meat. Moose and caribou start to mate, they do not eat anymore, they lose all their fat in a matter of five to six days. The animals' mating season is important to people, they have to know when it happens . . . Seasons and animals are big part of traditional life. (Kulchyski, McCaskill, & Newhouse, 1999, p. 408)

Nature's patterns clearly framed the Aboriginal family's experience (Friesen, 2000); their place in the world was defined by this close connection to the land and water they knew so well. Aboriginal people make sense of their world through their relationships with living things, with animals, plants, and people, and the natural environment. Instead of written protocols, literacy, for the Anishinaabe and other Aboriginal people across Canada, is located in symbolic systems that are deeply encoded across many dimensions of their environment. They knew when and where to pick berries and draw sap from trees through the rotation of the seasons. They knew where to hunt by land markers, and when to harvest crops by weather and time indicators. It is helpful to think of this rich knowledge as a form of literacy because it is imbued with a sense of reading what is written over the land. It is a productive, sustaining form of literacy out of which their lives were shaped by the dimensions of the environment, inscribed by memories of life on the land and with their families, toward a way of thinking to which Western literacy has paid too little attention. The weaving together of these patterns, phases, or cycles, as they are read by these people, represents the holism that is often articulated within an Aboriginal worldview. By describing the events in their lives, they are describing the ways in which they make sense of their world. For Aboriginal people, there is no separation between living and learning as they make meaning of the land and their lives within it. This worldview, reflecting an Aboriginal way of reading the world and transmitting from one generation to the next, is a key feature of Aboriginal literacy for the Anishinaabe of this study and for other Aboriginal people across Canada.

INTRODUCTION TO "PAPERS"

The long-standing insistence that Western literacy must supplant Aboriginal literacies, in order for Aboriginal education to take place, has presented the greatest challenges for Aboriginal peoples. Missionaries, who first introduced Aboriginal peoples to print literacy, particularly as a means of reading the Christian Bible, either destroyed, transformed, or neglected most of the Aboriginal literacies for their own purposes (Battiste, 1986). Education was an essential tool of colonialism. Formal schooling instituted English and/or French language only policies, emphasized print literacy, and devalued Aboriginal traditions. Yet, schooling is only emblematic of the broader forces that have acted to undermine Aboriginal literacies. Government policies, enacted in legislation such as the Indian Act, anticeremonial laws, and treaties, have contributed to Aboriginal peoples' marginalization from Canadian society, weakening their cultural base and marginalizing their literacies.

Many parents of the Anishinaabe in this study, if not most, wanted their children to be able to speak, as well as read and write, English and in that sense to become literate or "know papers," as our Saulteaux elder suggests. The ways of the world were changing, and Aboriginal people realized they needed to accommodate if they were to continue their preferred ways of life. Schooling in literacy offered a gateway, indeed *the* gateway, to the newcomer's world. For Aboriginal parents it was not a matter of either/or, but of both. Literacy, through schooling, would make it possible for the next generation to maneuver between two very different cultures. Ned reflected on how things had changed and on those who saw education as important to the future of their children:

> You have be educated and go to school and go to work. My dad eh, he said you go to school; it will help you in the long run. I think he saw something ahead of us, ahead, seeing ahead into the future. He'd seen the future, forecast, or whatever you call it. Seen ahead, what things are going to be like ahead. He told Leo one time, "just put your boys in school." They had an argument; they were calling back and forth. Some day, maybe we won't see it, but your boys are going to need it. They are the ones who will suffer. You see, there weren't the machinery that there is now. Mostly horses. Then there were no horses. It's all equipment, machinery. At that time all the machinery started coming in, that's where you need education.

Though the need for their children to learn literacy in English was the primary motivation for sending their children to school, Ned really questioned the good that it served at that time:

> You see at that time education wasn't that important, eh. You went out and you got a job right away and a lot of old people grew up that way believing in that . . . They just wanted to go out and work . . . They didn't need education. When they taught Latin in school, they didn't like that. They'd say, "What's Latin going to do for you?" It's not going to do you any good after you finish work, school. Work is what you need. You need to learn how to work. That is what the older people pushed, how to work in the bush.

If Aboriginal people, for the most part, accepted schooling as a means for acquiring skills needed to participate in a changing world, they did not anticipate that this introduction to formal education would be at the expense of their language, culture, and traditions. "While some Indians looked upon formal education with suspicion, other families felt there were practical advantages to be acquired through their offsprings' acquaintance with the dominant society, particularly where schooling could be acquired alongside a traditional education" (Ralston, cited in Barman, Hebert, & McCaskill, 1986, p. 5). Formal schooling for this generation of Anishinaabe resulted from a policy that required compulsory attendance at schools operated under control of the government and administered by religious institutions. For Edith, Thelma, and Annie, this meant going to the Indian day school located in the community. Irma, Millie, and Ned left the community to attend the Spanish Indian Residential School, located in northern Ontario, Canada.

The spread of missionary groups throughout Aboriginal communities led not only to the establishment of churches, but also to day schools on the reserves. Indian day school allowed those who attended to remain with their family while they went to school, continued to participate in community activities, and engaged in cultural traditions. Because most of their learning took place on the land, formal schooling was a new experience for these participants. Annie, who attended the Indian day school in her village, shared her sense of the importance and difficulty of learning English:

> They used to send me to school, to go to school, they sent us, all the kids. That is where you learn to speak English they say. Like in those days, eh, they may go out working and you know, you have to know what you are saying, like if you want to talk to the woodman . . . It was kind of hard [learning to speak English]. You didn't understand what the lady is saying. For me it was anyway. But I catch on pretty quick.

Edith, who began schooling at 8 years of age, says that her family always spoke Indian. It was at the day school in M'Chigeeng where Edith learned the English language and to read and write in English:

> I was the only one who went to school 'cause I guess it was somebody from the government's idea, I don't know. They said I should go to school. I started late. I was 8 years old when I started. We went here, West Bay. They had a school house. That's where I learned. I didn't even know one English . . . My mom took me to the school and said "You stay here all day." All day! How come? I didn't want to stay. And I couldn't understand the teacher. I didn't know what to say to her. I didn't even speak one English [word].

There were family circumstances within this generation of Anishinaabe that made staying home to attend the Indian day school impossible. Ned and Millie each had one parent who passed away when they were quite young. The surviving parent faced the hardships of raising their children on their own, eventually deciding that the residential school located at Spanish offered the best hope for their children. The St. Joseph's Residential School for girls and the Garnier Residential School for boys were referred to as one school called Spanish. "I went to school here [in the village] for a while," explains Ned. "About 2 years, and my mother died and it was real hard on us, like my Dad. So he put us in Spanish. We were there for about 3 years." Millie describes going to Spanish residential school as a refuge for many Indian children who faced difficult family circumstances. This refuge was not always a safe haven, but an only option for many Indian families. She describes her situation, "It was an environmental thing. My dad died when I was 4 years old. My mom had a hard time. So I went to Spanish and my brothers too. My mom remarried and my stepfather didn't accept his four stepchildren."

It would be inevitable that all Aboriginal children would eventually attend residential schools across Canada as part of a larger colonial agenda. "In the view of politicians and civil servants in Ottawa whose gaze was fixed upon the horizon of national development, Aboriginal knowledge and skills were neither necessary nor desirable in a land that was to be dominated by European industry and, therefore, by Europeans and their culture (Milloy, 1999, pp. 4–5). The government's response was to make assimilation the official policy goal for Aboriginal people, with the intent of eliminating the Indian from the Indian and ensuring their absorption into mainstream society. Assimilation through education gained momentum following Nicholas Davin's review of American Indian policy of segregated residential institutions in the United States. "Davin was much taken by the American schools, which he regarded as an especially successful aspect of the American policy of 'aggressive civilization' that had been implemented by the Grant administration in 1869" (Miller, 1996, p. 101). Day schools were proving ineffective, as the "influence of the wigwam was stronger than the influence of the school" (Davin cited in Milloy, 1999, p. 24). Assimilation could best be achieved if children were removed from the influences of their family and community; day schools and boarding schools were collapsed into a larger category known as *residential schools*, and these totalizing institutions proved to be one of the most powerful tools of assimilation and the most destructive force on Aboriginal cultures, traditions, and languages.

As residential schools became more centralized in a deliberate attempt to isolate children from the socializing structures of their lives, the schools' character became increasingly regulated in policy and practices. Children dressed in school uniforms, were given a number aligned to their Christian name, and assumed a rigorous schedule of prayer, school, and laboring. As the government provided limited funding for the schools' maintenance, the religious denomination that ran the schools relied on the children to sustain the daily operation of the school, limiting time in the classroom and academic opportunities. As Barman (2003) suggests, Aboriginal children were schooled for inequality, permitting their entry into mainstream society only at the lowest rungs.

The growing accounts of residential schooling shed light on the darker side of this history of institutional schooling, revealing the atrocities of abuse, denigration, and cultural genocide (Assembly of First Nations, 1994; Bull, 1991; Furniss, 1992; Haig-Brown, 1988; Ing, 1991; Jaine, 1993; Johnston, 1988; Knockwood, 1992; Secwepemc Cultural Education Society, 2000). Personal testimonies are damning:

> I don't know if anyone else ever got the strap. I felt like I was singled out to get the straps all the time. That's what it felt like to me. Sometimes they just told me it was because I lost one side of my sock. They were trying to teach us the ways of God and they called us savages and dirty Indians. (Secwepemc Cultural Education Society, 2000, p. 86)

Another student recalled:

> Other times I cried because I was terrified of hearing the footsteps that regularly crept up the fire escape to our dorm. Those nights, listening to little girls' frantic whisperings, muffled screams, and desperate cries, I jumped in bed with my sister, Carol, and fiercely clung to her for protection. (Acoose, in Jaine, 1993, p. 6)

The effects of residential schools have been devastating for generations of Aboriginal people. It has meant the loss of language and closely related elements of culture, along with the erosion of the Aboriginal family system. These essential structures of meaning for Aboriginal peoples caused a break in the cultural continuity that led to the passing on of knowledge and skills from one generation to the next. It meant a rupture of Aboriginal forms of literacy. Formal schooling, in both residential and day schools, assumed that displacing Aboriginal cultures and languages, and with them any notions of literacy outside the framework of mainstream culture, was a small price to pay for bringing these children within the folds of a civilizing Christianity. Ironically, the government mandate for public schooling among Aboriginal children, which was to educate them in skills of English reading and writing, actually acted to subvert the acquisition of Western forms of literacy.

Despite the increasing scholarship on residential schooling, with attention paid to aspects of schooling related to curriculum, teaching, and policy and practices of this schooling, few studies have focused on literacy (Goodburn, 1999). The strict language policies, emphasis on vocational training and religious instruction, and inadequate programming for learning were attributes of residential schooling that ensured that Aboriginal children did not achieve successful kinds of literacy learning, nor the academic and economic success associated with them. If language transmits culture, then any interruption to language continuity would result in a break to Aboriginal culture. Policy and practice were systematically aimed at eradicating Aboriginal culture and language. If not banned outright, both were so disparaged in school that they were among its casualties (Barman, 1996). Participants of this study came to school speaking only their Native language. Although instructed to speak only English or French, depending on the institution, many had difficulty adhering to this rule. Ned says about his experiences at Spanish, "Language was forbidden. They caught you talking Indian; you would get a rap over the hand. They told us nobody talk Indian." Irma confirmed this when she said, "We got caught speaking Indian all the time. We'd speak Indian and we get caught and they told us to get in the school and stand in the corner. They would strap us too . . . Yeah we would always get caught. We'd be standing and crying 'cause it hurts to be strapped." Thelma, who lived most of the time with her grandparents, explained that is why she left school after only a short time. She couldn't recall how long she remained at the Indian day school at M'Chigeeng. "I didn't stay. I don't think I even stayed there for a year. I got sent home because I would talk Indian . . . Every time they caught me speaking Indian, they'd spank me . . . We had to speak English all the time, but I didn't know how to speak English."

The inability to speak English or French on arrival at the schools posed considerable challenges for students and teachers:

> For many children, the language barrier they faced when they went off to residential school meant that weeks, months, perhaps in some cases even years of academic instruction were wasted . . . there was little understanding among authorities and teachers of the difficulties of teaching English as a second language, and probably there would have been little sympathy even if such knowledge existed. (Miller, 1966, p. 173)

Writing about her own experiences in the Shubenacadie Indian Residential School in eastern Canada, Knockwood (1992) recalls her own struggles with English language acquisition in residential school:

> We were trying to learn and understand English, which was completely foreign to us, and apply it to everyday life by watching others and imitating their behavior, acting through trial and error, sometimes with horrible consequences . . . The first three years went painfully slow as we struggled to learn our ABC's, to count, recite, sing and play, as well as pray. All this was either in English or Latin—both entirely new languages. (pp. 48–49)

Attempts to maintain language were met with harsh punishment, reinforcing to students that English was the only valid option, which was unsupported for students. As a consequence of such policies, many Aboriginal children lost the ability to speak their language so that the vast majority of Aboriginal languages in Canada are now threatened with extinction. Cree, Inuktitut, and Ojibway are seen as the most viable languages, given the number of speakers. Census data indicates that overall, Aboriginal languages are on the decline in both on- and off-reserve communities (Statistics Canada, 2003a, 2003b). The data show that 24% of the Aboriginal population in Canada reported they had enough knowledge of an Aboriginal language to carry on a conversation. This was down from 29% in 1996.

Although children were expected to learn academic skills in reading, writing, and arithmetic, residential schools emphasized domestic chores, manual labor, and religious indoctrination. Boys were given training in trades and skills such as agriculture, carpentry, blacksmithing, and shoemaking. Vocational training for girls was limited to skills that would prepare them for domestic work as wives, mothers, and housekeepers. They learned sewing, baking, knitting, laundering, and some minor cultivating. Student's participation in such a restricted curriculum served a more immediate goal, which was to keep these schools self-sufficient in their day-to-day operations, as the government provided limited funds on which they could run the schools. Haig-Brown (1988), in her book *Resistance and Renewal*, found that with the 13 Native people who attended Kamloops Indian Residential in British Columbia, "Memories of chores were mentioned by all those interviewed, frequently in greater detail than memories of academic work . . . Not only did work occupy considerably more time each day, it also occupied a greater portion of the students' consciousness about their lives" (pp. 69–70).

The belief that Indians were morally corrupt, and that traditional Indian religion was primitive, led missionaries to adopt a religious emphasis in the schools, which would assist in the assimilation process. But Indian people were really being judged by Euro-Canadian standards and racist attitudes held by missionaries who were in charge (Miller, 1996). As Haig-Brown (1988) explains, "The inculcation of [Catholic] values was of paramount importance. At the bottom of the list of priorities for both parties [church and government] was an introduction to basic reading, writing, and arithmetic" (p. 74). Given the schools' emphasis on vocational training and religious indoctrination, the support for academics and acquiring basic literacy skills of reading and writing is doubtful, let alone the mixed messages about literacy children would have experienced. Many former students of residential schools indicate that the education they received was minimal and the levels of academic achievement attained by many students was quite low (Barman, 1996; Bull, 1991; Haig-Brown, 1988, Ing, 1991; Knockwood, 1992; Miller, 1996; Milloy, 1999; Royal Commission on Aboriginal Peoples, 1996). Barman (1996) cites how ". . . up to 1920, four out of every five aboriginal boys and girls attending a federal school across Canada were enrolled in Grade 1, 2, or 3" (p. 281), indicating children acquired no more than a basic literacy.

The poor quality of programming, which contributed to dismal levels of literacy among Aboriginal students, manifested itself in a variety of ways. Children spent minimal time in the classroom, a system that was commonly known as the "half-day" system (Miller, 1996). It was not unusual for children to spend only 2 to 4 hours a day in the classroom. And as children got older or times of the year necessitated certain chores to be done, some children did not even go to class, a practice common among many of the schools. The need for children to maintain the schools and the lack of expectation for the Indian child by mostly unqualified teachers justified this practice. It was largely religious staff that instructed students, as schools rarely attracted qualified teachers. Miller asserts that, as the schools operated under the missionary influence, teachers who possessed a "missionary spirit," as opposed to a sound school or university training background, were preferred candidates to teach in the schools. Children attempting to acquire even the most basic of literacy skills met with little success (Assembly of First Nations, 1994; Miller, 1996; Royal Commission on Aboriginal Peoples, 1996).

Focusing on the literacy practices at an off-reservation government boarding school in the United States, the Genoa Industrial Indian School at Genoa, Nebraska (1834–1934), Goodburn (1999) examines three types of literacy artifacts of the school. These include the literary texts that students read, students' writing within the curriculum, and students' writing outside of the curriculum. Beyond a "just say no" campaign against speaking aboriginal languages, Goodburn identifies other forms of literacy instruction that shaped American Indian students' experiences at federal off-reservation boarding schools. Where reading was emphasized, literature provided an opportunity for American Indian pupils to learn patriotism and civic duty and eventually come to reject their culture, most obvious in her analysis of literary works where the aboriginal characters adopt and or replicate White values, with the exception perhaps of one novel found in the library which received much attention by students. Students' writings suggest that whereas topics and forms for writing were prescribed, students' essays reflect a variety of rhetorical stances regarding political and social issues that connected to their identities as American Indian students and illustrate how students used their literacy instruction to question and complicate the instructional values of the Genoa Indian School. Their own personal writings demonstrate how they used the dominant modes of communication to resist assimilative practices, writing petitions or letters to the administrative authorities asserting their position on personal and communal rights being ignored. The focus on literacy artifacts reveals how policies of institutional school for aboriginal children and youth were aimed at assimilation, but gives expression to the ways aboriginal students created space to name, define, and claim or reject their identities in the face of the most basic violation of human rights experienced by aboriginal people.

The Aboriginal participants of the study described made their own attempts to use the literacy of the schools as a means of connecting with their families, all the while being closely monitored by the residential school authorities who were clearly not comfortable with their programs. Ned described letters to his family that he viewed when he got home from school:

> I'd seen the letters after I got home. What I had wrote. A lot of words were taken out . . . things that were going on at the school . . . They kept it away from your parents . . . Whatever goes on there. What the priest was doing, who goes in the hospital in Espanola. Over two months, I broke my hip playing hockey and the priest would come over every day, bring my work, school work. He would say, "do you have any letters?" Yeah. They were all mailed from [Spanish]. When I say they got my letters, eh? I should have mailed them right from the hospital. They screened my letters . . . Crossed [being in the hospital] out. I told my Dad at home. You never said anything about you being in the hospital. You were in the hospital? Yeah. I was there for two months. I went back to the letters. There was stuff crossed out.

Ned's father confronted the priest at Spanish saying, according to Ned, "If anything goes wrong with my boys you let me know. Don't try and hide anything, 'cause I will find out anyway." Not surprisingly, the priest denied knowing anything of the incident that Ned had described.

Millie, another participant, experienced the same kind of literacy censure when writing to pen pals from school:

> I used to write to somebody out in Glace Bay, Nova Scotia, and somebody out in Manitoba . . . It was during this time that I was home that I was involved with pen pals. I didn't keep them up in Spanish because all of your letters there were opened. So I just wrote the family there. You weren't encouraged to communicate with friends. You were lucky to get a letter from home. And that was about the extent of what was tolerated in terms of communication . . . I don't know why, but to family . . . that was accepted, but they didn't encourage you to write to friends at all.

Despite attempts by school to control the kinds of literacy materials and activities, Aboriginal children resisted literacy impositions. Those interviewed in this elderly generation reflected on similar kinds of efforts to resist in their memories of the schooling. As the students were separated by gender, boys and girls sent notes secretly to one another inside their shoes. Ned, who worked in the barn sometimes doing shoe repair, would find notes in the shoes of girls to be distributed to many of the boys. Millie and Irma reported they wrote notes to boys and had them sent over, but also received correspondence from the boys.

For the Aboriginal men and women of this study, the way ahead required a firm hold on written text. They understood the need to "know papers," and even desired it, but not at the expense of what can best be thought of as Aboriginal literacy—a way of making sense of the world that is every bit as committed to meaning making as literate traditions associated with school-based learning. The convention of Western literacy has been imposed on cultures in the name of education, presenting itself as the only valid option. The very demands of schooling, both past and present, required Aboriginal children to relinquish their own literacy traditions. Because residential schools have had devastating impacts on generations of Aboriginal people, they represent an extreme form of Western schooling that isolated children and curricula from family and community. As a result, Alfred Manitopeyes cautions us that modern education, to which Western literacy is so closely associated, must not replace the traditional Aboriginal modes of teaching and learning.

"GOOD TALKING" AND "GOOD WALKING"

It is only by expanding the very sense of literacy—as systems of meaning making that encompass Aboriginal languages, oral and narrative traditions, and symbolic expressions—that we can begin to recover what was lost in the lives of these elderly Anishinaabe. Their literacies, which included close readings of landscapes and seasons, must be respected as meaningful ways of life with the potential to persist into the present. Approaches to education today need to include Aboriginal people's connection to the natural world as a legitimate text from which to learn alongside the print traditions learned in school, particularly as we attempt to define new traditions of living with the land.

This combination of Aboriginal and Western forms of literacy can be observed in the fast pace of global climate change taking place in the Arctic, which is affecting the livelihood of the Inuit people, even as it is giving back to the Canadian nation. Current research (International Institute for Sustainable Development, 2000) is underway that explores the contribution that traditional knowledge, local observations, and adaptive strategies can make to scientific research on climate change in the Arctic. By charting the recollections of Inuvialuit Elders and community members back through time to the earliest memories of local people, in this case back to the 1930s, changes in the environment and fish and wildlife behavior have been documented. One of the Elders interviewed indicated that Inuvialuit women have always had a deep understanding of weather patterns, as they were responsible for assessing conditions and preparing hunters accordingly. The result of this work with the Elders is contributing to a greater understanding of global climate change. It also provides a clear understanding of what is lost if climate change continues. But, more importantly, for the Inuvialuit, their understanding of previous landscapes informs their present hunting practices, as they look to different locations they may not have thought to hunt, fish, or gather berries in the past.

Yet this literacy is not only about the practical matters of weather and food. Cultural knowledge and teachings are expressed through oral traditions for Aboriginal peoples. Stories are passed from one generation to another, telling us who we are, identifying our place in this world, and directing us how to live in a respectful way. These stories speak to the most basic questions of origin. Anishinaabe teachings have both a creation and re-creation story, where in the creation story, the Creator gathered from Mother Earth life from the four sacred directions—north, south, east, west—and blew into them using a sacred shell. The union of the four sacred elements and the life breath gave rise to the Anishinaabe (Benton-Banai, 1988). Our re-creation story finds the world flooded, with only a collection of animals afloat on a log. While many of the water animals—the beaver, the otter, the loon—try to make their way to the bottom to find some earth, it is the muskrat who surfaces with a small piece of earth that is placed on the back of the turtle, whose shell is strong enough to bear the weight of the land that begins to grow and spread on the back of the turtle. The landmass in the water is known to Aboriginal people throughout North America as Turtle Island, where Aboriginal people, like the Anishinaabe, understand their origins to be.

In Canada, where Aboriginal title to the land for use, resources, and occupancy is not yet settled, and Aboriginal groups continue to negotiate treaties and pose challenges in the courts, it is the oral history that serves Aboriginal people as a record of their past. The Gitksan and Wet'suwet'en of northwestern British Columbia drew on their sacred oral histories and recollections of Aboriginal life on the land as evidence of their occupation of their traditional territories in their disputed land claim with the provincial government. The Gitksan houses have an *adaawk*, which is a collection of sacred oral tradition about their ancestors, histories, and territories, and the Wet'suwet'en each have a *kungax*, which is a spiritual song, dance, or performance that ties them to their territories (*Delgamuukw*, 1998). In a landmark court decision, known as the Delgamuukw decision, the Supreme Court of Canada ruled, "Notwithstanding the challenges created by the use of oral histories as proof of historical facts, the laws of evidence must be adapted in order that this type of evidence can be accommodated and placed on equal footing with the types of historical evidence that courts are familiar with, which largely consists of historical documents" (*Delgamuukw*,

1998). In other words, "stories matter." They stand as the record of a people. In a commentary on the Court's recognition of oral tradition in the Delgamuukw v. Supreme Court of Canada, Persky (1998) said:

> This recognition has practical consequences, since such histories are the primary means by which native nations can prove their claims to aboriginal title. But at a deeper level, what I read in the Court's decision on oral history is a more profound effort to reconcile how different people with different cultural traditions see the world. (p. 13)

The meaning and value of Aboriginal oral traditions has been overlooked in the literacy promoted by today's schools. It is given brief attention as part of multicultural education on myths, legends, and folklore, romanticized as part of our past. They are told without giving readers or listeners a context of place, meaning, or protocols associated with retelling these stories. Instead, they are implicitly measured against print texts, diminishing their purpose and worth. Although Aboriginal literacy projects aim to render Elder narratives in print, as if to preserve what could potentially be lost, efforts must also be made to preserve the integrity of the oral tradition alongside these initiatives with print, so as to ensure continuity in the cultural practices and knowledge in which the oral tradition is embedded. The protocols surrounding cultural knowledge need to be passed on, as do the skills of effectively communicating stories and deriving meaning from them, so that oral traditions may be protected. In his work with the Sto:lo Nation of British Columbia, historian Carlson (1997) reminds us that stories are shared in a dynamic and interactive fashion:

> Witnessing or participating in the performance of an oral narrative allows for vocal subtleties to be perceived such as intonations, pronunciations, and variations in voices (used primarily to distinguish between characters), as well as hand gestures, facial expressions, dances, drumming and so on. These performances are used not only to entertain an audience (although certainly this element is present in the events), but also, among other things, to instill and reinforce appropriate and socially acceptable behaviour in community members. As a result, these narratives convey aspects of Sto:lo culture which are often lost when frozen on audio tape or written text (media which usually record a story in isolation). The experience of witnessing an oral narrative performed versus simply reading one, is akin to seeing live theatre versus silently reading the script. (p. 189)

This begs the question of how this dynamic oral tradition can be incorporated into the literacy education of the young. Opportunities to hear stories shared orally by Elders and other cultural resource people are important for learners, just as important as opportunities to retell them. This may require educators to learn about the traditional territories of Aboriginal people on which their places of learning are situated. From there, they can learn respectful ways to approach community people of local Aboriginal communities, giving them meaningful ways to participate in programming. Learners, and likely many educators, will experience first hand how and why certain stories are told and strategies employed by the seasoned storyteller. For example, in Aboriginal tradition, some stories have ownership and may only be retold by the individual, family, or clan who own the story, and the story may only be shared at certain times.

Aboriginal languages are central to understandings of Aboriginal literacy. Establishing and promoting meaningful contexts for using traditional languages, in a society increasingly dominated by English, poses challenges for Aboriginal people. The Northwest Territories Literacy Council (1999) noted the precarious state of the language:

> The loss of Aboriginal languages in Canada is acknowledged as being far more serious than the loss of any other of the many languages used and spoken in this country. All other languages are immigrant languages and therefore have a "homeland" in another part of the world. French and English, Chinese, and Greek, for example, are all spoken in other parts of the world. If these languages are "lost" in Canada, they are not lost to the world . . . If the [Aboriginal] languages are lost here, they are lost forever to the world. (p. 9)

Battiste and Youngblood Henderson (2000) charge Eurocentric governments and academics with contributing to the destruction of Aboriginal languages:

> Canadian governmental officials and academics offer excuses that the Indigenous language problems are too complex, when in fact they do not perceive the value of Indigenous languages and thus do not care about their revitalization. They think all languages are merely communicative tools and that nothing significant is being lost with their non-use. They do not want to know about the consequences of destroying Indigenous languages, instead they seek to immunize themselves from blame. These thoughts are part of the bigger problem: the implicit state theory of European cultural and linguistic superiority. (p. 84)

Issues of language retention and revitalization are of great urgency in our communities. Status accorded to them through legislation, which would ensure the maintenance, promotion, and revitalization, is only a partial solution. Aboriginal people must move beyond the colonial myth that to learn English better requires learning only English and not their own languages (Battiste & Youngblood Henderson, 2000). Each language community, each culture, needs to see the benefit and necessity of their language so that the value it places on its own language is significant. Any language strategies aimed at language retention and revitalization must provide opportunities for the family, school, and community to work together.

Up to this point, the efforts of community-controlled and provincial schools to establish language maintenance and revitalization programs have produced only limited effects. Schools responding to culture and language differences generally prescribe remedial programming (Battiste, 2000; Noll, 1998). In an overview of Aboriginal language education in provincial school boards, Fettes and Norton (2000) noted the varied responses to Aboriginal language policies in Canada:

> No province has expressed a willingness to provide regular instruction through the medium of an Aboriginal language. In public schools, such instruction is common only in the school boards of northern Quebec and the Eastern Arctic (and only for the first few years of schooling). In the absence of strong, balanced bilingual programs, the overall effect of schools on Aboriginal language use and transmission is likely to remain negative. (p. 49)

Given the school's inability to support language in ways that ensure continuity, Aboriginal communities must establish their own language priorities, which involve all of the social networks of the community, including schools.

Our Aboriginal languages, which remain at the core of our consciousness and identity and provide a vehicle for the transmission of our worldview, have reached a critical state, evidenced in statistics on language decline and loss. Although we need to persist at language renewal and maintenance, we also need to ensure to continuity of Aboriginal culture in light of language struggles. Aboriginal ways of knowing must be given priority in classrooms, where students have opportunities to experience firsthand the language, knowledge, and traditions of their communities. This will necessitate traditional experiences within the contexts of land, family, and community, but also allow for new modes of expression, whether using dominant literacy forms or new forms of technology such as digital and video literacy, all while preserving cultural and linguistic integrity. Battiste and Youngblood Henderson (2000) caution imposing Eurocentric language and learning processes on Indigenous students:

> [T]he Mi'kmaw language is based on animacy, yet Mi'kmaw living relationships are translated in Eurocentric thought through the relative relationships of animacy and inanimacy and inclusion and exclusion. The English language holds that only things that are animate are alive; the Mi'kmaw language holds that all things have a spirit and a relationship. (p. 90)

Such mainstream approaches to teaching and curriculum are impediments to learning for Aboriginal children and can only serve to further marginalize our own literacies.

CONCLUSION

Returning to the words of the Saulteaux Elder, Alfred Manitopeyes, who views Western forms of education, and the literacy so closely associated with it, as a borrowed cultural product, we are reminded that Western forms of literacy were not something that was ours nor were we, as Aboriginal people, going to be possessed by it. The "good walks" and "good talks" shared by this Saulteaux Elder represent how our children learn to make sense of their world as Aboriginal people and are intimately connected to our rich cultural expressions, alternative systems of representations, and relationships with land and family. Our dance, music, and ceremonies are "text" that spells out meaning with each beat and step about who we are and our place in this world. Our stories, shared through oral tradition, ensure cultural continuity and define language, traditions, and identity. Aboriginal peoples' capacities of such meaning-making systems, which have been cast as Aboriginal literacy, are a direct challenge to the narrow and privileged meaning-making system that has been reserved for the name of literacy.

Consistently, reports on education (RCAP, 1996; Canada, 2002) have made clear the need for educational approaches that are inclusive of First Nations languages, cultures, and traditions, to which Aboriginal literacy is rooted. It would enable the schools to embrace something larger, finding the educational advantages to creating space for Aboriginal approaches to education. Aboriginal students would have the possibility of finding themselves among a range of cultural options and orientations, Western and Aboriginal, whether in acquiring the Aboriginal languages, developing Aboriginal narrative traditions, or learning about relationships to the land and environment. The school's inclusion of a wider range of cultural approaches would also, it almost goes without saying, enrich the education of non-Aboriginal students. It is necessary to have a far more inclusive understanding of literacy as one of education's basic principles, encompassing not only the print traditions of this society's dominant languages but also honoring the languages, narrative traditions, and rich symbolic and meaning-making systems of Aboriginal culture.

REFERENCES

Akan, L. (1999). Pimosatamowin sikaw kakeequaywin: Walking and talking. A Saulteaux Elder's view of Native education. *Journal of Native Education, 23*(1), 16–39.
Assembly of First Nations (AFN). (1994). *Breaking the Silence: An interpretive study of residential school impact and healing as illustrated by the stories of First Nations individuals.* Ottawa: Author.
Barman, J. (1996). Aboriginal education at the crossroads: The legacy of residential schools and the way ahead. In D. Long & O. Dickason (Eds.), *Visions of the heart: Canadian aboriginal issues* (pp. 271–303). Toronto, ON: Harcourt Brace Press.

Barman, J. (2003). "Schooled for Inequality: The Education of British Columbia Aboriginal Children." In J. Barman & M. Gleason (Eds.), *Children, teachers and schools in the history of British Columbia* (2nd ed., pp. 55–79. Calgary, AB: Detselig Enterprises, Ltd.

Barman, J., Hebert, Y., & McCaskill, D. (1986). *Indian education in Canada: The legacy* (Vol. 1). Vancouver, BC: University of British Columbia Press.

Battiste, M. (1986). Micmac literacy and cognitive assimilation. In J. Barman, Y. Hebert, & D. McCaskill (Eds.), *Indian education in Canada: The legacy* (Vol. 1, pp. 23–44). Vancouver, BC: University of British Columbia Press.

Battiste, M. (2000). Maintaining Aboriginal identity, language, and culture in modern society. In M. Battiste (Ed.), *Reclaiming indigenous voice and vision* (pp. 192–208). Vancouver, BC: University of British Columbia Press.

Battiste, M., & Youngblood Henderson, J. S. (2000). *Protecting indigenous knowledge and heritage: A global challenge*. Saskatoon, SK: Purich Publishing Ltd.

Benton-Banai, E. (1988). *The Mishomis book: The voice of the Ojibway*. St. Paul, MN: Red School House.

Bull, L. R. (1991). Indian residential schooling: The native perspective. *Canadian Journal of Native Education, 18*(supplement), 1–64.

Canada. Minister's Working Group on Education (2002). *Our Children—Keepers of the sacred knowledge*. Final Report. Ottawa: DIAND.

Carlson, K. (Ed.). (1997). *You are asked to witness: The Sto:lo in Canada's Pacific Coast history*. Chilliwak, BC: Sto:lo Heritage Trust.

Delgamuukw: The Supreme Court of Canada Decision on Aboriginal Title. (1998). Vancouver, BC: Greystone Books.

Fettes, M., & Norton, R. (2000). Voices of Winter: Aboriginal languages and public policy in Canada. In B. Castellano, L. Davis, & L. Lahache (Eds.), *Aboriginal education: Fulfilling the promise* (pp. 29–54). Vancouver, BC: University of British Columbia Press.

Friesen, G. (2000). *Citizens and nation: An essay on history, communication, and Canada*. Toronto, ON: University of Toronto Press.

Furniss, E. (1992). *Victims of benevolence: Discipline and death at the Williams Lake Indian Residential School, 1891–1920*. Williams Lake, BC: Cariboo Tribal Council.

Goodburn, A. (1999). Literacy practices at the Genoa Industrial Indian School. *Great Plains Quarterly, 19*, 35–52.

Haig-Brown, C. (1988). *Resistance and renewal: Surviving the Indian residential school*. Vancouver, BC: Tillicum.

Hare, J. (2001). *Aboriginal literacy: Making meaning across three generations in an Anishinaabe community*. Unpublished doctoral thesis, University of British Columbia, Vancouver, Canada.

Ing, R. (1991). The effects of residential schools on native child-rearing practices. *Canadian Journal of Native Education, 18*(Supplement), 65–118.

International Institute for Sustainable Development. (2000). *Inuit observations on climate change. Community adaptation and sustainable livelihoods*. Available at http://iisd.ca/casl/projects/inuitobs.htm.

Jaine, L. (Ed.). (1993). *Residential schools: The stolen years*. Saskatoon, SK: Extension University Press, University of Saskatchewan.

Johnston, B. H. (1988). *Indian school days*. Toronto, ON: Porter Books.

Knockwood, I. (1992). *Out of the depths: The experience of Mi'kmaw children at the Indian residential school at Shubenacadie, Nova Scotia*. Lockeport, NS: Roseway.

Kulchyski, P., McCaskill, D., & Newhouse, D. (1999). *In the words of Elders: Aboriginal cultures in transition*. Toronto, ON: University of Toronto Press.

Miller, J. R. (1996). *Shingwauk's vision: A history of native residential school*. Toronto, ON: University of Toronto Press.

Milloy, J. (1999). *A national crime. The Canadian government and the residential school system, 1879 to 1986*. Winnipeg, MB: The University of Manitoba Press.

Noll, E. (1998). Experiencing literacy in and out of school: Case studies of two American Indian youths. *Journal of Literacy Research, 30,* 205–232.

Northwest Territories Literacy Council. (1999). *Languages of the land: A resource manual for Aboriginal language activists.* Yellowknife, NWT: Author.

Persky, S. (1998). Commentary. In *Delgamuukw: The Supreme Court of Canada decision on Aboriginal title* (pp. 1–24). Vancouver, BC: Greystone Books.

Royal Commission on Aboriginal Peoples [RCAP] (1996). *Report of the Royal Commission on Aboriginal Peoples* (Vols. 1–5). Ottawa: Author.

Secwepemc Cultural Education Society. (2000). *Behind closed doors: Stories from the Kamloops Indian residential school.* Kamloops, BC: Author.

Statistics Canada (2003a). *Aboriginal Peoples Survey 2001–initial findings: Well-being of the non-reserve Aboriginal population.* Ottawa, ON: Author.

Statistics Canada (2003b). *2001 Census. Aboriginal peoples of Canada: A demographic profile.* Ottawa, ON: Author.

Sterling, S. (1995). Quaslametko and Yetko: Two grandmother models for contemporary Native education pedagogy. In M. Battiste & J. Barman (Eds.), *First Nations education in Canada: The circle unfolds* (pp. 113–123). Vancouver, BC: University of British Columbia Press.

Chapter 13

The Rainbow/Holistic Approach to Aboriginal Literacy

Ningwakwe/Rainbow Woman
National Indigenous Literacy Association

Ningwakwe/Rainbow Woman is an Aboriginal educator, researcher, and community leader. In her plenary address to the *Portraits of Literacy: Critical Issues in Family/Community/School Literacies Conference*, she drew on her knowledge and experience to propose a model for broadening understandings of Aboriginal literacies in ways that recognize the interconnections of mind, spirit, heart, and body. This model, the Rainbow/Holistic Approach to Aboriginal Literacy, is outlined here in an edited version of Ningwakwe's plenary address.

*   *   *

As a member of a community that historically does not recognise a different sort of geographical border, sometimes also referred to as the 49th parallel, the goal of encouraging dialogue between practitioners and researchers to stimulate public engagement in literacy issues that cross borders of family, community, and school literacies is very near and dear to my heart. In this chapter, I hope to show other limitations to borders, particularly those that involve Aboriginal literacies.

I have been truly blessed during the 15 years I've worked with Aboriginal literacy practitioners and learners. It is through sharing with me from their Hearts and Spirits that I have been able to make a few observations about print-based and print-related ways to nurture Heart and Spirit in literacy activities. It is my sincere desire that I do their words justice. The framework that I share here is really a story of a number of different literacies coming together.

In 1996, I was asked to work with the Ontario Native Literacy Coalition to develop some alternative understandings of literacy. The Ministry of Training, Colleges and Universities (1995) in Ontario had just come out with a document entitled *Program Reform*. This document defined literacy, who was eligible to learn literacy and who was not, what kinds of literacy activities could be used as "contact hours," and what the measurable performance indicators would be. Aboriginal language literacy was narrowly and restrictively defined. The *Program Reform* document considered only cognitive outcomes that would hopefully result in further education or training, getting a (better) job, or becoming more "independent." In searching for a possible solution to the restrictive definitions of literacy that shaped Aboriginal literacy work, I was introduced to the Medicine Wheel as a model of education by Diane Hill (1995), Mohawk, Six Nations of the Grand River Territory, who had been part of a teaching team with the First Nations Technical Institute (FNTI).

THE MEDICINE WHEEL

The Medicine Wheel is sometimes referred to as the Wheel of Life. It is based in Aboriginal traditional teachings that tell us that we are Spirit, Heart, Mind, and Body. To have a life of balance, we must recognize and nurture all four parts of ourselves. That is, I suggest that Aboriginal literacy is about recognizing the symbols that come to us through Spirit, Heart, Mind, and Body, interpreting them and acting on them for the improvement of the quality of our lives. This means becoming open to other ways of knowing, other forms of literacy. Denys Auger, an Elder from the Bigstone Cree First Nation in Alberta, expresses:

> In our traditional culture, we "read" nature (the environment). We must read and interpret the information we find there, so that we can survive. We use our eyes and brains just like you. We also use our other senses—smell, hearing, taste and touch—to read the coming weather, the presence of danger, and the health of the land, waters and air. When we don't hear the frog's song, we know the land and waters are polluted and cannot support life. (D. Auger, personal communication, October 15, 2002)

Further work by the FNTI included learning outcomes for each of the components of the Medicine Wheel. For example, *Spirit* is an attitude or insight; *Heart* is a feeling about oneself or others; *Mind* is knowledge; and *Body* denotes a skill. I interpret these four components and ways of knowing as interconnected and thus holistic, focusing more on process than on the outcomes of learning.[1] Over the years, I have felt inspired to superimpose the Medicine Wheel over what I call the Rainbow Approach to Aboriginal literacies.

THE RAINBOW APPROACH TO ABORIGINAL LITERACIES

The Rainbow Approach links each colour of the rainbow to a type of Aboriginal literacy. In this section, I describe the Aboriginal literacies that I have associated with each colour of the Rainbow. I then explain how these literacies link to the Spirit, Heart, Mind, and Body of the Medicine Wheel.

Red

Red is the first colour of the rainbow, and the colour understood by some Aboriginal cultures to mean confidence, which has within it the knowing, the ability to plan, to start a process. Red represents the language of origin of First Nations individuals and/or communities. Since time immemorial, Aboriginal Peoples have lived on this land now known as North America. We believe that the Creator put us here and that our ancestors did not cross the Bering Strait. We had our own Aboriginal languages. A press release from The Daily Statistics Canada (1998) states that, as of 1996, 50 Aboriginal languages, belonging to 11 major language families, existed in Canada. The Assembly of First Nations (AFN) did studies of Aboriginal languages in 1990 and 1991, and grouped our languages into the following categories: flourishing, enduring, declining, endangered, and extinct. They found that of the 50 or so Aboriginal languages still alive in Canada, only three were flourishing—Ojibway, Cree, and Inuktitut. As noted by Brant Castellano, Davis, and Lahache (2000), the importance of Aboriginal languages was summarized by the Assembly of First Nations as follows: "Language is our unique relationship to the Creator, our attitudes, beliefs, values, and funda-

---

[1]This piece focuses on the basis for a holistic approach to literacy within Aboriginal epistemology. However, a growing body of mainstream educational and scientific research corroborates the holistic approach embodied in the Medicine Wheel. Indeed, much current educational and scientific research challenges traditional Cartesian dualism with respect to the Mind/Body split and the associated dichotomies and hierarchies that favour cognitive "ways of knowing" or other forms of knowing. See, for example, the work of the HeartMath Institute (Childre & Martin, with Beech, 1999), which asserts that the electromagnetic frequencies of the heart are 5,000 times greater than that of the brain. That is, it is the heart that entrains the brain, not the other way around as we have been socialized to believe. Gardner (1993, 1999) put forward a theory on Multiple Intelligences that offers a model of human intelligence that is multifaceted, nonhierarchical, and integrated.

mental notions of what is truth. Our languages are the cornerstones of who we are as a people. Without our languages, our cultures cannot survive" (p. 29).

Only two languages have the status of being official in Canada and these are not the languages of the first people of this land. A policy or structure that does not recognize and affirm our language serves only to erode our culture, our worldview of interconnectedness. Fettes and Norton (2000) support this view, stating, "A linguistic renaissance must be an integral part of the evolution towards local self-government and the restoration of spiritual and physical health to Aboriginal communities" (p. 29).

Aboriginal literacy programs framed within a holistic approach contribute to the renaissance of Aboriginal languages. Joanne Boyer, of Mississauga # 8 First Nation in Ontario, recently involved learners in making medicine pouches. One of the learners knew how to tan deer hides and offered to teach that skill to the rest of the class. Learners received the relevant teachings, then went through the various steps of making their own medicine pouches—from tanning the deer hide to cutting and assembling the pouch. Learners had to calculate the costs of materials, as well as the time spent in making the pouch, to arrive at a price that would honour their time and energy, yet be attractive to their potential buyers. They identified and practiced the vocabulary they would need in English and Anishnawbemowin, in order to market and sell their pouches, then decided when and where they would only use Anishnawbemowin in their work together (J. Boyer, personal communication, November, 2002).

There are other special initiatives in the Aboriginal community to keep our languages alive. The Royal Commission on Aboriginal Peoples recommends granting special status to Aboriginal languages, providing formal education in the language, and conducting research (Norris, 1998). The First Nations Confederacy of Cultural Education Centres (FNCECC), located in Ottawa, is in the initial stages of developing protective legislation for the preservation, maintenance, promotion, and use of Aboriginal languages in Canada ("The First Nations Confederacy of Cultural Education Centres," 2004). Aboriginal people across language groups are helping one another to save their language.

Orange

Orange is the second colour of the rainbow, and the colour understood by some Aboriginal cultures to mean balance, the place of choice where we are taught to exercise self-confidence, self-assuredness, self-control, and self-esteem, in order to keep emotions, such as fear, in balance. Orange is often used to denote fire. The first source of fire is the sun, which is the centre of the universe. People are like the universe in that they also have a centre, a fire within. For Aboriginal Peoples, that centre is the teachings. Aboriginal teachings have been passed from generation to generation orally.

Orange symbolizes the skills and qualities required for oral literacy (speaking, listening, imagining, attending, and being aware). Since time immemorial, our culture has been an oral one. Many of our people are known for their oratory skills—in their own language of origin and in English. Many of our teachings have been passed down orally—either in ceremony, through songs, or through storytelling. In this way, Aboriginal literacies are oral, and many skills are required for oral literacy on the part of the speaker as well as the listener—outstanding listening skills, sometimes referred to as "wholly" listening, critical and reflective thinking, excellent memory, and the ability to make sense to many different kinds of people in different settings. Graveline (1998) describes these skills as a commitment ". . . to sit and attentively listen, allowing the wisdom of the teacher/speaker to really be heard" (p. 138). She says that, "Through respectful listening we are better able to enter into another's experience through their words" (p. 138). In a sense, our stories and our teachings are like learning spirals—we can hear the same story or teaching a number of times, but get a different "*lesson*" out of it, depending on where we are on our own "*journeys.*"

Aboriginal literacy programs value oral literacy by inviting Elders to share the teachings, and to conduct Talking Circles, either on specific topics or on something that is important to the learner that day. In this way, the learners can use the Circle as "the building block of community" (Graveline, 1998, p. 141). Certainly, I know that Leanne McLeod of Prince Albert, Saskatchewan, through her work in correctional institutions, found that such teachings by Elders gave learners who were in prison a solid foundation for sharing with others in the Circle, and for writing their stories (L. McLeod, personal communication, September 2001). To further quote Graveline (1998), such a process provides a space so that "those previously silenced are encouraged to find their voice and speak up" (p. 145).

Yellow

Yellow is the third colour of the rainbow, and the colour often used in reference to the moon, and the gathering of food. In Aboriginal tradition, crops are planted and harvested according to the phases of the moon. Some Aboriginal cultures understand yellow to mean creativity. Yellow refers to the creative means by which Aboriginal Peoples had to learn to communicate with others who spoke another language or through other than the written word, by using symbols (pictographs, and in contemporary times, artwork, music) and/or sign language. Creativity in the use of these symbols is another Aboriginal literacy.

Because of our different languages and linguistic groups, Aboriginal Peoples have always had to be creative in the ways in which we communicate with each other about trade, about events that have transpired, and about prophecies. We developed a kind of sign language. We used various art forms for our clothing, lodgings, and surroundings. Pictures or images and colours convey ideas or meanings without the use of words or sounds, but in a much more powerful way. Today we can often tell from a person's regalia what nation they are from.

One of our longest standing and best known art forms is the petroglyphs, which date back thousands of years. Petroglyphs stretch around the Pacific Rim from California to China. They record events and visions and are a form of storytelling. Keddie (1996), in referring to the current desire to "understand" the meanings and purposes of the petroglyphs, cautioned that these images cannot be understood from a Eurocentric, print literacy perspective.

I would be remiss if I did not mention the awesome totem poles found on the west coast of British Columbia. Each of these, too, has a rich story to tell. Literacy programs are using ancient and contemporary art forms as a way of helping learners to get in touch with their creativity. Learners at the Stardale Women's Association, Melfort, Saskatchewan are learning weaving, pottery, and quilting. One of the Elders who participated as a consultant to this project said that crafts are a way of helping learners to tap into ancestral memories, to our "Spirit."

Similarly, arts and cultural movements across Canada are providing ways for us to powerfully communicate ideas in ways other than the written word. At the Literacy, Museums, and the Arts Festival in Montreal in 2002, the dancer Lynn Snelling performed an interpretive dance. We were invited to speak into the microphones and share what words came to us, in whatever language they came. I could not find words to describe the welling up of emotion inside me as I picked up on the energy that she conveyed with her hands, eyes, and body movements. There are times when words are inadequate. Karla McLaren, a healer who specializes in the field of physical and emotional trauma, refers to this as the "straightjacket of language" (McLaren, 2000). Lynn shared later that she believes that the body has a literacy all its own. If we pay attention, it will let us know what feelings are being blocked and need to be moved (L. Snelling, personal communication, June 2002).

Green

Green is the fourth colour of the rainbow, and it is often interpreted to mean growth, with going beyond what is familiar, yet remaining true to the teachings. This allows us to live with respect and humbleness. It is used to represent grass and growing things on Mother Earth. Treaties and understandings with the newcomers often included the phrase, "*as long as the grasses grow and the rivers flow.*" Green refers to literacy in the languages of the European newcomers to this land, English and/or French, which have been given the status of official languages.

The English and French languages came to this continent only a little over 500 hundred years ago. Yet today, they enjoy the status of official languages in Canada. This status means that they are considered to be the languages of formal instruction, except in territories of the Yukon, the NorthWest Territories, Nunavut, and in Labrador, where some Aboriginal languages, such as Cree, Inuktitut, and Dene enjoy regional official status.

Aboriginal literacy practitioners are using literacy in the official languages as a way of reclaiming their voice. One example is the work of Larry Loyie and Constance Brissenden. Larry, a former learner with the Carnegie Centre in Vancouver, noticed that many books about Aboriginal Peoples are written by non-Aboriginal Peoples. He set out to encourage Aboriginal people to write their own stories, joining with Constance Brissenden to offer writing workshops across the country. The result was a book entitled *Acimowina, Storytelling* (Fofonoff, 2000), an anthology of the writings of learners in Wabasca-Desmerais, Alberta. Larry also wrote a play, *Ora Nobis*, about his experiences in residential school, which was performed across Canada.[2]

Blue

Blue is the fifth colour of the rainbow, which some Aboriginal cultures understand to mean truth. Knowing the truth means staying true to your vision, and here commitment is most important. Blue is also used to symbolize the colour of the sky. With the coming of the Europeans, the skyline changed, and now contains the tools of technology, such as towers and satellite dishes, that send and receive signals. Blue refers to the skills required to communicate using technology.

For the purposes of describing literacy programming, I focus on computers and online learning. I recognize that there are many other types of technology. Computers and computer literacy offers Aboriginal Peoples, many of whom live in isolated communities, a way to keep in touch with the rest of the world. Sometimes this is a good thing; sometimes it is not. An Internet site where Aboriginal people can post their own Web pages can be found at http://myknet.org. A brief viewing of this site reveals a wide variety of symbols that people select to depict their culture.

---

[2]Larry Loyie and Constance Brissenden offer workshops to support and encourage Aboriginal writers. These are called *Self to Story—Creative Writing* and *Bring Stories to Life*. More information about these workshops can be found at: http://www.firstnationswriter.com/

The examples of Web sites posted on http://myknet.org suggest the great range and depth of Aboriginal literacies, and the potential of technology to support these, when literacy is broadly defined. Indeed, technology is now an important way that Aboriginal Peoples from around the world share their stories, which helps to support many other forms of Aboriginal literacies. For example, Pat Paul, Maliseet from the Tobique First Nation, New Brunswick, put a request over a number of Aboriginal listservs, looking for publishers for Aboriginal stories. Among the many responses was one from a woman in Australia who said that she had a Web site, and wondered if Pat would be interested in posting one of his stories there. Pat sent the story, *Geow-lud-mo-sis-eg: Little People*.[3] The story prompted a flood of messages from around the world that resulted in new connections, relationships, and work in support of Aboriginal cultures and Aboriginal literacies. For example, teachers included the story in their curriculum. People from around the world who were doing genealogy research and wanted to make links to their ancestors, shared other "little people" and "creation" stories, including several examples of "little people" who helped to heal serious illnesses. Messages arrived from Aboriginal groups around the world wanting to make links with Aboriginal Peoples in Canada. Requests for information came from Europeans who are deeply interested in the North American Native cultures. People originally from Tobique reconnected with Pat and some of their relatives. As well, students contacted Pat for help with their research. These new relationships, and the new work and new ideas that flow from them, are all about literacy.

Indigo

Indigo is the sixth colour of the rainbow. It is often referred to as the colour of the nighttime sky, the dream-time, when Aboriginal Peoples are more open to receiving messages from the Spirit World. This colour also refers to the "third eye chakra," which means "spiritual seeing." Indigo refers to the skills required for spiritual or cultural literacy—the ability to interpret dreams, visions, or natural events, which are seen to be messages from the Spirit World—the sighting of an animal, the shape of a cloud, seeing a certain person at a particular point in time, etc.

Since time immemorial, Aboriginal Peoples have believed in a Spirit World, what we often refer to as our "unseen helpers"—unseen with the naked eye, that is, but most certainly seen with the Spirit Eye. We believe that the Spirit speaks to us in imagery, thoughts, sounds, and feelings. Some cul-

---

[3]Pat Paul's "Little people" story can be found at http://www.ilhawaii.net/~stony/lore10.html [Accessed January 17, 2004]. Or search under the terms "Pat Paul" and "Little People."

tures call this clairvoyance, claircognizance, clairaudience, and clairsentience. The legacy of the Cartesian era, and a social system that values only what can be validated through the scientific method, has socialized spiritual ways of knowing out of many peoples, not just Aboriginal Peoples.

Violet

Violet is the seventh colour of the rainbow and is often thought to be a healing colour. Some Aboriginal cultures understand violet to mean wisdom, the ability to understand things, to have true power (inner and spiritual), to respect, and to know in a holistic way. Violet refers to the holistic base to Aboriginal literacy, the ways in which all of the literacies I have just described are integrated—facilitating spiritual, emotional, mental, and physical learning outcomes, striving for balance.

This is where the Medicine Wheel comes in. From the beginning, Aboriginal Peoples have recognized the importance of nurturing Spirit, Heart, Mind, and Body. We have long looked to the teachings of the Universe to help us. In fact, in my Anishnawbe language, the word for teach, *ahkinomagai*, means "the earth is our teacher." Through its cyclical changes, through the animals, through every aspect of Mother Earth, we learn about embodying caring, sharing, respect, honesty. And we learn these things through the many forms of literacy available to us—those of the colours of the rainbow I have laid out for you.

ABORIGINAL LITERACY PRACTITIONERS

Literacy practitioners strive to bring the rainbow colours of Aboriginal literacies into balance with the Medicine Wheel. When life is out of balance, the most important thing is to ask yourself, "In what ways am I nurturing myself in my spirit, heart, mind, and body?" There are many ways in which practitioners put the Medicine Wheel into practice as part of their literacy work. These include the way we treat learners when they first walk in our doors, listening closely to their needs and ideas and facilitating supportive groups where learning can happen, to the extent that many come to think of the literacy group as their family. We strive to work with the whole person. Often it is the first time that somebody has treated them like that. They're used to getting shuffled from one program to another, each with its stringent criteria and requirements that so often serve as barriers to learning. Rita Buffalo, a learner from Thunder Bay on the NADC, speaks of her experiences as a literacy learner in this way:

> It was important for me to know that I was always welcome in the program. There was no such thing as failure. When I did badly in some of the work,

someone sat down with me and patiently taught me the right way to do the work. I was encouraged and praised to go on, and not forced to complete work in a certain amount of time. (R. Buffalo, personal communication, June, 2000)

The success of the Medicine Wheel approach to literacy is supported by mainstream research that shows that students rate the quality of their relationship with their instructor as the number one factor in whether or not they enjoy learning (Rose & Nicholl, 1997).

CONCLUSION

I would like to relate an incident that occurred 2 years ago that really brought home, for me, the impact of losing, or being denied, the holism of Aboriginal literacy in the residential school system and the mainstream education system. I was participating in the Adult Literacy Research in Practice preconference, which was held just before the *Portraits of Literacy* conference at the University of British Columbia in July, 2002. As we arrived in the morning, the organizers asked us to use the array of arts and crafts materials on the tables to make a symbolic representation of our research interests. It seemed to me that people just dove in and started to assemble their pieces. I walked around looking at what others were doing, hoping that I might get an idea. Time was running out. When we were told that there were only a few minutes left before we would share our work with others, I panicked. I grabbed some different coloured wire-like pieces, and started to assemble a rainbow on the right-hand side of a piece of flipchart paper. On the left-hand side of the paper, I drew a chart to show the linear nature of the process that literacy practitioners are required to use in Ontario.

In those few seconds, I realized that by not having my Spirit and Heart recognized and nurtured in the residential school or the two-room school on the reserve that I attended, in having to conform to the paper- and print-based ways of expressing myself, I was "robbed" of the creativity that others seemed to possess so naturally. I felt what other learners must feel when they see others able to use many literacies to express themselves, and realize that they cannot do this, or that they must fit into the restricted views of literacy in Ontario's *Learning Outcome Matrix* and similar restricted definitions of literacy across the country. I was struck by the many kinds of literacies we use, and we need, in our everyday lives and I recommitted myself to helping learners recognize their "gifts," their ways of expressing themselves, and not to put the emphasis on only one form of literacy, to the detriment of others.

My Heart and Spirit go out to all literacy practitioners. We need to see beyond cognitive outcomes. We need to help learners to recognize their "gifts," only one of which is the ability to read and write in English. We need to go that extra mile to provide an atmosphere that makes space for the learner to grow as a whole person. Each and every day, we make a difference in someone's life.

In conclusion, I would like to acknowledge the Spirit World. Life has taken on a different tone for me since I learned to put my trust in the Creator to guide and direct my work, my life. It's a privilege to walk with the Creator and to share with you this sacred journey.

Gichi Miigwech! (Ojibway for 'Thank you.')

REFERENCES

Brant Castellano, M., Davis, L., & Lahache, L. (Eds.). (2000). *Aboriginal education: Fulfilling the promise.* Vancouver, B.C.: University of British Columbia Press.

Childre, D., Martin, H., with Beech, D. (1999). *The HeartMath Solution.* San Francisco: Harper.

The Daily Statistics Canada. (1998). *Canada's Aboriginal languages, 1996.* Retrieved December 14, 1998, from http://www.statcan.ca/Daily/English/981214/d981214.htm

"The First Nations Confederacy of Cultural Education Centres." (2004). Retrieved December 11, 2004, from http://www.schoolnet.ca/aboriginal/ab-lang/noframes/conte-e.html

Fettes, M., & Norton, R. (2000). Voices of winter: Aboriginal languages and public policy in Canada. In M. Castellano & L. Davis (Eds.), *Aboriginal education: Fulfilling the promise* (pp. 29–51). Vancouver, B.C.: University of British Columbia Press.

Fofonoff, A. (Ed.). (2000). *Acimowina: Storytelling.* Edmonton, AB: Voices Rising/Learning at the Centre Press.

Graveline, F. J. (1998). *Circle works: Transforming Eurocentric consciousness.* Halifax, NS: Fernwood Publishing.

Gardner, H. (1993). *Multiple intelligences: The theory in practice.* New York: Basic Books.

Gardner, H. (1999). *Intelligence reframed.* New York: Basic Books.

Hill, D. (1995). *Aboriginal access to post-secondary education: Prior learning assessment and its use within Aboriginal programs of learning.* Deseronto, Ontario: First Nations Technical Institute.

Keddie, G. (1996). *Aboriginal Defensive Sites* [Electronic version]. Retrieved December, 2001 from http://www.rbcm.gov.bc.ca/hhistory/aboriginaldef-sites1.html

McLaren, K. (2000). *Emotional genius: How your emotions can save your life.* (Cassette Recording): Boulder, CO: Sounds True.

Ministry of Training, Colleges and Universities (1995). *Program reform.* Toronto, Ontario: Queen's Printer for Ontario.

Norris, M. J. (1998, Winter). Canada's Aboriginal Languages. In *Canadian Social Trends.* Ottawa: Statistics Canada.

Rose, C., & Nicholl, M. J. (1997). *Accelerated learning for the 21st century.* New York: Dell Publishing.

Chapter 14

Creating Change in Literacy Programs: Taking Account of Violence

Jenny Horsman
Spiral Community Resource Group

The impact of violence[1] is traditionally seen as separate from education and viewed as a matter for therapeutic interventions.[2] Dominant discourses of education[3] shape what we know as "proper" literacy work and make it hard to change programs in ways that might support learning for those who have experienced violence. These discourses—language and practice—shape policy, expectations, shared assumptions about appropriate pedagogy, and necessary resources. They also lead "us" to "know" the general form of

---

[1]Throughout this chapter, I use the term violence to signal a broad range of oppressive experience. I have included the assumptions I make about violence in Appendix A (Morrish, Horsman, & Hofer, 2002).

[2]When I began the research, I thought that literature on violence and learning must exist if I could only find it. After many lengthy searches, I realized that it is not there because education and therapy are commonly seen as entirely separate, and experiences of violence are seen to need medical and therapeutic interventions. There are some exceptions to this overwhelming absence, for example, a manual on teaching English as an additional language to newcomers to Australia, recognizing what topics and approaches might remind students of war and torture (Martinez, 1997); an article on how to diagnose literacy learners suffering from Post Traumatic Stress Disorder (Wolpow & Askov, 1998); and articles on memory deficits and learning difficulties (e.g., Bremner et al., 1995; Gardner, 1971), but I found nothing that recognizes that survivors of trauma will be present in every classroom and examines how educators and educational programs of all sorts should take account of this.

[3]Language and practices that shape educational pedagogy, teaching methodology, and concepts of the good and bad teacher and student, are easily taken for granted as simply the way education must be carried out.

training that is necessary for those working in literacy—paid and volunteer—to support literacy work. For example, if we believe that education is entirely separate from therapy and all the "stuff" about the self and emotions is matter for therapy sessions, not the classroom, then a relaxed, comfortable, and inspiring learning environment is simply a luxury, learning about counseling is not seen as part of the work of a teacher, and supports for teachers witnessing trauma are not expected to be needed. Changing these perceptions and questioning mainstream discourses about adult literacy and education more broadly is a challenging endeavor.

BACKGROUND TO THE RESEARCH

I was initially drawn to exploring the impact of violence on learning, prompted by both research and practice. In research with women in rural Nova Scotia exploring the daily practices of literacy in their lives, most of the women I interviewed revealed layers of violence in their lives (Horsman, 1990). I began to question the connections between these experiences of violence and their difficulties with literacy learning, as children and as adults. These women spoke of childhood violence at home and in school, of violence as adults living with violent men, of the damage to their bodies from physically demanding, monotonous jobs, and the humiliation of living on an inadequate welfare allowance. In the context of that research, I began to see a broad range of violence as the backdrop against which I was examining the promise of literacy (Horsman, 1994b).

In-depth interviews with women, their accounts of the literacy practices in their lives, and their desires for change led me to situate my own understanding of literacy alongside those who question the unitary and autonomous concept of literacy—a "thing" or "skill" to be acquired—and instead recognize the socially and historically situated and contested nature of literacies (e.g., Bennett, 1983; Cook-Gumperz, 1986; Sola & Bennett, 1985; Street, 1984).[4] I also came to value feminist poststructural theory (e.g., Weedon, 1987),[5] the concept of discourse and its relation to power and social practices (e.g., Foucault, 1982). As Weedon (1987) explains: "Once language is understood in terms of competing discourses, competing ways of

---

[4]More recently, Barton and Hamilton elaborated this approach with elegance (e.g., 2000). In a recent workshop for counsellors exploring the links between violence and learning, I wrote my current assumptions about literacy that frame my thinking about connections between violence and illiteracy (see Appendix B).

[5]Although I still find Weedon's book a valuable core text, the recent work of Davies has been particularly useful in my attempts to understand the construction of meaning and the possibilities of change (e.g., 2000).

giving meaning to the world, which imply differences in the organization of social power, then language becomes an important site of political struggle" (p. 24). As I grappled with the concepts of discourse and agency, (Horsman, 1990) trying to clarify the idea that we both "assume a subject position within discourse" and "become subjected to the power and regulation of the discourse" (Weedon, 1987, p. 119), I went on to explain:

> It is this dual sense of being a subject that is crucial to discourse. People are seen neither as helpless puppets subjected to control through discourses, nor as the traditional rational individual who makes free choices. Discourses are not monolithic. Although discourses which are made powerful through institutional frameworks are an important form of control, we can also contest and challenge them. As we participate in resistant discourses, we are part of a process of changing perceptions of experience and forming new subjectivities. (Horsman, 1990, p. 23)

This focus moves us from looking for the "truth," and instead to seeking to reveal discourses and how they shape our understandings of truth or reality in a particular time and place.[6] Both of these theoretical frameworks underlie my more recent research.

I believe the language we use to understand what we do is crucial.[7] Seeing our language and practices as discourse offers a tool to get outside a focus on what is "right" and draws attention to examining how discourses open or close possibilities. Some discourses are dominant, reinforced by social institutions and widely used. Others are minority discourses of resistance. Such an analysis directs us to notice our own language closely and explore its implications. As literacy workers discuss the impact of violence on learning, we begin to create possibilities for new understandings of literacy work. Discourses are not fixed for all time. They do not operate independent of people. When we come to see the ways that particular discourses shape our thinking—especially those we may initially have trouble seeing,

---

[6]I had puzzled over the contradictory accounts of the Nova Scotian women I interviewed, determined to find an interpretation that did not suggest that they were foolish. On one hand, they did not think improved literacy skills could make much difference in their lives; on the other, literacy was going to open up an entirely different life. I began to see that, to some extent, the women bought into common, dominant discourses about the value of literacy. They wanted to believe, as everyone says, that literacy changes lives. On the other hand, they resisted these discourses and offered alternate explanations. They knew by their own experience that it did not make sense—that there were very few jobs in their rural area, and even fewer well-paid jobs that anyone would hire a woman for—so they did not really believe literacy would change *their* lives.

[7]A clear introduction to a poststructuralist understanding of meaning, and the responsibility to explicate social practices that disadvantage some, is offered by Gee (1993).

because they just reveal "the way it is"—we become more able to create, or participate in, resistant discourses that may open possibilities for new practices that can support learning for all.

When I returned to Toronto after completing the Nova Scotian research study, one member of a women's literacy group in a community literacy program commented in a session I led that "things happen to children that shouldn't." I described where this led us in an early article:

> Several years ago, when a woman from the women's literacy group I was facilitating called me to apologize for speaking about her unhappy childhood in our last group session, I said she had no need to apologize. This was the beginning of a relationship I had no experience to handle. This woman had never told anybody else about her childhood. This telling, and my acknowledgement that it was fine that she spoke of it, led to a difficult process where she at first wanted to tell me the horrors of her childhood and wanted more and more of my time and my support. I kept backing off and then feeling bad—scared that she was asking more of me than I could give, but unwilling to let her down. Finally I suggested that I could try to give her support through a regular meeting where she could speak, read and write about her memories of childhood and the abuse she experienced then. She decided to meet with me and we began a long process of negotiating how we would work together, which evolved into a special kind of tutoring situation. (Horsman, 1994a, p. 56)

This agreement launched me into an intense literacy tutoring relationship, and reflection, writing and presentations as I explored the issue of violence and how it affects literacy learning (e.g., Horsman, 1994a, 1995a, 1995b, 1996a, 1996b). The desire to learn more led me to a new research study[8] interviewing therapists, counsellors, literacy workers,[9] and literacy learners to explore the discourses that shape therapists' and educators' understandings of those who have experienced violence (Horsman, 2000a) and to learn how literacy programs might be improved to support learning for these students. As I sought to build on this research, I took it into practice through conceptualizing and leading a course for women in a community-based program, Parkdale Project Read, Toronto (Horsman, 2000b), designing training for literacy tutors in Saskatchewan (Horsman, 2001b), and working with adult educators from New England teaching in a wide variety of settings (Morrish, Horsman, & Hofer, 2002).

---

[8]The research was funded by the National Literacy Secretariat of Human Resources and Skills Development Canada and sponsored by the Canadian Congress for Learning Opportunities for Women (CCLOW).

[9]By "literacy workers" I mean people in a whole range of roles in the adult literacy, adult basic education field, for example, coordinators of community programs, instructors in community college and school board programs, group facilitators, and individual tutors.

THE RESEARCH PROCESS

I also embarked on further research,[10] reported here, to systematically observe this process of change in different educational organizations and to learn more about the discourses that might help and hinder possibilities for changing programs and addressing the impact of violence on learning.[11] Focus groups and individual interviews with practitioners became sites for collaborative exploration, as we all listened carefully to the discourses that shaped our thinking about violence and literacy education, and looked for possibilities for changing practice. Partners in this action research study were two organizations where I was actively involved: *Parkdale Project Read,* Toronto, Ontario and *World Education,* Boston, Massachusetts, along with two organizations where key staff had organized focus groups and participated in my earlier research: *The Learning Centre,* Edmonton, Alberta and *Malaspina University-College,* Duncan, British Columbia.

At *Parkdale Project Read,* my local community-based literacy program, the course I facilitated allowed women time to explore their lives and build their strengths as learners.[12] The course gave me the opportunity to put learning from my earlier research into practice. I led the group with the support of a therapist who gave occasional workshops. I also met with her bi-weekly to discuss the group work and explore the value of a process of "supervision" similar to that regularly used by therapists. A focus group[13] attended by program staff allowed us to reflect on the group and its impact on the program.

---

[10]The research was funded by the Social Sciences and Humanities Research Council and the National Literacy Secretariat of Human Resources and Skills Development Canada, and carried out along with Dr. Susan Heald of The University of Manitoba.

[11]In discussion with Mary Hamilton (Summer 2003), she helped me realize that I had been ignoring that my acceptance of social practice theories of literacy had played a role in making it possible for me to even imagine that impacts of violence were relevant to understanding how to teach literacy. This theory itself enables a discourse of multiple literacies and includes the social and historical context within which literacy is taking place. Mary pointed out that social practice theories are multidimensional, including such aspects as confidence and embodied learning within the theoretical frame.

[12]This course, funded jointly by the National Literacy Secretariat and the Ontario Ministry of Colleges, Training and Universities, led to a manual of approaches and learning activities called *Moving Forward.* We had hoped to work with a range of programs interested in using the manual in their own setting and adding further activities and reflections to make it appropriate to different communities and contexts, but as we failed to secure funding, we continue to distribute it in its current draft form (Horsman, 2000b).

[13]Susan Heald and I jointly led focus groups in each location (except Douglas College, which I led alone). Individual interviews were carried out either by Susan Heald or me individually, or both of us together. Focus groups and individual interviews were a process of collective and collaborative exploration of the discourses that shape our understandings of education, violence, and possibilities for changing education.

World Education[14] in Boston selected six programs from different states in New England to work collaboratively with organizations working on violence in their community on a joint project. Programs included an adult education school in a maximum security prison, a literacy and GED program in a homeless shelter, a community-based centre that offers native language literacy and basic education, a welfare-to-work program, a family literacy program that works with families in their homes, and a program for immigrants and refugees with English classes for speakers of other languages. As a trainer and consultant for this project, I met with the participants working in these diverse organizations every 3 months. During training I listened to program workers talk about the challenge of making changes in their programs and followed up with interviews and focus groups with some participants at the end of the first year.[15]

At the *Learning Centre* and other programs in Edmonton and Camrose, staff have been developing initiatives for holistic education, drawing on the arts and writing to support learning and change. These initiatives do not explicitly focus on violence, but were planned with recognition of the prevalence of violence in learners' lives and an interest in exploring the value of holistic education. Focus groups in Edmonton were attended by staff of the Learning Centre, *Edmonton John Howard Society*, and the *Write to Learn* project in Camrose.

At *Malaspina University-College*, instructors at all levels of education—from adult basic education (ABE) to university level courses, within the college and in a new storefront reading and writing centre in the community—have been interested in exploring how to support learning for those who have experienced violence. A focus group with ABE instructors and individual interviews with several instructors, administrators, and counsellors explored the potential for change and the barriers they envisaged in a college setting. Also in British Columbia, as a result of my earlier research, *Douglas College* in New Westminster has been running a course to support women "with violence in their background or foreground" in their learning in the college. Interested in learning more about this group, I went into a group session, and held a focus group with the instructor and other ABE instructors at the college. An informal discussion with this group and the president of the college allowed us to continue collectively to reflect on the issues.

---

[14]Funding from the U.S. Department of Education under the Women's Educational Equity Act Program was directed to help adult educators and family violence services explore together how best to work with women who experience violence and support them in pursuing their educational goals.

[15]Susan Heald also interviewed workers from each of these programs, focussing on their conceptions of their work and role.

In various workshops, presentations, and discussions, I have been able to introduce my earlier research study and issues of violence and learning to many more literacy workers in British Columbia, Alberta, Saskatchewan, Ontario, Massachusetts, and New York State. An online discussion allowed me to reach literacy workers in various parts of the world.[16] Participants who contributed identified themselves as working in Nepal, England, Canada, and the United States. Throughout these sessions, whether they were billed as part of the research study or more generally about violence and learning, I listened carefully to how workers speak about the issues and the possibilities and limitations for creating change in their programs. Susan Heald and I generated initial themes from interview notes and during reflection sessions immediately following focus groups and interviews. I continued to look for patterns in data and to document emergent themes I identified in notes from interview and focus group tapes and jottings from workshops and informal discussions. I took the first paper Susan and I wrote (Heald & Horsman, 2000) back to partners in the research, and to participants in academic and practitioner conferences, exploring themes further in an extensive process of collaborative analysis. Toward the end of the research, I wrote a lengthy discussion paper and consulted with all those whom I had quoted to check whether they were happy with their words and the meaning I was making of them in the paper, and to confirm whether and how they wished to be identified. This paper was then posted online, and I invited academics, administrators, and literacy educators from Canada, the United States, and elsewhere to join in a participatory process of negotiating interpretations of the research.[17]

DISCOURSES ABOUT VIOLENCE

Many literacy workers, even those who had heard many stories of violence, said during workshops that they had not previously thought about how violence might impact on learning. Several workers said they simply thought of violence as part of poverty and had not taken account of it separately. At a workshop focussing on the impact of violence on learning, one experienced literacy worker mused about how obvious the issue seemed as soon as she began to think about it. She was surprised at herself and her organiza-

---

[16]I was invited to lead a discussion on violence and learning on the U.S.-based National Institute for Literacy's women and literacy list moderated by Daphne Greenberg during September 2000.

[17]The paper was posted at www.alphaplus.ca and discussion was carried out on the Alphacom discussion system during June 2001.

tion for not recognizing and addressing the issue previously. But she also commented that many teachers who regularly attend training had not chosen to attend this workshop.

Knowing about experiences of violence had led some teachers to recognize that violence impacts on learning and had to be addressed, even though it was not spoken about. When I asked one educator whether she talked to colleagues about the issues, she said:

> No, on my personal level in working with people, but not with other teachers. We never really looked at it, identified it, said we need training in this area . . . I just felt that this was something I needed to deal with as a teacher. These were issues coming up and they were interfering with what I was trying to do as a teacher. (Interview, Janice Armstrong, Farmington, Maine, May 2001)

I still question what has enabled some literacy workers to "know" that issues of violence are part of their work as a teacher, even though dominant discourses lead them also to "know" that violence issues are not part of literacy work. The belief that the issue is outside education leads to teachers' silence on the issue, and allows many workers to avoid any focus on it.

Silence

A profound silence about issues of violence in society preserves violence as an individual experience outside the "normal," even though it is an everyday experience in women's lives. Both this silence and the widespread experience of violence are reflected in literacy programs. The suggestion is often that it is better or wiser not to talk, that it serves no purpose to open up the issues.

The phrase "it's a can of worms" is one I often hear in response to talk about issues of violence. The image of breaking silence as opening something far too complex, too messy, too nasty to deal with, is a compelling one, telling us that it is simply not wise to open the can. Comments that "it" is too big, too specialized an area, often follow. Although the development of training will be enormously important if the literacy field is to be able to take on issues of violence with a sense of competence and capacity, as workers spoke, it usually sounded less like a request for training, and more a way to say that it should not be taken on. This leads me to question the origins and purposes of discourses that tell us what belongs, and does not belong, in education.

The question of what counts as violence also silences attempts to open discussion about the impacts of violence on learning. One workshop participant said attempts to take up the issue were often blocked with the argument that "this isn't violence," so "stop making a fuss." In a later conversation, she spoke more about her sense that the extent of violence in organizational life in most workplaces leaves workers so steeped in a culture of violence it can simply seem "normal," something I heard many times from literacy workers. While enduring violence themselves, it may be difficult for workers to take on addressing violence issues for others. They may have a tendency to feel, "If I can put up with it, why can't you?"

Teachers working with students of a different ethnicity reported that the students didn't perceive as violent experiences teachers identified as such, and often told me they could not do anything about issues of violence. I was told repeatedly that some particular ethnic group accepted more violence against women than other groups—often a group that represented the "other" for that speaker. Talk about violence can easily slide into talk about "them" as if "they" are not also us. It seems much easier to talk about the problems "they" have rather than our own, whether the "they" refers to learners or to another class, culture, or religion. I've found it useful to identify that most cultures seem to accept some aspect of violence against women and children, but at the same time activists in every culture struggle to make change. As a way of opening space for discussion, I have suggested that literacy workers find activists from within the same religious, cultural, or ethnic group as their students and invite them into the classroom to talk about their struggle and open the possibility of changing conceptions.

Often violence is excused with the explanation that the person is only violent when drunk and so is not responsible. Kate Nonesuch, a literacy worker in British Columbia, suggested:

> I think [men] know that if they drink, they may beat their partner, and they get drunk anyway—or maybe they get drunk so that they will be able to beat her up and then have an excuse for doing it. Here we give stiff penalties to people who drink and drive, especially people who kill or injure people while they are drunk at the wheel. The law says that they are responsible for whatever they do in a car while they are drunk. I think the same should apply to men who drink and batter.
>
> More positively, I am amazed at the change in attitudes to drinking and driving. While some people still do it, the idea of a designated driver who does not drink but who drives for the rest of the people who are partying, has made its way into the popular culture. Surely we could make the same sort of change in attitudes to violence. (NIFL Women in Literacy Forum, 2000)

What counts as violence is contested terrain. Reframing drinking and violence provides an example of how to change the discourse and shift away from an acceptance of violence to a focus on new possibilities.

Even when they were trying to break silences about the issues, literacy workers—and I include myself here—often found ourselves being indirect, worrying about embarrassing the person we were talking to, wondering whether she wanted to speak about it, and not wanting to "break down" the person's defenses. We struggled with how to acknowledge violence without excluding women. If a group is billed as one that will address issues of violence, or as for survivors of violence, many women don't attend. Some women said they had been through too much violence and didn't want to talk about it. When I began a women's group, I did not name violence directly in the advertising or calls to prompt women to attend. I quickly realized I could not mention violence to family members or on answering machines because that could escalate violence for any woman at risk. In person, I still did not speak directly about violence. I didn't want women to decide not to attend the group out of fear they would be labeled as going to "that" group, or to decide that it wasn't for them because they didn't perceive themselves as having experienced violence. I was told about one student attending a women's empowerment group, who said she hadn't experienced violence like other women in the group, and later mentioned in passing that her husband had tried to kill her several times.

I also did not want to separate out women who have experienced violence, to avoid imposing a division between "normal" learners and "others" who have experienced violence and need special treatment. Educational programs need to change so that everyone, survivor or not, will be able to learn effectively, rather than to simply provide something special for those who have experienced violence. A direct approach, which appears to open up talk about violence, may unintentionally recreate silence. The challenge is to create ways to avoid complicity in recreating silence—to name violence while avoiding increasing danger or threat in any way.

The frames "It's safer not to open it up" or "I don't know what to do so it's better to do nothing" suggest silence is safer than saying the wrong thing, and doing nothing is a way of doing no harm. As I search for discourses that offer routes to support addressing the impact of violence on learning, I have found it helpful to focus on the dangers of silence. I frequently tell another story I heard from Kate Nonesuch, the instructor in British Columbia:

> [Kate] reported that when she checked in with a woman student to see if a male student's behaviour was bothering her, the woman remarked that she had seen the instructor watching the interaction. The student said that because the instructor did nothing immediately, she had assumed that meant that the instructor thought the man's behaviour was acceptable. This is a powerful reminder that if an instructor does not take action when she sees violence—such as harassment in the classroom, or a woman's bruises—students witness that silence and lack of action and take a message from it. (Horsman, 2000a)

After one talk I gave, a man approached me and said he was very wary about taking on the issue of violence. He seemed to be particularly worried that "as a man" this was not something he could address. I responded with the story I have just told. I argued that there is no neutral place for a man. He is either identified with the abuser or offers a different model of a man, one who respects the woman's right to be free of violence and to set her own boundaries. One male computer instructor recognized during a workshop that if he was careful about distance as he helped women at the computer and always asked before taking over the mouse or the keyboard, he would model respectful boundaries. In this way he could reduce the possibility that women were fearful of his presence and distracted from learning by their anxiety. Students from another program also told me that the gentle man who taught them computer skills and was very careful about touch and distance had been extremely healing, helping them to learn and also to imagine the possibility of men who would not be violent.

Another male instructor at a workshop talked about his discomfort at his own silence when women came into his class with bruises. Because he was not from the same culture as the students and they were not telling him that the injuries were caused by male violence, he felt unable to say anything. Together, we thought about what he could say that respected their silence, did not make him the judge of their lives, yet was not complicit. His plan in future was to say: "I don't know how you got those bruises, but if somebody hurt you I want you to know that I don't think violence against another person is ever OK. Nobody ever deserves to be hurt."

Preparing a response to a range of possible situations can be very helpful for both men and women in literacy, helping to avoid silences that give messages we would rather not send. There is no neutral place men or women can reach by staying silent. We can break the silence using posters, pamphlets, reading materials for students and teachers,[18] and workshops. We can set ground rules about violence, and respond clearly to violence and to the pressure to "get over it." We can provide a clear message that violence is not acceptable.

Naming the presence of violence does not mean moving to a place with no boundaries where all stories can be told at all times. Recognizing this may also enable literacy workers to feel more prepared to open the "can of worms." After teaching a 3-month intensive course with a group of women, I know few details of the abuse they have all experienced. I heard a little about the crises they lived through as they sought to find a way to continue their studies and hold their lives together. I saw tears often, as they remem-

---

[18]Materials addressing how to break silences include Horsman, 2001b, 2000b; Morrish et al., 2002; Murphy, 2004.

bered how badly they had been mistreated in the past. But the acceptance that violence was present in their lives, the availability of counseling supports, and their own acknowledgement that each other's stories would be too hard to hear, meant they were all careful to limit what they shared.

One literacy worker mentioned that the disclosures she hears in groups using the arts to explore well-being and support women's learning do not burn her out the way disclosures did in the course of more traditional teaching work. She thought the difference was that the stories emerge within the class as part of each woman bringing her whole self to learning. She realized she had previously been exhausted by hearing stories presented in a frame that said, "I have this problem—fix it" while this was also not an accepted part of her literacy work. This recognition might be useful to other workers afraid that opening up the issue will be overwhelming.

Janet Isserlis, a literacy researcher from Rhode Island who focuses on issues of violence and learning, suggested that it is important to notice that when we begin to name violence, many of us are drawn to all-or-nothing approaches. She suggested it might be helpful to explore middle ground— ways of "layering into considerations of violence that bring it to light gradually, subtly" (e-mail correspondence, 2001). We can explore ways to speak about violence in education, to insist that violence is not just "the way it is," and instead provide a clear message that violence is not acceptable and its aftermath must be addressed in educational programs. In this way, we may be prepared to believe we can open the "can of worms" without chaos erupting!

Medicalizing Violence

The aftermath of violence is spoken about primarily in medical terms. This sets the scene for an approach to issues of violence in education that is clearly focused on diagnosing who has a problem and referring them for help. One educational counselor said when he told his supervisor that one of his students needed more support or was in danger of dropping out, his supervisor asked whether it was "appropriate for her to be here in the first place? Would it make more sense for her to be somewhere else?" Literacy workers commented that saying, "You need to talk to a counselor" can be silencing, giving the impression that the person who has begun to tell is not normal and has special problems that need to be dealt with outside of the classroom. The person needs to change, but the education system can remain the same.

I often heard teachers say, "I'm not a therapist," the implication being that they cannot address issues of violence in any way. The discourse of the professional fosters the belief that teachers are not trained as therapists, and emotional and violence issues are properly subject matter for therapy, therefore teachers should not take up issues of violence. Students also share this discourse. On several occasions when I talked about emotions blocking learning with a literacy group, students have asked whether I am a psychiatrist or therapist, or questioned whether we are still doing literacy. They remind me that I have strayed away from the expected ground of education. This assumption, that anything to do with violence or emotions must be therapy, limits the possibilities for exploring new educational practices. I do not want to suggest that teachers should "do therapy," although we may want to learn from the therapeutic field as we explore new practices. Through such exploration, we may redefine the divide between the work of educators and therapists. This may include a range of collaborations with the therapeutic field: coleading groups with therapists; adapting training traditionally offered to counselors for literacy workers; designing new curriculum that enters the terrain of emotions; offering teachers supports traditionally offered to therapists, such as supervision and peer support.

During focus groups, literacy workers commented with surprise that they were talking about their own experiences of violence, and gave the sense that this rarely happens in the literacy field. We heard a discourse that suggested literacy teachers should have "dealt with it," in relation to any violence they themselves had experienced. This discourse parallels the pressure on learners to go away and heal if experiences of violence are getting in the way of learning. Pressure to have "dealt with it" increases the separation between workers and learners: professionals give help, they don't need help. This silences possibilities for workers to talk about how their work impacts them. One worker said that when working with students triggered her own memories of abuse, she took a leave of absence and wondered whether she had disqualified herself as a literacy worker. Several literacy workers talked about the difficulty of trusting colleagues and of asking for support if they are triggered in the classroom. For survivors of violence, there is danger in opening up issues of violence in the classroom. This may lead them to avoid anything that might reveal to themselves or others that they haven't "dealt with" their past.

Lewis (1999) offers an alternative conceptualization to the medical model of sickness and healing, the image of "living beside the violation." She asserts that experiences of trauma live on and suggests a new frame, "familiarity with violence:"

> Living beside the violation becomes much more possible if I understand myself as someone who is familiar with violence rather than someone whose life experience is pathologized. My familiarity with violence contributes to my knowledge, my sense of strength and my capacity for empathy rather than be-

ing something tainted with pathology that must be overcome. (Unpublished presentation, 1998)[19]

Though medical diagnoses can be reassuring (and sometimes useful)[20] to a person who has experienced trauma, they can also be a trap, identifying a sickness to be cured and leading to self-blame or blame from others when she is not cured fast enough or cannot get on with "normal" life again and learn successfully. This trap can be particularly acute in literacy. The experience of taking part in a literacy program can reveal possibilities for living beside trauma, but if literacy workers have absorbed the medicalizing and pathologizing discourses, then workers and learners will seek to show they have left violence and its impacts behind or risk the judgement that they are not "ready" to be there.

The metaphor of people who have experienced violence as "canaries in the mine"[21] is useful for shifting from more pathologized views to approaches that recognize that nowhere is free of violence and there is no safe place to retreat to and heal. Instead, it suggests that those who have experienced violence offer a warning that the levels of violence in society are toxic to us all. It is not they who must return to "normal," but society that must change and reduce the ongoing possibility of violation, particularly for women and children. This invites all survivors, whether learners or teachers, to honor their experience of trauma and impacts on the self, rather than to seek to deny and hide them.

These new discourses also allow for a recognition of the value of tears. In my group, I often heard myself and others say, "Don't cry." Other White instructors were aware that they, too, had sought to quell tears even though they wanted to recognize the value of them. They, too, drew on the phrase "Don't cry" when seeking to offer comfort. Yet this denies the value of expressing feeling. I heard from several First Nations instructors that, in their traditions, tears are to be valued as life giving, a means of honoring the grief and those present who are being trusted to bear witness to the grief. Lewis' concept of honoring traumatized parts of the self is consistent with this tradition of valuing tears:

> Living beside means acknowledging the traumatized parts of self as they arise in daily life. It means honouring them and giving them space for expression. As soon as I resist and refuse these parts of myself, I quickly move back into re-

---

[19]These concepts were articulated by Lewis (1999) as part of her thesis defence and developed in depth in the book drawn from her thesis. I thank her for the tremendous insight such metaphors offer for enabling a vision outside medicalizing discourses.

[20]Thanks to Nicole Ysabet-Scott for her insights about the value of medical diagnoses to assist students in bargaining concessions from the academic system in order to gain entry or achieve success within the formal academic system.

[21]Thanks to Susan Heald for this concept and for all her help in recognizing the discourses of violence and education.

lationships and a sense of self that reflect past patterns of survival. When I honour the trauma, I gain the flexibility to move into different parts of myself to create new possibilities. (Lewis, 1999, p. 120)

DISCOURSES ABOUT EDUCATION

In our first paper on this research (Heald & Horsman, 2000), we described several discourses of education that became visible to us through the research. These are outlined briefly here.

Violence as a Barrier to Learning

The concept of violence as a barrier to learning initially seemed as if it might open up possibilities for addressing issues of violence and arguing for funding to address these issues. However, I have gradually come to see that although it may reveal women's felt experience of ceasing to learn after an incident of abuse, it does not reveal what is learned through violence or the ways in which that learning is in accord or in conflict with other learnings for females in western society.[22]

This discourse also contributes to assumptions that only literacy learners will have experienced violence, as those who have successfully negotiated the education system cannot have experienced these barriers. This allows other educational institutions to ignore the issue entirely. Or this approach can, as happened in one of our focus groups, lead to questions about how those who do succeed in education despite having experienced violence did so, with the idea that maybe this knowledge could be helpful for those who have failed. This direction opens many questions about what counts as success, and success at what cost?

The Severed Head[23]

One possible cost is the "severed head." The educational system can be a place of escape for the mind, but can, at the same time, contribute to a fragmentation of the whole person. For those who have experienced vio-

---

[22]In an interview Judy Titzel, a literacy worker from Providence, Rhode Island, modified this approach by stressing the widespread existence of violence as a systemic barrier to women's learning. She argued "the pervasiveness of violence is preventing equal access to quality education for women." This approach allows attention to move from the individual who experiences violence to a consideration of what quality education might look like and to the broad range of systemic barriers to creating that quality for all students in all levels and types of educational setting.

[23]Sylvia Fraser (1987) speaks of taking her severed head to college and seeking to bury emotions and self-hate through putting together a "rational and successful person" she could respect (p. 130).

lence and already feel fragmented, this further severance may be particularly costly.

To attempt to bring the whole person into the teaching and learning process is to go against the widely shared sense of the "real" work of education. Those who have sought to draw the whole self into the learning process have been able to do so when they can find a space outside the discourses of "proper teaching" and "acceptable outcomes." This may mean working in the guise of research or with the protection of special project funding. When time is short, instructors recognized that they were drawn back to practicing math, for example, and steered away from spending time on supporting students to reflect on their learning, even when they believed in the importance of the alternative approach. Similarly, when I speak about the importance of focusing on issues of violence, my listeners often veer into talk about the methodology of teaching reading. In response to one talk about the necessity of shifting discourses of education in order to encompass the experience of violence, I was asked in the silence that followed about the merits of whole language over phonics. Violence was not mentioned again.

The "correct" ways to be a student or teacher are well known. The apparent neutrality of this discourse makes it appear that one's competence as a student is a function of the presence or absence of personal qualities, rather than biases concealed within the discourse. Learners who don't conform to the description of the good student are judged as not motivated, not ready, or not committed. This frame allows the educational system to continue unchanged, as if everyone knows how to learn and to be a student, and those that don't ought to.

Drawing the Line

The existing discourse draws a line between the preparation work to be done by the student and tasks appropriate to be carried out within the institution. The work that might be necessary to help a student get to a point where she or he is ready to learn is made invisible in the institution, a task for the student alone to deal with, instead of recognizing that there might be a crucial role for the institution and the teacher in support of that process.

"Drawing the line" is also often used to divide literacy work and therapy. This divide helps to rule inadmissible any talk that might be identified as doing therapy in the classroom. But, over and over again, we heard that counselors in institutions often focus on "advising" instead of counseling, and that counseling hours are insufficient for many students to see counselors. In community-based programs without counselors on-site, teachers worry about the long waiting lists and lack of appropriate, free counseling in the community. These pressures lead some teachers to feel they have no option but to counsel. If they do so, they take on the work illicitly, without resources, office space, supports, or time, and with the risk of being blamed for becoming "overinvolved." Institutions benefit from this unpaid, unacknowledged work, while teachers risk being framed as the problem.

What Is Missing?

We also heard often about the ways in which lack of resources framed expectations about education. In various settings, instructors spoke about the challenge of taking up issues of violence given the lack of institutional support for their work and the outright hostility of some colleagues. Structural constraints, such as attendance policies and waiting lists for places in programs, increased the challenge. Literacy workers at Parkdale Project Read, a community-based literacy program in Ontario, mused about whether they would need to move away from using volunteer tutors if they were to adequately address issues of violence. Committed literacy workers were open to thinking about this challenge, but lack of funding to make this a realistic option, along with lack of time for reflection and professional development, limits possibilities for radical solutions. In the same program, the level of stress was revealed as they talked about the difficulty of taking on this work in the absence of supports:

> I think we could do more, I think we could take more chances without feeling irresponsible about it, because *you open up this can of worms*, possibly, with people, you encourage this kind of speaking about their feelings and then—my sense is that there are no resources in the community. So, people have their defense mechanisms for a reason, and *who are we to try and pry them open* and then they have no supports to . . . but if there was this on-site counselor . . . we'd always know that there's extra supports.
>
> Even if we went to get information from a counselor and talked about students . . . We could deal with some of the problems better if we had some backup. (Interview, Toronto, Ontario, March 2000)

As long as support is not forthcoming, the discourses outlined earlier—the "can of worms" and the fear that naming is demanding disclosure—remain in place.

Safety Is Fundamental

In the first paper from this research, we argued that the lack of a discourse about safety limited what instructors could take on and leaves teachers responsible to cope with everything that happens in the classroom. When we

took this paper back to instructors, Kate Nonesuch disagreed, saying that
she made use of a discourse of safety in her class:

> I often have a reason for walking behind the guy who's on the Internet. One
> day in class I said that I felt unsafe when I noticed on the screen that people
> were talking about what kind of sexual things they were going to do to
> women, that I felt unsafe when the guy came off the screen and walked over to
> ask for help doing math, that it made me uncomfortable knowing that he had
> just finished talking about sex and a particular kind of sex. So, I wanted to
> know if other people felt unsafe and what kind of agreement we could make.
> People went around and agreed that this wasn't conducive to safety.

Later, they wrote an Internet policy for the program to confirm this agreement. A discourse of safety can open talk about a broad range of what
might be required to maintain safety and what exactly it might look like in
context.

INTEGRATING NEW DISCOURSES

When literacy workers imagined creating new practices in adult literacy,
they often spoke of constraints within their own institutions and within government discourses. They struggled with limitations imposed at the highest
levels. Teachers might feel constraints from the administration, but administrators were clear that they were limited by provincial or state constraints
and that policy change was needed at that level. In many provinces and
states, literacy workers itemized a direction of government policy that they
saw as opposite to what was needed if the lives of learners were to be taken
into account and issues of violence taken up within educational practice.

In programs lacking flexibility to carry out new ideas, workers talked
about trying to cope and feeling unable to stretch to even *think* about new
approaches. Where space has been created—through professional development, supportive colleagues and supervisors, project funding, and counseling supports—literacy workers are carrying out groundbreaking work. This
work, described next, can take place when "space" is created to explore new
approaches and new conceptions of the work and to experiment with new
collaborations that make the concept of drawing new lines between healing
and learning a material reality.

Provide Legitimacy for New Concepts of Education

Literacy workers who took part in special projects talked glowingly about
the opportunity to explore the unknown and to launch into unlikely exper-
iments. Funding paid for and legitimized talk about new collaborations and

made it possible to try out new curricula, such as learning about learning, self-empowerment, and creative arts. It is only within such a space that new models can be generated to demonstrate the success of shifting what counts in education and provide a basis for challenging policy.

Literacy workers in the World Education project in New England often talked about the shift from isolation they experienced and the value of creating a supportive group working toward a shared goal. Being part of this group allowed them to withstand the expectations of others about what constitutes the work. They became more aware of what was going on in students' lives, which helped them to shift the common tendency to blame students for "not trying hard enough," and reminded them of what they "know but may not regularly think about."

Many of the programs transformed the physical space where groups met and were able to justify spending on things that might usually have been seen as frills, such as flowers and food. As Char Caver, a literacy worker in New England, said: "Food has symbolic meaning. Food as nurturance has been an important part of the program. People feel taken care of" (Interview, Dorchester, Massachusetts, March 2001). The opportunity to try making change in a way that might often be judged frivolous and inessential allowed them to see hoped-for changes in women. Transforming the physical space did transform the "inner spiritual space" of the women. Creating change in this way allowed the workers and the students some "space" outside the everyday experience of violence, and engendered the possibility of hope. To make learning possible for women who have been devalued, this message may be the most crucial.

Char Caver valued a training she took part in that confirmed her own belief in the importance of "acting outside the oppression" in order not to "repeat the oppression." She questioned the prevalent attitude in human services of working from a poverty model, always making do with "less than." Workers in several programs talked about how easily their own way of working with each other and with students could be part of the "whole structure of violence." Taking part in a project that offered a little extra space allowed literacy workers the opportunity to create some well-being for themselves and their students. For many who participated, the question was how to get that message heard more broadly in a climate that was, as several said, getting worse, not better.

Draw New Lines Between Healing and Learning

Project funding also created the time and space to explore building connections and collaborations with therapists and healers, and to integrate the creative arts into learning opportunities. Literacy workers had permission and support to explore drawing new lines to link work that is connected within each person, to imagine new programming. Workers often spoke about the insights these collaborations gave and about the freedom of knowing that they had support in the form of someone to whom they could take their professional tensions and worries. Programs explored coleading groups with a counselor, having local counselors offer training for staff, meeting with counselors in study circles to learn more about the intersections of their work, and meeting individually or in staff teams with counselors who could help them think through problems.

My own experience meeting regularly with a counselor offered me insights into myself as a facilitator, ideas for how to work with the group, support to try new ways of interacting with some students, and new language to talk about the work with others. I noticed that sometimes we could slide into approaches that felt too close to therapy, but other times we were able together to discover new modes that did not invite me to act like a therapist, or stay in the old model of teacher, but instead invented a new place from which to act. For example, I placed an easy chair in the corner of the room as a place for women to retreat to when they wanted a rest from participating in the group, but wanted to continue to listen. I gradually recognized that this arrangement provided space for emotions and a container for the tension and fear of taking on difficult work and so supported learning. After my reports on the value of working with a therapist, the staff at Parkdale Project Read were eager to experience it themselves. So the staff began to meet with the therapist when they felt it would be useful, individually and together. They valued these sessions so much that when we ran out of money, we knew our first priority was to find a way to continue the practice.

Women in several programs spoke eloquently about the gains they saw in women who participated in innovative classes. Programs began groups they labeled empowerment, wellness, love yourself, mindfulness, and so on. The common ingredient was allowing space for women to explore themselves and their lives. Programs used a mix of journal writing, meditation, yoga, relaxation, collage, quilting, and other healing arts in a variety of ways. They brought in counselors, artists, and a wide variety of teachers. Teachers were full of stories of the transformation they saw through this process. One central challenge that remains is which of these valuable supports to learning and growth will continue and be integrated into on-going programming after special project funding ends.

WHERE TO FROM HERE?

Drawing new lines linking literacy and healing offers great potential for learning. A key question now is whether the literacy movement will be able to build on the discourses that support diverse possibilities for teaching in ways that recognize the widespread nature of violence and the impact of violence on learning. Change is already occurring in many individual literacy programs. As new discourses become more broadly recognized, the simple divide between literacy and therapy may shift. Addressing the impact of violence on learning may seem less of a "can of worms" and more enticing, offering the potential for creating nurturing spaces for workers and learners alike. Or as Tammy L. Stockman, a job coach based in New England, suggested, maybe we can come to see worms as life giving and necessary for growth, not something to be contained at all cost. Although incremental change is taking place, I am still left with questions about what will enable a truly radical shift in discourses of violence and education, rather than merely marginal resistance. The challenge is to move from changing conceptions and practice in the privacy of individual classrooms, or when legitimacy is gained through special projects, to major shifts in the dominant discourses of literacy policy and practice, to enable permanent and universal transformation of the whole terrain of literacy work.

ACKNOWLEDGMENTS

This chapter draws from the final paper of the research study (Horsman, 2001a) and an earlier paper by Heald and Horsman (2000). The research study was the result of collaboration with many wonderful people. I could not have even begun without the support and collaborative conceptual work of Susan Heald. Many literacy workers talked to us in focus groups and interviews and thought through the issues along with us—I learned wisdom from many more than are quoted here. Working with participants in the World Education project and Women's Success Group at Parkdale Project Read gave me many insights. Jennifer Woodill and Nicole Ysabet-Scott provided much needed support with notes and transcription. Janet Isserlis, Judy Hofer, and Elizabeth Morrish offered crucial help when I was blocked, talked through ideas, read drafts, and generally made it possible for me to keep going. Moon Joyce listened to my struggles through the whole course of this project. Ann Decter and Nicole Ysabet-Scott pared clarity out of my words even within the tightest deadlines. I offer a heartfelt thank you to everyone whose wisdom is reflected here and who supported the process of research and writing in any way.

APPENDIX A

Assumptions About Violence

Violence Is Pervasive and Takes Many Forms.   It is important to see the whole range of violence in one picture, including state and individual, public and private. Violence includes childhood sexual, emotional, and physical violence; "domestic" violence and stalking; rape and the threat of rape in the public sphere; dangerous working conditions, and state-sanctioned violence. Racism, ableism, homophobia, poverty, sexism, and other oppressions foster violence.

Different Forms of Violence Are Intertwined.   All kinds of violence build on each other in one person's experience. When a woman is made vulnerable by one form of oppression, each additional violence has increased impact and deepens the first violation.

Violence Affects All of Us.   All women are vulnerable to and shaped by the presence of violence. Whether or not we experience life-threatening violence directly, we all live with the possibilities of violence, and all women, and many marginalized men, are diminished daily as a result of violence and our willingness as a society either to accept it or to turn a blind eye to it.

Violence Is Institutionally Supported.   Violence is not only perpetrated by individuals, it is also systemic. The institutions and systems of society support and allow violence to continue. When a court gives a suspended sentence to an abusive husband, when the limitations of welfare leave a woman trapped with an abusive partner, when the only jobs available in a racist, sexist society do not allow a woman to afford safe transportation, day care, or accommodation, institutions are perpetuating violence.

Institutions Harm; We All Participate in Those Institutions.   We cannot avoid participating in institutions that perpetuate the violence our society supports.

APPENDIX B

Assumptions About Literacy

Literacy Is Best Described as a Set of Social Practices, Rather Than Simply a Skill.   If we think of literacy only as a skill, then it is easy to slide into seeing the person as simply lacking something he or she should have, and needing remediation to counteract the deficit. If we see it as a set of social practices, then it is easier to see that some societies have chosen to privilege certain forms of literacy and that using print is only one way to obtain knowledge or to communicate.

Illiteracy Is a Social Problem, Not an Individual Problem.   Although society's practices and policies construct illiteracy, individuals who fail to learn to read well are judged lazy, unmotivated, stupid, and an economic drain on the rest of "us."

Illiteracy Does Not Cause Other Social Problems. Many social problems—such as poverty, violence, racism, and ableism—are interconnected with illiteracy. They are not caused by illiteracy. In a society shaped by inequality and oppression, illiteracy is one factor that can lead to marginalization and mistreatment.

Violence Contributes to Learning Difficulties. When children are hurt, abused, or put down, they learn that they are stupid and worthless. When they are humiliated or discriminated against because of their class, race, sexual orientation, physical or mental ability, or some other aspect of their selves, learning is made harder.

Illiteracy Is Created Through the Education System. Because schools share societal assumptions, they teach and validate the forms of literacy practised and taught within White, middle-class families, and devalue and even obscure awareness of the diverse literacy practices and multitude of different ways of knowing practised within other cultures and communities. Students who fit, learn.

People Who Have Difficulties With Literacy Are Not Childlike. Nor are they stupid, helpless, imprisoned, "poor souls," or abnormal. They have strengths and weaknesses and "read" many things well. These stereotypes lead people who do not easily understand print or professional language to avoid professionals, or to conceal their difficulties, for fear of being judged.

REFERENCES

Barton, D., & Hamilton, M. (2000). Literacy practices. In D. Barton, M. Hamilton, & R. Ivanic (Eds.), *Literacy practices.* London: Routledge.

Bennett, A. T. (1983). Discourses of power, the dialectics of understanding the power of literacy. *Journal of Education, 165*(1), 53–74.

Bremner, J. D., Randall, P., Scott, T. M., Capelli, S., Delaney, R., McCarthy, G., & Charney, D. S. (1995). Deficits in short-term memory in adult survivors of childhood abuse. *Psychiatry Research, 59*, 97–107.

Cook-Gumperz, J. (1986). *The social construction of literacy.* Cambridge: Cambridge University Press.

Davies, B. (2000). *A body of writing: 1990–1999.* Walnut Creek, CA: AltaMira Press.

Foucault, M. (1982, Summer). The subject and power. *Critical Inquiry 8*(4).

Fraser, S. (1987). *My father's house: A memoir of incest and of healing.* Toronto: Doubleday.

Gardner, G. E. (1971). Aggression and violence—the enemies of precision learning in children. *American Journal of Psychiatry, 128*(4), 77–82.

Gee, J. P. (1993). Postmodernism and literacies. In C. Lankshear & P. L. McLaren (Eds.), *Critical literacy politics, praxis, and the postmodern.* New York: State University of New York Press.

Heald, S., & Horsman, J. (2000). Rethinking violence and learning: Moving research into practice. In T. J. Sork, V. L. Chapman, & R. St. Clair (Eds.), *AERC 2000, An International Conference. Proceedings of the 41st Annual Adult Education Research Conference.* Vancouver: University of British Columbia. Available: http://www.jennyhorsman.com

Horsman, J. (1990). *"Something in my mind besides the everyday": Women and literacy.* Toronto: Women's Press.

Horsman, J. (1994a). Working on memories of abuse. . . . *Australian Journal of Adult and Community Education, 34*(1).

Horsman, J. (1994b). The problem of illiteracy and the promise of literacy. In M. Hamilton, D. Barton & R. Ivanic (Eds.), *Worlds of literacy.* Clevedon: Multilingual Matters.

Horsman, J. (1995a, Spring). Violence and illiteracy in women's lives: Proposal for research and practice. *International Journal of Canadian Studies, 11.*

Horsman, J. (1995b, Fall). It must be my fault. *Twelve Pages: The Newsletter of Adult and Continuing Education, 4*(3), The City University of New York.

Horsman, J. (1996a). Responding to disclosures of abuse in women's lives. Canadian Congress for Learning Opportunities for Women (CCLOW). *Making connections: Literacy and EAL curriculum from a feminist perspective.* Toronto: CCLOW.

Horsman, J. (1996b). Exploring learning and identity. Canadian Congress for Learning Opportunities for Women (CCLOW). *Making connections: Literacy and EAL curriculum from a feminist perspective.* Toronto: CCLOW.

Horsman, J. (2000a). *Too scared to learn: Women, violence and education.* Mahwah, NJ: Lawrence Erlbaum Associates.

Horsman, J. (2000b). *Moving forward: Approaches and activities to support women's learning.* Toronto, Ontario: Parkdale Project Read.

Horsman, J. (2001a). *Creating change in literacy programs: Talking about taking account of violence* (ERIC ED 461 077). Available: http://www.jennyhorsman.com

Horsman, J. (2001b). *Drawing the line: Dealing with affective issues in literacy.* Saskatchewan Literacy Network: Saskatoon. Available: http://www.nald.ca/Province/Sask/SLN/Resource/newordrs/drawline.htm

Lewis, T. (1999). *Living beside: Performing normal after incest memories return.* Toronto: McGilligan Books.

Martinez, A. (1997). *Teaching survivors of torture and trauma.* Sydney: TAFE Multicultural Education Unit/ Northern Sydney Institute of TAFE Multicultural Education Coordinator.

Morrish, E., Horsman, J., & Hofer, J. (2002). *Take on the challenge: A source book from the Women, Violence and Adult Education Project.* Boston: World Education.

Murphy, J. (2004). *Women's journeys in self discovery: Literacy, life skills and learning: A resource book.* Edmonton John Howard Society & Elizabeth Fry Society of Edmonton: Edmonton.

National Institute for Literacy. (2000, September). *Women in Literacy Forum, Archives.* Available: www.nifl.gov/lines/discussions/nifl/-womenlit/women_literacy.html

Sola, M., & Bennett, A. T. (1985). The struggle for voice: Narrative, literacy and consciousness in an East Harlem school. *Journal of Education, 167*(1), 88–110.

Street, B. V. (1984). *Literacy in theory and practice.* Cambridge: Cambridge University Press.

Weedon, C. (1987). *Feminist practice and poststructuralist theory.* Oxford: Blackwell.

Wolpow, R., & Askov, E. N. (1998). Strong in the broken places: Literacy instruction for survivors of pervasive trauma. *Journal of Adolescent & Adult Literacy, 42*(1). September.

Chapter 15

The People Write Back: Community Literacy Practices and the Visibility of the Ordinary Writer

David Bloome
The Ohio State University

This chapter presents a portrait of literacy across three institutional settings: schooling, business, and law court. This portrait of literacy is not a typical case although the issues raised through this portrait may extend widely. The portrait is perhaps best viewed as a "telling case" (Mitchell, 1984), a case whose particularity and difference make visible hidden social, cultural, and political processes in the nature, structuration, and multiplicity of literacy practices (Street, 1995).

To present this portrait of literacy, I examine three sets of data collected as part of a larger study of literacy practices and the Mass-Observation Project.[1] The first set of data comes from an interview I conducted with Mrs. Wright,[2] (also known as W632),[3] a middle-age woman (49 years old at the time of the interview) from a working class community in southern England who describes her school experiences. Her description is similar to descriptions by other women who also wrote for the Mass-Observation Project. In brief, Mrs. Wright and the other women report what we call a "derailed" education. A "derailed" education is one in which reasonable expectations for schooling (a reasonable educational trajectory) are negated by actions of either the school, family, or other circumstance. The second set of data is

---

[1]Dorothy Sheridan, Brian Street, and I report the broader study in a book titled *Writing Ourselves: Literacy Practices and the Mass-Observation Project* (2000); however, the data presented, analysis, and discussion here are not presented in the book.

[2]Pseudonym.

[3]This is the number assigned to her by the Mass-Observation Project.

about Mrs. Wright's writing in her job as a midlevel manager (a senior clerk) for a major utility company. The third set of data is a written contribution to the Mass-Observation Project sent by Mrs. Wright about a court appearance related to the "poll tax." I examine that written text with concern for how uses of written language operate in the events she describes, and in specific for the kinds of writing positions made available.

The thesis that I argue, based on these three sets of data, is that writing is a socially structured process, and that the structuration of writing practices is supported across social institutions. As currently organized, who can write what, when, where, and how is hierarchically structured and that hierarchy is maintained by the structuration of writing in schools, business, and other settings. Although some people are wholly encapsulated (colonized) by the hierarchical structuration of writing, others create and engage in writing practices that eschew that structuration. This argument is grounded in a view of literacy as a social and cultural process (Barton & Hamilton, 1998; Bloome, 1983, 1985; Heath, 1983; Street, 1995; Willinsky, 1990). In brief, rather than assume literacy to be a predetermined and decontextualized set of cognitive and linguistic processes autonomous of situational and contextual processes, questions are asked about how people use written language to create and maintain social relationships; communicate intentions, feelings, knowledge, and so on; structure power relations; sustain, challenge, resist, construct, and reconstruct their cultural lives; and establish who they are and who others are within and across particular social situations (Bloome, 1985). In this chapter, I focus on how people create and constrain social positions for writing. Recent discussions of writing have suggested that people write, as well as talk and interact in general, from social positions (e.g., Brodkey, 1987; Christian & Bloome, 2004; Fairclough, 1992; Gee, 1996; Ivanic, 1994; Street, 1995). These social positions may be provided by the social institutions of which they are a part (schools, businesses, the courts, family, etc.), they may be created as part of daily life, or they may be provided by alternative social institutions, such as local writing communities and the Mass-Observation Project.

I begin with brief descriptions of the Mass-Observation Project and of the research project from which the data in this chapter comes. Then I present each of the three sets of data. Finally, I discuss the three sets of data taken together.

THE MASS-OBSERVATION PROJECT[4]

The Mass-Observation Project started in 1937 as a "people's anthropology" of life in Britain. Ordinary people were asked to write about their daily lives

---

[4]Additional information about the Mass-Observation Project can be found in Sheridan (1993) and Sheridan, Street, and Bloome (2000).

and the events in their community. Other methods were also used to collect information about the lives of ordinary people: surveys, observations, interviews. The first phase of the Mass-Observation Project occurred from 1937 until 1950, with a good deal of attention devoted to the recording of civilian life during the Second World War. The papers from that research were brought to The University of Sussex, and the Mass-Observation Project Archive opened in 1975.

The second phase began in 1981. Professor David Pocock and Mass-Observation Project Archivist Dorothy Sheridan recruited people from all parts of the United Kingdom to write about their lives. These volunteers are known as Mass-Observation correspondents. So that people could write without being personally identified, a system of numbers was introduced in 1983. Each year, three or four directives are sent to the Mass-Observation correspondents. Each directive contains up to three themes, divided into sections. Most of the themes relate to personal experience, feelings, and opinions on a subject (holidays, health, old age, education, etc.); some ask for a one-day diary for a specified day; some ask for a more continuous record (for example, monitoring reactions to media coverage of the Gulf War). Since 1981, an enormous bank of written information about life in the United Kingdom has been accumulating, including over 400,000 pages of typed and handwritten material representing the combined contributions of over 2,500 volunteer writers. Researchers, students, and others come to the Archive and read what has been written.

It is important to note that Mass-Observation correspondents vary considerably in the degree to which they feel bound to respond within the guidelines presented in the directives. Whereas some follow the guidelines closely, responding to each item requested, many do not, and some take great liberties redefining the writing task and their responses to it. Nor is there any specific genre that characterizes a response to a directive or that can be confidently predicted. Responses may include expository texts, narratives, descriptions of events, lists, poems, copies of print found in the environment, diary entries, editorials, vita, or letters, among others, orchestrated in various ways. Some Mass-Observation correspondents have also written both as part of their response or directly to Archivist Dorothy Sheridan their views about the appropriateness, interest, or construction of a particular directive or set of procedures employed by the Mass-Observation Project. A small but substantial number of Mass-Observation correspondents have sent unsolicited material to the Mass-Observation Project including diaries, descriptions of events, or creative material they have written (e.g., a book of poems, among others).

In Spring 1991, a directive (open-ended questionnaire) was sent to the 700 people who wrote for the Mass-Observation Project at that time, asking them to describe their usual literacy practices, including the daily reading and writing they did and how they typically wrote responses to the Mass-Observation Project directives. They were also asked to keep a diary of literacy activities over a 3-day period, and they were asked to complete a directive about their educational experiences. We conducted follow-up, in-depth interviews with 40 people. Two years after the original directive on literacy practices, a directive on reading was sent out that was informed by the earlier directive and the interviews. The data on which the findings are based come from the interviews, the responses to the 1991 and 1993 directives, as well as from other writings submitted to the archive by the people interviewed.

WRITING AT SCHOOL—DERAILED EDUCATIONS

Mrs. Wright's education began in London; then, when her father was moved to southern England for his job, she transferred to a school there. At the time, secondary schools were differentiated between Secondary Modern Schools and Grammar Schools. The Secondary Modern Schools were for the students who failed their 11+ examinations (the examination taken by students at 11 years old). The Grammar Schools were reserved for the students who passed their 11+ examinations.

As a child, in primary, junior, and secondary levels, Mrs. Wright had a special interest in essay writing. However, as her interview indicated, her interest in expressing her ideas was frustrated by her teachers' attention to spelling and grammar:

> I've always been interested in, I mean, English essays at school—I was keen on writing, when I didn't have the spelling or the language sentence—the power to be able to—put sentences together, I still had ideas that I wanted to get down, and it was frustrating not being able to write—properly—to write as I could read. Reading books was another thing that I always enjoyed doing, and I could—wanted to write like that, you know, without going through the learning stage. . . . I had the ideas that I wanted to get down on paper that I thought were interesting stories, and that I wanted to write about, but it was the—my brain was going faster than the spelling and the sentences could be made, the—grammar would come, and I found that irritating, you know, that I couldn't put down my thoughts then. [DB: But that's not your feeling about how you write now.] No, no, no, I can express most of the time, express what I mean to. [DB: And, what happened to make a change?] Oh it was just continuous practice I think, reading a lot and picking up the sentence formation and—it was just a lot of practice and keep on try, try, try, you know I mean like—like riding a bike you know you keep falling off and getting back on again and—if its' something you really want to do, if you don't want to do it then you just throw the bike away and say I'll walk . . . I wanted to do it, yes. . . . It was a long time ago, but I think some children are excitable and express

themselves outwardly, and I was the middle one in the family, so perhaps at home I was rather quiet, but I don't know—I felt as though I was quiet at home and that this was my way of expressing myself, to be able to write it down. I remember I used to get annoyed when papers came back from marking and there was all these big S's through the spelling mistakes and so on, and I'd say, "But what did you think of it?" and never got much of a satisfactory answer to that. What did you think of what I'd written, you know, not alright, it's wrong, you know, but—and I can see—I know the English is wrong, but what about what I've written, and I don't feel as though that was taken into consideration enough. So I had to get the spelling and grammar right in order for people to listen or want to read what I was writing. [DB: And once you did then they listened ? or not, or?] Oh, I don't know—I suppose once I could do it then perhaps the interest waned—I know I buried myself in books a lot—perhaps I didn't do so much writing then—once I knew I could do it. Escaped into books instead of thinking my own thoughts.

The issue Mrs. Wright's description of her school raises is not whether spelling and grammar should be taught, but rather the gate-keeping role played by grammar and spelling instruction. Indeed, the issue, I believe, is not about grammar and spelling at all, but rather about the structuration of the teaching of writing in such a manner as to create "bottlenecks of access." In order to be designated a writer, in order to have someone in authority declare your writing worthy of attending to the ideas, you must be able to display achievement of whatever criteria are being used to designate worthy writing. Not everyone's writing will be evaluated as worthy. In Mrs. Wright's case, the criteria were spelling and grammar (at least, those were one level of criteria). Of course, Mrs. Wright had already passed through one "bottleneck of access" with regard to her writing by being competitively selected for a Grammar School. Whether the bottleneck of access works by explicitly eliminating some people or by sufficiently frustrating them that they give up (which may have been the case with Mrs. Wright) matters little.

The fact than Mrs. Wright attended a Grammar School suggests that she was identified as having a trajectory that would have taken her to education beyond the end of secondary school, perhaps to university or polytechnic. However, as her interview makes clear, that did not happen:

I went to a Grammar School, so you couldn't leave at fifteen, which—all the secondary modern children left at the age of sixteen—the Grammar School system was supposed to be the top twenty per cent and it was enough to have got there, without having to do anything or pass exams or so on, and—you'd reached the standard, and to have a Grammar School education therefore whether you'd passed the exams or not you were considered bright enough. Employers nowadays don't seem to go along that—they want the bits of paper that go with it, the certificates and so on. But no I left school as soon as I could—I had a bit of disruption because we moved down from London and I

changed schools and the school that I came to was—well, it was just so completely different to what I'd been to. I'd been to a little inner London school,
was a tiny pocket-handkerchief playground and the rooms were so over-
crowded, the equipment was so old—we were bused out to playing fields in
the suburbs, which would take all morning, just to get us out to a games lesson
and back—and moved down to a school in XXXXX and there were all these
huge green fields around, there were these huge great classrooms, so light
and airy, all modern equipment, sewing machines and—they didn't have
computers but they had all the latest scientific equipment, and there was one
each, you know—no sharing or anything, and it was just completely different
world. I'd say it took me the time I was there just to settle in, the two years, that
I was there, to be in that environment, you know—to slow down from London, where you'd always be on the rush and the go and the tear, and just to
come down to their pace of sauntering along the corridor, you know—. . . it
was just a completely different world . . . I wouldn't say I enjoyed it, and I didn't
stay on any longer than I had to. I wanted to take shorthand and typing so that
I would have a career, or alone to go out into the world . . . and I suppose I
wanted to do office work. I'd have preferred perhaps to go to Art School, the
only subjects that I was good at really—art and illustrations . . . I just wanted to
get out of school and I went into an office—the headmistress was not very
happy about giving me permission to go to evening school to learn shorthand
and typing, she said that was what the secondary school children did—they
were the typists, we weren't, so unless you were going on for further education
they did tend to lose interest in you—in your development after that. But I
found coming out to work that if you were a shorthand typist you were forever
taking orders—you didn't instigate the work, you were given work to do, so after failing the typing and shorthand exams, I went purely clerical.

The move from the crowded school in London to what Mrs. Wright describes
as a school with better facilities in the south of England would, at first, seem
to have been a positive move for Mrs. Wright's education. But it was not. She
did not adjust well, dropped out as soon as she could, and deviated from the
educational and career trajectory the school had planned for her.

I am less interested in the cause of the derailed trajectory than in the
fact that it *was* a derailed trajectory. Instead of a trajectory that may have
gotten her through the bottlenecks of access with regard to writing, Mrs.
Wright found herself on trajectories that provided no access to social positions for writing. Typing and shorthand are not writing as they don't "instigate the work."

The derailed trajectory Mrs. Wright experienced is similar to the derailed trajectories of education experienced by a large percentage of the
women Mass-Observation correspondents who responded to the Education
directive. Of the 29 women Dorothy Sheridan, Brian Street, and I interviewed, 23 had what could be described as derailed educational trajectories.
Reasonable expectations for pursuing education were obstructed or redi-
rected in ways that were disappointing and that made life difficult.

One type of a derailed education is that the person was doing well in school academically (even if they disliked it) when something happened that disrupted their education trajectory. For example:

- A616 failed her university examinations.
- A1733 won a scholarship to grammar school but her father died when she was 7 and with her mother working, it was impossible to go.
- C108 could not attend higher education because she became sick.
- C1883's parents thought school was unnecessary and forced her to leave.
- H260's mother would not let her sit for a scholarship examination because they did not have enough money for the uniform or bus fare.
- W569's teachers thought she was a bright student but she failed her 11+ examinations.
- W571 was not allowed by the headmaster of her school to sit for the examination to be admitted to a School of Art.
- Y1514 had to drop out at 14 as her father could not afford to pay for her schooling.

Several of the women described having to overcome a father who did not believe in education for women. Some were able to overcome their father's prejudice with the help of their mothers. For example, W640's mother was able to prevail against her father in large part because she saw that other girls were going on to further education. W1835's mother faked her father's signature so she could go to Nurse's Training School instead of staying home and marrying a farmer. But it wasn't always just the father who derailed the education, sometimes it was both parents and teachers. For example, the parents of one Mass-Observation correspondent would not let her take the entrance exam for Grammar School because they did not believe that she needed that kind of education, although her teachers encouraged her. Another ran into trouble with her school, as she sees it, for no fault of her own other than being inquisitive, and was denied earned recommendations by her teachers.

The fact that so many of the women who write for the Mass-Observation Project may have had a derailed education may explain at least part of the reason they write for the Mass-Observation Project. But beyond that, it gives insight into the relationship between social structure and writing as a social practice. Schooling provides access to legitimate writing positions. The access can be described as a bottleneck because the process appears to be one in which there are limited numbers of people who can gain access to legitimate, designated, recognized, and established positions as writers. Mrs. Wright is not one of the people with such access.

INTERVIEW WITH MRS. WRIGHT
ABOUT WRITING AT WORK

Mrs. Wright lives in a working-class suburb of a major city in southern England, with her husband and youngest son. She comes from a working class family. Her father had moved from a small village to London before she was born because he did not want to be a coal miner and her mother did not want to stay in domestic service. She has three sons and is a grandmother.

It is a short walk from the railway station to their flat. She works for a public service company just outside London, taking the train to work daily. Her youngest son was living at home and attending one of the local, new universities. Her husband is home full time on a disability leave from his job, the result of a stroke. Before the stroke, he did worked as a rigger, doing repair work on power stations, which required him to be away from home for lengthy periods of time. They had a one-floor flat that they bought on the second floor in a complex of council estates. They had a living room, small kitchen (not big enough to eat in), and two bedrooms. Behind the kitchen was a small room with a small table and two chairs.

During the interview I had with her, she spoke at length about writing on her job. I have included a long excerpt from that interview to illustrate three points: the technical expertise Mrs. Wright has, the way her job positions her among other employees, departments, and external groups (consumers), and the kinds of writing that she does:

> I work in—for XXXXX[5] in XXXXX and I work in the planning department—and that's for customer accounts planning. And if there's any mandatory changes that come through by the government, then we have to update our billing system to be able to cater for these changes. And so that's my job—to be between the user and the systems—computer systems people, and to translate what each one's saying, so that the user says I want this, and the systems people are saying XYZ—formula, you know, and I'm saying will that produce this? And I test that out and make sure that this is what we want, the business is being met—the business requirements are being met. The last mandatory project I had was the average calorific value . . . Before, the accounts were billed on the calorific value projected three months ahead from previous, estimated from previous heat value of the gas. And now we've decided instead of estimating, projecting ahead what the heat value is going to be, that we will take it on a weekly basis, and it will be based on the actual heat values as measured averaged over their bill. So the bill period is thirteen weeks, we add up the heat values for each week and divide it by thirteen, and that is calorific value that their bill will be used, will be charged at, and in order to put that in I had to liaise with an awful lot of people within [the utility company], not just

---

[5]Some identifying information has been masked to protect confidentiality.

the systems people but also with headquarters because they're the ones that were saying that they wanted this in, also with another region where it had been in for a 3-month trial period. They can give you guidelines but [the utility company] is divided into 12 regions, and each region has a different system. So although you get guidelines from them as to how the system can be changed to accommodate this, it won't work, you have to develop your own. [DB: It seems like there is a lot of writing and reading on your job, and a lot of writing and reading with other people]. Yes. Formulating training notes, so with each group, with each, might only be one person, but with each section I would be writing and writing and writing, "Is this what we want, is this what you're saying we're getting?" to make sure . . . At work, it's taking away their ideas and testing them out and producing them for somebody else to read and say, "Well, can you do this?" and for them to say "Well, we can do X, Y, and Z but we can't do that particular bit," and then I'm thinking different ways round this—"Well, could we do it if we did it this way, or could we go about it that way? Can we get it from another type of record? this information that we want and draw it in from there." And it's not being too involved with either group, either the computer people, who love jargon, and, if you don't understand anything I say "What was that you said then?" you know, and it brings them up. They get so used to talking it to, in their language, "Oh we'll have a program here" and I say, "What is that?" and they have to stop and think, well, what is a program, you know, because they're so used to talking in that language. And then the end users I understand more because I was an end user, but they start saying, "Well, I want this, that, and the other," and I say, "Well, that's not in the scope of the project, I'm sorry that's something completely different, we haven't got the money to do all the changes that you'd like. This is the part that we're changing and if we just look down this road, we'll see about them another day." And so it's, it's been in the middle, really, but also talking to an awful lot more people. The training instructors are the best ones to get through to because if you can get it straight with the training instructors then they will take it out and teach it correctly. If you fail with them, nobody will do it right. So, in that case you might just as well have not put the project in. [DB: At work you mostly write memos, training programs, and . . . ???] procedures, very formal procedures. If you do this, this will happen. If you do that, you will expect this end result. And it must, every tiny little movement or wrong movement must be written down to say what exactly what happened.

The writing that Mrs. Wright does at work is not writing in which she expresses her ideas. Rather, her job is to work with people at the company to find a way to accurately and effectively express their ideas to each other. To do so, she needs enough technical knowledge to be able to talk with the technical people and help them translate their jargon into plain language. She also needs skills for interacting with consumers and others in the company who may not understand whatever initiative the company is trying to pursue. Furthermore, she needs acumen in writing in a wide variety of genres, training manuals, formal procedures, memoranda, letters, and so on, to a wide range of audiences.

Despite her expertise in bringing people together to create the needed written texts and to create effective communication, she is not viewed and does not view herself as a "writer." For example, consider her comments about writing for the Mass-Observation Project:

> ... it's a pleasure because it's writing about my thoughts and feelings, rather than straight correspondence—you know, like business letters and so on. . . . It's flattering, really, to think that somebody's going to sit there [at the Mass-Observation Project Archive] and read it all, you know and I think it's rubbish most of the time that I write . . . I feel as though nobody's interested in my opinions, really.

What Mrs. Wright writes at work is not her opinions or ideas. Perhaps the criterion for being considered a "writer" is that the writing must be an expression of one's own ideas or opinions. Of course, given that Mrs. Wright brings people together to create the concepts and language that end up in her workplace writing, one could argue that the ideas and opinions are hers. However, I would argue that what is at issue is whether Mrs. Wright occupies a social position at her workplace recognized as that of a "writer." As a senior clerk, someone who lacks—to use her words—"the bits of paper that go with it, the certificates and so on," she does not have access to those positions that might be recognized as a "writer."

The argument here is not that Mrs. Wright could never occupy a position at her workplace recognized as "writer" or that occupying such a position is dependent on "bits of paper," but rather that those positions are limited and, as a consequence, are hierarchically structured. Mrs. Wright's comments about the "bits of paper" are one indication of the relationship between schools and businesses with regard to "writer" positions.

The availability of "writer" positions is also an issue in other social institutions, which is explored in the next section.

MRS. WRIGHT'S WRITTEN DESCRIPTION OF GOING TO COURT FOR FAILURE TO PAY THE POLL TAX

The Poll Tax was a popular term for an additional tax promulgated by the Conservative government that taxed each individual at a particular level without regard to income. It received the name Poll Tax because the government used the list of names from the voting lists to determine taxation. People who did not want to pay the Poll Tax or who could not afford to do so might avoid having to pay it by keeping their names off of the voting lists.

The Poll Tax was very controversial and subject to a great deal of debate and protest. Those people who refused to pay the Poll Tax were summoned to court. Mrs. Wright and her husband were two of the people taken to court. Mrs. Wright wrote about her experiences in court and sent the description to the Mass-Observation Project:

1   My husband and I went to court today to answer the summons for non-
2   payment of the community charge. We arrived 15 mins before the court was
3   due to start at 10 A.M. The entrance was crowded with people waiting in line
4   to see the clerk, about fifty answering the same summons that we received.
5   The clerk advised everyone to go and talk to the counselors about payment ar-
6   rangements, they had a room set up at the courts for that purpose, I said I
7   would see them after I had seen the Magistrates, and my name was entered on
8   a list and I was given [next page] a raffle ticket. There was several people
9   there that we knew but gradually the crowd thinned out and there was only
10 about sixteen people left. We had a cigarette and coffee when names started
11 to be called. I was seventh, my husband wasn't called. I was the only woman.
12 There were eight altogether and all the others were young Jack the Lads' un-
13 der 30. We were given a page of instruction saying what we couldn't dispute
14 and what we could, these were six items like not living at the address stated, al-
15 ready paid & having proof of payment, the forms not properly served etc.
16   Each person was called to the stand and asked if they had paid in full, to
17 which the answer was no in every case, and whether they had a defence as
18 specified in the instructions. Several brought in points such as can't afford to
19 pay—they were advised to see a counselor, disagreed with the Law—they were
20 advised to contact their MP and one contested the amount of the court
21 costs—ours was L20 whereas another area charged L10.60 to which the Magis-
22 trate's clerk said they could set a charge of any amount that the court decided
23 was reasonable. All these points had been listed in the instructions as matters
24 not in the jurisdiction of the Court.
25   When it was my turn I took an Affirmation, rather than an oath on the Bi-
26 ble, and was asked the first two questions, had I paid in full—no and did I
27 have a defence as listed in the instructions to which I said "No, I am here as an
28 Act of Civil Disobedience in protest at this regressive tax and it will be re-
29 corded for History to judge."
30   The magistrate laughed and said "So you are going down in history," I said
31 "yes my grandchildren will read about this." He said "I have no alternative but
32 to grant the liability order, unfortunately the reporter has just left so you
33 won't be in the newspapers." I said "Thank you, perhaps next year."
34   I joined my husband in the entrance foyer and waited for him to be called.
35 A court clerk was asking everyone if they had been seen to assess how things
36 were going. I said I had been in court and was waiting til my husband was
37 called, she was perplexed, they hadn't put him on the list as he hadn't made
38 clear his intention of going before the Magistrate. Apparently all the other
39 people who turned up at court had gone to talk to the counselors and didn't
40 go into court, so there had only been the one sitting that I attended. My hus-
41 band said not to bother them, we would just go and make an arrangement
42 with the council advisors. A chap with the court clerk said well he would at-
43 tend to us now. So we stayed where we were and he joined us. He turned out

44   to be the manager of the District Council's Recovery Department. Although I
45   had put money aside each month to pay the Poll Tax once we had been to
46   court, it seemed that wasn't expected so we agreed to pay it in five monthly in
47   stallments so it was cleared in this financial year. He asked if we would like to
48   make an arrangement for next year and we said no we will go through the
49   same procedure again. We sat chatting to him for half an hour, talking about
50   the unfairness of the system and he [top of next page] seemed to think that
51   the social services would be adjusting benefits to pay the 20% liability of bene-
52   fit recipients' Poll Tax direct in future. He told us that he recommends peo-
53   ple to pay their mortgage first as it would cause the Council more problems if
54   their property was repossessed than if the Poll Tax wasn't paid. He said he has
55   agreed payments as low as L2 per week, which would take years to clear, be-
56   cause he lives in the real world and knows the hardship some residents suffer.
57   I had a lovely morning altogether, the atmosphere of the people at Court
58   was friendly and helpful. The attitude of the other defendants was jocular or
59   amiably defiant & there were no banner-waving, angry militants to be seen so
60   my husband was relaxed. I will be there again next year unless the whole sys-
61   tem is scrapped.
62   Altogether 47 non-domestic and 200 domestic liability orders were made
63   in that one court on that one morning, the media have given us no clue as to
64   how prevalent the discontent has been but these figures must be published
65   some day. I believe it was the cause of the Tories losing the safe seat at
66   Eastbourne in the byelection but again the media didn't mention this aspect
67   as a reason at all. (W632, 16 November, 1990)

Mrs. Wright's description of going to court was an unsolicited contribution to the Mass-Observation Project; it was not a response to a directive.

There are at least four institutional contexts that are either implied or
mentioned explicitly in the first four paragraphs: Mrs. Wright's family (she
and her husband); the Court, legal, and governmental systems; the media;
and the Mass-Observation Project. The last, of course, is not mentioned
explicitly but is implied because the text was written for and sent to the
Mass-Observation Project. Indeed, it is our knowledge that this is so that un-
dercuts the magistrate's comments about being too late to be recorded for
history and that allows us to understand a meaning of Mrs. Wright's statement, "It will be recorded for history," that is not known by the magistrate.

It is important to note that Mrs. Wright's description of events at court
on that day is only one of many different descriptions possible. Presumably, official court records give another description, and descriptions that
would be written by the court clerk, the magistrate, the counselor, or a
newspaper reporter would all differ, in large part because of the different
social positions from which they would be writing. Part of what is important about Mrs. Wright's recount of events at court is that it describes how
ordinary people may not be provided a social position from which to
write. Mrs. Wright writes about the event from the social position of a

Mass-Observation correspondent. Yet, that social position is not a public social position. There was no mention of it at court, and most Mass-Observation correspondents (Mrs. Wright included) do not tell people other than close family that there are Mass-Observation correspondents. Furthermore, there is no established genre for writing as a Mass-Observation correspondent and thus no established social position to take up. This is especially so given that Mrs. Wright's writing was unsolicited and thus the social position from which she was writing was not structured by questions on a Mass-Observation Project directive. In the analysis that follows, I focus on (a) how and where Mrs. Wright locates various types and uses of written language (in what institutional domains), and (b) where and how she locates herself as a writer (the social position she assumes).

Mrs. Wright begins by locating herself as a family (My husband and I—line 1) being brought into the court. As an institution, and as shown throughout the text, the court deals with individuals, not with families. Each person is given a number (line 8), and there are continual references to the number of people there (e.g., "fifty [people]"—line 4, "everyone"—line 5, "sixteen people"—line 10, "I was seventh"—line 11). Within the first few words then, Mrs. Wright has set up a tension between how the court conceptualizes people (i.e., personhood) and how people are conceptualized with the family as social institution.

This tension has implications for understanding authorship. Implicit in definitions of writing is individual authorship. Even if one writes as a co-author, authorship is an individual contribution, not the result of a collective or group.[6] This definition of personhood implied in authorship is related to issues of accountability and ownership in writing, each of which involves intricate structures and processes in social institutions like law, schooling, and business.

The first mention of writing is the summons, which is located in the court context (line 1). Indeed, almost all of the types and uses of writing are located in the court context (list, raffle ticket, page of instructions, Bible), and the court uses of writing were to control people (to bring them before the court), to constrain what they could and could not say (lines 13–15), and to define them as individuals. The magistrate recognized only the media context as an institutionally available writing position outside of the court (lines 32–33), a position not available to Mrs. Wright.

The tension between the court and how it was controlling and positioning Mrs. Wright through writing climaxed immediately after Mrs. Wright said, "I am here as an act of Civil Disobedience in protest at this regressive

---

[6]At some universities, the individual nature of co-authorship is revealed by requiring faculty seeking promotion or tenure to indicate the percentage of their contribution to the written work.

tax and it will be recorded for History to judge" (lines 27–29). Mrs. Wright's statement is a defiance of what the list of instructions provided as allowable statements. The authority of the instructions derives in part from the court—it is a court document and presumably the court can enforce the content of the instructions; but its authority also derives from the status often attributed to particular genres of written language in British and other Westernized societies. Information and directives in a textbook, a written contract, a legal document, a newspaper, et cetera, are treated as more valid and true than information given in spoken form. Mrs. Wright is not only defying the court's authority to constrain what may be spoken in court but is also violating a widely shared cultural significance for certain genres of written language.

Mrs. Wright may have intended several meanings when she stated, "recorded for History to judge": recorded in the court records, as well as in newspapers, in her writing at home, and in her writing for the Mass-Observation Project. The magistrate recognized only one available space for Mrs. Wright's protest to be recorded in history and that was in the media, in the newspapers. There is no institutionally recognized position from which she can write, from which she can put her protest in written history (other than the Mass-Observation Project, but that is not a publicly acknowledged presence). It is not just that the reporter has left, but that the magistrate does not assign to Mrs. Wright a personhood associated with writing. Stated in another way, if Mrs. Wright had been a newspaper reporter herself, a university-based historian, or held a position of power, she would have been viewed as having available to her various writing positions. Mrs. Wright is only an ordinary person, without any available writing positions for having her protest recorded in history. From the magistrate's perspective, Mrs. Wright is powerless to get her protest in history and powerless to change her personhood (as an individual protester and as an individual who did not pay the poll tax) inasmuch as there are no writing positions available to her to do so.

Of course, the magistrate is being represented by Mrs. Wright's writing. But what is at issue is not whether the magistrate actually said the specific words or acted exactly as described by Mrs. Wright, but rather what Mrs. Wright is showing us about how she sees herself, as an ordinary person, being positioned by various forms of written language and by various government authorities, and how she sees herself resisting the constraints that government authorities and the allied media have placed on her—both with regard to what she can say and write, and with regard to who she is (her personhood).

Mrs. Wright does not have available to her institutionally recognized positions in the media, the court, or in other dominant institutions. However, there are writing positions open to her within the family context (signaled by her reference to "my grandchildren," line 31) and through the Mass-Observation Project. By writing up the event and sending it the Mass-Observation Project, Mrs. Wright did record her protest for history.

In the second half of her description, she describes the conversations ("chatting") she and her husband had with "a chap with the court clerk." Her husband is not called to the magistrate as his name was not entered on the list (line 37). Within this paragraph (lines 34–56), the tension reappears between the family context and the court context that only recognizes individuals: Mrs. Wright "joined her husband" (line 34) versus the "court clerk asking every*one* if they had been seen . . ." (line 35, emphasis added); "My husband . . . we . . . us" (lines 40, 41, 43) versus "he hadn't made clear his intention" (line 37). From line 40 to the end of the paragraph, all of the references to Mrs. Wright are to the family unit (she and her husband, together). The one exception ("I had put money aside"—line 44—is also a reference to the family context as Mrs. Wright handled all of the financial matters in her family).

The last paragraph is important with regard to the construction of a social position from which to write. Mrs. Wright is no longer telling an autobiographical story but has assumed a writing position perhaps of a historian or political observer. Her use of details, technical jargon, the repetition of "that," and the distancing of the first person singular in the first part of the sentence—"Altogether 47 non-domestic and 200 domestic liability orders were made in that one court on that one morning, . . ." (lines 62–63) reposition her as an observer and reporter for the Mass-Observation Project. She is no longer invoking the family context as social identity but the writing position of ordinary people ("us"—line 63) who live in the "real world" (line 56), in opposition to the authorized writing position of the media, who are described as aligned with the court and the Tories (line 65) and who attempt to construct reality by what they do not publish (line 66). Of course, the social position from which she is writing is invisible to the Court and to most other social institutions. Although the Mass-Observation Project is associated with an established and hierarchically structured social institution, the university, the Mass-Observation Project itself is not recognized as being present in the machinations of dominant institutions like the legal system the same way that the media are, for example.

FINAL COMMENTS

In the previous sections, I presented data from Mrs. Wright's written contributions to the Mass-Observation Project and from an extended interview with her to highlight the structuration of writing in three social institutions: school, business, and court. Although the structures and social processes were not the same, in all three institutions, writing positions were limited and hierarchical (if not elitist). Mrs. Wright did a great deal of writing in her job, and enjoyed writing and did a lot of it in school (at least for part of her schooling). In court, there was no writing position available to her, although she used her position within the Mass-Observation Project to write about the court.

People who want to engage in writing to create a new social situation, set of relationships, contribute to social change, or merely participate in the status quo, find it difficult to do so because no writing practice institutionally exists, is recognized, made available to them, or is authorized. For example, many Mass-Observation correspondents described writing for the Mass-Observation Project as providing a "platform" or a "voice" for "ordinary" people (see Appendix). The issue is not one of access to various genres or to established literacy practices, but the absence of institutionally available positions and spaces within which to engage in and orchestrate various writing practices and genres. Many of the comments made by Mass-Observation correspondents noted that the Mass-Observation Project provided a space in which their writing (their thoughts, views, observations, etc.) would be read and taken seriously when otherwise they might not be. Yet, at the same time, being a writer for the Mass-Observation Project is "invisible." Mrs. Wright did not reveal she was a Mass-Observation correspondent to the court, and most Mass-Observation correspondents tell few people, if any, that they are Mass-Observation correspondents. This invisibility helps provide protected positions from which people may write, create, and, to some extent, provide for themselves some means of promoting change (e.g., Mrs. Wright was able to record her protest for history). It is ironic that the only social position that Mrs. Wright can occupy as a writer is one that is "invisible."

There are, of course, a number of organizations that provide opportunities for ordinary people—those not designated as "writers"—to be "writers." The Plaistow Poets, in East London, for example, provides an opportunity for ordinary people to take up positions as writers. Indeed, one of the Mass-Observation correspondents I interviewed, Mr. Reed (R450), was a member of the Plaistow Poets and published poems in their poetry booklets (described in detail in Sheridan, Street & Bloome, 2000). He saw himself as a writer/poet, but he also saw himself as a writer on the margins (and certainly as a writer in opposition to the establishment). Throughout England and elsewhere, there are many such writing groups as the Plaistow Poets, but they remain on the margins, a barely visible part of writing in dominant society.

Studies such as Barton and Hamilton (1998), Heath (1983), Street (1993), Richardson (2002), and Kugelmass and Boyardin (1998), among others, provide rich, detailed descriptions of writing activities that occur outside of dominant social institutions, yet all are nearly invisible beyond the locality or beyond a discrete, marginalized group. Regardless of how numerous such activities might be, writing education in schools orients primarily to writing in dominant institutions through how it is structured. The cultural models of writing promulgated include the structuration of writing positions.

In discussions of classroom education, especially around questions of relationships between schools, families, and communities, there has been much attention to issues of access. Questions have been asked about how cultural, linguistic, and economic differences affect access. With regard to writing education and literacy education in general, pedagogies and assessments have been devised to provide access to those often denied because of cultural and linguistic variation.

The issue that I tried to raise here is one that acknowledges the importance of studies and curriculum development around issues of access and cultural and linguistic differences, but raises questions about the need to address the structuration of writing positions within dominant social institutions. If it is the case, as the interpretation of the data presented here suggests, that writing positions are limited and hierarchically structured, and are used to control the behavior within those institutions (as occurred in court) and to control the representation of history, then extant pedagogical approaches may provide more equitable access (e.g., access not based on culture, language, and economic background), but not overall greater access nor create a "writer" population. The power relations involved in the structuration of writing positions within social institutions such as the court will need to be addressed, as well as the distribution and valuing of roles and expertise within business institutions. Schools will need to reconsider the orientation of their writing programs. If their pedagogical efforts with regard to writing are to be something more than rationalization of a hierarchical system of limited and limiting writing positions, then they will need to consider how to provide students with the social, cultural, and political insights and skills to create new writing positions for themselves and for their communities.

APPENDIX

Excerpts from Interviews and Written Responses to Mass-Observation Project Directives

1. W: it's flattering, really, to think that somebody's going to sit there and read it all (laughs) you know and I think it's rubbish most of the time I write . . . I feel as though nobody's interested in my opinions, really (laughs)—I mean my husband doesn't ask what I think about all these things (laughs) so why should somebody else be interested in what I think about them? (W632, interview)

2. I don't think ordinary people get the same chance as many perhaps academics, or so-called educated people, and people in the media, to have their say. (M1498, Interview)

3. Ordinary people writing about their lives. In fifty years time it will be fascinating. That's what history is all about, but the history of ordinary people has to be written while it's happening as there is no surviving source material otherwise. (B1106, interview)

4. When we watched TV and read the papers people like us seemed to be extinct. Working class people . . . whoever reads mine might understand working class people better. (S496, response to directive).

5. It is a platform that a working man would never have in his everyday life, exhilarating—like my songs which nobody ever hears, but which are wonderful tonic to me. (R450, response to directive)

6. I remember the fairly opprobrious label "history from below" was placed on the kind of work Sussex [the Mass-Observation Project] was instrumental in making happen. Fucking right on, I say. I'd rather have that sort of history than history written by eminent ass-lickers, honours-junkies and apologists for state crimes. (R1671, response to directive)

7. ordinary people rather than the professional media think about events. (P2250, response to directive)

8. The ordinary voice . . . the person who wouldn't have a voice otherwise. (B1106, interview)

9. It's very difficult really; I don't think anybody's really ordinary . . . And I thought well I'm fairly ordinary. I think ordinary really, you think of yourself as someone who hasn't perhaps achieved fame, or great success; just live a sort of normal, everyday life, going to work and with your family. . . . Well, the way I tend to think of it is, perhaps that there are some people who have more power in society to change things, in government for instance, and often I think you feel you're ordinary because you don't have this power, and so you have very little influence sometimes over the big decisions, like ecological decisions and world decisions. (M1498, interview)

REFERENCES

Barton, D., & Hamilton, M. (1998). *Local literacies.* London: Routledge.
Bloome, D. (1983). Reading as a social process. In B. Hutson (Ed.), *Advances in reading/language research* (Vol. 2, pp. 165–195). Greenwich, CT: JAI Press.
Bloome, D. (1985). Reading as a social process. *Language Arts, 62*(4), 134–142.
Brodkey, L. (1987). *Academic writing as social practice.* Philadelphia: Temple University Press.
Christian, B., & Bloome, D. (2004). Learning to read is who you are. *Reading Writing Quarterly, 20*(4), 365–384.
Fairclough, N. (1992). *Discourse and social change.* Cambridge: Polity.

Gee, J. (1996). *Social linguistics and literacies: Ideology in discourses*. London: Taylor Francis.

Heath, S. (1983). *Ways with words*. Cambridge: Cambridge University Press.

Ivanic, R. (1994). I is for interpersonal. *Linguistics and Education, 6*(1), 3–16.

Kugelmass, J., & Boyardin, J. (Eds.). (1998). *From a ruined garden: The memorial books of Polish Jewry*. Bloomington: Indiana University Press.

Mitchell, J. C. (1984). Typicality and the case study. In R. Ellen (Ed.), *Ethnographic research: A guide to general conduct* (pp. 238–241). New York: Academic Press.

Richardson, E. (2002). "To protect and serve": African American female literacies. *College Composition and Communication, 53*(4), 675–704.

Sheridan, D. (1993). "Ordinary hardworking folk?" Volunteer writers in M-O 1937–1950 and 1981–1991. *Feminist Praxis, 37/38,* 1–34.

Sheridan, D., Street, B., & Bloome, D. (2000). *Writing ourselves: Literacy practices and the Mass-Observation Project*. Cresskill, NJ: Hampton Press.

Street, B. (Ed.). (1993). *Cross-cultural approaches to literacy*. Cambridge: Cambridge University Press.

Street, B. (1995). *Social literacies*. London: Longman.

Willinsky, J. (1990). *The new literacy*. London: Routledge.

Chapter 16

"First We Must Dream. Nothing Is Harder": Toward a Discourse on Literacy Across the Life Span

B. Allan Quigley
St. Francis Xavier University

DECONSTRUCTING "THE EDUCATIONAL GAME"

Jonathan Dale, a Quaker who has spent much of his life as a community worker, once wrote: "First we must dream. Nothing is harder . . . Dreaming has to break through the constantly reinforced assumption that 'There Is No Alternative' " (1996, p. 1). This takes on special poignancy when we look at the world through the eyes of those with low literacy skills; particularly since one of the great tragedies of Western civilization is that the concept of "lifelong learning" has never been taken particularly seriously.

The promise of accessible educational opportunities for *all* citizens remains part of the Western world's legacy of education rhetoric. Far from a coherent system, we have a fragmented series of competing, disconnected education systems which have a major breakpoint at the end of public schooling. For many, public education ends at approximately age 16—comprising less than one quarter of the normal lifespan for North Americans (Tuijnman & van der Kamp, 1992). For others who choose to go on, the educational challenge is only beginning in earnest. Consider, for example, the institutional barriers that arise within and between the countless preschool, elementary school, middle school, and high school systems across North America. Consider how the maze of postsecondary training schools and colleges spreads out across provinces and states, and winds its way into the Byzantine world of requirements and barriers in the competing "city states" of our universities. Just the transferability issues around course credits, certificates, and degrees alone require entire admissions and registrar departments in educational institutions and provincial governments to try to monitor inquiries. Somehow employers, the public, and aspiring students must find their way along these roads to knowledge. Most debilitating of all, now try to imagine how this labyrinthine set of "accessible" roads must appear to those with low literacy skills. Those who left school early and, now, having heard about "access," want to make a "fresh start."

As early as 1976, census data in Canada revealed that 37.2% of Canadians over 15 years of age had less than a Grade 9 education (Thomas, 1976). Repeated literacy surveys since have revealed that the levels of reading, writing, and numeracy skills among Canadian adults remain a major issue (Calamai, 1987; OECD & Statistics Canada, 1996, 2000). The most recent study conducted under the auspices of the OECD and Statistics Canada (2000), the *International Adult Literacy Survey*, found that approximately 43% of the Canadian adult population suffers from some level of problem dealing with reading, writing, and numeracy, and a full 22% of these face severe literacy difficulties (OECD & Statistics Canada, 2000). The situation is very similar in the U.S.A., with some 23% at the lowest level and up to 51% in the two combined lowest levels of prose, document and quantitative proficiency (Kirsch, Jungeblut, Jenkins, & Kolstad, 1993).

However, the "game" does not end there. It is well documented that, of the thousands of youth and adults that walk away from our public schools, few *ever* return to formal adult education (Cervero & Fitzpatrick, 1990; Henry & Basile, 1994; Quigley & Arrowsmith, 1997). Less than 10% ever return to literacy education programs across North America (Quigley, 1997). For the millions with low literacy skills, or who lack the requisite formal education required in today's job market, the "educational game" is inexorably working against them.

However, lifelong learning, by definition, consists of much more than educational systems (Cross, 1982; Jarvis, 1990). Lifelong learning in today's Information Age involves accessing knowledge through myriad learning opportunities everyday (Barton & Hamilton, 1998; Heath, 1983). One such means is the ubiquitous Internet. However, like so many avenues to knowledge, this too is not accessible to everyone. Shohet stated this new literacy problem of the 21st century succinctly:

> We mouth platitudes about living in an age when access to, and control over, information constitute a new form of capital. If the metaphor is viable, then we are in a process of creating a new underclass of the dispossessed and the exploited in all those adults who lack the skills to accept, choose and use the information that is multiplying faster than the most literate among us can comprehend. (cited in Hautecouer, 1994)

If we are seriously concerned about almost half of the adult population across North America, and the thousands of children and youth dropping out of school systems that sustain these numbers, not to mention issues of recidivism in literacy skills, we need to ask: Can we not make an effort to build a more coherent path of informal learning and formal education that focuses on the common foundation of lifelong learning—literacy across the lifespan? If the fundamentals of how to build solid foundations for buildings are well known in the building trade across all nations, and these fundamentals are understood and applied daily despite the size or complexity or location of the building to be constructed, is there a reason why researchers, practitioners, and policymakers cannot cooperate to develop a more comprehensive, accessible, meaningful path for literacy learners—irrespective of age—in our so-called "learning society?"

I believe there are at least two broad approaches we could and should take to change the game rules for the future of literacy. Both are based on the belief that we can "imagine a better state of things" (Greene, 1988, p. 16) and can build a discourse to achieve change.

A HISTORY OF LITERACY IMBALANCE
ACROSS THE LIFESPAN

Unfortunately, history is not on our side. With the possible exception of Scandinavian countries, where initiatives such as the Folk High School Movement have made a lasting intergenerational impact (Stabler, 1987), and examples of family literacy in North America (discussed later), literacy education has never been equitably distributed over the period of a normal lifespan in any Western country.

A glance at the history of reading is useful. Most scholars agree that reading is some 6,000 years old (e.g., Fischer, 2003). And, reading has historically been part of adults' lives, not necessarily of children's. From the earliest Sumerian signs of a writing system that appeared in Mesopotamia, to the written and pictorial communications systems of Egypt, to writing and reading in the Iranian Plateau, through the Aegean to Greece, Rome, and on to Europe as we know it today, the evolution of reading has been about adults communicating with other adults, and adults educating adults in the ways of reading. Today's vast discipline and practice of adult education (i.e., Wilson & Hayes, 2000) is founded on the ancient history of teaching reading, writing, and numeracy to adults (Quigley, 1997). Adult education is infinitely older than today's institutionalizing efforts to educate child and youth. It was only in the late 19th century that governments began investing heavily in organized educational systems for children; in fact, it was only in 1904 that G. Stanley Hall's two-volume book *Adolescence* appeared, introducing the concept of a special "intermediate period of transition . . . between the end of childhood and the acceptance of full adult responsibilities" (Button & Provenzo, 1983, p. 210).

The Club of Rome has forcefully argued that "the preoccupation with the training of the young and the neglect of the needs of adults" (Botkin, Elmandjra, & Malitza, 1982, p. 66) is a serious problem within the quest for true lifelong learning in society. They argue that, "In a period of rapid changes and rising complexity, it no longer makes no sense to cram education into the first eighteen to twenty-odd years of life" (Botkin, Elmandjra, & Malitza, p. 66). Yet, today's imbalance between education for adults and education for children and youth is a relatively recent issue considering the ancient history of adults and literacy. Ironically, today, adults who are attempting to learn or enhance their reading, writing, or numeracy skills are often being taught by volunteer or part-time tutors or teachers, if indeed such a local program is even available within the community or geographic region (Quigley, 1997). Can we not seek a better balance?

The beginning point, I believe, is to try bridge the huge chasm between school-based literacy and adult literacy education. Perhaps it is quixotic to try. Perhaps nothing will change between such entrenched hegemonies, but I am reminded of Martin Buber, theologian and philosopher, who once wrote about various translations of our phrase "far away." Buber (1958) noted there is a Fuegian term that "soars above our analytic wisdom" (p. 18). It is "a seven-syllabled word whose precise meaning is, 'They stare at one another, each waiting for the other to volunteer to do what both wish, but are not able to do' " (1958, p. 18). My hope is that the strategies I offer here may help us build a discourse toward a better future for literacy across the entire life span.

LEARNING VERSUS EDUCATION: A NEW LIFESPAN FRAMEWORK FOR LITERACY DISCOURSE

Until now, literacy educators from the school system and adult literacy educators have often found themselves talking at cross purposes. We work in different environments with different assumptions. Children and youth are legally required to attend school, and a review of the literature reflects how much of the traditional body of school-based research inevitably contends with the institution of schooling itself. By contrast, adults spend comparatively little time in formal educational settings—that is, in school-like, institutions. For adults, education occurs only occasionally in postsecondary institutions, and only for some. Instead, learning occurs for adults in nonformal or informal settings every day. The discipline of adult education has long made a distinction between "education" and "learning." These are not seen as the same thing (e.g., Lindeman, 1926/1961; Wilson & Hayes, 2000). The distinctions between "pedagogy" and "andragogy" are but one example (Knowles, 1980). Simply put, there are two huge areas involved for the discipline and practice of adult education around (a) learning in nonformal and informal settings, and (b) formal education in educational settings (Merriam & Cunningham, 1989).

Looking at learning more closely, Courtney (1989) explains that "*Informal* [learning] means . . . [where] adults inform themselves about life and its possibilities" (p. 18). This enormous area of learning is supported by a body of literature that has grown up since the 1970s around autodidactic self-directed learning (Brockett & Hiemstra, 1991; Candy, 1991; Tough, 1971), incidental learning (Marsick & Watkins, 1990), and transformative learning (Cranton, 2000; Mezirow, 1991). The research around self-directed learning asks how and why adults learn on their own (Courtney, 1992; Rose, 1989, p. 211). By contrast, "*Nonformal* means organized adult education outside the established formal system" (Courtney, 1989, p. 19). Typically, nonformal involves groups of learners in, for instance, the plethora of community-based or institutionally organized general interest, skill development, personal interest, and other noncredit learning events, often, but not necessarily, with some organizing activity, task, or curricula involved.

In this framework, *learning* can be seen as occurring in informal and nonformal settings with learners alone or in groups; by contrast, formal education can be understood as occurring in or through institutions where the educational activities are often given formal recognition, such as course credit. If learning is seen as being essentially driven by learners, and education is understood as mainly teacher and profession based, then adult education and school-based education have two common bridges to build literacy on. We can now begin to talk and share with a common language around learning *without* continuous reference to an institutional base, and we can talk about education *with* sets of understandings germane to institutions. This framework could help us across the literacy lifespan and put us on common ground for discourse, as seen next.

LEARNING ABOUT LEARNING THROUGH THE NEW LITERACY STUDIES MOVEMENT

The New Literacy Studies Movement, which has arisen out of school-based literacy education, offers a very helpful—very hopeful—thrust for both children/youth *and* adult educators to build on. In this movement, the emphasis shifts from classrooms with decontextualizing analyses of texts (Apple, 1993) and traditional teacher-based literacy pedagogy (Gee, 1997), to a more situated, contextualized understanding of language and literacy—to literacy as "social history," as Heath (1983) describes it; as sociocultural discourses, as Gee (1997) discusses it; or, as Street (2001) explains, as "social practices rather than technical skills to be learned in formal education" (p. 17). Across the Movement, we see the turn toward literacy in lived contexts, what adult educators might think of as learning in everyday life, both in informal and nonformal settings.

The New Literacy Movement is articulating well what many adult literacy educators have advocated for years. For instance, Fingeret (1983) conducted ethnographic research into the rich social networks of adults with low literacy skills in a major urban centre, but did not take the ethnography as far into levels of theory as Heath (e.g., 1983) has done. Gowen (1992) has followed the development of English skills among immigrant workers in the midst of workplace politics, but has not taken the issues to a wider level of discourse, as, for instance, Barton and Hamilton (e.g., 1998) have done. Fingeret and Jurmo (1989) have helped build the movement for participatory adult literacy; groups of literacy practitioners in British Columbia have begun investigating ways low-literate adults learn in social context without educational classrooms (Niks, Allen, Davies, McRae, & Nonesuch, 2003); and a few of us (e.g., Quigley & Arrowsmith, 1997) have begun investigating how learning occurs among low-literate adults based on international data, but the nature of language and linguistics and the uses of language are not part of these initiatives as they are with, for instance, Fairclough's work (e.g., 1989) and Gee's research (e.g., 1990).

For purposes of discourse, one obvious connection is found in Gee's (1997) sociocultural approaches to language and literacy where literacy usage inexorably leads to " 'critical literacy' " (p. xvii). This research connects with the multidefinitioned life of critical literacy in adult literacy (e.g., Quigley, 1997). Gee (1997) reveals how the very ambiguity of language and the various, competing interests behind the usage of language creates contestations. This is a welcome addition in adult literacy. From language itself, we see how "interests, goals, and power relationships" (p. xviii) become unmasked.

If informal literacy learning were explored across the life span, adult literacy educators and youth/child literacy educators might work together to consider critical literacy, as discussed in the New Literacy Movement, alongside the living history of liberatory, or radical, adult education seen in mainstream adult education (i.e., Beder, 1989; Hellyer & Schulman, 1989), or as found throughout the history of liberatory literacy (Quigley, 1997). For example, the work of perhaps the most famous adult educator, Paolo Freire (e.g., 1973), the activism of radical adult educator Rev. Moses Coady of the

Antigonish Movement (e.g., Welton, 2001), the work of Myles Horton and Highlander Folk School (e.g., Horton, 1989), and the ongoing work of Martin (e.g., 1981) and others focused on literacy and workers' unions all speak to critical literacy in the lived struggle for social justice (Heaney, 1984).

Taken further, researchers in the New Literacy Movement, like Lankshear (1997) and Harris (1993), have also taken literacy directly to politics and gender issues. Similar work is being conducted in the areas of adult literacy policy studies (e.g., Blunt, 2001), and research by feminist adult literacy researchers such as Horsman (1999), with her work on issues of women and violence in literacy (and see Luttrell, 1996), provides multiple living examples across the lifespan. Likewise, adult critical literacy work is occurring around the threatened cultures of First Nations people in Canada (i.e., Haig-Brown, 1995); in research and action with literacy and minorities in the United States (i.e., Sheared, 1994), and in the work of many literacy researchers and activists in Europe and nations of the South (i.e., Flecha, 2000; Hautecouer, 1994). Building bridges across the age divide would expand the lived possibilities of literacy as learning for researchers, practitioners, and policymakers, and would create healthy new directions for adult literacy education (Hautecouer, 1994).

Yet, despite the many promising connections between the New Literacy Movement and adult literacy learning, as seen here, and despite the fact the New Literacy Movement is not particularly "new" today, the impact of this movement is only now being felt in adult literacy education in Canada. Recently, Ewing (2003) began to point out that the New Literacy Movement can "bring communities into programs" (p. 17), that "A literacy program must be more than a place where one can learn the technical skills required for using written language" (p. 17), and that the New Literacy both "encourages people to invent literacy practices" (p. 18) and can "help learners to adapt and expand their literacy practices" (p. 19).

The opportunities to build a bridge of informal and nonformal learning out of the New Literacy allows us in practice, policy, and research to understand the huge world of literacy learning more fully, irrespective of age, cross-discipline barriers, or the confines of institutional histories.

BUILDING BRIDGES ACROSS A FRAGMENTED FORMAL FIELD

Bourdieu (1971) once observed, "Reality is not an absolute . . . it differs with the group to which one belongs" (p. 195). There are a great many realities involved in working toward a better balance of literacy learning and education across the life span. The earlier discussion was concerned with ways adult and child/youth-centered *learning* could be better connected. Turning now to our "mutually exclusive" *education* systems, Grabill's (2001) argument is helpful. He notes that, "Literacy [in most Western contexts] only has meaning because it is given meaning by institutional systems" (p. 9). Where might bridges be built across our education terrain for children, youth, and adults seeking literacy education?

In Table 16.1, we compare many of the various populations and programs of the school-based and adult literacy systems. Children and youth literacy education systems appear in the first column, literacy programs for adults are in the third column, and there is the "meeting ground" in the middle with family literacy. What this figure seeks to depict is how our two sets of mainstream educational systems virtually mirror one another. Looking at the parallels, it is immediately obvious how education programs separate learners by age groups for purposes of student management—not for reasons of pedagogy or lifestage learning development.

Looking more closely at this map of literacy, some clear commonalities emerge. We have, for instance, common "beginners–intermediate–advanced" learning levels for youth, families, and adults (Martin & Fisher, 1989; Street, 2001; Taylor, 1989). We have the commonality of teaching reading, writing and, often, numeracy in our public, family, and adult educational domains. Why can we not share and learn from these at our mutual levels of content and teaching/learning methodology across the life span? Why can we not evolve a better process of referral to formal literacy programs throughout the life span? Why not see youth moving smoothly into adult tutoring or adult basic education programs, for instance? Why can we not see more adults and youth studying together across the life span in educational programs? What could we all learn, and contribute, to family literacy, inasmuch as it draws methods and materials from both sides of the map (Thomas, 2001)? Families—the first educators—grow together and live to-

TABLE 16.1
Mapping Mainstream and Traditional Literacy Education
by Learner Population and Program

I. Child & youth literacy		*II. Family literacy*		*III. Adult literacy*
1) Emergent literacy (preschool & kindergarten)	↔	Collaborative family literacy programs	↔	1) (Basic) Literacy
2) Early literacy (primary grades)	↔	Collaborative family literacy programs	↔	2) Adult Basic Education ABE levels 2–3, etc.
3) Transitional literacy through to literacy fluency	↔	Collaborative family literacy programs	↔	3) GED/Adult Basic Education 11–12 basic education, Level 4, etc.

gether in Western nations, but are not "allowed" to attend the same educational institutions. What is the potential here for discourse? We are restricted only by archaic policies and encrusted hegemonies.

A MAP OF LITERACY AS LANGUAGE AND PRESERVATION OF CULTURE

There are even more remarkable commonalities if we look at a second map. As seen in Table 16.2, there are structural similarities across the language teaching institutions of literacy. In Canada, we have a long history of beginner–intermediate–advanced learning levels (and multiple variations of these) across programs for English and French language acquisition—either as languages or as dialects of languages—but there are also many heritage language programs that serve learners of all ages. In this language area, culture becomes critical. For instance, in Canada, Inuktitut is taught to adults and children/youth alike in Nunavut; the Mi'kmaq language is taught in Nova Scotia, Cree in Saskatchewan—all working to preserve cultural literacies. Similarly, Canada's heritage languages, together with English and French, also carry political as well as deep cultural ramifications in literacy work, as depicted in Table 16.2. What could we learn across the life span if the ageism barriers were challenged? Even a cursory search of the literature suggests there is little sharing of language and culture practice knowledge or research across the life span (see Auerbach, 2001; Goldgrab, 1992; Orem, 1989). "Research follows form" in academic and language literacy, meaning, just as learners are so often separated by age, so is the wider field separated by institutional program constructs. The single exception,

TABLE 16.2
Mapping Mainstream and Traditional Literacy Language
Education by Learner Population and Program

I. Child & youth literacy	II. Family literacy	III. Adult literacy
First and second language programs & schools	Multiple family	First and second language programs & schools
Reclaiming Aboriginal languages and FSL & ESL	1st and 2nd language programs in French, English, and indigenous languages	Reclaiming Aboriginal languages and FSL & ESL
Heritage language programs for youth including Germanic, Romance, Asian, etc.	Heritage language programs for families	Heritage language programs for adults including Germanic, Romance, Asian, etc.

again, is family literacy. Surely the issues of culture are so deeply embedded in family structures that this "map" could be a wider topic of discourse within a more inclusive field of literacy across the life span.

A MAP OF SPECIALIZED LITERACY POPULATIONS AND PROGRAMS

A third depiction of literacy across the life span is possible if one considers the more specialized areas of literacy education—"specialized" in the sense that they serve more specific needs of learner groups, as seen in Table 16.3.

As indicated on the first line of Table 16.3, there are multiple examples of alternative schools for youth and children across North America, and we have a wide variety of community-based adult literacy programs as well

TABLE 16.3
Mapping Specialized Institutional Literacy Education
by Learner Population and Program

I. Child & youth literacy	II. Family literacy	III. Adult literacy
Alternative school models	Community-based models	Community-based models
Home schooling/education Parents and students' homes	Home-based and home visitation models	Tutoring Volunteer tutors, one-on-one, in adult's homes, from literacy programs
Technical/Vocational Community placement programs	n/a	Workplace literacy Multiple work settings
Juvenile & Corrections Corrections programs for youth	In-corrections institutional models	Corrections literacy Prisons/penitentiary
Aboriginal Reading Dev't First Nations, Inuit schools & programs	Family-literacy models	Aboriginal literacy First Nations, Inuit, colleges, community based
(Health curriculum specific in some schools)	Curriculum-specific in some programs	Health literacy Hospitals and community health settings
Inclusive Education Integrated and "pull out" programs	n/a	Learning Disabilities/"Emergent Literacy" at sheltered settings, and new inclusive programs in colleges and universities
Alternative Schools "storefront programs"	n/a	Literacy for the homeless at shelters and various community locations

(Fagan, 2001; Sussman, 2001). By way of parallel, adult literacy education systems have a centuries-old history of one-on-one, volunteer tutoring (Quigley, 1997) and, for children and youth, home-schooling is a major alternative in North America. As in the earlier figures, however, it is *family literacy* that draws from both sides of the life span for materials and teaching methodologies. Turning to literacy for vocational purposes, this entire stream of programming has much to share between the technical/vocational educational programs that one finds in virtually every major public school and the adult workplace literacy programs found in virtually every Canadian city (i.e., Blunt, 2001; Gowan, 1992; Thorn, 2001). However, in all three cases, sharing is extremely rare.

Programs that involve juvenile and adult corrections systems—from minor court sentences to prison incarceration—offer the potential for sharing across youth, family, and adult literacy (Horvath, 1982; Wolford, 1989). Here is a virtual subculture in literacy, but little is shared in the literature and practice on mutual struggles, successes, or issues (Baird, 2001; Rafter, 1982; Watterson, 1996).

Health literacy is an emerging field of study and practice in adult literacy (e.g., Rudd, 2001). To date, it has had its primary focus on hospitals and other institutional health settings, but there are numerous programs in family literacy programs and mainstream adult literacy, not to mention curricula in the school system, that contain health content and health literacy. Furthermore, schools have a long history of education with the intellectually challenged and youth with learning/behavioral disabilities. Whether it is the so-called "pull-out" special education programs in schools or the school-integrated programs, adult education has much to learn from, and much to share with, the school system. The learning disabilities literature in adult literacy (i.e., Corley & Taymans, 2001)—sometimes referred to as *emergent literacy*—has made some headway. However, the issues of literacy across the life span could clearly benefit from shared research and more shared practice concerning youth, adults, and entire families.

Finally, as seen in Table 16.3, we can find special programs for the homeless or those in deep poverty from both schools and adult systems. At the adult level, Frontier College (e.g., Morrison, 1989) has a history of working with street people in adult literacy, storefront programs exist for homeless children, and specialized programs for families have emerged in Canadian cities. Once again, adult, youth, and family programs work in systemic isolation from one another in education and adult education could easily benefit from more cross-over research and combined practice.

These three figures illustrate how, in formal literacy education settings, we have reinforced fragmentation through the very institutions and policies that define and support literacy. These fragmentations create serious needs and dilemmas for learners, but the policies and practices we live with are rarely challenged (Taylor, 2001).

BUILDING AN AGENDA FOR LITERACY DISCOURSE ACROSS THE LIFE SPAN

Literacy across the life span offers multiple opportunities for sharing and building a better field. A few examples follow, beginning with some of the common points for discourse that may well arise from this discussion:

• We have learner interests and needs in common and can explore these through the mutual area of the New Literacy Studies and multiple adult settings as informal and nonformal learning occurs throughout the life span. Secondly, we have a virtual mirror image of each other's educational programs through our parallel structures of literacy education. Why can we not enter a better discourse across these points of learning and education?

• We have family literacy as a common "meeting ground." What can be learned from this area of practice and research, and how can this be applied throughout the lifespan?

Such exploratory discourse could lead to far greater efforts for research and collective advocacy. The following is a sample of questions and concerns that suggest themselves:

• What do young adults experience when they drop out of school? Why do they drop out of school? How does this affect their learning patterns and their dispositions to further learning? How does it impact on further education? What steps can be taken to address the issues and effects of dropout across the life span? What can we learn to improve formal education systems and pedagogy across the life span?

• What can we learn from one another on issues of learner gender, ethnicity, cognitive development, learning style, and participation patterns throughout the literacy life span?

• What strategies, what methods, what new ideas do we have to more successfully understand and "measure" learner progress for purposes of evaluation across the literacy life span?

• What better strategies, what improved methods, what new ideas do we have to teach and tutor literacy learners of all ages, in all settings, across the life span?

• How, when, where, why do children/youth/adults with limited literacy learn *on their own* through the life span? What is it within learners' formative years that equips or motivates them for processes of learning in their adult years?

• How can we work together to more effectively refer/assist/guide learners through the institutional structures of literacy education across provinces, states, and regions?

• We have common professional development goals and, if compared, common successes and failures. What can we learn from each other in literacy work?

• How can we more effectively lobby and support each other for more resources and far greater recognition for literacy—in our institutions, in our communities, with our governments, and across our societies? Must literacy education be a compartmentalized set of contradictory, competing educational policies on the margins of more mainstream policies and systems?

CONCLUSION: BEYOND BENIGN GOODWILL

After over some 40 years of adult literacy campaigns, programs, and countless "fresh initiatives" in adult literacy (Arnove & Graff, 1987), and endless programs of "school reform," we enter the 21st century with approximately half of our North American adult population affected by low literacy skills and schools that are helping to keep these numbers high. For those of us in adult literacy, it is all too easy to become cynical, to feel no progress is being made—or can ever be made. Yet, if we take our lead from learners of every age, literacy is about hope, not about cynicism or discouragement. Researchers and practitioners from all walks of literacy *can* take steps to build a better field of literacy education—and do so collaboratively.

We could have a more collaborative literacy field that explores possibilities across borders, that challenges the hegemony of "what is," that seeks to learn from one another across the life span, and that works to share knowledge for the benefit of learners and potential learners, of all ages. However, to do so will require more than "benign good will." We need to argue for "literacy across the life span" as part of the political and research agenda for this new century (Quigley, 2001). We need to argue the case for literacy education across the life span in such as national health policies, in national employment and training initiatives, and in arenas of public education funding. If we are to live in a better century—a century that will take literacy as a basic right for everyone, irrespective of gender, race, *or age*—first we must dream. Then we must act.

REFERENCES

Apple, M. (1993). Between moral regulation and democracy: The cultural contradictions of the text. In C. Lankshear & P. McLaren (Eds.), *Critical literacy: Politics, praxis, and the postmodern* (pp. 193–216). New York: State University of New York Press.

Arnove, R., & Graff, H. (1987). *National literacy campaigns: Historical and comparative perspectives.* New York: Plenum Press.

Auerbach, E. (2001). "Yes, but . . . ." Problematizing participatory ESL pedagogy. In P. Campbell & B. Burnaby (Eds.), *Participatory practices in adult education* (pp. 267–306). Mahwah, NJ: Lawrence Erlbaum Associates.

Baird, I. (2001). Shattering the silence: Education, incarceration and the marginalization of women. In P. Sissel & V. Sheared (Eds.), *Making space: Reframing practice in adult education* (pp. 168–181). Westport, CT: Greenwood.

Barton, D., & Hamilton, D. (1998). *Local literacies.* London: Routledge.

Beder, H. (1989). Purposes and philosophies of adult education. In S. Merriam & P. Cunningham (Eds.), *Handbook of adult and continuing education* (pp. 37–50). San Francisco: Jossey-Bass.

Blunt, A. (2001). Workplace literacy: The contested terrains of policy and practice. In M. Taylor (Ed.), *Adult literacy now!* (pp. 89–108). Toronto: Culture Concepts.

Bourdieu, P. (1971). Systems of education and systems of thought: New directions for the sociology of education. In M. E. D. Young (Ed.), *Knowledge and control* (pp. 189–207). London: Collier Macmillan.

Botkin, J., Elmandjra, & Malitza, M. (1982). *No limits to learning: Bridging the human gap.* New York: Pergamon Press.

Brockett, R., & Hiemstra, R. (1991). *Self-direction in adult learning: Perspectives in theory, research and practice.* New York: Routledge.

Buber, M. (1958). *I and thou* (2nd ed.). New York: Charles Scribner's Sons.

Button, H., & Provenzo, E. (1983). *History of education and culture in America.* Englewood Cliffs, NJ: Prentice Hall.

Calamai, P. (1987). *Broken words: Why five million Canadians are illiterate.* Toronto: Southam News Group.

Candy, P. (1991). *Self-direction for lifelong learning.* San Francisco: Jossey-Bass.

Cervero, R., & Fitzpatrick, T. (1990). The enduring effects of family role and schooling on participation in adult education. *American Journal of Education, 99*(1), 77–94.

Corley, M., & Taymans, J. M. (2001). Adults with learning disabilities and the role of self-determination: Implications for literacy programs. *The Canadian Journal for the Study of Adult Education, 15*(2), 149–167.

Courtney, S. (1989). Defining adult and continuing education. In S. Merriam & P. Cunningham (Eds.), *Handbook of adult and continuing education* (pp. 15–25). San Francisco: Jossey-Bass.

Courtney, S. (1992). *Why adults learn. Towards a theory of participation adult education.* New York: Routledge.

Cranton, P. (2000). Individual differences and transformative learning. In J. Mezirow & Associates (Eds.), *Learning as transformation: Critical perspectives on a theory in progress* (pp. 181–204). San Francisco: Jossey-Bass.

Cross, P. (1982). *Adults as learners.* San Francisco: Jossey-Bass.

Dale, J. (1996). *Beyond the spirit of the age: Quaker responsibility at the end of the twentieth century.* London: Quaker Home Service.

Ewing, G. (2003, Spring). The new literacy studies: A point of contact between literacy research and literacy work. *Literacies, 1*, 15–21.

Fagan, W. (2001). The dominant literacy: Subdued lives. In M. Taylor (Ed.), *Adult literacy now!* (pp. 51–66). Toronto: Culture Concepts.

Fairclough, N. (1989). *Language and power.* London: Longman.

Fingeret, A., & Jurmo, P. (1989). *Participatory literacy education.* San Francisco: Jossey-Bass.

Fingeret, H. (1983). Social network: A new perspective on independence and illiterate adults. *Adult Education Quarterly, 3*(3), 133–145.

Fischer, S. (2003). *A history of reading.* London: Reaktion Books.

Flecha, R. (2000). *Sharing words: Theory and practice of dialogical learning.* New York: Rowman & Littlefield Publishers.

Freire, P. (1973). *Pedagogy of the oppressed.* New York: Seabury Press.

Gee, J. (1990). *Social linguistics and literacies: Ideology in discourses.* London: Falmer Press.

Gee, J. (1997). A discourse approach to language and literacy. In C. Lankshear (Ed.), *Changing literacies,* xviii–ix. Philadelphia: Open University Press.

Goldgrab, S. (1992). The preservation of Franco-Ontarian language and culture. In J. Draper & M. Taylor (Eds.), *Voices from the literacy field* (pp. 295–306). Toronto: Culture Concepts.

Gowen, S. (1992). *The politics of workplace literacy: A case study.* New York: Teachers College Press.

Grabill, J. (2001). *Community literacy programs and the politics of change.* New York: State University of New York Press.

Greene, M. (1988). *The dialectic of freedom.* New York: Teachers College Press.

Haig-Brown, C. (1995). First Nations Adult Education. In M. Battiste & M. Barman (Eds.), *The Circle Unfolds* (p. 281). Vancouver: UBC Press.

Harris, K. (1993). Critical literacy as political intervention: Three variations on a theme. In C. Lankshear & P. McLaren (Eds.), *Critical literacy: Politics, praxis, and the postmodern* (pp. 57–80). New York: State University of New York Press.

Hautecouer, J. (1994). *Alpha 94: Literacy and cultural development strategies in rural areas.* Toronto: Culture Concepts.

Heaney, T. (1984). Action, freedom, and liberatory education. In S. Merriam (Ed.), *Selected readings on philosophy and adult education* (pp. 113–122). Malabar, FL: Kreiger.

Heath, S. (1983). *Ways with words: Language, life, and work in communities and classrooms.* New York: Cambridge University Press.

Hellyer, M., & Schulman, B. (1989). Worker's education. In S. Merriam & P. Cunningham (Eds.), *Handbook of adult and continuing education* (pp. 569–582). San Francisco: Jossey-Bass.

Henry, G., & Basile, K. (1994). Understanding the decision to participate in formal adult education. *Adult Education Quarterly, 44*(2), 64–82.

Horsman, J., (1999). *Too scared to learn: Women, violence and education.* Toronto: McGilligan Books.

Horton, A. (1989). *The Highlander Folk School: A history of its major programs, 1932–1961.* Brooklyn, NY: Carlson Publishing.

Horvath, G. (1982). Issues in correctional education: A conundrum of conflict. *Journal of Correctional Education, 33*(3), 8–15.

Jarvis, P. (1990). *An international dictionary of adult and continuing education.* New York: Routledge.

Kirsch, I., Jungeblut, A, Jenkins, L., & Kolstad, A. (1993). *National Adult Literacy Survey.* Washington: U.S. Department of Education.

Knowles, M. (1980). *The modern practice of adult education.* New York: Cambridge Book Co.

Lankshear, C. (Ed.). (1997). *Changing literacies.* Philadelphia: Open University Press.

Lindeman, E. (1961). *The meaning of adult education.* Montreal: Harvest House. (Original work published in 1926)

Luttrell, W. (1996). Taking care of literacy: One feminist's critique. *Educational Policy, 10*(3), 342–365.

Marsick, V., & Watkins, K. (1990). *Informal and incidental learning in the workplace.* San Francisco: Jossey-Bass.

Martin, D. (1981). Conscious romantics: A trade unionist's reflections on the politics of learning. In M. Taylor & J. Draper (Eds.), *Adult literacy perspectives* (pp. 103–112). Toronto: Culture Concepts.

Martin, L., & Fisher, J. (1989). Adult secondary education. In S. Merriam & P. Cunningham (Eds.), *Handbook of adult and continuing education* (pp. 478–489). San Francisco: Jossey-Bass.

Merriam, S., & Cunningham, P. (1989), *Handbook of adult and continuing education.* San Francisco: Jossey-Bass.

Mezirow, J. (1991). *Transformative dimensions of adult learning.* San Francisco: Jossey-Bass.

Morrison, J. (1989). *Camps & classrooms: A pictorial history of Frontier College.* Toronto: Frontier College Press.

Niks, M., Allen, D., Davies, P., McRae, D., & Nonesuch, K. (2003). *Dancing in the dark: How do adults with little formal education learn?* Vancouver: Malaspina University College.

OECD & Statistics Canada (1996). *Reading the future: A portrait of literacy in Canada.* Ottawa: Statistics Canada.

OECD & Statistics Canada (2000). *Literacy in the Information Age: Final report of the International Adult Literacy Survey.* Ottawa: Statistics Canada.

Orem, R. (1989). English as a second language. In S. Merriam & P. Cunningham (Eds.), *Handbook of adult and continuing education* (pp. 490–501). San Francisco: Jossey-Bass.

Quigley, B. A. (1997). *Rethinking literacy education: The critical need for practice-based change.* San Francisco: Jossey-Bass.

Quigley, B. A. (2001). Living in the feudalism of adult basic and literacy education: Can we negotiate a literacy democracy? In C. Hansman & P. Sissel (Eds.), *Understanding and negotiating the political landscape of adult education* (pp. 55–62). San Francisco: Jossey-Bass.

Quigley, B. A., & Arrowsmith, S. (1997). The non-participation of undereducated adults. In P. Belanger & A. Tuijnman (Eds.), *New patterns of adult learning: A six-country comparative study* (pp. 101–130). New York: Elsevier Science Ltd.

Rafter, N. (1982). *Judge, lawyer, victim: Women, gender, race and criminal justice.* Boston: Northeastern University Press.

Rose, A. (1989). Nontraditional education and the assessment of prior learning. In S. Merriam & P. Cunningham (Eds.), *Handbook of adult and continuing education* (pp. 211–220). San Francisco: Jossey-Bass.

Rudd, R. E. (2001). A maturing partnership. *Focus on Basics, 5,* 1–8.

Sheared, V. (1994). Giving voice: An inclusive model of instruction—A womanist perspective. In E. Hayes & S. Colin III (Eds.), *Confronting racism and sexism in adult education.* San Francisco: Jossey-Bass.

Stabler, E. (1987). *Founders in education—1830–1980.* Edmonton, AB: University of Alberta.

Street, B. (2001). Contexts for literacy work: the "new orders" and the "new literacy studies." In J. Crowther, M. Hamilton, & L. Tett (Eds.), *Powerful literacies* (pp. 13–22). Leicester, UK: National Institute of Adult Continuing Education.

Sussman, S. (2001). The demographics of low literacy. In M. Taylor (Ed.), *Adult literacy now!* (pp. 81–86). Toronto: Culture Concepts.

Taylor, M. (1989). Adult basic education. In S. Merriam & P. Cunningham (Eds.), *Handbook of adult and continuing education* (pp. 465–477). San Francisco: Jossey-Bass.

Taylor, M. (Ed.). (2001). *Adult literacy now!* Toronto: Culture Concepts.

Thomas, A. (1976). *Adult basic education and literacy activities in Canada.* Toronto: World Literacy of Canada.

Thomas, A. (2001). Family literacy: Issues and directions for research and practice. In M. Taylor (Ed.), *Adult literacy now!* (pp. 71–192). Toronto: Culture Concepts.

Thomas, A. M. (2001). Introduction: How adult literacy became of age in Canada. In M. Taylor (Ed.), *Adult literacy now!* (pp. xvii–xxv). Toronto: Culture Concepts.

Thorn, I. (2001). Literacy is a labour issue. In M. Taylor (Ed.), *Adult literacy now!* (pp. 123–136). Toronto: Culture Concepts.

337

Tough, A. (1971). *The adult's learning projects: A fresh approach to theory and practice in adult learning.* Toronto: Ontario Institute for Studies in Education.

Tuijnman, A., & van der Kamp, M. (1992). *Learning across the lifespan. Theories, research, policies.* New York: Pergamon Press.

Watterson, K. (1996). *Women in prison: Inside the concrete womb* (Rev. ed.). Boston: Northeastern University Press.

Welton, M. (2001). *Little Mosie from the Margaree: A biography of Moses Michael Coady.* Toronto: Thompson Educational Publishing, Inc.

Wilson, A., & Hayes, E. (2000). *Handbook of adult and continuing education.* San Francisco: Jossey-Bass.

Wolford, B. (1989). Correctional facilities. In S. Merriam & P. Cunningham (Eds.), *Handbook of adult and continuing education* (pp. 356–368). San Francisco: Jossey-Bass.

Part **IV**

LITERACY POLICY ISSUES

Thinking Globally About English and New Literacies: Multilingual Socialization at Work

Patricia Duff
University of British Columbia

In 1998, an article appeared in *The New York Times* about a German newspaper company, *Berliner Morgenpost*, that had just launched a major advertising campaign in its drive to become the leading newspaper in Berlin and, it was hoped, in the new capital of Europe (Cohen, 1998). Surprisingly, the advertisers settled on an English slogan, not a German one, for their campaign, even though the newspaper is published in German. The slogan, "Simply the Best," was borrowed from the song by American pop singer Tina Turner. The company's marketing manager reportedly felt that the slogan was "young, fresh, simple and [was] sure to get people talking. German words are just too long." Cohen, a writer for *The New York Times*, explained the significance of the slogan, given that the German translation, "Einfach besser" was really not longer at all:

> English, of course, is advancing everywhere, propelled by the Internet and the dominance of American popular culture. It is the most widely studied foreign language in German schools, where most children start learning it at age 11. But its advance has been particularly marked here [in Berlin], strong enough to set off a debate on what it is to be a German. (p. 1)

The German newspaper saw English as crucially linked to its own ambitions as well as those of the city and country within the new Europe. This advertising campaign illustrates the changing, and thus sometimes socially unsettling, role of English in corporate, educational, and popular cultures in

341

various parts of the world, particularly in times of socioeconomic and political transition. English, like pop culture, can be a unifying factor or an alienating, segregating factor across groups and across generations (e.g., Duff, 2002); both have the potential to provide access to cultural information and to social interactions or to serve as formidable obstacles or barriers to social progress and integration.

This chapter focuses on changing language and literacy practices in contemporary societies affected by a number of factors, including the pressures of globalization, English as an international language, multilingualism, and human migration and mobility. I provide an overview of research trends connected with globalization and workplace language and literacy issues drawing on recent studies involving second language learners or members of linguistic minorities trying to enter and succeed in primarily, but not exclusively, English-dominant occupational networks and communities. I then discuss some of the complexities of face-to-face and electronic communications, new media, and other oral and written aspects of work in these evolving global environments. Finally, I consider some of the challenges and opportunities that exist for educators preparing others to participate more fully in the new workplace.

THE CHANGING STATUS OF ENGLISH:
IMPLICATIONS FOR EDUCATION,
GLOBAL MEDIA, AND WORK

In the *New York Times* article previously referred to, the connection is made between the English language and countries' socioeconomic and political ambitions because of the pervasiveness and power of English globally. Similar uses of English in business and in advertising are commonly found in Asia because of the mass appeal of English, regardless of its form or meaning in some cases. Goodman (1996) captures the situation with the clever title "Market Forces Speak English." Graddol (1996) highlights the sociolinguistic prestige and cachet commonly assigned to English:

> In many countries, the social elites with disposable income are those who are bilingual in English. English-medium advertising can thus effectively target higher income groups. Increasingly, in Asian advertising fragments of English are used symbolically in what linguists refer to as "language display": to connote western cultural values and status. (p. 216)

English obviously has important symbolic and functional roles internationally and is therefore part of what Robbins (1996) dubbed "the new media order," which extends well beyond magazine advertisements to CNN,

Sony, Disney, and other all-powerful global corporations. It serves other legitimate and perhaps more basic interests and needs as well. For that reason, it is now being taught, learned, and used by rapidly growing numbers of people around the world, coming from a variety of first-language backgrounds and cultures. In fact, Crystal (1997) estimated that as many as 1.5 billion people, or a quarter of the world's population, now use English as either their first language (L1) or as an additional language and also notes that most international organizations use English in an official capacity. People's reasons for learning English vary, but increasingly their goals are academic and professional, not just recreational or cultural, as used to be more common. Moreover, English is no longer simply a required subject at school, an examinable subject for high school matriculation or university entrance with little transactional value otherwise. It is a medium of learning from primary to tertiary education, a requirement for professional certification and for workplace interaction, and also a lingua franca or language of wider communication in multilingual communities in many countries (e.g., in Africa; Cleghorn & Rollnick, 2002).

Those learning English or upgrading their language and literacy skills now often come from untraditional educational backgrounds as well. They may be older students, immigrants, teachers, and others being retooled or retrained for the "new economy" or in response to policy reforms over which they have little control. One example was the massive retraining of thousands of former Russian teachers as English teachers in Hungary in the early 1990s, when Russian's previously mandatory status as a school subject was changed and English took its place (Duff, 1993). Another example is contexts of unemployment in Ontario that qualify workers for retraining programs in such fields as refrigeration mechanics, which have specific English language, literacy, and technical requirements, and pose difficulties for second-language and second-dialect speakers of English (Bell, 2000).

This current surge in English language teaching and learning for intranational and international communication is a phenomenon with no historical precedent on the present scale. It also coincides with the shift in many parts of the world from agrarian to industrial and, now, highly interconnected information-based economies using new technologies. Recognizing the importance of multilingual competence in contemporary society, the European Union now emphasizes that citizens in member countries should become proficient in three languages, one of which is usually English. This policy is evident in the school curriculum, and in European mobility initiatives for teachers, students, and workers, which help make it possible (Council of Europe, 2001).

Hungary, being one of the newest member countries to join the European Union, provides a good example of the shift toward trilingualism and functional multilingual/multiliterate competencies for European Community, higher education, and work purposes. In follow-up interviews I conducted in 2002 with about 20 Hungarians in their late 20s who had attended newly established English-Hungarian bilingual secondary schools 10 years earlier (first described in Duff, 1993, 1995), many indicated that in the intervening years, they had become fluent in German and other languages (e.g., Dutch, French, Russian, and even Japanese) and many used English and additional Western European languages on a regular basis in connection with their work inside and outside of Hungary. They worked for universities, ministries, private-sector companies, hospitals, language schools, public schools, and in their own businesses in Hungary. Much of their use of other languages was, furthermore, mediated by technologies (e.g., fax, e-mail, TV, mobile and landline telephones, instant messaging, mobile phone text messaging) that were all relatively uncommon in that country just 15 years earlier, when many homes did not have telephone lines or cable/satellite television. Perhaps not surprisingly, given the times, a number of the graduates had found multilingual employment in the information technology sector.

Therefore, the commodification and spread of "global English" (Nunan, 2003), although welcome in some parts of the world such as Hungary (generally speaking), especially after years of Soviet/Russian domination, has its detractors (e.g., Francophones in Quebec) and often incites social, linguistic, and political backlashes (Pennycook, 1994). Nevertheless, English has been introduced in school curricula in many countries in Asia and elsewhere in recent years, including Korea, at earlier grade levels than before. Many countries, in their pursuit of a competitive edge over their neighbors, are now racing to lower the age at which English is first introduced from Grade 7 to Grade 3 and, it would seem, inevitably to Grade 1 or earlier, leading many community members to ask how this will affect the young generation's first language skills and ethnic identity (Duff, in press; Nunan, 2003; Tucker, 2001). Further up the age spectrum, many adults continue to engage in English education long past their graduation from university, often for their work in education, business, and other sectors. This represents a trend in lifelong education or, phrased differently, linguistic socialization across the lifespan (Duff, Wong, & Early, 2000; Li, 2000). For example, the University of British Columbia's Faculty of Commerce and the Centre for Intercultural Communication (M. Chase, personal communication, 2003) have for many years run programs for managers in companies like Korea Telecom to improve their understanding of the impact of language and culture on business communications. The Korean managers' use of English *within* their company and within Korea is apparently somewhat limited, but English is vital to executives and midmanagement personnel in their communications with non-Koreans inside and outside of Korea and for their access to information in English. English is thus their principal language of communication with non-Korean colleagues.

Programs developed for international and exchange students at many Western universities also support the desire of individuals in both emerging and developed economies in such regions as the Asia-Pacific region to become more proficient in the languages and cultures of business, trade, and higher education and to return with those skills to enhance their careers and their nations' knowledge base. However, that often involves learning to write and speak using genres of academic discourse that were never well developed in the students' own languages, as preliminary data from my ongoing research with Korean and Mexican communities of students reveal. The students are often highly adept at using PowerPoint and other current business-related technologies, but more traditional ones, such as essay writing or preparing oral presentations, may be underdeveloped, even in their first language. Students are often unaware of the ways in which they will need to use English orally or in writing either in their current studies or their career aspirations. Many of the students are expected to become business leaders in their countries, so follow-up research (such as I have undertaken to a limited degree in Hungary) is being planned to investigate the extent and manner in which the same students ultimately require English language and literacy skills in their lives and work in Korea and Mexico.

In many companies around the world, English has also become the *official* language for communications both within and between countries. Nunan (2002) reports that a major multinational consulting conglomerate, KPMG Latin America, has chosen English as its company language, although the majority of employees in that region are Spanish and Portuguese speakers. Because many of the employees may not currently have high levels of English language proficiency, workplace policies such as this have serious implications for the recruitment, training, assessment, advancement, and identities of workers. The major Swedish telecommunications company, Ericcson, also requires Swedish employees to communicate with each other using English (Warschauer, 2000).

RESEARCH ON ENGLISH FOR WORK

Important trends such as those reported here have attracted the attention of the international TESOL organization and other groups, which have developed research priorities and agendas to explicitly address the current needs of adult ESL learners (see, e.g., Brindley, Baynham, Burns, Hammond, McKenna, & Thurstun, 1996; Brindley, Curtis, Davidson, Duff, Scott, & Tucker, 2000; Center for Applied Linguistics, 1998; Duff & Bailey, 2001; National Clearinghouse for ESL Literacy Education at the Center for Applied Linguistics, 1998). Informed by such research agendas and related sociolinguistic and policy concerns, a growing body of current scholarship by language and literacy specialists documents the changing literacies presently associated with work in society (Duff & Labrie, 2000; Garay & Bernhardt, 1998; Gee, Hull, & Lankshear, 1996; Hull, 1997; Roberts, Davies, & Jupp, 1992; Taylor, 1997). With a relatively mobile and migrant labour force, and with transformations in the nature of work and in modes of international communication, teachers, scholars, government agencies, employers, and employees need to understand how languages such as English are being used for work and how best to prepare people linguistically for this eventuality. Second language (L2) research has historically focused on other concerns, such as early syntactic development, basic oral fluency, and academic oral or written English for kindergarten to university levels. Examining the contextualized experiences of individuals interacting in different languages (L1, L2, or L3) in work environments and closely examining the new literacies and competencies required for work provides a basis for improving work conditions, productivity, mutual understanding, and, it is hoped, cooperation within and among employees and management teams. This kind of concerted effort within workplaces—or what are sometimes referred to now as "learning organizations" to stress ecological or systemic aspects of how they function (Senge, 1990)—is said to benefit both workers and society more generally, particularly in times of intensive globalization.

Nunan (2001) poses the following research questions (among others): "What are the English language needs of workers in a wide range of workplaces and occupations, from multinational corporations to government and quasigovernmental institutions such as hospitals? What are the implications of the changing workplace and economy globally for the teaching, learning and use of English, often with speakers of other language or varieties of English?" (pp. 605–606).

These are, indeed, fundamental questions that warrant more empirical research. Nunan (2002, 2003) has been exploring some of these research questions in his recent research in Asia and revealing, for example, the impact of the upcoming 2008 Olympics in Beijing on the English-language preparation of ordinary Chinese workers. Answers to these sorts of questions are also starting to appear in well-contextualized workplace English studies.

Extensive interview-based survey research conducted by Cooper (1998) in Hong Kong examined hundreds of vocational training program graduates in 26 firms in 13 disciplines (e.g., design, accountancy, and computer studies). Cooper then looked at categories of activities for which English was required in the workplace, such as conversation, correspondence (often a combination of speaking, reading, and writing), extracting or receiving information with follow-up activity, providing information to others in oral or written form, giving personal reactions in oral or written form, understanding information based on general world knowledge, dealing with different English accents and cultures, and using organizational and thinking skills. The results revealed that English remained the "principal language of international communication" in Hong Kong "and virtually no other European languages are used, even for communication with Europe. Spoken in-company communication is mainly in Cantonese with English second, whereas written follow-up is usually in English" (p. 135). Cooper noted, as well, that junior employees frequently needed to do translation and interpreting. Also, employees' perceptions about their future English-language use at work differed from the actual requirements, which included faxing, e-mail, and direct interaction with customers, which "created a need for greater cross-cultural knowledge and for an ability to give personal reactions" in English and not to have to rely so heavily on supervisors for English editorial and communicative assistance (p. 136). Cooper summarized the findings as follows:

> The workplace communication situation is far more complex than some had supposed. Interpersonal, informational and creative use of language, cultural and general knowledge, and organizational and thinking skills are required even at junior levels, though in varying degrees . . . In addition, it was clear that the higher up the career ladder the greater the requirement to use these aspects when using English for communication in the workplace. (p. 139)

Vandermeeren (1999) investigated the role of English as a "lingua franca in written corporate communication" across European companies (p. 273). Her survey research found differences in language choice among 415 companies surveyed in Germany, the Netherlands, France, and elsewhere in Western Europe, in their international export-related dealings with one another. In her analysis, the use of English by a company was considered "standardization," whereas the use of the other trading partner's national language was "adaptation." The use of the language of one's own company/country and not that of another country was "nonadaptation." The results showed that about 40% of German companies surveyed wrote contracts in English for French companies (standardization), and 30% in French. French companies, on the other hand, were more likely to use German (adaptation, 47.5%) than French (7.5%) or English (27.5%) for the same type of document with German companies. Overall in their business dealings with each other, in addition to the use of English as a lingua franca, French and German companies tended to use each others' languages as a form of reciprocal adaptation, in recognition of the relative strength and equality of the two languages, particularly in "before-sale" documents (e.g., advertising, offers, catalogues). In after-sales correspondence (e.g., confirmations, contracts, invoices) between the two countries, German companies used English more and French less, and French companies used German more and English less. The German companies, on the other hand, tended to use German—and not English—in their dealings with Dutch companies, and vice versa (from 57% to 73% of Dutch or German companies reported this mutual use of German). Clearly, there are many sociolinguistic factors to be taken into account in analyses of how English is used in international corporate discourse and the impact of language choice on not only communication but differential power, geoeconomic alignments, and so on.

Regardless of policies or routine practices regarding workplace English-language use, the actual levels of L2 orality and literacy required for work depend on employees' hierarchical status within a profession and the linguistic competence of their interlocutors. Mercer (1996) provides an example from Macao, a region that depends to a great extent on the manufacturing and exporting of textiles to the United States, Europe, and Japan. Describing a study by Cremer and Willes (1994), Mercer writes that "even though English is in daily use as a working language in Macau and other parts of south-east Asia, its use is confined to specific domains:"

> Most of those who use English in this daily traffic [of securing and delivering international import–export orders] would not claim to know the language well, and are uneasy where they correspond with counterparts in North America. They are altogether more confident in interaction with agents in Sweden (say) or Spain, where both parties to the correspondence handle the only available medium of communication with some difficulty and, even if they recognize each other's errors, disregard rather than tolerate them. (Cremer & Willes, 1994, p. 7; cited in Mercer, 1996, p. 92)

Mercer (1996) provides another example of an Asian context where English is widely used as the company language, in this case in central southern India, in a company called Wipro Fluid Power, which makes hydraulic equipment. Whereas most of the workers speak Kannadu, company policy dictates the use of English for most communication. English is promoted in this way as both a national lingua franca, uniting Indian workers whose first languages are different, and also for international trade purposes.

THE COEXISTENCE OF ENGLISH AND OTHER LANGUAGES IN THE NEW GLOBALIZED WORKPLACE: CONFLICTING STANDARDS OF BI/MULTILINGUALISM, PROFESSIONALISM, AND COMPETENCE

Ironically, just as English has, over time, achieved the status of a powerful—some would say hegemonic—language of work in many spheres from India to Sweden, many workplaces in English-dominant countries are becoming more multilingual or non-English. The role of English is sometimes secondary to Chinese and Spanish, the only two languages with more native speakers worldwide than English. Indeed, despite top-down pressures to adopt English, many communities naturally rely on other linguistic resources to function, sometimes as a way of maintaining their sense of solidarity, ethnic identity, efficiency—or even resistance to linguistic and cultural domination and possibly exploitation. Even when workers know English and have been in a country for as long as 20 years, they may choose to use their L1 almost exclusively and reject opportunities to improve their English for a variety of sociocultural reasons.

This observation is particularly salient in high-stakes and time-sensitive situations such as those found in manufacturing jobs where employees must meet challenging production quotas and are penalized for mistakes or the delayed completion of jobs. Even for highly skilled bilingual Vietnamese-American workers, it can be risky to negotiate technical issues in English in case of miscommunication and delays in solving problems (Kleifgen, 2001).

In her in-depth critical ethnography of an English-owned manufacturing company in Toronto, Goldstein (1997) reported that a large number of Portuguese-Canadian employees, and especially women, used Portuguese and not English on the factory production lines. There were many practical and socioaffective reasons for this phenomenon, including efficiency, speed, and worker morale, despite the workers' many years of residence in Canada, their knowledge of English in some cases, and their professed need for English for greater social integration in Canadian society. Maintaining solidarity with their Portuguese-Canadian co-workers and friends on the factory floor through the reciprocal use of Portuguese was seen to be preferable to the women in Goldstein's study to the less predictable, potentially alienating social consequences of breaking connections with them and moving up or out into positions involving greater use of English and more responsibility. Some of the women in the study even chose not to attend subsidized ESL classes at work specially designed for them. Duff, Wong, and Early (2000) also revealed that entry-level, low-paying (e.g., blue-collar) jobs that do not require high levels of English often attract new nonnative English-speaking immigrants. Many of those same jobs (e.g., sewing, cleaning) either require relatively little language at all because of the isolated nature of the work, the noise of machines, or the physical location of co-workers, who may not face one another (McAll, 2003), or they are done within same-L1 cultural groups or ethnic enclaves. Employers may, in fact, encourage workers to remain within their L1 groups because it promotes better communication between management and workers (assuming that "translators" or go-betweens exist), promotes better harmony within groups, and at the same time may also reduce opposition to management practices if workers are not organized and do not communicate well across language groups (Goldstein, 1997; McAll, 2003).

With further education or layoffs that result in retraining subsidies, immigrants previously isolated in low-skill manufacturing jobs often seek out opportunities to learn and use English and other skills to a greater extent. Our research conducted within a Canadian immigrant services program teaching immigrants English and nursing skills for careers as resident care aides in hospitals or other longterm care facilities revealed the extent to which English and other languages and literacies proved essential to workers' successful workplace communication (Duff et al., 2000).

Surprisingly, our in-depth longitudinal interviews with 20 program participants or graduates (the majority of whom were Asian women) revealed that in many urban multilingual workplaces and communities, such as those in Vancouver or Toronto, English is not used in the workplace to the extent that students, teachers, funders, and the general public expect. In jobs in the service sector, languages such as Chinese may be used by the majority of co-workers and their interlocutors (clients and patients)—but unfamiliar dialects may predominate. Even Mandarin- or Cantonese-speaking workers face challenges communicating with speakers of other dialects, such as Toisanese, a language of rural southern China. Successful workplace communication in inner city hospitals and care centres of the sort reported in Duff et al. (2000) and Wong, Duff, and Early (2001), therefore, depends on workers' ability to develop excellent communication skills and new literacies, both nonverbal and verbal, including the ability to "read" bodily texts in the deaf, blind, aphasic, or otherwise disabled populations (e.g., those with dementias), the ability to use language pragmatically in a wide range of situations (e.g., when talking about private bodily functions in ways that are both comprehensible and inoffensive to interlocutors with varying levels of English proficiency; talking with co-workers about medical situations; discussing delicate care issues with patients' or residents' families; interpreting and using humor; or when writing and processing care reports according to expected genres and conventions). Interview excerpts from the resident care aide program participants follow:

> I was expecting y'know English speakers, but there are other languages, so it's hard to communicate. Especially from today, the one [resident] I got she's a blind and also deaf . . . so it's hard communicate but there is always a way to do something, so I was using my touching. So it's quite okay. (Chinese speaker, female)

> They are Chinese but they speak in Cantonese, right? They couldn't understand English. I'm a Chinese but I speak Mandarin [laughs] so they can't understand English [and] they can't understand Mandarin so it's really hard to communicate. . .I need to learn Cantonese. But my English is not good. I

need to learn English and Cantonese too. It's too hard. (Mandarin speaker, female)

For example if I'm cleaning a lady she's paraplegic, for example, right? She doesn't move anything. Stroke and everything, right? But when I feeding her, she doesn't want something, she just clench her mouth like that. I know she doesn't like it. But—so I switch something else, I explain it. We're gonna try the peach pie, or whatever. And she ate, so she liked eh. So I find out, if you give them love, we get love back. Um, I know the language is a barrier but . . . I can jump the barrier. (Spanish speaker, male)

Therefore, the monolingual-English communities that students, workers, and even ESL teachers might envision in a so-called English (or ESL) setting, or into which many new immigrants expect to gain relatively rapid membership, are out of reach for many or simply no longer exist in many urban communities.

In the United States, Spanish coexists with English in a growing number and range of work environments, whether agricultural, service sector, or white collar. A non-Spanish-speaking immigrant in the United States may need to learn both English and Spanish to function optimally there. Thus, at the same time as many non-English-dominant countries insist on greater access to English resources and education, in English-speaking countries with many immigrants, multilingualism—and not just English language mastery—is becoming more advantageous and necessary. In Asia, one might speculate that multilingualism involving English, Mandarin, and Japanese may someday represent the norm for politicians, diplomats, business executives, and other internationally networked professionals, rather than Chinese–English or Japanese–English bilingualism.

At the same time as the use of English is spreading internationally into ever-new spheres by new populations, media, and technologies, valiant attempts are also being made to revitalize and support indigenous, heritage, and other languages of local or wider communication and to understand what role these languages might play in our evolving, more networked but sometimes fragile multilingual societies (e.g., Hare, chapter 12, this volume; Hornberger, 2003). In the Canadian province of Quebec, there has been a concerted and quite successful resistance to English domination in professional fields and in society since the 1960s, so much so that within the span of just two or three decades, there has been a significant shift in policies regarding workplace language use and in the ethnolinguistic composition of the upper tiers of companies (Heller, 2002; McAll, 2003). Prior to the late 1960s, the English-speaking minority in Quebec had disproportionate levels of power over the socioeconomic affairs in the province, marked by economic and linguistic ownership and control over public- and private-sector company management.

The (nonimmigrant) French-speaking majority, on the other hand, now representing approximately 83% of the population, were relegated to inferior positions within the labor market, economy, and society. French was therefore associated with low-skill and low-status positions (McAll, 2003). This situation has been reversed to a great extent, and the French language now occupies a much more central place in the daily affairs of most workplaces at all levels, with some notable exceptions.

McAll (2003), a Montreal sociologist, describes this ethnolinguistic transformation in higher professional tiers but notes that having Francophones in those positions does not mean that French is necessarily being used, especially in the private sector. For example, Béland (1991) found that just over half of the Francophones working in the Montreal private sector in the late 1980s were working in French. In a Montreal pharmaceutical company, French might be used in the factory but not in administration (physically as well as linguistically separate domains; Tremblay, 1993). The reasons for this, according to McAll, are not only the integration of Montreal into international markets dominated by English, but also internal sociolinguistic dynamics in the workplace.

As McAll (2003) reported:

> White collar workers we interviewed see the development of their own professional competence and career advancement as being somehow associated with working in English, particularly in that working in French (in the context of this company) is associated with production and blue-collar work. (p. 242)

He contrasts this case with the aerospace industry in Quebec, which has become largely French-dominant at all levels, with the exception of engineering because of insufficient numbers of highly trained Francophone engineers (the absence of a critical mass), the predominant use of English in "language-intensive" aspects of engineering, and the frequency of English borrowings ("Anglo-French jargon") even in French usage of manufacturing discourse, and finally, the greater tendency for the Francophone engineers to be bilingual and for the Anglophone engineers to be monolingual or not highly proficient in French. Thus the presence of Anglophone monolinguals requires accommodation to their needs in English. Even with the international ascendancy of English within fields such as engineering, tensions characterized variously by resistance, accommodation, or exclusion in bilingual settings become evident. McAll (2003) concludes that in language-intensive work contexts, "language difference" maintains inequalities between groups and that for both immigrant and nonimmigrant populations, access to (official-language) language competence and access to coveted sectors of the labor market are crucial.

Labrie, a French-Canadian sociolinguist, together with his colleagues (e.g., Heller, 2002; Labrie, Belanger, Lozon, & Roy, 2000; Roy, 2000, 2003) in Canada and Europe, has been examining other changes in language and literacy requirements within certain fields of work. In some parts of Canada and in some professions, the two official languages, English and French, may no longer be sufficient for workers, as tourism and other business interactions require proficiency in additional languages such as Spanish, German, and Japanese. This trend is likely to grow stronger as the North American Free Trade Agreement and growing trade relations with other parts of Latin America increase communications with Spanish-speaking countries and as new tourist markets open up (e.g., in Mainland China).

Furthermore, Labrie et al. (2000) report that some bilingual French-Canadian speakers in minority communities in Ontario, an English-dominant province, unlike Quebec, may be comfortable communicating orally in French (their L1) and are encouraged to maintain their French for future jobs. However, their French literacy skills may be inadequate for particular types of work-related communication that now involve e-mail exchanges and other more standardized communication with speakers of other varieties of French from outside those local Francophone communities, or their work-related communication may require more formal registers and greater accuracy in writing than was previously the case.

Much Canadian, American, and European work-related sociolinguistic research is taking place in call centers (see Cameron, 2000; Roy, 2000). In these work settings, employees must learn to respond to e-mail and telephone inquiries from around the world in standardized ways that involve a great deal of repetition, low-pay, and the training, surveillance, evaluation, and enforcement of tightly scripted interaction patterns requiring, for example, a soft, empathetic, and feminine voice quality by females (Cameron, 2000) and an impersonal approach to talking on the phone. These factors are reported to create stress, turnover, and ultimately the devaluation of workers' own communicative abilities, identities, and prior literacies. Based on her ethnographic study in a rural Franco-Ontarian call center, Roy (2003) observed:

> Francophones in the community frequently used French–English code-switching, as well as English terms and French colloquialisms. These vernacular usages were not seen by company management as sufficiently professional to ensure work as a bilingual in the call center; and the meaning of "bilingual" came to be redefined as speaking both languages well, in a standard way. Thus in the name of "professionalism," an ideology of language purity replaced an earlier value placed by community members on the local vernacular. (pp. 269–270)

Yet, the call center provides important work for local community members, both monolingual and bilingual, in an otherwise economically depressed area, and helps maintain the French language and culture because bilinguals are paid more than monolinguals, and obtaining work locally reduces the need to move to larger (English-dominant) centers. In this way, it sets a new, professional standard for bilingualism (particularly for French) that even local native French speakers who are fluent in English often cannot attain, and they are often hired as monolingual English-speakers instead, undermining their bilingual—and especially Francophone—histories, identities, and aspirations.

Therefore, new forms and means of telecommunication in the service industry, coupled with intensive globalization and market pressures, are associated with new forms of oral skills and literacy, new measures of control, and new combinations of languages. Ideologies of competence and politeness, and views of exemplary, standardized, sociolinguistic behavior may clash across cultures that coexist in workplaces (Katz, 2000; Li, 2000; Scollon & Scollon, 1995). For example, Cameron (2002) provides the following example from Hungary:

> Since the end of the communist era there has been an influx of Western business organizations, and controversy has been caused by the insistence of some of these multinationals that customers be addressed (in Hungarian) using the informal, egalitarian styles which is the norm in most Western companies, though this flouts local expectations and well-established rules of Hungarian usage. (p. 81)

In addition to these examples about call center and other workplace ideologies that stress pure, standardized bilingualism, professional language use, or, in some cases, egalitarianism, there have been other related changes in workplaces connected to the ostensible distribution of power and responsibility, in the name of both democratization and efficiency. "Fast capitalism"—which requires flexibility, speed, multitasking, problem solving, information technology, communication skills, and so on—may actually disadvantage workers not previously trained to perform work in settings where responsibilities are increasingly distributed horizontally across workers, rather than vertically or hierarchically among different layers of management (Lankshear & Gee, 1997).

Katz (2000) and Hull (e.g., 1997) have documented some of the English oral and written skills that multilingual immigrant workers require in high-tech Silicon Valley companies in California. They describe culturally challenging expectations or ideologies in workplace discussion sessions, in which employees, in the presence of their co-workers and managers, are expected to volunteer their personal opinions and publicly demonstrate their abilities. According to Katz, to do so might be viewed as culturally inappropriate or boastful in cultures valuing cooperation and solidarity over independence and individual self-expression among workers. Katz reported that in her study, the message conveyed to a very cohesive group of Mexican-American workers was that, to be considered for promotion, you need to "show what you know" and "speak your mind." However, as Tannen (1994) points out, group membership may be threatened when people are singled out for recognition in this way; moreover, boasting has negative connotations in some workplace contexts and cultures, or among certain members of society (e.g., women), who may be socialized early in life *not* to behave in that manner. These factors in Katz's study seemed to conspire against minority women, in particular, taking risks to make open suggestions in English about management practices in the presence of their peers and, thus, they also lost opportunities for praise and validation as a result.

In a related situation, Li (2000) found that multilingual workplace ideologies and socialization are at times contradictory, not only when different norms exist between home and workplace cultures with respect to language and literacy use, but also when native-speaker peers, mentors, or superiors themselves, whom one might otherwise consider sociolinguistic models of target-language and cultural conventions, behave inappropriately, rudely, or inconsistently. Li describes one Chinese immigrant woman who, on one hand, was being coached successfully by her Anglo-American office co-workers in a medical equipment company to assert her right to fairer work conditions, but at the same time was sometimes dealt with rudely and without consideration by the same colleagues. She had to learn how to be assertive yet pragmatically effective in such a way as to not jeopardize her employment or relationships with her co-workers or to either lose face herself or cause others to lose face, which would also make her ongoing situation unpleasant. Therefore, ideologies of workplace sociolinguistic competence often pose dual challenges for workers, beyond just understanding what the target ideologies and practices are: First, the ideologies may conflict with the cultural values and orientations of newcomers, and second, the practices of English-speaking co-workers from whom newcomers might reasonably expect to receive mentoring may themselves be highly problematic and inconsistent. Both of these sources of conflict, in turn, may undermine workers' performance and chances for promotion.

GLOBALIZATION AND ELECTRONIC LITERACIES

Electronic communications have impacted the teaching, learning, and use of English in seemingly all facets of work and life. One ongoing Canadian study (Chase, Macfadyen, Reeder, & Roche, 2002; Reeder, Macfadyen, Roche, & Chase, 2004) is examining cross-cultural, English-mediated, electronic communication for educational and work purposes and the poten-

tial for misunderstandings or pragmatic failure based on discursive differences in the form and content of messages, which may be read as overly
direct, indirect, and so on, depending on the culture (see also Li, 2000).
One aspect of their research focuses on threaded Internet bulletin board
discussions in international and intranational interactions connected with
distance education (e.g., between Canada and Mexico or Europe; and
among Canadians of different ethnolinguistic backgrounds). This work
points to new areas for research, looking at electronic communication between and among native and nonnative speakers of English. Indeed, given
the disparity between the number of native speakers of English and the
much larger number of nonnative but highly proficient speakers of English
who use that language as a medium of instruction/learning and for occupational communication, the new international norm is for electronic communication in English among nonnative users of English.

The potential for the mixing or switching of languages and registers in
multilingual electronic literacies and other forms of communication is also
great, as the studies previously cited illustrated, signifying different stances,
identities, and contextualization cues (Gumperz, 1978). Examining e-mail
use in a multinational corporation in the Netherlands, Nickerson (1999)
observed the following:

> One typical chain of four messages began with a message in English by an
> English-speaking employee at another Dutch division sent to a Dutch em-
> ployee in the same division. This was then forwarded by that Dutch employee
> to another Dutch employee in a different department at the original Dutch
> manager's division with a cover note in English! [emphasis in the original].
> This Dutch employee then forwarded both English messages on to the origi-
> nal Dutch manager, with a cover note in Dutch, and he completed the chain
> of transmissions by forwarding all three messages on to a member of his
> group with a cover note in Dutch. (p. 45)

The ever-expanding use of the Internet for information acquisition and
transfer as well as for education itself has implications (Crystal, 2002). We
read and write differently with a keyboard and screen in front of us and
while multitasking and accessing support materials in various nonpaper
and nonprint textual forms than when we read a textbook or write with paper and pen. We now routinely send attachment files back and forth among
colleagues and coauthors, some of whom may never have met face-to-face,
to compose, edit, and respond to reports in ways that were simply too cum-
bersome before. These texts are highly intertextual, involving bits of text
and voices from different sources. Multiparty report writing and editing is
becoming very common in many workplaces, dictated by the need and
capacity for rapid turn-around time and quick message dissemination. Understanding the different genres required for different oral and written
purposes and audiences, and understanding processes for writing collabor-

atively well, have become paramount. However, new written literacies are not all that is required. Writing about the "technologizing" of workplace discourse in Britain, Fairclough (1992) observes that oral skills are also evolving (see also the previous discussion from Katz, 2000):

> Even within manufacturing, there is a shift away from isolated work on a production line to team work, and workers are seen as needing more complex "communicative skills." One interesting development is that discussions of such skills increasingly highlight abilities in face-to-face interaction, group discussion and decision-making, "listening skills," and so forth—abilities which have previously been seen . . . as general "life skills" rather than vocational skills. (p. 4)

An intriguing example of the new focus on multiple literacies, electronic networks, and team-based education and work appeared in an American *Time Magazine* supplement, *Time Global Business*, in June 2001. The article described a program for executive "global M.B.A. students" enrolled at Duke University in North Carolina, USA. The heavily enriched coursework is described as follows:

> Students and professors meet for three two-week sessions, visiting pairs of industrial and developing economies, such as Germany and the Czech Republic or China and Hong Kong. Students stay in hotels, tour factories, get face time with CEOs and attend lectures on topics like global finance. Back at their jobs, they are assigned to teams with members stationed around the world [a third of the class are foreign nationals], in part to simulate the pressures of operating across time zones. Teams use instant messaging and online forums to work on case studies. They develop a PowerPoint presentation—say, accessing Brazil's economic prospects—and post their results online. Professors distribute CD-ROMs of lectures and leave assignments on a school website. Says [a student and Pfizer manager], "You learn to resolve conflicts without being in a physical room together. It's like the real world." (p. G9)

The "real world" described here represents the new manner in which both work and studies are being conducted, at least in the field of international business. It is not clear, however, to what extent lower proficiency nonnative English speakers, native speakers, or instructors are being prepared for these new forms of interaction in more traditional undergraduate degree programs.

CONCLUSION

Educators' approaches to language and literacy education must reflect some of the new realities and priorities associated with English-mediated, multilingual, and multimodal communication at work locally and in the wider community. We must also base these approaches on situated research, not just on static target-language texts and other materials workers or students are expected to use. It is important to understand the social practices that accompany the texts and not just their linguistic components. For intermediate to advanced level students, superficial task-based teaching focusing on low-level conversational skills or focussed on grammar and writing exclusively probably will not serve the long-term needs of the future multilingual, highly intercultural "knowledge worker" well (Wallace, 2002). Instead, this type of teaching must be supplemented with more sustained, and more cognitively and sociolinguistically demanding, content-based activities or projects that involve various kinds of literacies, including electronic literacies (depending on the course context), and various kinds of collaboration (e.g., Warschauer, 2000).

Apart from the issues of register, face-to-face versus online/remote communication, and other pragmatic issues in workplace communication (Li, 2000; Roberts et al., 1992), there is growing realization that academic and professional discourses are not generic but are highly context-specific. Education preparing people for those dominant discourses must therefore expose students to the specific genres that fulfill particular communicative functions within particular settings. At the same time as expanding students' linguistic and discursive repertoires, there must be attempts to understand and validate their own languages, cultures, and preferred modes of communication, to the extent possible. The genre-based approach to academic and professional discourse, especially in literacy education, has had a long history in Australia, the United Kingdom, and the United States, and is often associated with Australian Systemic Functional Linguistics and more recently with corpus linguistics (e.g., Bargiela-Chiappini & Nickerson, 1999; Dias, Freedman, Medway, & Pare, 1999; Johns, 1997; Mercer & Swann, 1996). As illustrated in Cooper's (1998) study, previously mentioned, researchers need to examine school- or university-to-work transitions, in terms of the social and linguistic practices in writing in particular, in learning to compose the kinds of texts required across a range of fields. We must also try to increase access to English for immigrant and international learners who may need it for academic and occupational advancement as well as for day-to-day survival.

In conclusion, language educators must become better informed about the current language, literacy, and communication demands in workplaces in order to prepare students and new workers to be more proficient, flexible, and confident users of language and other modes of communication. Furthermore, we must prepare citizens with the capacity not only to participate but also to effect social change in highly intercultural, interconnected, and multilingual societies.

As Heller (2002) reminds us, there are many "sites of struggle" when communities are confronted with the pressures of globalization, the commodification of languages (e.g., what constitutes "good French" or "good English" or "bilingualism"), and new understandings of what might constitute authentic and legitimate competencies and identities. There is, therefore, a concomitant need to provide advocacy for people's opportunities to access and learn the new skills they may need for their personal advancement and also to understand their own vernacular languages, indigenous cultures, and ways of knowing.

REFERENCES

Bargiela-Chiappini, F., & Nickerson, C. (Eds.). (1999). *Writing business: Genres, media and discourses.* Harlow, UK: Longman/Pearson.

Béland, P. (1991). *L'usage du français au travail, situation et tendances* [The use of French at work: Situation and trends]. Québec: Conseil de la langue française.

Bell, J. S. (2000). Literacy challenges for language learners in job-training programs. *Canadian Modern Language Review, 57,* 173–200.

Brindley, G., Baynham, M., Burns, A., Hammond, J., McKenna, R., & Thurstun, J. (1996). *An integrated research strategy for adult ESL, literacy and numeracy.* Sydney: Macquarie University.

Brindley, G., Curtis, A., Davidson, F., Duff, P., Scott, S., & Tucker, G. R. (2000). *A research agenda for TESOL.* Available: http://www.tesol.org/s_tesol/seccs.asp?CID=236&DID=1708

Cameron, D. (2000). *Good to talk? Living and working in a communication culture.* Thousand Oaks, CA: Sage.

Cameron, D. (2002). Globalization and the teaching of "communication skills." In D. Block & D. Cameron (Eds.), *Globalization and language teaching* (pp. 67–82). London: Routledge.

Center for Applied Linguistics. (1998). *Research agenda for adult ESL.* Washington, DC: Author. Available: http://www.cal.org/ncle/agenda/adult.html

Chase, M., Macfadyen, L., Reeder, K., & Roche, J. (2002). Intercultural challenges in networked learning: Hard technologies meet soft skills. *First Monday, 7*(8). Available: http://firstmonday.org/issues/issue7_8/chase/index.html

Cleghorn, A., & Rollnick, M. (2002). The role of English in individual and societal development: A view from African classrooms. *TESOL Quarterly, 36,* 347–372.

Cohen, R. (1998, December 6). Berlin Journal; Berlin has a word for it's ambitions: English. *New York Times,* Final edition, Section 1, p. 1, column 4.

Cooper, A. (1998). Mind the gap! An ethnographic approach to cross-cultural workplace communication research. In M. Byram & M. Fleming (Eds.), *Language learning in intercultural perspective: Approaches through drama and ethnography* (pp. 119–142). Cambridge: Cambridge University Press.

Council of Europe. (2001). *Common European framework of reference for languages: Learning, teaching, assessment.* Cambridge: Cambridge University Press. Retrieved Dec. 31, 2003, from http://culture2.coe.int/portfolio/documents/0521803136txt.pdf

Cremer, R. D., & Willes, M. J. (1994). Overcoming language barriers of international trade: A text-based study of the language of deals. *Journal of Asia Pacific Communication, 15,* 3.

Crystal, D. (1997). *English as a global language.* Cambridge: Cambridge University Press.

Crystal, D. (2002). *Language and the Internet.* Cambridge: Cambridge University Press.

Dias, P., Freedman, A., Medway, P., & Pare, A. (1999). *Worlds apart: Acting and writing in academic and workplace contexts.* Mahwah, NJ: Lawrence Erlbaum Associates.

Duff, P. (1993). *Changing times, changing minds: Language socialization in Hungarian-English schools.* Unpublished doctoral dissertation, University of California, Los Angeles.

Duff, P. (1995). An ethnography of communication in immersion classrooms in Hungary. *TESOL Quarterly, 29,* 505–537.

Duff, P. (2002). Pop culture and ESL students: Intertextuality, identity, and participation in classroom discussions. *Journal of Adolescent and Adult Literacy, 45,* 482–487.

Duff, P. (in press). Foreign language policy, research, and practice: A Western perspective. In Y. Zhao, R. Floden, & Q. Dong (Eds.), *Cross-cultural perspectives on education reform: The Asian-Pacific experience.* Beijing: Beijing Normal University Press.

Duff, P., & Bailey, K. (2001). Identifying research priorities: Themes and directions for the TESOL International Research Foundation. *TESOL Quarterly, 35,* 595–616.

Duff, P., & Labrie, N. (Eds.). (2000). *Languages and Work.* Special Issue of the *Canadian Modern Language Review, 57,* 1.

Duff, P., Wong, P., & Early, M. (2000). Learning language for work and life: The linguistic socialization of immigrant Canadians seeking careers in healthcare. *Canadian Modern Language Review, 57,* 9–57.

Fairclough, N. (1992). Introduction. In N. Fairclough (Ed.), *Critical language awareness* (pp. 1–29). London: Longman.

Garay, M. S., & Bernhardt, S. A. (Eds.). (1998). *Expanding literacies: English teaching and the new workplace.* Albany, NY: State University of New York Press.

Gee, J. P., Hull, G., & Lankshear, C. (1996). *The new work order: Behind the language of the new capitalism.* Boulder, CO: Westview Press.

Goldstein, T. (1997). *Two languages at work: Bilingual life on the production floor.* New York: Mouton de Gruyter.

Goodman, S. (1996). Market forces speak English. In S. Goodman & D. Graddol (Eds.), *Redesigning English: New texts, new identities* (pp. 141–164). London: Routledge.

Graddol, D. (1996). Global English, global culture? In S. Goodman & D. Graddol (Eds.), *Redesigning English: New texts, new identities* (pp. 181–217). New York: Routledge.

Gumperz, J. (1978). The conversational analysis of interethnic communication. In E. L. Ross (Ed.), *Interethnic communication* (pp. 14–31). Athens, GA: Georgia University Press.

Heller, M. (2002). Globalization and the commodification of bilingualism in Canada. In D. Block & D. Cameron (Eds.), *Globalization and language teaching* (pp. 47–63). London: Routledge.

Hornberger, N. (Ed.). (2003). *Continua of biliteracy: An ecological framework for educational policy, research, and practice in multilingual settings.* Clevedon, UK: Multilingual Matters.

Hull, G. (Ed.). (1997). *Changing work, changing workers: Critical perspectives on language, literacy, and skills.* Albany, NY: State University of New York Press.

Johns, A. M. (1997). *Text, role, and context: Developing academic literacies.* New York: Cambridge University Press.

Katz, M.-L. (2000). Workplace language teaching and the intercultural construction of ideologies of competence. *Canadian Modern Language Review, 57,* 144–172.

Kleifgen, J. (2001). Assembling talk: Social alignments in the workplace. *Research on Language and Social Interaction, 34,* 279–308.

Labrie, N., Belanger, N., Lozon, R., & Roy, S. (2000). Mondialisation et exploitation des ressources linguistiques: les défis des communautés francophones de l'Ontario [Globalization and the exploitation of linguistic resources: The challenges for Francophone communities in Ontario]. *Canadian Modern Language Review, 57,* 88–117.

Lankshear, C., & Gee, J. P. (1997). Language, literacy and the new work order. In C. Lankshear (Ed.), *Changing literacies* (pp. 83–102). Buckingham: Open University Press.

Li, D. (2000). The pragmatics of making requests in the L2 workplace: A case study of language socialization. *Canadian Modern Language Review, 57,* 58–87.

McAll, C. (2003). Language dynamics in the bi- and multi-lingual workplace. In R. Bayley & S. Schecter (Eds.), *Language socialization in bilingual and multilingual societies* (pp. 235–250). Clevedon, UK: Multilingual Matters.

Mercer, N. (1996). English at work. In J. Maybin & N. Mercer (Eds.), *Using English: From conversation to canon* (pp. 84–107). London: Routledge.

Mercer, N., & Swann, J. (Eds.). (1996). *Learning English: Development and diversity.* London: Routledge.

National Clearinghouse for ESL Literacy Education at the Center for Applied Linguistics (1998). *Research agenda for adult ESL.* Washington, DC: Center for Applied Linguistics.

Nickerson, C. (1999). The use of English in electronic mail in a multinational corporation. In F. Bargiela-Chiappini & C. Nickerson (Eds.), *Writing business: Genres, media and discourses* (pp. 35–56). Harlow, UK: Longman/Pearson.

Nunan, D. (2001). English as a global language. In P. Duff & K. Bailey (Eds.), Identifying research priorities: Themes and directions for the TESOL International Research Foundation. *TESOL Quarterly, 35,* 605–606.

Nunan, D. (2002, April). *English as a global language: Counting the cost.* Featured plenary presentation, TESOL, Salt Lake City.

Nunan, D. (2003).The impact of English as a global language on educational policies and practices in the Asia–Pacific region. *TESOL Quarterly, 37,* 589–613.

Pennycook, A. (1994). *The cultural politics of English as an international language.* London: Longman.

Reeder, K., Macfadyen, L., Roche, J., & Chase, M. (2004). Negotiating cultures in cyberspace: Participation patterns and problematics. *Language Learning & Technology, 8*(2), 88–105.

Robbins, K. (1996). The new spaces of global media. In S. Goodman & D. Graddol (Eds.), *Redesigning English: New texts, new identities* (pp. 225–228). New York: Routledge.

Roberts, C., Davies, E., & Jupp, T. (1992). *Language and discrimination: A study of communication in multi-ethnic workplaces.* New York: Longman.

Roy, S. (2000). La normalisation linguistique dans une entreprise: le mot d'ordre mondial [Linguistic standardization in a company: Global issues]. *Canadian Modern Language Review, 57,* 118–144.

Roy, S. (2003). Bilingualism and standardization in a Canadian call center: Challenges for a linguistic minority community. In R. Bayley & S. Schecter (Eds.), *Language socialization in bilingual and multilingual societies* (pp. 269–285). Clevedon, UK: Multilingual Matters.

Scollon, R., & Scollon, S. (1995). *Intercultural communication: A discourse approach.* Malden, MA: Blackwell.

Senge, P. M. (1990). *The fifth discipline: The art and practice of the learning organization.* New York: Currency Doubleday.

Tannen, D. (1994). *Talk from 9 to 5: How women's and men's conversational styles affect who gets heard, who gets credit, and what gets done at work.* New Haven: Yale University Press.

Taylor, M. (Ed.). (1997). *Workplace education: The changing landscape.* Toronto: Culture Concepts.

Tremblay, L. (1993). L'utilisation du langage et des langues dans une entreprise du secteur biomédical [The use of language(s) in a company in the biomedical sector]. In C. McAll (Ed.), *L'utilisation du langage et des langues dans quatre milieux de travail á Montréal* (pp. 1–23). Montréal: Research report submitted to the Office de la langue française, Gouvernnment du Québec.

Tucker, G. R. (2001). Age of beginning instruction. In P. Duff & K. Bailey (Eds.), Identifying research priorities: Themes and directions for the TESOL International Research Foundation. *TESOL Quarterly, 35,* 597–598.

Vandermeeren, S. (1999). English as a lingua franca in written corporate communication: Findings from a European survey. In F. Bargiela-Chiappini & C. Nickerson (Eds.), *Writing business: Genres, media and discourses* (pp. 273–291). Harlow, UK: Longman/Pearson.

Wallace, C. (2002). Local literacies and global literacy. In D. Block & D. Cameron (Eds.), *Globalization and language teaching* (pp. 101–114). London: Routledge.

Warschauer, M. (2000). The changing global economy and the future of English teaching. *TESOL Quarterly, 34,* 511–535.

Wong, F. P., Duff, P., & Early, M. (2001). The impact of language and skills training on immigrants' lives. *TESOL Canada Journal, 18*(2), 1–31.

Chapter 18

Connecting the Local and the Global: A Pedagogy of Not-Literacy

Elsa Auerbach
University of Massachusetts at Boston

> *The most profound, far-reaching and significant impact of literacy on people's lives is its empowering potential. To be literate is to become liberated from the constraints of dependency. To be literate is to gain a voice and to participate meaningfully and assertively in decisions that affect people's lives. To be literate is to become politically conscious and critically aware and to demystify social reality. . . . Literacy helps people to become self-reliant and resist exploitation and oppression. Literacy provides access to written knowledge and knowledge is power.*
>
> —"International Task Force on Literacy Newsletter,"
> as cited in James, 1990, p. 16

This statement epitomizes the claims made for the empowering potential of literacy, claims that have become a mantra for many justice-minded literacy educators. My hope is that the quote makes you a little uncomfortable.

A great deal has been written about the flaws of the "literacy myth"—the myth that literacy is the key to economic and cognitive development (Graff, 1979). I argue that this discourse of empowerment may, likewise, contribute to a different version of the literacy myth—one in which literacy is seen as the motor force for social change. My premise is that, just as it's not literacy that leads to cognitive or economic development, it's not literacy per se that leads to social change or community empowerment. Whatever transformative power it may have comes from how it is contextualized and placed in service of broader struggles. Thus, in considering the role of literacies in schools, families, and communities, it is important to guard against a remystification of literacies. This means being quite explicit about what literacy can do and what it can't do, about how we contextualize our work and how we position ourselves as researchers, educators, practitioners, and activists.

The line of argument that subordinates literacy education to ongoing sociopolitical struggles is entirely common sense for people who are not literacy professionals—for social change activists and community organizers. For example, in the opening speech at a literacy conference in Cape Town, Asmal (2001), a long-time antiapartheid activist and the current Minister of Education in South Africa, interrogated the claim that literacy yields empowerment. He argued that, on the contrary, text is often used as an instrument of separation, alienation, and oppression. To the extent that literacy is elevated above orality and the knowledge of ordinary people, it can become disempowering. It's only when knowledge is not limited to the knowledge constructed through text that people will gain more control over their lives. Asmal's point is that we have to be careful not to privilege literacy as the key to liberation. To posit that literacy is the source of knowledge and that knowledge leads to power is not only misleading, but, in fact, can become justification for a new apartheid, one in which *literacy* rather than *race* is the fault line for segregation.

Like Asmal, James, a radical educator and activist in the San Francisco bay area who works with youth on health, employment, drug prevention, and other social issues, argues that the notion that literacy is empowering is naïve and counterproductive. In an article entitled "Demystifying Literacy," from which I drew the opening quote, James (1990) says:

> Many literacy educators and programs today would hope their programs were indeed transformative. The new interest [in literacy for transformation] has also generated an inclination to mystify literacy, to ascribe to it catalytic properties far beyond its actual utility. It has captured the imaginations of many activists and educators for whom it represents a panacea for social and political inequities. (p. 15)

He goes on to say that "Literacy alone rarely guarantees privilege, access, or political leverage. When practitioners naively accept this idea, they sabotage their credibility with their students, who, in many cases, have an ability to recognize such idealism and know when to reject it" (James, 1990, p. 15). The problem with ascribing such power to literacy, according to James, is that it "undermines the importance of the context itself" (1990, p. 18).

Within literacy studies, context has, of course, come to take on enormous significance. The New Literacy Studies paradigm replaces the focus on individual mental processes of the cognitive tradition with a focus on sociocultural contextual factors in literacy acquisition and usage (Street, 1984). Findings from this research suggest that people acquire language and literacy by being informally socialized into the practices and values of contexts in which they are immersed. As such, literacy research has shifted beyond school settings to include domains such as homes, communities, workplaces, and religious institutions, examining the multiplicity of literacies enacted in these domains. A central tenet of this paradigm is the view that recognizing, valuing, and including local ways of knowing, literacy practices, languages, and cultural knowledge shifts the balance of power promoted by traditional schooling.

James (1990) would argue that this stance continues to frame literacy (or "illiteracy," as he says) as a social or educational problem, rather than as a symptom of larger political contradictions. In this analysis, the antidote to problems of inequity and oppression is organizing for change through concerted political action, rather than educational interventions per se. This is the lesson of the civil rights movement; it is the lesson of the struggle in South Africa; it is the lesson of the labor movement; it is the lesson of the struggles of First Nation peoples. In each of these movements, literacy education has played a role—as a vehicle or context for analysis—but rarely as the structural framework out of which the struggles emanated. What James (1990) is calling for is not educational activity with "relevant" content, but, as he says, political processes with an educational character (p. 18). It is the context in which literacy education takes place and the struggles in which it is embedded that are the forces for change, not literacy itself.

My argument is that social justice-minded literacy educators need to define "context" not just as situational or institutional domain in the New Literacy Studies sense, but also in broad geopolitical terms. In these times, the forces of globalization that shape families, communities, and school must be considered in any analysis of literacy. The primary reality that contextualizes our work is, on one hand, globalization—or as many have called it, global economic apartheid—and on the other hand, resistance to globalization. These two contradictory forces have been called, respectively, *globalization from above* and *globalization from below* (Brecher, Costello, & Smith, 2000). The former consists of transnational forces that are consolidating power and wealth in the hands of the few while increasing the impoverishment of the many. The latter refers to the widespread emergence of local organizations challenging the forces of transnationalism and neoliberalism.

Although there has been considerable discussion about globalization within literacy circles, most of it has focused on the impact of globalization on literacies and how literacy education needs to accommodate these changes. There seem to be two tendencies within this discussion. On one hand there are those who focus on the study of multiple, local literacies and the ways in which globalization threatens local identities, discourses, and literacies (Barton & Hamilton, 1998). On the other are those who focus on the ways in which new technologies have profoundly changed communication within and between regions, requiring new attention to multimodalities, multimedia, critical media literacy, the discourses of power, and so on (New London Group, 1996). Often the local and the global are framed as contradictory: Some argue the need to protect the local and others argue the need to provide access to the global. This debate is particularly sharp within TESOL education circles, where it plays itself out around the question of English as a global language. Warschauer (2000) says that the overriding contradiction posed by globalization is the contradiction between the power of global forces and the struggle for local identities.

I think this debate misses the mark on two counts. First, it focuses too much on the changing nature of literacies at the expense of understanding the changing nature of the economic and political context of learners' lives. Second, it constructs a false contradiction between the global and the local. I want to turn the question of how globalization shapes literacy education on its head and ask instead: How can literacy education contribute to shaping and resisting the dominant forces of globalization? I propose aligning our work with the multitude of local organizations and movements around the world that are challenging globalization from above, as such linking the local with the global. This argument necessitates first, an understanding of geopolitical economic forces that contextualize literacies in families, communities, and schools, and second, an understanding of the global movement to resist them.

GLOBALIZATION FROM ABOVE

It is impossible to fully describe the mechanisms of globalization from above here, but a brief overview can give a sense of the scope and power of this new world order. According to Brecher et al. (2000), 51 of the 100 largest economies in the world are corporations, not countries; $1.5 trillion flows *daily* across international borders. Other features of globalization from above include:

- Global assembly lines linking the North and South: sweatshops, child labor, and the maquilladora system.
- Changing structures of work: recommodification of labor; flexible workforce.
- Global markets for buying/selling of goods, labor, and services.

- Transnational finance, financial institutions (IMF, WTO, World Bank) that supercede national governments.
- Corporate restructuring: centralization of control, transnational mergers.
- New technologies.
- Privatization, deregulation.
- Trade: tariff agreements, open markets, NAFTA.
- Neoimperialism: economic control taken out of the control of poor countries; structural adjustment, et cetera.
- Accelerating migration.
- Militarization.
- Dismantling of welfare.

Brecher et al. (2000) characterize the impact of this system as follows:

- Increased impoverishment and inequality: concentration of wealth, growth of poverty.
- Global ecological and environmental damage.
- Economic volatility.
- Permeability of borders/migration cycles.
- Decimation of human rights.

GLOBALIZATION FROM BELOW

In recent years, organizations have begun emerging all over the world in social locations that are marginal to dominant power centers, in order to challenge the negative impacts of globalization from above. While engaging in local struggles, they are at the same time forming global alliances that constitute a new transnational resistance movement, a movement that has come to be called the "globalization from below movement" (Brecher et al., 2000). This movement recognizes the inevitability (and potential benefits) of a globalized world, but aims to shape globalization in the interests of the poor. It recognizes, too, that the combined force of the local movements is greater than the sum of individual forces, invoking what has come to be called the "Lilliput strategy" because, just as the tiny Lilliputians captured the giant Gulliver by tying him up with hundreds of threads, there are hundreds of local struggles banding together to take on the globalization from above movement.

As such, the local struggles are seen to be different facets of a broader movement based on solidarity that crosses boundaries of nations, identities, and narrow interests. These networks of local movements, with diverse interests and geographically diverse starting points, have come together under the slogan "Another world is possible;" they have formed the World Social Forum with global meetings like those in Porto Alegre, Brazil, as well as organizing demonstrations in opposition to IMF, G-8, and World Bank meetings such as those in Seattle, Davos, and Calgary (see, for example, http://www.portoalegre2003.org/publique/index02I.htm). This movement is characterized by forms of political and social action that include:

- Organizing against runaway plants.
- Organizing against child labor.
- Union organizing.
- Protection of indigenous peoples/cultures and languages.
- Resistance to engineered food.
- Environmentalist movements.
- Debt cancellation campaigns.
- Antiglobal sweatshop campaigns (Nike, Gap).
- Human rights campaigns.
- Health, medication costs, HIV/AIDS campaigns.
- Struggles for women's rights, reproductive rights, against welfare "reform."

The strength of this movement has become evident through its recent focus on opposing war in Iraq. In a recent article, Danaher and Mark (2003) say:

> The huge worldwide peace marches in mid-February 2003 were of historic importance. For years progressive activists have trumpeted the promise of "grassroots globalization"—an alternative to the current corporate-led globalization. The planetary peace rallies showed the force of such a people's globalization. They proved that grassroots globalization is getting real.

They go on to say, "The currents of discontent are rising into a wave of citizen activism with the potential to re-order international relations and reinvigorate efforts for human rights and democracy. As *The New York Times* put it: 'There may still be two superpowers on the planet: the United States and world public opinion'" (Danaher & Mark, 2003). As I am writing this on the eve of Bush's attack on Iraq (March 15, 2003), the contradictions between the two forms of globalization are becoming sharper by the minute. The international dialogue about what kind of a world we want is happening in every home, community, and school.

IMPLICATIONS FOR LITERACY

What does all this mean for literacy studies? At this moment, whether or not we want a world that is controlled by the forces of greed or a world that protects democracy is the single question contextualizing all of our work. It seems abundantly clear that major global forces, not individual competence, shape life possibilities, and that to promote new multimodal literacies as the key to participation in the globalized world risks becoming a new version of the literacy myth. At the same time, this analysis challenges the view that preserving local literacies will provide protection, access, or power in the face of the onslaught of global apartheid. Rather than positioning literacy education as the key to social change, as so many critical literacy educators (myself included) have done, this analysis suggests that change is possible, not when individuals improve their skills or expand their repertoire of practices, but when they join with others in challenging specific conditions and forces that are undermining their communities.

My argument is that an understanding of global forces necessitates recontextualizing the work of critical literacy educators in service of the grassroots globalization movement. This means framing the acquisition and use of local and globalized literacies as part of political projects that challenge oppression. As James (1990) says, it means not just positioning literacy as educational activity with "relevant" content, but linking it to political processes with an educational character. As such, it is a "pedagogy of not-literacy" that recognizes that the struggles in which literacy education is embedded (as opposed to literacy itself) are the forces for change. The focus shifts from individual literacy acquisition to literacy in service of furthering struggles informed by the "think globally, act locally" ideology. As such, its content is determined by local conditions, and its structural/institutional location may not be educational at all. It entails collaboration with community organizations and participants, where they have a lead role in shaping the pedagogy.

This argument is really old news in many countries of the two-thirds world—just not the countries of the "North." Martin and Rahman (2001) write about the lessons that we in the North can learn from literacy work in Bangladesh, saying, "Learning is a process of political struggle, and education is an instrument to be used in this struggle . . ." (p. 125). They argue in favor of what they call "really useful literacy," which entails, among other things:

- acquiring practical knowledge to help people act on their world,
- harnessing learning to a social purpose,
- splicing the people into sustainable development,

- enabling people to take power,
- ensuring democratic control over the curriculum and the development of literacy materials,
- addressing gender inequities, and
- respecting but also trusting the people. (pp. 122–125)

They conclude by saying:

> One of the political lessons of globalization is that the local and specific struggles of ordinary people all over the world can become part of the wider, international struggle for democracy, social justice and equality. As we all, in our different ways, live out the meaning of 'globalization from above', the question is: how can we make our work part of an alternative and deeply subversive 'globalization from below' . . . ? (Martin & Rahman, 2001, p. 130)

There are already many forms of literacy education with social change and social justice agendas. What is somewhat different, I believe, about the notion proposed here is that its driving force is not literacy education per se, but rather a political project that connects the local and the global. Given the realities of policy mandates regarding literacy education, the possibilities for a social justice agenda within officially sanctioned (and funded) adult education programs seems to be diminishing. Existing adult education settings have less and less space to incorporate change-oriented curricula. In the United States, at least, the right-wing agenda that is waging war on Iraq is also waging war on all the social programs that support families, communities, and schools. Funding for adult and family literacy is both diminishing and being tied to a neoconservative agenda. In fact, fighting for the very existence of democratic education is precisely one of the facets of the grassroots globalization movement.

DIVERSIFYING CONTEXTS FOR LITERACY EDUCATION

What this analysis of geopolitical forces suggests is a vision and a set of principles that may shift the emphasis and the location of the work of social change-minded literacy educators. It is a vision in which sites of struggle become sites of learning. This entails making linkages with existing grassroots organizations—with women's centers and union halls, with those struggling for tenants rights, access to health care, or against environmental pollution and domestic violence. It entails molding instruction in service of analysis, skills, practices, and discourses that enable people to participate in organizing for change as part of a global network. In addition to existing grassroots organizations, other structural locations are potential sites for integrating literacy education with local struggles. For example, community education centers could become spaces where community members identify and investigate issues, and then learn skills that will help them address the issues, as well as connecting with other organizations. Collaborations or partnerships between organizations (for example, educational institutions and community groups) can also become spaces for this kind of work. And finally, of course, the traditional language or literacy classrooms can become contexts in which to explore local issues as a means to connect to broader community/global struggles.

The seeds of this model have already been planted. In domains other than literacy, popular education and participatory action research approaches have been integrated into labor organizing drives and women's organizations (e.g., Louie & Burnham, 2000; Barndt, 1999; Lee, Krause, & Goetchius, 2003); community education centers have taken up local issues (e.g., Kirkwood & Kirkwood, 1989) and taught skills for democratic participation; collaborations and partnerships between literacy providers and community groups have shifted their focus from literacy to community action (e.g., Auerbach, 2002); and adult education classes have led to community organizing initiatives (e.g., Nash, 1999). Although few of these endeavors situate literacy education squarely within grassroots struggles, they provide evidence of the potential of that direction. The remainder of the chapter focuses on examples of projects that have planted the seeds for a model based on the ideology that "another world is possible."

Social Change Organizations or Movements

One organization that integrates literacy education as a tool in service of social change is the Right Question Project (RQP) in Boston (http://www.rightquestion.org/). RQP teaches community members to research power dynamics in a variety of contexts so that they can then ask "the right questions" in advocating for their children, dealing with a range of institutions, and challenging inequitable policies. Their strategy includes teaching people to formulate good questions and to target key decisions of public institutions. They say:

> Our strategy is so powerful because it directly helps ordinary citizens in their encounters with the various outposts of government. We believe this is the level at which people can best begin to help themselves, and in the process create new "pockets of democracy" or what we call Microdemocracy. This can then help all of us by building a stronger, more inclusive and connected democracy. (http://www.rightquestion.org/)

The RQP educational strategy has been used in struggles relating to citizen participation and economic development, health care and social services, public education, adult education, and parent involvement.

Community Education Centers

The Adult Learning Project (ALP) in the Gorgie/Dalry community of Edinburgh, Scotland exemplifies a community center whose goal is to connect local struggles with educational projects (Kirkwood & Kirkwood, 1989). The Freire-inspired model of this center, which has been in existence since the early 1970s, entails intensive investigation of community issues (sometimes taking up to 2 years), codifying community issues through graphic representations, discussion of codification with community participants, development of curricula around themes identified, learning programmes, and action outcomes. One issue that emerged in recent years centered on plans for the construction of a superstore/car park on community land. Through an educational program that investigated land use regulations, and, interestingly, regulations regarding endangered plants, the community developed strategies for confronting and ultimately stopping the construction. According to a pamphlet produced for the Gorgie/Dalry Community Council, the local Community Council fought against the development at public hearings and successfully prevented the construction of the car park based on arguments related to the importance of open space and biodiversity (Saville, 2002). They identified a rare species of moss on the community land that "played an important role in safeguarding the Park from development" (p. 4). The space became a community park. Based on recent investigations of community issues, ALP is now developing programs to address issues related to racism and "fear of the other," with particular attention to how globalization is impacting the Gorgie/Dalry community.

Another example of community education in service of social change comes from Milwaukee, Wisconsin. Baez and Mack (1996) write about parents studying education law as they work to develop community control in schools, neighbors learning research methods so they can document pollution caused by the waste products of a closed factory; and community members learning script writing and video production so they can share their concerns and redefine the community to a wider audience (p. 42). Other possibilities they envision include adults working with teenagers in projects such as street theater that serve as an alternative to street life, and participants developing the writing and computer skills necessary produce a community newspaper, and learning public speaking skills so they can participate in PTA, city council, and school board meetings.

Collaborations and Partnerships

Additional data supporting the notion of literacy education in service of community action comes from a collection of case studies of community partnerships which I edited (Auerbach, 2002). The projects described in the book were located all over the English-speaking world including the Nunavut province in Canada's far north, South Africa, London, England, New Zealand, and the United States. Beyond geographic diversity, the projects reflected age diversity (elder-, youth-, and early-childhood-focused projects), gender diversity (projects for women only, men only, and mixed gender groups), linguistic diversity (mixed language vs. single language projects) and diversity of national origin (single nationality, multiple nationalities, and, in one case, mixed American and immigrant groups). Some projects were home-based, others community-based, and still others school-based. As the chapters started coming in, I realized that although they reflected this incredible diversity, there were some striking common recurring themes so I decided to look at them as "data" and to analyze them in terms of factors contributing to productive partnerships and strategies for constructing them. A few of the key findings from this analysis are relevant to the argument of this chapter.

One of the most important "lessons" of the partnerships was that, although many of them were set up as ESL or literacy projects, the participants wanted opportunities to become more active and proactive in community life. The result was that many partnerships took the form not of classroom or school-related programs, but rather, much like Baez and Mack (1996), of programs focusing on community enterprises, computer education, addressing community problems, writing about community problems, and, in some cases, recreation. English and literacy acquisition were by-products of these initiatives rather than being their primary focus.

The authors repeatedly stressed the importance of contextual factors in designing partnerships. These factors range from the broad political climate, to economic factors, to social and logistical ones. Not surprisingly, the two chapters from South Africa addressed the role of the political context most explicitly (Mashishi, 2002; Schofield, 2002). Both described the legacy of apartheid in shaping the culture of schooling and argued that it is impossible to conceive of educational change without embedding it in community change. Both were structured to promote the democratic participation of parents who had, under apartheid, been denied any voice or role in either school or community development. In one community, global economic shifts, including the shift toward high technology and the deskilling of much of the workforce, resulted in community members being unprepared to meet labor market demands, rising unemployment, and "unprecedented social dislocation" (Schofield, 2002, p. 161). The understanding that educational problems originated outside the education system led to a strategy for integrating school and community reconstruction through a wide range of economic development projects linked to schools. Parents and community members decided to set up a vegetable cooperative, a day-care business, computer training facilities, training programs for ceramics, bricklaying, and metalwork, and a community park. The vegetable garden was a response to malnutrition and poverty and, as one parent said, "It impacts on learning because a hungry child cannot think. . . . So our garden helps learning" (Schofield, 2002, p. 166). A day-care center was set up by community women who addressed school attendance problems and at the same time shifted traditional gendered economic roles within the community.

In a project in El Paso set up through Even Start funding, participants learned to analyze political decisions that affected them, resulting in the parents taking action to challenge a decision made by the housing authorities (Huerta-Macias, 2002). Projects in Chicago (Adams & Hurtig, 2002) and Oregon (Keis, 2002) used writing and literature workshops to critically analyze conditions of their lives. One thing that I found interesting in these projects was that often the negative political climate (which devalued parents, their culture, their language, and their knowledge) seemed to have made the work of the partnerships even more powerful: Precisely because participants faced these forms of oppression on a daily basis, the projects took on meaning as a positive force for change.

One theme that emerged over and over again was the theme of participant "ownership" of collaborations: Partnerships really began to flourish when there was a shift from outsider to insider control. There were four interrelated factors that promoted "ownership:" (a) involving community members in planning; (b) ensuring nonhierarchical relations between partners; (c) staffing the project with people from the learners' linguistic and cultural backgrounds; and (d) promoting leadership of community members. Partnerships that were unilaterally initiated by dominant institutions (universities or service agencies) based on their "expert" perception of community needs often met community resistance (usually in the form of nonparticipation). Simply put, nobody came. On the other hand, projects that originated in the communities themselves or that involved communities in planning from the beginning did not encounter these difficulties. As Elmi, Folarin, Moalin, and Rees (2002) argued, people won't participate if someone else tells them what they need or should do. This finding can be seen as a metaphor for the overarching struggle between the dominant forces of globalization and the grassroots forces.

Another key factor in many of the projects was letting go of the plan. In fact, many of the authors attribute the success of their partnerships precisely to the ways they deviated from the original proposal. As the professionals began to listen to community members, they realized that the goals they had established did not reflect community realities and aspirations. Conventional educational interventions are often designed by experts who decide what the "target" groups need, how it is to be "delivered" and, these days, what the outcomes will be. But most of the partnerships in the book attributed their success, at least in part, to the fact that what happened was unexpected, unplanned, and unpredictable, or, as Schofield says, "wild" (2002, p. 166). He argues that the extent to which program coordinators or initiators are willing to let go of control and genuinely share decision making with community participants often determines the viability of the partnership. The book is full of examples of this process. In London, England, the project was initially designed as a series of courses for Somali women, but when the women didn't participate, it became evident that the adults could only be reached through working with children (Elmi et al., 2002). The Somali staff then set up a football club for the youth and a number of other strands that did eventually involve the adults, one of which was a "men's project" motivated by high unemployment among men and their resulting sense of dislocation. Likewise, a number of the projects that provided concrete paths for leadership development helped to situate control in community hands in many of the projects.

As a corollary to this, many of the authors agreed that partnerships should build on or link with preexisting community organizations rather than create new organizations that would compete with those already in place. The Nunavut project, for example, stressed the importance of connecting community initiatives with each other and filling gaps, rather than duplicating or adding new entities (Crockatt & Smythe, 2002). The effect of this strategy is to strengthen organizations that already have histories and ties in the community, rather than to draw resources away from them. These factors were important not only in terms of the planning and administration of the project, but also in terms of their pedagogical components. Recurring themes in this regard were: (a) hiring staff who are tied to the participants' communities and who speak the learners' language/s; (b) valuing and inviting use of learners' first languages even in ESL projects (in some cases, inclusion of the heritage language was a political statement: In Nunavut, indigenous languages had been officially excluded until recently, so promoting community choice in language/literacy use was a stance supporting local control); and (c) involving community participants in the selection of program and curriculum content: Once participants became involved in the process of selecting program/curriculum content, they chose to focus on issues such as stable housing or gardening, rather than literacy or language per se.

Taken together, these studies reinforce the point that the way to promote language/literacy goals may be by not focusing directly on language and literacy in self-contained educational programs, but rather on community-based activities identified by participants. They reinforce a pedagogical model that positions community members not as language/literacy learners, but as sources of knowledge, understanding, and wisdom in their own right; they demonstrate that when participants take the lead, they may focus more on key issues arising from their social contexts than on language and literacy instruction per se.

Classrooms

Finally, of course, since the early 1980s, there has been a rich tradition of Freirean pedagogical approaches that promote critical analysis and action emanating from the classroom. Practitioners have developed strategies for identifying social/community issues with participants, which can become curriculum content and lead toward initiatives outside the classroom. One of the most refined models for integrating this kind of analysis into literacy/ESL education was developed in South Africa at the end of the apartheid regime in order to promote skills for participatory democracy (Kerfoot, 1993). In that model, educators elicit learners' experience through the presentation of photos, readings, objects, skits, videos, and such. They then compare and analyze their experiences through structured dialogue and identify common community themes or issues. They research the themes and get new input through readings, published materials, invited speakers, and numeracy (graphs/charts), developing language/literacy skills in the process. They go on to develop skills for participatory democracy: speaking; chairing meetings; handling conflict; writing letters, petitions, and reports; conducting debates; and using these skills in order to participate in the transition to a democratic government.

A recent volume that includes accounts of many such initiatives in North America is entitled *Civic Participation and Community Action Sourcebook* (Nash, 1999). It includes pieces about GED students taking action when their food stamps are held up, students challenging local police about their approach to controlling drug traffic, women organizing against family violence, formerly homeless women studying the history of welfare policy and then teaching others about the issue, and students researching and organizing for public transportation in their rural community. Another book, *Participatory Practices in Adult Education*, likewise documents projects and practices that promote participant activism (Campbell & Burnaby, 2001).

To the extent that these projects and examples focus on local issues and local actions as ends in themselves, they are a step away from the model that I propose. This model suggests exploring possibilities for connecting local initiatives to the wider global forces that contextualize them (in terms of analysis, research, and critique), as well as forging linkages with grassroots organizations or movements that are challenging the forces of globalization from above. Of course, all of this is easier said than done; as Martin (2001) argues, a critical component of such work is acknowledging participants' existing understandings of their own positionings and socioeconomic dynamics as well as examining factors that make it difficult to take action.

My guess is that there are hundreds of grassroots globalization organizations or projects that embed literacy work in them, but are "invisible" to literacy educators because they do not define themselves as literacy projects. This is an area that requires further research and documentation.

CONCLUSION

In this chapter, I tried to put forward a vision for "thinking globally and acting locally" in relation to family, community, and school literacies; I described the seeds of a "pedagogy of not-literacy" that locates literacy education within grassroots movements and seeks to connect it with global struggles to create a better world. This vision and many of the examples presented here are guided by some common underlying principles:

- A "pedagogy of not-literacy" starts with participants' concerns, preoccupations, interests, and wisdom (rather than with "needs assessment" ré literacy skills). It rests on the assumption that participants come to learning with enormous strengths, life experiences, and struggles. Uncovering and building on these is key.
- Because it's issue-based, rather than skills or literacies driven, it allows for different kinds of participation. It encourages participants to contribute according to their strengths, drawing on local literacies, knowledge, and experiences, but connecting them to new literacies and "transportable" analytical processes.
- Critical analysis that connects the individual and the local with the broader socioeconomic forces is central. Through structured dialogue, students can see the commonalities and patterns of their individual experiences; they can come to see that the challenges they face are not due to their individual inadequacies or deficiencies. This entails challenging the notion that their problems will be solved with better language or literacy skills.
- Research is also integral. This entails investigating historical information and information about rights, looking at economic factors, and looking at how similar struggles play themselves out in other places (and in the process acquiring research skills). This kind of analysis also leads to the un-

derstanding that collective action, rather than individual action is often most effective.

- Skills are taught in service of analysis and action. Overt instruction focusing on specific skills, competencies, structures, and conventions is integrated as needed to address issues.

I end with two paradoxes. The first goes back to the opening quote: It is only by debunking the myth that literacy in itself is empowering that we can position ourselves to contribute to shifting the balance of power. By acknowledging the limitations of our work as literacy practitioners, we can support a broader vision of democratization that challenges the forces of top-down globalization. In other words, humility about what we can and cannot do is key. The second paradox draws on the wisdom of Myles Horton, the founder of the Highlander School, a school that was influential in the civil rights, labor, and environmental movements. In his autobiography, Horton (1998) made the point that if you have a goal that you can attain in your lifetime, it is the wrong goal (pp. 226–228). In other words, we need to both hold on to our vision and to recognize that we will not achieve it and that that is all right. We need to put our local work into perspective, to see ourselves as Lilliputs, taking small steps that contribute to something bigger. The point of an ideal is not to reach it; it is to let it guide your journey. What I proposed here is a direction, not necessarily an attainable goal. And, as Horton says, once we decide what our vision is, all we can do is "just hack away on it" (1998, p. 228).

REFERENCES

Adams, H., & Hurtig, J. (2002). Creative acts, critical insights: Adult writing workshops in two Chicago neighborhoods. In E. Auerbach (Ed.), *Case studies in community partnerships* (pp. 147–158). Alexandria, VA: TESOL Publications.

Asmal, K. (2001). Keynote Speech. *Literacy and language in global and local settings: New Directions for research and teaching.* AILA Conference, Cape Town, South Africa.

Auerbach, E. (Ed.). (2002). *Case studies in community partnerships.* Alexandria, VA: TESOL Publications.

Baez, T., & Mack, E. (1996). Reclaiming and transforming community through adult education. In C. Walsh (Ed.), *Education reform and social change: Multicultural voices, struggles, and visions* (pp. 37–43). Mahwah, NJ: Lawrence Erlbaum Associates.

Barndt, D. (1999). *Women working the NAFTA food chain.* Toronto: Second Story Press.

Barton, D., & Hamilton, M. (1998). *Local literacies.* London: Routledge.

Brecher, J., Costello, T., & Smith, B. (2000). *Globalization from below: The power of solidarity.* Cambridge, MA: South End Press.

Campbell, P., & Burnaby, B. (Eds.). (2001). *Participatory practices in adult education.* Mahwah, NJ: Lawrence Erlbaum Associates.

Crockatt, K., & Smythe, S. (2002). Building culture and community: Family and community literacy partnerships in Canada's North. In E. Auerbach (Ed.), *Case studies in community partnerships* (pp. 91–105). Alexandria, VA: TESOL Publications.

Danaher, K., & Mark, J. (2003). Grassroots globalization gets real. *AlterNet*. Retrieved March 6, 2003, from http://www.alternet.org/story.html?StoryID=15327

Elmi, J., Folarin, M., Moalin, A., & Rees, S. (2002). From isolation to education: Working with Somali families in South London. In E. Auerbach (Ed.), *Case studies in community partnerships* (pp. 79–90). Alexandria, VA: TESOL Publications.

Graff, H. (Ed.). (1979). *The literacy myth: Literacy and social structure in the 19th century city.* London: Academic Press.

Horton, M. (1998). *The long haul: An autobiography.* New York: Teachers College Press.

Huerta-Macías, A. (2002). Getting an even start: A story of family literacy through participation and collaboration. In E. Auerbach (Ed.), *Case studies in community partnerships* (pp. 121–131). Alexandria, VA: TESOL Publications.

James, M. (1990). Demystifying literacy: Reading, writing, and the struggle for liberation. *Convergence, 23*(1), 14–25.

Keis, D. (2002). Building community with books: A case study of the Libros y Familias Program. In E. Auerbach (Ed.), *Case studies in community partnerships* (pp. 133–146). Alexandria, VA: TESOL Publications.

Kerfoot, C. (1993). Participatory education in a South African context. *TESOL Quarterly, 27*(3), 431–447.

Kirkwood, G., & Kirkwood, C. (1989). *Living adult education: Freire in Scotland.* Milton Keynes, UK: Open University Press.

Lee, P. T., Krause, N., & Goetchius, C. (2003). Participatory action research with hotel room cleaners: A case study of first steps in a policy change campaign guided by community based participatory research. In M. Minkler & N. Wallerstein (Eds.), *Community-based participatory research for health* (pp. 390–404). San Francisco: Jossey-Bass.

Louie, M. C., & Burnham, L. (2000). *Women's education in the global economy: A workbook.* Berkeley: Women of Color Resource Center.

Martin, I., & Rahman, H. (2001). The politics of really useful literacy: Six lessons from Bangladesh. In J. Crowther, M. Hamilton, & L Tett (Eds.), *Powerful literacies* (pp. 121–130). Leicester: The National Organization for Adult Learning (NIACE).

Martin, R. (2001). *Listening up: Reinventing ourselves as teachers and students.* Portsmouth, NH: Boynton/Cook Heinemann.

Mashishi, L. (2002). Using a community-based curriculum to promote literacy in Soweto. In E. Auerbach (Ed.), *Case studies in community partnerships* (pp. 107–120). Alexandria, VA: TESOL Publications.

Nash, A. (Ed.). (1999). *Civic participation and community action sourcebook.* Boston: New England Literacy Resource Center (http://literacytech.worlded.org/docs/vera/index1.htm).

New London Group. (1996). A pedagogy of multiliteracies: Designing social futures. *Harvard Educational Review, 66*(1), 60–92.

Saville, B. (2002). *The wildlife of Dalry Community Park.* Edinburgh: Gorgie/Dalry Community Council.

Schofield, A. (2002). Wild power: School–community partnerships in a South African school district. In E. Auerbach (Ed.), *Case studies in community partnerships* (pp. 159–169). Alexandria, VA: TESOL Publications.

Street, B. (1984). *Literacy in theory and practice.* Cambridge: Cambridge University Press.

Warschauer, M. (2000). The changing global economy and the future of English teaching. *TESOL Quarterly, 34*, 511–535.

Author Index

Subject Index

Note. *f* indicates figure; *n* indicates footnote; *t* indicates table.

A

Aboriginal languages, 10
Aboriginal literacies, 9, 10, *see also* First Nations; Medicine Wheel (Wheel of Life) model of education; Multiple literacies, Aboriginal; Rainbow Approach, to Aboriginal literacies
  adult program, 329*t*, 331*t*
  borders and, 265
  print-based literacy and, 265
Academic knowledge, 25
Additive bilingualism, 8, 175–178
Adolescence (Hall), 324
Adolescent literacy, *see* Literacy for All project; Youth Literacy program, in British Columbia; Youth Millennium Project
Adult Basic Education (ABE), 327, 328*t*
Adult education, *see also* Lifespan, learning across
  informational learning in, 325
  nonformal learning in, 325
  role in community organizing, 371
  roots of, 324
  tutoring and, 324, 330, 331*t*
Adult Learning Project (Scotland), 372

Adult literacy, 9–11, *see also* Mass-Observation Project
  traditional vs. critical, 327
Afghanistan, *see* Literacy for All project
Alternative school model, 330–331*f*, 332
Anishinaabe, *see* Multiple literacies, Aboriginal
Apartheid, 364, 365, 369, 373–374, 376
Armenian heritage language community, 150–155
  Armenian day schools, 152–155
  Armenian language, *literate/literacy* in, 149, 154
Arts-based literacy, 3, 8 (10), *see also* Children's drawings study
Assembly of First Nations, 267–268
Auger, Dennis, 266
Authorship, 313
Autonomous model of literacy, 1

B

Basic literacy, school-based vs. adult literacy, 328*t*
Behavioral disabilities, adult literacy and, 331*t*

389